Praise for *The Killer of Little Shepherds*

'Starr's book . . . evokes what might otherwise be thought an idyllic rural France in all its ghastly 19th-century ignorance, suspicion, violence and fear.'
Guardian

'Starr has created a book with every bit as much tension as a thriller, as much detail as a meticulous police procedural, and a court-room drama that's up there with the best. Furthermore, much of what occurred in 1890s France still has meaning today, and techniques developed then led to the procedures we use today. Lacassagne called for the government to set up a nationwide agency to collect data on crime; almost half a century later, Interpol came into being. "CSI Belle Epoque"? It's not as crazy as it sounds.'
Independent on Sunday

'[Conveyed] with such lucidity and urgency. Starr, very intelligently . . . allows readers to draw their own conclusions in his fine book.'
Spectator

'Starr uses this story as a hook to draw us into his main subject, which is the development of forensic science to track down criminals. Will appeal to viewers of CSI and Silent Witness.'
Daily Mail

'So fascinating and beautifully written that it reads as much like a novel as a real-life account as it navigates the twists, turns and drama that followed fresh developments in forensic science.'
Sunday Express

'Deftly explains the birth of forensic science in Europe and beyond.'
Independent 'Best Summer Reads'

'Starr manages his material superbly and turns this study of the birth of forensic science into a gripping, sometimes horrific, sometimes funny page-turner.'
Daily Telegraph

'An intriguing read . . .'
Bookseller

D0270914

The Killer
of
Little Shepherds

The Case of the French Ripper
and the Birth of Forensic Science

DOUGLAS STARR

**SIMON &
SCHUSTER**

London · New York · Sydney · Toronto · New Delhi

A CBS COMPANY

First published in Great Britain by Simon & Schuster UK Ltd, 2011
This edition published in 2012
A CBS COMPANY

1 3 5 7 9 10 8 6 4 2

Simon & Schuster UK Ltd
1st Floor
222 Gray's Inn Road
London
WC1X 8HB

www.simonandschuster.co.uk

Simon & Schuster Australia, Sydney
Simon & Schuster India, Delhi

A CIP catalogue for this book is available
from the British Library.

ISBN: 978-1-84983-328-8

Printed and bound by CPI Group (UK) Ltd, Croydon, CR0 4YY

For my parents

The wild beast slumbers in us all. It is not always necessary to invoke insanity to explain its awakening.

—Dr. Edward Spitzka, 1901
postmortem report on Leon F. Czolgosz,
assassin of President William McKinley

Contents

PART THREE: AFTERMATH

Illustrations follow page 146

Author's Note

This book is a work of nonfiction. I have taken no liberties with facts or the context in which the events related in the book occurred. All quotes and dialogue were taken from the participants' letters, books, affidavits, and court testimony, or from verifiable contemporary journalistic sources. In those instances where I attribute thoughts to someone, the thoughts appear in italic and are based on that person's writings or testimony. The serial killer Joseph Vacher's state of mind was reflected in a surviving collection of his letters, in affidavits of contemporaries who encountered him, in records of the asylums in which he was confined, and in the reports of investigators and alienists who interviewed him. Details of his crimes were gleaned from original crime-scene analyses, autopsy reports, newspaper accounts, and the oral histories of the modern-day inhabitants of the villages he terrorized. Dr. Alexandre Lacassagne's personality and state of mind were revealed by his voluminous writings and scientific reports, the writings of his many colleagues and friends, and the stories and artifacts shared by his descendants.

Most of the source material is in late-nineteenth-century French. Sometimes I shortened sentences and simplified the language in order to make the quoted material accessible to modern readers. Although numerous people helped with translations, any oversimplifications that may have resulted are my own.

Part One

Crime

*The werewolf of legends
Has now been surpassed . . .*

—Popular verse about Joseph Vacher, 1898

One

The Beast

On a drizzly spring evening in 1893, in the French provincial city of Besançon, nineteen-year-old Louise Barant was walking along the riverside promenade when she crossed paths with a man wearing the dress uniform of the French army. His name was Joseph Vacher. "Ugly weather, isn't it?" he said, and automatically she responded, "For sure." Normally Barant, tall and wholesome-looking, with curly blond hair, would not have spoken to a stranger, especially one as brutish-looking as he; but Vacher projected a kind of disarming innocence, and the sergeant's chevrons on his sleeve reassured her.

So they chatted and walked and shared dinner in a café. They learned that they both came from small towns: she from Baume-les-Dames, a pretty village near the Swiss border, and he from Beaufort, a nondescript hill town southeast of Lyon. As they lingered over shared stories about their pasts, he told her he had never felt this comfortable with anyone, and she, too, sensed she could speak freely and easily. Yet she felt a shiver of doubt when she looked up from her meal and saw his eyes burning into her. Later that evening, he ardently proposed marriage. When he vowed that he would kill her if she ever betrayed him, she realized she had made a terrible mistake.

In the weeks that followed, he pursued her relentlessly. Like other men who live easily with violence, Vacher knew how to interweave threat, regret, self-pity, and charm in an attempt to prolong the relationship. Louise, who was a stranger to the town and worked as a housemaid, tried desperately to avoid him, inventing endless excuses for not being available. Once, taking pity as victims sometimes do, she agreed to meet him at a dance. They were standing awkwardly among the merrymakers when a soldier approached to talk to Louise. Vacher lunged at the man with such fury that the soldier and Louise ran from the dance hall.

Now she knew that she would never be safe in the same town as Vacher. Too afraid to reject him directly, she made up a story that her mother had forbidden their marriage and had ordered her home. The distance did nothing to quell his obsession. He kept mailing her love letters. Finally, she responded in the clearest possible way: "It would be best if you stopped writing to me . . . Everything is finished between us; I do not want to go against the wishes of my mother. Furthermore, I do not love you. Adieu, Louise."

She hoped that would finally end things between them. Besides, she knew that if he left his unit to find her, he would face charges of desertion. But her departure and final letter had sent him into such a series of rages that the regimental doctor diagnosed him as having "nervous exhaustion" and gave him a four-month medical leave. He immediately headed to Baume-les-Dames, stopping to buy a revolver along the way.

Any of the soldiers in Vacher's barracks would have told Louise not to get involved with the twenty-three-year-old sergeant in the first place, for something wild and violent dwelled within him. They had witnessed his manias and explosive temper: How once, when a soldier lagged in formation, Vacher swiftly and without warning kicked him in the groin; or how, during alcohol-induced tantrums, he would hurl heavy wooden bureaus across the room, roar like an animal, and rip handfuls of hair out of his forearms. Another time, when he was passed over for promotion, he drank himself senseless, tore apart the barracks, and slashed with a razor at anyone who came near. He ended the episode by taking the blade to his own throat. After that incident, he was hospitalized and transferred to another company.

Yet at times, Vacher could appear deferential, and, when necessary, even charming. Undoubtedly, he behaved that way when he first met Louise, although under the stress of rejection the beast had reemerged.

Arriving in her village, he spent days trying to persuade her mother and family to accept him, only to succeed in frightening them as well. On the morning of June 25, 1893, he went to the house of Louise's employer for a final confrontation before taking the train back to Besançon. Louise opened the door, recoiling when she saw him.

"Why are you afraid, Louise?"

"I'm not afraid," she said unconvincingly.

"Look, I don't want to harm you. I've come here peacefully to demand the things that you owe me."

He had become obsessed with reclaiming the letters and trinkets he had given her, and the money he had spent taking her to dinner. She gave him all that he demanded, but still he kept talking about needing more. As he rattled on about his various resentments, she furtively backed her way up the marble stairway. The more he spoke, the more agitated he became.

"When I think that you don't want me, Louise . . . We would have been so happy! Listen, you don't know what I am capable of doing. I have already told you and I repeat: I'm crazy about you! Come away with me."

She told him that if he did not leave immediately, she would wake her boss, who would eject him. Vacher slipped his right hand into his pocket.

"So you do not want to come with me, then?"

"No!"

He pulled out the revolver and began firing. The first bullet entered her mouth, shattered two teeth, ripped through her tongue, and exited her cheek. She screamed and collapsed. Two more shots grazed the top of her head as she fell and another smashed into the wall. Then Vacher turned the gun on himself, firing two bullets into his face.

The explosions echoed so loudly in the hallway that her employer's family rushed down from their bedrooms and passersby ran in from the street. They found Louise crumpled on the stairs, Vacher staggering blindly, his face covered with blood. He lurched four or five steps out the door before collapsing in the street.*

And so began the public life of Joseph Vacher, one of the most notorious serial killers of his century, who slaughtered more people than the infamous Jack the Ripper. Although the incident with Louise Barant was the first of Vacher's legal encounters, he had perplexed and discomfited the people around him for years. Neighbors in Beaufort remembered him as a child who was quick to pick an argument, and unusually violent in schoolyard scuffles. Once, when asked to guard the family's livestock, he took the animals to a meadow and broke some of their legs. He spent a couple of his teenage years in a monastery but was expelled for unspecified indiscretions. He was drafted and stationed with the Sixtieth

---

*Both survived, because the dealer who had sold Vacher the revolver loaded the cartridges only with half charges—just enough powder to stop an aggressor but not necessarily to kill him.

Regiment in Besançon. Although he thrived under the army's strict discipline, he showed violent outbursts there, as well. All along, people found him strange, but as he himself had said to Louise, they had no idea of what he was capable.

Crimes of passion were notoriously common at the time, leniently punished, and often blamed on the victim. After he shot Louise, Vacher spent a couple of weeks in a hospital. He was then sent for observation to the public asylum in the nearby city of Dole, where doctors were to determine if he was sane enough to stand trial. The "Certificate of 24 Hours," documenting the patient's first day in the asylum, reported he was "calm, responds meekly to questions and regrets the act he has committed." It described in detail how the shooting had disfigured him: a scarlet furrow ran the length of his right jaw; yellowish pus oozed from the right ear—stigmata that would mark him for life. With each breath, his right cheek fluttered like an unfettered sail, for one of the bullets had severed a facial nerve. When he spoke, he could barely open his mouth, and the voice that emerged was nasal and slurred.

He seemed a defeated man, rather than a menacing one. Yet over the weeks, as Vacher healed and became stronger, a more paranoid and violent character emerged. Quietly at first, and then more stridently, he accused the doctors at Dole of plotting against him. Day after day, he demanded to see a surgeon to remove the bullet from his ear. When medical personnel arrived for the procedure, Vacher accused them of trying to kill him and bolted from the operating room.

On July 20, according to hospital records, he experienced a "crisis of agitation." He screamed at doctors and fought with his roommates. Sometimes he sat rocking on the side of his bed. "At certain moments he raises his head and focuses his eyes as if listening to invisible voices," wrote Dr. Léon Guillemin, adjunct doctor at the facility. "During such times he has the facial expression of a madman."

Inwardly, Vacher seethed. He hated the institution and everyone in it. According to him, the doctors were heartless and the patients were swine. Later, in a long, embittered letter to the authorities (Vacher would prove to be a prolific letter writer), he would write that the asylum was "everything that is dirty and abominable," where he was forced to sleep "on a grubby flea-infested mattress." The food was barely edible, he said, and the guards often stole it. Unsupervised patients often abused one another and took special delight in tormenting the blind. "They pushed them and spit in their faces. Some even pushed them outside naked in the snow." At times, he thought of killing himself. "And I was not the only one . . . some people could not take this treatment, and committed suicide."

Contrary to Vacher's accusations, the alienists at Dole considered themselves sympathetic and attentive. (*Alienist* was the era's term for a psychologist, as mental patients were seen to be "alienated" from themselves.) Printed materials from the asylum described their treatments as "gentle, tolerable, humane, and more in agreement with modern ideas." Unlike in the past, inmates were not shackled to the walls or beaten for offenses they unwittingly committed. "All the coercive methods that tortured the sick patients have been abandoned . . . the fate of the sick [who come to the asylum] is nothing other than completely humane."

When Vacher was admitted, the asylum's director was preparing to move the patients to a new facility, a cluster of pavilions in a pastoral setting just outside of town, a notable improvement on the present fortresslike edifice. Scores of such facilities were being built throughout Europe.

Still, conditions at Dole were not what they should have been. A late-nineteenth-century visitor to the asylum noted that many patients still lived behind bars in dank cells and received inadequate personal care. In truth, this asylum, like many others, had far too many inmates. The population of insane people had exploded in France (and throughout Europe and in the Americas, as well) due to the epidemics of alcoholism and syphilis, and to the increasingly common diagnosis of mental disease. In time, insanity became a catchall diagnosis for all sorts of deficiencies, including dementia, homelessness, and criminal behavior. As a result, asylums became dumping grounds for the overflow from prisons, almshouses, workhouses, and the streets. By the time Vacher entered the asylum, the state-run system was housing more than twice the capacity it was designed for. Dole, built for five hundred patients, was bursting with more than nine hundred—at least 15 percent of whom were criminals. (Faced with such impossible conditions, even the most dedicated alienist could lose heart. When the director of the Villejuif asylum in Paris was asked what he found most effective for patients, he replied, "We wait for them to die.")

Doctors had put Vacher in a special high-security wing, but, as in many asylums at the time, oversight was lax. On the night of August 25, 1893, Vacher sneaked out of his room, found a long wooden beam, leaned it against the wall, and shimmied over it to freedom. He was heading to Baume-les-Dames to find Louise. An all-points bulletin went out over the telegraph, with a special notification to the police in Louise's village. It would not be hard to identify the fugitive: He wore the asylum's standard-issue gray cotton shirt and trousers, and there was no mistaking his disfig-ured face.

A couple of weeks later, some soldiers in Besançon caught sight of him. Local policemen jailed him. A few days later, he was put on a train, headed back to the asylum. His guards had instructions to handcuff him and to keep him in view at all times. As the train rumbled on, Vacher asked the guards if he could get off at the next stop to go to the bathroom. "You'll have to wait," they said. They had no intention of letting him off the train, even if manacled, for a minute. He persisted. Finally he offered to stand right in front of the guards and urinate out the door. They paused; the train was flying along at top speed, and it seemed there was no way he could even think of making that leap and surviving. He shuffled to the door, opened his pants, and, before they could react, heaved himself out. He hit the talus, then rolled and scampered off like a jackrabbit as the train roared away.

Two days later, police, alerted by some village children, found him eat-ing dinner at a farmer's house. They took him to the Dole asylum in chains. His condition grew worse. Increasingly "in the grip of melancholic ideas," he tried to commit suicide by slamming his head against the cor-ner of a wall. "We frequently have to take energetic measures to prevent him from harming himself," wrote the doctors in a "situation report" of October 26, 1893.

Meanwhile, Dr. Guillemin had arrived to make an official assessment of the inmate's sanity. He interviewed Vacher, physically examined him, spoke to his minders, and pored over his records. Guillemin diagnosed Vacher as "a deliriant with a persecution complex of the first order." He had suffered this condition for most of his life. The symptoms, not always evident, would occasionally and dramatically appear. The rejection by Louise aggravated the condition as never before, the doctor said, and trig-gered the homicidal behavior. At the asylum, Vacher continued to suffer severe paranoia, aggravated by auditory hallucinations. He imagined the "entire world is in league against him," wrote Guillemin. "From the moment he arrived at Dole, [Vacher felt] his doctors neglected him, ignored him, did not want to care for him, and wanted him to die. We have done our best for him, but he accuses us of trying to kill him, and shows no signs of being cured."

In conclusion, Guillemin wrote: "(1) Vacher suffers from mental alienation characterized by a persecution complex, and (2) He is not responsible for his actions."

The local court issued a finding of not guilty by reason of insanity, transforming Vacher's legal status from that of an accused criminal to that of a mentally damaged ward of the state—more specifically, a ward of his home district, or *département*, Isère, in the east of France. He would be taken to the state-run asylum there, outside of Grenoble, and stay until his doctors decided he was cured.

They put him on a train for Saint-Robert, the new asylum, along with two guards. In a note to accompany the transfer, Guillemin described Vacher as "currently really quiet. He only wishes to return to his region [and to] be back with his family soon." Guillemin expressed confidence that Vacher would behave during the transfer. "However, because of a history of suicide attempts and escapes, I recommend serious supervision. Two reliable guards should suffice." Inexplicably, he made no mention of the attempted homicide, the voices, or Vacher's murderous impulses and dangerous paranoia. As far as the people at Saint-Robert were concerned, they were preparing to receive a depressed and suicidal man, but not one who was dangerous to others. Vacher later recalled that as the train pulled away from the station at Dole, all he wanted was "to see blood running everywhere."

Vacher had promised to behave during the transfer. In an effort to appeal to his reason and dignity, the doctors allowed him to wear his regimental uniform instead of the asylum grays. But the uniform only awakened his sense of outrage, and he resolved to escape and tell the world about Dole. On the platform, he tried his "urination" escape; the guards quickly grabbed him and shackled his hands and feet. Once on the train, he tried to create the maximum amount of disturbance. Seated between the guards in a third-class carriage, he lurched his body this way and that, trying to break free. When that failed, he shrieked anarchist slogans and screamed about his treatment at Dole—especially at stations, when lines of people were shuffling through the car. His ravings made women on the train cower and weep.

Vacher's destination, the Saint-Robert asylum, was "one of the best institutions in France," according to a British survey of hospitals and asylums at the time. Constructed on the grounds of an ancient priory, it commanded a majestic view of the surrounding Alps, where its inmates could savor the brisk mountain air. The facility had been designed according to the latest psychological theories, which emphasized bringing normalcy to patients' lives, rather than simply confining them. The institution was built as a campus, with separate men's and women's residences and a common building in the center, all in a neoclassical style. Beyond the main edifices stood buildings and streets reminiscent of those in a quaint rural village, along with acres of trees and cultivated fields. The totality of the setting, from the scenery to the architecture to the attitude of the staff, was intended to lighten the spirits of the inmates who lived there.

The staff's attitude reflected gentleness, as well. Unlike their colleagues at other asylums, doctors at Saint-Robert used straitjackets only two or three times a year, and only "in temporary and exceptional cases, when it is clear that a patient will injure himself," as the asylum's director, Dr. Edmond Dufour, explained to a group of visiting alienists. Saint-Robert's employees never resorted to the common practice of using freezing showers to discipline their patients, or the "Scottish showers" of alternating hot and cold water. They never shackled the patients, even the violent ones. They busied their inmates with esteem-building employment such as cobbling and sewing, and with theatrical and musical productions. They always spoke respectfully and with kindness. It was all part of an effort to restore dignity to patients, and to appeal to the better part of their intelligence.

So it was with tenderness and humanity that the orderlies greeted the man who arrived late on the night of December 21, 1893, whose face portrayed a history of violence. Knowing that he posed a suicide risk, they assigned Vacher to the high-security section, placing him in a room with a calming view of the mountains. He had been there barely twenty-four hours when he began to show improvement. Apparently responding to the benevolent atmosphere, he stood up and offered a communal grace before dinner: "Dear Friends, let us praise God to have been born in a region where our caretakers are so loyal and humane. Thank God we were born under such a benign and benevolent sun."

The words seemed to arise from an inner gentleness, and augured well for the patient's recovery. No one who heard those words of benediction could ever imagine how misleading they would be.

Joseph Vacher walked into history at a time of expectation and dread. The period at the end of the nineteenth century and the beginning of the twentieth, known as the Belle Époque, was an era of peace and prosperity, of advances in science and the arts. It was a time when Sarah Bernhardt lit up the stage and Toulouse-Lautrec and Degas illuminated the art world; when Gustave Eiffel was building his tower and Louis Pasteur was developing his germ theory of infection.

Everything seemed bigger, faster, newer, more efficient. The new train networks sped passengers across continents, and steamships bore them rapidly across the seas. Telegraph wires carried messages at the speed of light across the countryside and under the Atlantic. The Olympics were revived. The cinema was born. Modern burlesque halls opened in Paris, where they featured a lively new dance called the cancan.

People could truly aspire to *enjoy* life, not just endure it. They shopped in the new department stores, bought the new ready-to-wear clothing, and pedaled their new bicycles, which had taken the middle class by storm. Women especially flocked to the bicycle as an independent means of transportation. Posters and full-color newspaper ads—themselves innovations of the era—portrayed new customers as liberated goddesses, flying naked across the heavens on their bikes.

Yet amid all the optimism ran an undercurrent of anxiety. For every happy, well-off family, many more lived in poverty and destitution. Everyone could sense the instability, the rumblings from below. Anarchism, an international terrorist movement, was growing: Bombs were exploding at markets, government offices, and train stations. The authorities responded with brutal repression, and the cycle of reprisals continued. By the end of the century, anarchists would bomb targets throughout Europe and assassinate the presidents of France and the United States. Some intellectuals saw modern society, with its vulgar amusements and avant-garde lifestyles, as evidence of a species gone soft, of a reverse evolution, of a social degeneracy.

Crime rates were rising, and fear among the populace was inflamed by the new tabloid press. It was not simply crime that alarmed people but also the emergence of a criminal *class*. Londoners learned to fear the "residuum," New Yorkers saw the rise of ethnic street gangs, and Parisians knew to avoid the "apaches"—roaming bands of youths who swarmed over the gentry who might wander from the beaten path. Legions of the dispossessed—vagabonds from the countryside, street gangs from towns, the criminally insane who escaped from the asylums—all seemed bent on victimizing good citizens.

In this climate of hope and anxiety, an international group of experts emerged that took a scientific approach to crime. Like the other great logicians of the era, they viewed the problem not as sin or the workings of the devil, but as a scientific challenge. (This, after all, was a scientific age.) Trained in medicine, law, psychology, and anthropology, they established new institutes for criminal research, published their work in scholarly journals, and debated their theories at international conferences.

Theirs was the first generation of modern criminologists, and they developed the techniques that characterize forensic science to this day. They learned to read meaning into the chaos of a crime scene by measuring and mapping; by recording scuff marks, prints, and fibers; and by performing methodical autopsies and collecting biological samples. They employed the new science of psychology to create profiles of suspects and to interview them calmly and effectively upon capture (in contrast to the brutal techniques of their predecessors). To understand larger patterns of crime, they created databases of maps and statistics. To explore the roots of deviant behavior, they dissected the brains of executed criminals. Their studies opened realms of discussion formerly reserved for priests and philosophers: What impulses for good and evil naturally existed within human beings? What modified those impulses along the way? What were the limits of free will and sanity? Could the impulse to do evil be understood, predicted, redirected, or cured?

If the doctors at Saint-Robert looked kindly on their new patient, he seemed to feel the same about them. "When I arrived here I thought I had entered Paradise," he wrote in a letter to the director, Dr. Dufour. Later, in a long letter to Louise (to the end of his days, he never stopped writing her), he wrote of his delight at arriving at the new asylum:

> Imagine my surprise. . . . I arrived by train through a little valley surrounded by snow-crowned mountains, and there it was, glowing by the light of the moon . . . this clean and rich establishment lit by electricity (for I arrived at night). The main door opened and there in front of me were two friends

who I had thought would be executioners. We crossed gardens as beautiful as any in Grenoble.

They put me in a building that was frequented by rabble, but they were nothing like the walking dead [at Dole]. Whereas in Dole we were surrounded by guards who might as well have been executioners, here there are guards who embody Vigilance and Humanity.

That is not to say that Saint-Robert was a summer camp. Like their colleagues elsewhere, the alienists had a fear of free time that bordered on paranoia and left not a moment for idle hands or deviant thoughts. Wake-up call came at 5:00 a.m. (6:00 a.m. in the winter), followed by a half hour of room cleaning and then breakfast. Patients spent the morning cultivating the fields or laboring in one of the asylum's workshops. Lunch was served exactly at noon, followed by a half hour of recreation and then the afternoon work shift. Dinner was at 6:00 p.m. (5:00 p.m. in the winter), followed by quiet activity, such as dominoes or cards, reading or strolling the grounds, and then bedtime at 8:00 p.m.

Days moved forward in lockstep progression: Friday was for haircuts, beard trimmings, and hair washing; on Saturday, new sheets were given out; and on Sunday, patients received clean clothes before mass. Sunday was also concert day, and the patients would stage a variety of shows, plays, and musical performances for the other residents and people from the community. Patients could write one letter every two weeks to someone in the outside world, and censors would review it. The concept was simple: The order and discipline of a daily routine would help alleviate the disorder and chaos of the patients' minds.

Amid all this "normalizing" activity, doctors administered physical and psychological therapies. In part, they relied on the era's pharmacopeia: leeches to calm excitability; purgatives to cleanse the system by provoking vomiting and diarrhea; and light doses of opium, belladonna, or chloroform, depending on the symptoms they were trying to relieve. They often used hydrotherapy—long, hot baths to calm patients with mania and cold baths for depressed patients who needed stimulation. Sometimes they applied mild electrical shocks to calm a manic or hallucinating patient—a procedure known as "the touch of a brass paintbrush." Doctors would also engage the patients in talking about their problems and their hopes for a better life.

Vacher spent three months in Saint-Robert. The alienists who treated him knew he was manic and sometimes suicidal, so they likely administered calming hydrotherapy. They may have given him electroshock treatments—in a letter to the asylum director in January 1894, Vacher asked him not to "electrify part of my head." Certainly they employed talk therapy; the doctors recorded in their notes that they listened to and accepted his version of the incident with Louise. He spent most of his time alone, reading.

Saint-Robert's status reports portray a very different man from the one who behaved so wildly at Dole. He *responded* to treatment, or at least appeared to. Within two weeks of his arrival at Saint-Robert, doctors could report that he no longer heard voices, that he was becoming "docile and polite." He wrote fawning letters to and about Dr. Dufour. ("He should be governing all of France rather than administering this establishment full of rabble.") On January 29, 1894, Vacher wrote that he understood the crime he had committed, deserved the punishment he had received, and felt that he had been able to cure himself despite the previous six months in Dole. Soon he described a plan to put his life back in order after his release.

The letters, together with his "inoffensive" behavior, persuaded Dufour that his patient was recovering. As he explained, they demonstrated two critical elements: that Vacher accepted responsibility for his crime and that he showed an ability to plan for the future. "He also made it clear to me and insisted on this point that we don't have the right to hold those insane people who are completely cured," Dufour later told a newspaper reporter. "And it is my obligation to set them free." Meanwhile, the local government of Isère, chafing at the expense of running a world-class asylum, had been pressuring Dufour to release patients as soon as their symptoms abated.

In early March of 1894, Dufour wrote to the prefect of Isère that Vacher, having suffered a fairly ordinary nervous breakdown triggered by his broken engagement, was now cured. The prefect issued a release order. On April 1, 1894, less than ten months after Vacher tried to murder Louise, guards opened the wrought-iron gate. Vacher hugged his doctors and fellow inmates. Then he walked free.

A newspaper would later describe that moment as "opening the door to the cage of a wild beast."

Two

The Professor

In mid-November 1889, Dr. Alexandre Lacassagne, head of the department of legal medicine at the University of Lyon, got a request from the city prosecutor to help with a particularly nasty case. Four months earlier, a body had been found in a sack by the Rhône River, about a dozen miles south of the city. The corpse had been autopsied by another doctor, who could not arrive at an identification. Now, because of new developments in the case, the body was being exhumed. Granted, there would not be much left of the cadaver, but could Dr. Lacassagne perform a new autopsy? Perhaps he could find something the previous doctor had missed.

It was not unusual for Lacassagne (*Lackasanya*) to be called in where others had stumbled, for he had established a reputation as a skilled criminologist. As the author of textbooks, the developer of many new forensic techniques, and the investigator of several celebrated cases, he was first among equals in an international cadre of experts in the new field of legal medicine.

The subject of this autopsy was presumed to be a missing Parisian named Toussaint-Augustin Gouffé. A bailiff by profession, and a widower with two daughters, Gouffé was a prosperous man and had a reputation for being a sexual adventurer. On July 27, Gouffé's brother-in-law, whose name was Landry, reported to police that Gouffé had gone missing. Police paid little notice at first—this was, after all, the summer of the Paris World Exposition, with many unscheduled comings and goings. But when three days passed without Gouffé's reappearance, they took the case seriously, and referred it to Marie-François Goron, renowned chief of the Paris Sûreté, the city's investigative unit.

Three weeks later, a body turned up about three hundred miles southeast of Paris, near the village of Millery, south of Lyon. A few days after that, some snail gatherers in the woods found a broken wooden trunk, which reeked of death and bore a shipping label from Paris.

Could the body and the trunk be connected to the missing man? Goron telegraphed a description of Gouffé to the medical examiner's office in Lyon. At the time of the discovery, Lacassagne was away, so a colleague and former student, Dr. Paul Bernard, conducted the autopsy. He found little that matched the corpse to the missing person. True, the cadaver, like Gouffé, had large and strong teeth and was missing the first right upper molar, but that was about all. The corpse measured about five feet seven inches, while the missing man stood about five eight. The corpse had black hair; Gouffé's hair was chestnut-colored. The cadaver was between thirty-five and forty-five years old, according to Bernard's estimate; Gouffé had been forty-nine. Just to be sure, Goron sent Landry to Lyon, along with a deputy. Landry took a brief, gasping look at the bloated, greenish body and saw not the slightest trace of his relative. Case closed. The men returned to Paris and the body went into an anonymous pauper's grave.

That might have been the end of the affair, but in the fall Goron received an anonymous tip. Just before Gouffé disappeared from Paris, he had been seen at the Brasserie Gutenberg in the company of a con man named Michel Eyraud and his consort, Gabrielle Bompard. The couple left Paris the day after Gouffé went missing. Meanwhile, Goron had taken the shipping label from the trunk and showed it to the clerk at the Gare de Lyon in Paris. Records showed that the trunk had been shipped to Lyon the day after Gouffé's disappearance. Its weight was registered at 105 kilograms—just about the combined weight of a fully grown man and a stout wooden trunk.

Everything tied the victim to Gouffé—except for the autopsy. Goron felt there must have been a mistake. He contacted the authorities in Lyon and asked them to exhume the body and reexamine it. They resisted: By now the victim had been dead for four months; no one could possibly identify the remains. But Goron, legendary for his persistence, remained adamant. And so the hideous job of conducting an autopsy on a body that had previously been dissected and had lain rotting underground fell to the one man in Lyon—perhaps in all Europe—who stood the slightest chance of solving the mystery.

Dr. Jean-Alexandre-Eugène Lacassagne already was well respected in his field when he encountered the case that would make him world-famous.

As one of the early scholars and innovators of legal medicine, he had helped devise many new techniques in crime-scene analysis, such as determining how long a body had been putrefying and how to match a bullet to a gun. He showed investigators how to determine whether a dead body had been moved by examining the pattern of blood splotches on the skin. He developed procedures by which even simple country doctors could perform professional autopsies if called to a crime scene.

Colleagues admired him not only for his contribution to science but as a scholar, teacher, and friend. As people often did in those days, they saw his character revealed in his appearance—and a noble physiognomy it was, with a high forehead, handlebar mustache, burgomaster's girth, and a "strong, rhythmic step and ever-cheerful eye." With his energy and talent, he could have done anything, but he had chosen the nascent field of criminology. To his mind, it encompassed the scale of the human experience, from the workings of a single brain to the forces that shape civilization. But even that occupied only part of his intellect. He immersed himself in poetry, philosophy, literature, and art. He could recite from memory pages of Dante in the original Italian and entire acts from the work of his favorite French playwrights. He sponsored young artists. He was never without a book—either reading or writing one. His friends thought him a Renaissance man, except for one flaw: He lacked the ability to appreciate music.

He was born in 1843 to innkeepers in Cahors, a quiet town in southwest France. A gifted student but too poor to afford a private education, he attended the military's medical school in Strasbourg, where he wrote his first thesis, on the side effects of chloroform. He studied military medicine in Paris for a year and then returned to Strasbourg. He arrived during the Franco-Prussian War, and for thirty-nine days the Germans bombarded the city before its ultimate surrender. As one building after another collapsed, Lacassagne and his fellow medical residents set up a clinic in the hospital basement, piling mattresses against the windows as explosions blew fiery debris all around them. In September, a Swiss delegation evacuated the wounded and doctors to a hospital in Lyon. It was Lacassagne's first view of the city that would become his home and a world capital for the investigation of crime.

With the Strasbourg medical school destroyed, Lacassagne continued his studies in Montpellier. He wrote a thesis on putrefaction, manifesting an early interest in biological phenomena that affect both the living and the dead. To fulfill his military obligation, he traveled to Algeria, where he was assigned to be the doctor for a disciplinary brigade. Normally, it would have been a dreary assignment, but not to a man with an intellect as lively as Lacassagne's. He became fascinated by the miscreants in his care. Many bore tattoos with strange and exotic images: Joan of Arc, the scales of justice, hearts pierced by knives, two hands clasped with a flower rising between them, and naked women with sexual features exaggerated to cartoonlike proportions. The inscriptions were equally fascinating: "No luck"; "Death to unfaithful women"; "Vengeance or death"; "Born under an unlucky star." Convinced that the tattoos revealed insights into criminal subculture, he developed techniques to transfer the patterns to paper and then categorized them according to imagery and body location. By the end of his service, Lacassagne had categorized some two thousand tattoos from hundreds of soldiers. When he presented his research to an international meeting of anthropologists, the American journal *Science* described it as "one of the most entertaining and instructive anthropological papers which have appeared in a long time."

From that point, his career path rose steeply. In 1876, he published a book entitled *Précis d'hygiène privée et sociale* (Synopsis of Private and Public Hygiene), a more than six-hundred-page volume about personal, public, and occupational health. Two years later, he wrote an equally weighty tome, entitled *Précis de médecine judiciaire* (Synopsis of Judicial Medicine), which summarized the nascent field of legal medicine. It was hailed as a small masterpiece. In 1880, he was named to the recently established chair of legal medicine at the University of Lyon. In this hardworking, bourgeois, insular city, he became popular among the students, not only for his knowledge but for his refreshing enthusiasm and warmth.

Beyond solving individual crimes, Lacassagne became fascinated by the criminals themselves—their thought processes, subculture, and way of life. Why did they feel compelled to behave in a manner that was contrary to the rules of society? Why did they take such a difficult path? He made it his life's work to find out, and studied them as assiduously as a zoologist would scrutinize a favorite species. He visited them in prison, collected their writings, and dissected the brains of those who had been guillotined.

His findings, and those of his colleagues from Europe, Russia, and the New World, appeared in a journal he founded, *Archives de l'anthropologie criminelle* (Archives of Criminal Anthropology). For twenty-nine years, it served as the preeminent forum in the field. In its pages scholars would discuss the key developments of their day—crime-scene analysis, criminal psychology, capital punishment, the definition of insanity. There were also many practical reports, in which Lacassagne and his colleagues would describe how they used the latest forensic techniques, as in "the Thodure Affair" (pieces of an old man's body found around a village), "the Father Bérard Affair" (a priest accused of sexual perversion), and "the Montmerle Affair" (a woman found hanged and stabbed in the throat). There were articles on celebrity cases, such as that of Oscar Wilde, in which a French expert on homosexuality wrote about the writer's trial and imprisonment. Jack the Ripper appeared in its pages, as did Jesse Pomeroy, the boy killer of Boston. On two occasions the journal reviewed the newly published stories about Sherlock Holmes. (The verdict: fascinating procedures, but why did Holmes never conduct an autopsy? Also, real medical experts recruited teams of specialists, while Holmes worked alone, with Watson as a mere sounding board.) The journal was populated by the castoffs of society: thieves, murderers, child molesters—the human face of the degenerate instinct.

To assist in an autopsy with Dr. Lacassagne was to participate in a memorable educational experience. Medical students would have seen hospital autopsies before, but forensic dissections were something quite different. Here they saw tableaux of violent death, displayed in a medium of shredded tissue and broken bone. Death leaves a signature, and they would learn to read the meaning: a peaceful death versus a violent one; a death by accident, suicide, or criminal intent. By removing an infant's lungs and seeing if they floated, they would learn to determine whether the baby had been stillborn or had lived long enough to take its first breath. They would learn that a frothy liquid in the airways indicated drowning; that a furrow around the neck pointed to a rope hanging; that break points on opposite sides of the larynx showed that the victim had been strangled with two hands. They would use the angle of a stab wound to determine the trajectory of the arm that had held the knife, and the pathway of a bullet to deduce the location of the gun. They would employ chemical reagents to identify stains from blood, semen, fecal matter, and rust (often mistaken for blood). "The students all flocked to him," recalled Dr. Edmond Locard, a student who himself became a prominent criminologist. And so, several times a month for the thirty-three years that Dr. Lacassagne taught at the medical faculty of Lyon, students would cluster around their beloved professor, who, with no mask on his face and no gloves on his hands, would slice into a cadaver to reveal the mysteries of the last moments of the deceased.

No crowd of students surrounded Lacassagne as he prepared for an autopsy on the morning of November 13, 1889—only a small number of medical assistants and police officials were in attendance. On the table lay the remains of someone who had died almost four months before. Was it Gouffé? Following the autopsy in August, after the body had been buried in an anonymous pauper's grave, a clever lab assistant named Julien Calmail had a hunch that the body would be needed again, so he scratched his initials on the outside of the coffin and put an old hat on the cadaver's head, creating a means of identification.

By Lacassagne's side stood Dr. Paul Bernard, who had conducted the first autopsy, and an assistant, Dr. Saint-Cyr. There was also Dr. Étienne Rollet, Lacassagne's student and brother in-law, whose recently completed thesis would prove invaluable to the case. The state prosecutor from Lyon stood close by, as did Goron, determined to get to the bottom of the mystery. Up in the far reaches of the amphitheater, with a handkerchief pressed against his face, stood one of Goron's colleagues, Brigadier Jaume.

One could forgive Jaume for keeping his distance, as the sight must have been appalling. A four-month-old cadaver retains little of the appearance that once identified it as human. Having been ravaged by insects and having passed through several stages of putrefaction, the body is little more than shapeless clumps of organs and flesh and odd tufts of hair clinging to a bone structure. The stench is even worse than the appearance. It is a mixture of every repulsive odor in the world—excrement, rotted meat, swamp water, urine—and invades the sinuses by full frontal assault, as though penetrating through the bones of the face. One reacts with a deep-seated revulsion. The neck hairs jump to a state of alarm, and the nervous system sends out a message to flee. It is an olfactory memory not easily forgotten.

Lacassagne had stopped noticing those sensations, having performed hundreds of autopsies, often in hot, unventilated conditions. The only complaint he and his colleagues sometimes voiced was that the smell on their fingers would linger for days.

Lacassagne liked to use aphorisms in teaching. A favorite was: "A bungled autopsy cannot be redone," emphasizing the need for care and precision. Bernard must have dozed through that lesson, judging by the state of the cadaver. He had examined the brain, as recommended, but in order to reach it, he'd smashed off the top of the head with a hammer—not with a saw, as his mentor had taught—eliminating any chance of detecting head trauma. He'd opened the chest with a chisel, as prescribed, but completely destroyed the sternum, making it impossible to see if there had been a traumatic chest injury. The organs had been removed and placed in a basket. Many bones were out of place.

No matter—the master would work with whatever materials he had. First he needed to determine the victim's age. There were several places he would normally have looked to make an estimate. The junctions of the skull bones would have been one, if they had not been rendered useless by the hammer blows. Instead, he directed his attention to the pelvis. He examined the junctions between the sacrum—the triangular structure that contains the base of the spine—and the hip bones on either side of it. Those junctions are obvious in a child and progressively become fused as a person reaches adulthood. He also examined the fibrous junctions among the last few vertebrae in the coccyx, which also become fused over the years. Lacassagne examined the victim's jaws and teeth. The teeth were in good shape, but years of gingivitis had caused a loss of bone around the tooth sockets. The bone of the tooth sockets, normally well defined and sharp at the edges, had resorbed into itself and presented a ratty appearance. The state of all those age-related changes characterized a person between forty-five and fifty years old—not thirty-five to forty-five, as Bernard had stated.

The next step was to determine the victim's height. Standard practice at the time was to stretch out the cadaver and add four centimeters (one and a half inches) to roughly account for the loss of connective tissue. But that was too inaccurate for Lacassagne. Instead, he made use of the newly developing field of anthropometrics—the statistical study of body dimensions. Researchers had been experimenting with methods of deducing the size of a body from individual bones, but no one had done the kind of comprehensive studies that would make their correlations precise and authoritative. Lacassagne knew about this shortcoming, so he assigned Étienne Rollet to write a thesis on the relationship between certain bones of the skeleton and the length of the body. Over the years, Rollet obtained the cadavers of fifty men and fifty women and measured more than fifteen hundred bones, down to the millimeter. He focused on the six largest bones, including the three bones of the upper and lower leg (the femur, tibia, and fibula) and the three of the upper and lower arm (the humerus, radial, and ulna). He carefully charted the bone lengths of men and women—right-handed and left-handed people of various ages.

As he recorded and charted hundreds of measurements, Rollet began to see certain regularities. Within a given gender and race and general age cohort, the length of individual long bones of the skeleton bore a constant correlation to the overall body length. For example, a man's thighbone measuring 43.7 centimeters (1 foot, 5 inches) corresponded to a body height of 1.6 meters (5 feet, 3 inches). If his upper arm measured 35.2 centimeters (1 foot, 2 inches), he probably stood at 1.8 meters (5 feet, 11 inches).

The findings were so predictable and consistent that Rollet realized he could create a forensic tool. He compiled two charts—one for men, one for women—with six columns for bone lengths and one for the overall calculated body length. By looking up the size of any of the six major bones, a doctor could move his eye across the chart and estimate the length of the entire body. The chart had limited accuracy, however: The thighbone lengths, for example, increased in increments of six centimeters, and the overall body lengths by increments of two. To make the estimates more precise, Rollet developed a simple mathematical equation that would increase the accuracy to within half a centimeter. The method seemed almost too simple; yet he tested the procedure on several cadavers, including that of a recently executed criminal, and found it quite precise.

Lacassagne consulted his student's chart as he cleaned away the flesh that remained on the cadaver's arm and leg bones. Because he had an entire cadaver with all six major bones available, not just a few, as often was the case, Lacassagne could double- and triple-check his results. He averaged the numbers to estimate a body height of five feet eight inches. Bernard's estimate had been about an inch and a half shorter.

Gouffé's family was unsure about his exact height, so Inspector Goron telephoned the victim's tailor and the military authorities in Paris, who had measured him at his time of conscription. Both agreed: He was five feet eight. Further measurements and other calculations told Lacassagne that the victim had weighed about 176 pounds—again a match to Gouffé.

Now for the hair. One of the key reasons that Bernard and Gouffé's brother-in-law had failed to identify the cadaver was that Gouffé's hair was chestnut brown and the cadaver's was black. Lacassagne asked Goron to order his men to go to Gouffé's apartment in Paris, find his hairbrush, and send it by courier to Lyon. Lacassagne could see that the hair from the brush was chestnut in color, just as Gouffé's relatives had described. Then Lacassagne took the bits of black hair that remained on the cadaver and washed them repeatedly. After several vigorous rinsings, the grimy black coating that had built up from putrefaction dissolved, revealing the same chestnut color as the hair from the brush. To make sure the hair color was natural, Lacassagne gave samples to a colleague, Professor Hugounenq, a chemist, who tested them for every known hair dye. He found none. Next, Lacassagne microscopically compared the hair samples from the brush with those from the cadaver's head. The samples all measured about 0.13 millimeters in diameter.

That would have been enough for most medical examiners: the victim's age, height, approximate weight, hair color, and tooth pattern. But it was not enough detail for Lacassagne, who taught that "one must know how to doubt." He had seen too many errors by medical experts who had fit most pieces into place but not all of them. And so he pushed on.

In the days before DNA testing, nothing could rival a fresh cadaver for an accurate identification. A fresh body would reveal facial features and identifying marks, such as scars and tattoos. Relatives could be called to identify the cadaver, which is why morgues at the time included exhibit halls. And yet skin, the great revealer of identity, concealed certain aspects of identity, as well. Skin could erase history. An old injury, such as a bone break or deformity, would exhibit no trace in the healed-over skin. Bones, on the other hand, were "a witness more certain and durable" than skin, wrote Lacassagne. Long after the soft tissues had decayed, the bones would remain just as they had been in the moment of death. So with little more than bones and gristle to work with, he searched for whatever history those bones might portray. He spent hours scraping bits of flesh off the skeleton, examining the points where ligaments connected, measuring bone size, and opening the joints. Something drew his eye to the right heel and anklebones. They were a darker brown than the bones around them. He cut away the tendons that held the two bones together and examined the inner surfaces of the joint. Unlike the clean and polished surfaces of a healthy joint, these bone ends were "grainy, coarse, and dented"—signs of an old injury that had improperly healed. The ankle could not have articulated very well. The victim probably had limped.

Moving forward on the foot, he examined the joint between the bone of the big toe and the metatarsal bone. The end of the metatarsal bone had accrued a bony ridge, which extended clear across the joint and butted into the toe bone. The victim would not have been able to bend his right big toe. Lacassagne suspected that the victim had gout, a disease in which the body loses the ability to break down uric acid. Over time, the chemical accumulates as crystals in the joints, particularly the big toe. In advanced cases, the bone ends build up a chalky deposit, sometimes enough to painfully immobilize a joint.

Lacassagne worked his way up the right lower leg. The fibula, the narrow bone running alongside the calf bone, appeared slimmer than that of the left leg. This meant that the muscle must have been weakened, for without the pull and pressure exerted by muscles, the bones beneath would lose mass. The right kneecap was smaller than the left and more rounded. The interior surface of the kneecap showed several small bony protuberances. None of these features previously had been noticed because the first examination took place three weeks after death. At that stage, both legs could have been bloated with gas. It was only now, with the skin and muscles removed, that this aspect of the victim's medical history was revealed.

To confirm his observations, Lacassagne called Dr. Gabriel Mondan, chief of surgery at the world-famous Ollier clinic in Lyon. Mondan carefully studied the leg and foot bones, sketching their irregularities, treating them with chemicals to remove the bits of flesh, and drying and weighing them. He found that the bones of the right foot and leg weighed slightly less than those of the left, individually and collectively. He confirmed Lacassagne's observation of the kneecap, and of the subtle withering of the lower part of the right leg. He noted that the right heel and anklebones were "slightly stunted." He placed both sets of bones on a table. The bones of the left foot sat normally, with the anklebone, or talus, balanced on the heel. The anklebone of the right foot kept falling off.

Meanwhile, in Paris, Goron's men had been gathering information about Gouffé. They interviewed Gouffé's father, who recalled that when his son was a toddler he fell off a pile of rocks and fractured his ankle. It never healed correctly. Ever since then he'd dragged his right leg a bit when he walked, although many people did not notice. Gouffé's cobbler testified that whenever he made shoes for him, he made the right shoe with an extra-wide heel and used extremely soft leather to accommodate his tender ankle and gouty toes. "His big toe stuck up when he walked," the cobbler said.

Gouffé's physician, a Dr. Hervieux of Paris, attested to a variety of leg problems that had plagued his patient for years. In 1885, Hervieux treated him for a swelling of the right knee. The condition had been chronic, Hervieux reported: Another doctor had considered amputating the leg. Hervieux instead prescribed two months of bed rest, after which Gouffé returned to work. In 1887, Hervieux saw his patient for a severe case of gout in the big toe of his right foot. This, too, was a chronic condition, he said, and caused so much painful swelling that Gouffé could not bend the toe joint. Hervieux sent his patient to a spa at Aix-les-Bains for six weeks. A document from the spa stated that Gouffé had suffered a relapse in 1888.

By now, enough evidence had accumulated for Lacassagne to satisfy even *his* doubts. The victim had been five feet, eight inches tall, weighed 176 pounds, and was about fifty years old. He had chestnut-colored hair and a complete set of teeth, except for the first upper molar on the right. The man had been a smoker—Lacassagne surmised that from the blackened front surfaces of the incisors and canine teeth. Sometime in childhood, the victim had broken his right ankle, an injury that had never properly healed. Later in life, he had suffered several attacks of gout. He had also had a history of arthritic inflammations of the right knee. All these injuries had contributed to a general weakening of the victim's lower right leg, reflected in the reduction of bone mass. He must have frequently suffered pain in that leg and perhaps walked with a slight limp. "Now we can conclude a positive identity," Lacassagne reported. "The body found in Millery indeed is the corpse of Monsieur Gouffé."

Once the body had been identified, the pieces of the case quickly fell together. Goron had a replica of the trunk made and displayed it in the Paris morgue. It caused a sensation: Within three days, 25,000 people had filed past it, one of whom identified it as having come from a particular trunk maker on Euston Road in London. Goron traveled to London and obtained the receipt, which showed that the trunk had been purchased a few weeks before the crime by a man named Michel Eyraud. Goron quickly sent bulletins with descriptions of both Eyraud and Bompard to French government offices on both sides of the Atlantic. He dispatched agents to North America, who followed the couple to New York, Quebec, Vancouver, and San Francisco—always just a few days behind them.

Finally, in May 1890, a Frenchman living in Havana recognized Eyraud and alerted Cuban police. His girlfriend, meanwhile, had stayed in Vancouver, where she met and fell in love with an American adventurer. Eventually, he persuaded her to turn herself in.

With both suspects in custody, the bizarre story of the crime emerged. Bompard and Eyraud had known of Gouffé's wealth and reputation for sexual adventure, and they'd heard that he spent most Friday nights at the Brasserie Gutenberg after emptying his office safe. So they had set a trap. Eyraud went to Bompard's apartment, where he attached an iron ring to the ceiling in an alcove behind her divan. He passed a sturdy rope through the ring, then hid the apparatus and himself behind a curtain. Bompard, meanwhile, went to the café, found Gouffé, and started flirting with him. She persuaded him to go back to her apartment, where she took off her clothes and slipped into a robe. Seductively drawing Gouffé close to her, she playfully slipped the sash around his throat. She passed the ends to Eyraud, who affixed them to the rope and, pulling with all his might, hanged Gouffé before he could react. To their horror, however, when they rifled his pockets, they found that he had left all his money behind somewhere.

They needed to get rid of the body, and fast. They trussed it up in a canvas sack, packed it in a trunk, and bought tickets on the next morning's train to Lyon. Once in Lyon, they spent a night in a rooming house with the body, then rented a horse-drawn carriage to travel into the countryside. They rode about a dozen miles south of the city, then dumped the body on a steep hill leading down to the Rhône River. On the return trip, Eyraud purchased a hammer, smashed up the trunk, and threw the pieces in the woods.

They had expected the body to roll into the river and float downstream, never to be seen again. Unfortunately for them, it got hung up in a bush and became the key piece of evidence that led to their convictions. The world saw it as a miraculous turn of events, and Lacassagne as the wizard who had made it happen. The feat was unprecedented. To think that the corpse had been autopsied and buried for months! Not even Gouffé's relatives could identify it. But Lacassagne, using the tools of a new science, enabled the victim to exact justice from beyond the grave. "It was no miracle," his former student Locard protested, "because modern science is contrary to miracles." Yet as a work of deduction, it was truly "a masterpiece—the most astonishing, I think, that ever had been made in criminology."

After a massively attended and publicized trial, Eyraud received the death penalty and Bompard was sentenced to twenty years in prison. On Feburary 4, 1891, Eyraud went to the guillotine. Thousands of people mobbed the event, straining to glimpse the notorious killer. Street vendors circulated among them, selling miniature replicas of the infamous trunk. Inside each was a toy metal corpse bearing the inscription "the Gouffé Affair."

Three

First Kill

Standing outside the Saint-Robert asylum, Joseph Vacher felt certain that God loved him. How else could he explain the fact that both he and Louise had survived the shooting, that he had lived through the horrors at Dole, and that he had survived his jump from a speeding train? As he later recalled in his testimony and letters, who but God would have placed him in Saint-Robert, where kindly alienists truly understood him? Who but God would have guided their decision to set Joseph free after only three months in confinement? And now that he was released from the asylum, Vacher felt certain that God would tell him what to do.

Meanwhile, he needed to find lodging and work. He had 170 francs in his pocket from the paid field work he had done in the asylum, as well as a certificate of honorable discharge from the army, his knife, and a pistol. He started wandering. He found odd jobs and slept in haylofts along the way. After a couple of weeks, he grew tired of this existence and bought a train ticket to Menton, a Mediterranean resort town, where his sister Olympe worked in the Monte Carlo Café. Olympe had always been leery of her youngest brother. She remembered how he would run wild in the fields, brandishing a club.

Nonetheless, she agreed to take him in. For the next several days, he stayed in his room for the most part, writing, sometimes emerging to regale her with unsettling stories about the asylums. After a week, she gently suggested he go elsewhere—perhaps he could stay with the monks again. She took him to the train station and bought him a ticket to Saint-Genis-Laval, the site of the monastery that once housed him. She promised to send money whenever he needed it.

After he left, she noticed a pile of crumpled-up letters in the fireplace. She flattened them out and found page after page of passionate scribblings to Louise Barant, the woman he had shot. *He really is completely crazy,* she thought. She set fire to the letters and hoped she would never see him again.

Vacher rode north in the direction of Lyon, through landscapes that changed from Mediterranean to temperate. Palm trees gave way to chestnuts and pines; dry, ragged countryside yielded to shadowy valleys and paths lined with impenetrable hedges. Six miles before reaching Lyon, he got off in Saint-Genis-Laval, an ancient walled village near the banks of the Rhône. He recalled with pleasure the years he'd spent wandering among the monastery's arched passageways while contemplating the mysteries of the Trinity. Surely the monks would remember, too, and take him in.

The monks had very different memories of Vacher, and they turned him away.

He caught a train to Lyon, where he worked at a few odd jobs. Finding that urban life did not agree with him, he wrote to his sister for train fare out of town. She declined; so he left the city on foot, headed for his native town of Beaufort. He walked south along the Rhône, taking towpaths and carriage trails that wended their way between the riverbank and the vine-covered hillsides. May was a hopeful time along the banks of the Rhône: The apricot and peach buds held the promise of ripening fruit, the lavender and rosemary bushes released their perfume, and the squawk of the magpie punctuated the air. When he came to the small city of Vienne, he turned left and crossed the iron bridge across the river. His route would take him up into the hills, where, after a few days of begging and stealing, he would find himself in the town of Beaurepaire. With God looking over him, he felt that things were certain to work out his way.

Eugénie Delhomme was an attractive twenty-one-year-old woman who worked at the silk mill of Monsieur Perrier, on the outskirts of Beaurepaire. It was one of hundreds of such factories scattered throughout the villages that fed the burgeoning textile industry of Lyon. Inside the mill, hundreds of silk reels mechanically twitched as they wound the threads from skeins onto bobbins. Amid the staccato clatter, an army of women monitored the apparatus, deftly reaching in and straightening tangled fibers. It was a grueling day that began at 5:00 in the morning and lasted, with a lunch break, until 8:30 at night. Eugénie received twenty-four sous per day, barely enough to buy a pound and a half of bread. She sent part of her salary to her elderly father in another town.

It was a tough life, but a decent one for Eugénie and her companions. They lived in the factory dormitory together, ate in the factory dining hall, and spent evenings gossiping at the Café Dorier in town. Many of them had love affairs with the local men; Eugénie, in particular, was known to have had several. People remarked that if you walked along the lane that bordered the factory, you could often hear kissing on the other side of the hedge.

On Saturday evening, May 19, 1894, Eugénie got up from her workstation about an hour before quitting time and headed out the factory door. She had just eaten a dinner provided by the company. She wore a red-and-white-striped smock and Molière shoes—a popular style with open tops, stumpy heels, turned-up toes, and fancy laces. They were named for the playwright, whose foppish characters wore similar footwear. "Where are you going?" her supervisor asked. "It's beginning to rain."

"Oh, I'm just going to take a walk in the alley. I'll be back right away."

No one knew if Eugénie had planned a rendezvous with a lover or whether she just needed some air. In any event, she did not return to work for the rest of the shift, nor did her friends see her in the dormitory that night. The next morning, Monsieur Perrier did not see her, either, which surprised him, because she had always been reliable.

That afternoon, a local woman was grazing her sheep near the mill when she saw a pair of Molière shoes protruding from under a hedge. She knew this was a place where lovers would lie in each other's embrace, but became curious when she noticed only one pair of feet. She wandered over to take a closer look.

Eugénie's body, only two hundred yards from the factory door, looked like it had been attacked by a wild beast. On hearing the woman's screams, the workers poured out, and they recognized the victim. Under the horrified eyes of the crowd, the police took notes on the crime scene; then they transported the body to the hospital in Beaurepaire, where a doctor named Claude Brottet conducted an autopsy.

Under French law, any local doctor could be required to perform an autopsy if called upon by the authorities to do so. There were only a few proper morgues in the country, and only a few modern anatomy labs. Conditions in the rural areas were especially primitive. Police would carry the body to the nearest farm or perhaps to a municipal building. There, working over a kitchen table or a functionary's desk, breathing the stench of a putrefying body, and working without gloves, a doctor would attempt to do an autopsy skillful enough to be admitted as evidence in court.

"I can recall almost none of these operations without deep feelings of repugnance and discouragement," wrote Dr. Henri Coutagne, a colleague and friend of Lacassagne who sometimes was called upon to do rural autopsies.

> If the temperature is not too cold, we would put the cadaver for better or worse in the open air in a courtyard or in a barn on some planks propped up on some barrels or casks. We would get water . . . linens . . . and operate slowly, completely exposed to all the changes in temperature, without help, and consider ourselves lucky if the policeman acts as a clerk. But if it is cold the question becomes more complicated; the body is transported for better or worse (for there are no stretchers available in the countryside) into a community building, such as City Hall, the police station, or school. . . . One time we were obligated to operate on the municipal council's meeting table . . . the mayor afterwards faced a veritable revolt on the part of the administrators.

Sometimes he would have no choice but to operate in the victim's house, often on the "victim's own dinner table."

For this miserable, dangerous work, doctors would receive twenty-five francs for an ordinary autopsy, thirty-five francs if the job required an exhumation, and from fifteen to twenty-five francs for a newborn, depending on whether it was fresh or had to be exhumed. (The new rates were instituted in 1893 after lobbying by Lacassagne and his colleagues. Previously, the payments had been about a tenth of that amount.) The procedure was designed to move forward in stages. On arriving at the scene, the doctor would fill out a form with his name, the names of other officials, and whatever background he could supply about the case. He would describe the immediate area: Were there traces of blood? Ripped clothing? Trampled bushes or other signs of struggle? Then he would describe the position and condition of the body and then—still without touching it—go over every inch of the cadaver, noting all identifying characteristics and describing and measuring every wound. Then he would turn the cadaver and continue to examine it minutely. He would be sure to note which insect larvae were colonizing the body and how far along they were in their development, a signal as to the date of the death. Only then would the team be ready to move the body to a protected place for the autopsy.

With the cadaver on a table or on a clear stretch of ground, the doctor would make sure to open and examine the head, neck, thorax, abdomen, and stomach. Given the uneven state of medical training, Lacassagne assumed nothing when he published instructions for medical examiners. Finally, the medical examiner was to register, in a written protocol, the facts and his conclusions.

Brottet generally followed the procedures. He duly noted the location of the body, and the evidence that it had been dragged from the crime scene, a short walk away, where he found trampled, bloody bushes and chewed-up ground. He carefully described the external wounds and abrasions; then, during the autopsies, he noted the corresponding damage to internal organs.

Based on his examination, Brottet concluded that Eugénie had been attacked in the alley about 7:00 or 8:00 p.m., about an hour after her last meal. (He had found partially digested bread, cheese, and alphabet pasta in her stomach.) The attacker had grabbed her throat, thrown her to the ground, and started strangling her with two hands, as evidenced by the finger marks on both sides of her throat. She must have resisted fiercely, judging from the trampled vegetation and the bruising of her palms. The assailant had tried to stifle her cries by forcing his hand over her mouth (evidenced by the inner surface of her lower lip, which has been torn by her front teeth) and pinned her with his hands and feet (evidenced by footmarks on her left knee). The suffocation must have been almost complete when, in order to hasten her death, he stabbed her several times. Wounds on the right side of the victim's neck indicated that the killer had stabbed with his left hand as he continued to strangle her with his right. Eugénie must have been dead by that point, but the killer was frenzied. He repeatedly stomped her around the torso, chest, and pubis. He then used his knife to dig out the areola of her right breast and threw the bloody tissue away. There was no evidence of rape. In the end, the killer dragged his victim away from the crime scene and left her behind the hedge.

As complete as the autopsy was, Bottet missed some key observations. He departed from Lacassagne's handbook by neglecting to note the condition of the rectum, which might have revealed signs of anal rape and told him more about the nature of the predator. Nor was he, nor the police, able to make plaster casts of footprints, because the rain had made the ground a muddy soup. The trail began and ended with the body.

Police fell back on the investigative methods they had followed for decades, relying on denunciations, rumor, and innuendo, even when physical evidence pointed to the contrary. They would round up suspects on the merest suspicion and hold them in jail until, police hoped, one of them cracked.

Assuming that the murder was a crime of passion, they arrested the victim's most recent lover, a young man named Eugène Dorier. There was no physical evidence against Dorier and the young man had an alibi, but the police held him for twenty-nine days.

Next, they arrested a young man named Louis François, who they felt had had a motive to harm the victim. Eugénie had an illegitimate baby and for a time claimed it belonged to François. Searching a trunk of Eugénie's belongings, police found some letters from him in which he angrily denounced her allegation. A couple of witnesses thought they had glimpsed François near the crime scene, though they could not agree on the time. His clothing bore no traces of mud or blood, and friends of Eugénie said she had long since conceded to François that the baby was not his. Despite this, he was arrested and remained in jail for four months without trial.

Meanwhile, someone had come forward with a bloody knife and a cap from the crime scene. The police made no attempt to find their owner.

Their final suspect was Louis Lacour, a servant of the factory owner. Lacour had lost his watch a few days before the crime, and it turned up in a rivulet not far from the struggle. It mattered not to the police that Lacour had an alibi; arresting him would show that they were active and eager. In a clumsy attempt to build a case against Lacour, they visited the parents of François. The police insisted to the mother that the only way she could clear her son was to inculpate someone else in the killing.

"Could it have been Lacour?" asked an officer. "Yes or no—*do you accuse Lacour?*"

The mother said she could not. The police made it clear that until she did, her son would remain in jail. In time, she relented, and the police arrested Lacour.

The police now had three suspects in jail, based on no evidence. Had they bothered to cast a wider dragnet, they might have talked to Victorine Gay, a fifty-five-year-old woman in a neighboring town who had been stalked by a stranger while guarding her sheep earlier in the day the killing occurred. He got close enough for her to see the scar on his cheek and his sagging right eye before she took flight. That same day, a Beaurepaire woman named Eydan had been tracked by a disfigured vagabond, but she was rescued by her husband before the stranger could attack. A third woman, Mélanie Pallas, saw the same vagabond creeping up on her from about thirty yards away. She kept walking and loudly conversed with an imaginary companion, convincing the stranger that she was not alone.

All three women described the same stranger, and the last incident took place only a few hundred yards from where Eugénie Delhomme was killed. In fact, the very night of Eugénie's killing, half of Beaurepaire was out looking for the mysterious stalker; the police never made the connection between those events and the murder. They already had their suspects. It was not until three thousand citizens signed a petition that the police granted François his freedom. They released the other young men, as well. Still, with the murder unresolved, suspicion in the small town remained high, making life so difficult for the young men that they all had to leave. Lacour found work in the small city of Vienne, in the Rhône Valley, about halfway between Beaurepaire and Lyon. François and Eugène enlisted in the army for service in Algeria.

Eugénie Delhomme's elderly father had walked eighteen miles from the village of Charmes to attend his daughter's funeral. Along the way, he collected flowers and lovingly wove them into a bouquet. During the funeral, attended by all the factory workers, he placed the bouquet over the crude wooden cross that stood as Eugénie's marker. Then he threw himself into the open grave and wailed. He stayed at the cemetery, crying piteously, for days. He became a ghostly presence in the town, calling out for his daughter, handing out rosaries, and asking strangers to pray for her. Eventually, his family confined him to an asylum, where, after a few months, he died.

This, the first murder Joseph Vacher had committed, surprised even him. He remembered slogging up the trail and coming upon a young woman. Something about the moment—a bump, a flash—ignited a strange feeling inside him.

"A kind of fever came over me . . . of revulsion and craziness," he would say later. "I tried to contain myself, but the rage made me stronger. I let go of everything and threw myself at my victim."

After he dragged the body behind a hedge, he washed himself in a rivulet and kept walking. Soon he was in another *département*, where no one had heard about the crime.

And so began "this terrible, errant, and mysterious life, not knowing where I was going," he would say. "Ever after that, to the four corners of France, I have been shaking out this bag of burdensome abominations that I inherited at Dole."

Four

The Institute of Legal Medicine

The Institute of Legal Medicine in Lyon occupied two floors of a building across the Rhône River from the Hôtel Dieu Hospital and up the street from the university's medical faculty. There, amid the graceful dignity of the university's domed buildings, Alexandre Lacassagne devoted his career to bringing the study of forensics into the modern era. It would be a new kind of work, based on practical training, extensive research, and the translation of that research into standardized procedures. It did not carry the glory of Pasteur's discoveries or the history-changing paradigms of Darwin's. Perhaps for those reasons, his name is mostly forgotten. But in terms of human benefits—villains brought to justice, innocent people freed, the overall *civilizing* effect on society—the impact of Lacassagne's work was immense.

The science of forensics was a recent development compared with the millennium-old history of medicine. Scholars allude to early roots of forensics in Roman and Greek times and the Middle Ages, but those references are more rhetorical than real. Many cite a thirteenth-century Chinese book entitled *Hsi-yuan lu* (Instructions to Coroners) as the first text on how to investigate cases of suspicious death. The document advised investigators to mark carefully the wounds that appeared on the body, taking note of those that appeared above vital organs and comparing their shapes with any weapons found at the scene. But it also gave information more folkloric than true—for example, that all male accidental drowning victims floated facedown and all female victims floated faceup. In 1533, the Holy Roman emperor, Charles V of Germany, enacted a penal code, the *Constitutio Criminalis Carolina,* requiring a "serious examination and, if necessary, opening of the body" in cases of violent death. The document, while creating a legal foundation for forensic science, was very much a product of its age. Rather than sanctioning whole-body autopsies (a practice frowned upon by the Church), it advised coroners simply to widen the wounds to determine their angle and depth. It also prescribed penalties for witchcraft and laid out guidelines for obtaining confessions through torture.

As the Church loosened its prohibition of autopsy, a better understanding of human anatomy emerged. Doctors learned that the body did not consist of four humors sloshing to and fro in a delicate balance, but of organs, such as lungs and a heart that pumped blood. The effects of violence on that anatomy also became clear. In 1575, Ambroise Paré, a barber-surgeon and battlefield physician who became surgeon to four kings, wrote the first of his *oeuvres* (works), which instructed investigators about wounds, fractures, and damage to internal organs. Later, Paolo Zacchia of Rome, physician to two Popes, wrote medical texts about detecting signs of poisoning, abortion, and violent death. German physicians developed the "hydrostatic test" to use in cases of suspected infanticide. They removed the lungs and put them in water. If the organs floated, it meant the infant had been born live and taken its first breaths; if not, the baby had been stillborn.

Still, these works bore the limitations of their times. Most authors continued to give credence to sorcery and provided medical guidelines on the use of torture. Well into the eighteenth century, physicians believed that a woman could be impregnated by the devil, and that severe alcoholics sometimes died from spontaneous combustion. Many believed that if a murderer was brought into the presence of his victim, the wounds of the corpse would "bleed afresh."

It was not until the nineteenth century that a related series of social and scientific developments made modern legal medicine possible. After the French Revolution, control of the nation's hospitals passed from the Church to the state and the medical profession, and many more bodies became available for autopsy. (Many "heroes of the guillotine" were dissected.) Torture was on the wane throughout the modern world, which forced prosecutors to turn to other methods, such as analyzing evidence, to solve crimes. Chemistry was rapidly maturing as a science. It became possible to use laboratory tests to identify poisons such as arsenic, which— odorless and tasteless and producing cholera-like symptoms—previously had been undetectable.* The science of bacteriology, pioneered by Pas-

*In 1840, Mathieu Orfila, dean of the Faculty of Medicine in Paris, caused an international sensation when he employed laboratory tests to demonstrate that Madame Marie Lafarge used arsenic to poison her coarse and boorish husband.

teur and Robert Koch, helped medical examiners understand the process of putrefaction and the changes that take place in a corpse over time. The medical autopsy was becoming routine, along with the microscopic examination of tissues and the spectroscopic analysis of blood. Many of the great universities of Europe had established chairs in legal medicine, including Edinburgh, Berlin, Kraków, Prague, Vienna, and Moscow.

Yet, as with any new science, the state of the art outpaced its practice. Knowledge and expertise spread slowly in that era. Justice informed by misconstrued forensic evidence produced irregular, even monstrous, results.

That was the case in the notorious prosecution of Pauline Druaux in the small town of Malaunay, northeast of Paris, in 1887. On Easter morning, passersby heard a woman screaming for help out the window of her apartment. Rushing inside, they found Pauline Druaux standing over the bodies of her husband and brother-in-law. Madame Druaux seemed woozy and flushed, as though she had been drinking. Two local doctors examined the bodies. They saw no external markings or wounds, but they did observe rose-colored blotches on the skin, some bloody foam around the lips, and a reddish tint to the urine that had seeped from the bodies. In their autopsy report, the doctors referred vaguely to some bleeding in the victims' stomachs, bleeding and congestion of the lungs, and bloody lesions in the intestines. The blood seemed exceptionally red. The doctors also noticed tiny particles of a local beetle species in the cadavers' fecal matter and vomit. This, they felt, gave them the clue that they needed. They had heard stories that one could produce a poison from beetle bodies, known as "Spanish fly." They had never seen this poison before nor isolated it from the victims' stomachs or tissues. But based on the lesions in the digestive tract, the traces of foreign matter in their excretions, and the fact that Pauline had caught her husband in bed with another woman, they turned in a report of death by poisoning. After a short trial, she was convicted and sentenced to life imprisonment.

That would have been the end of the case, but within a year another couple had moved into the apartment and had died. Sometime after that, another young couple moved in and became gravely ill with symptoms that included light-headedness and vomiting, but they survived. Their cat was found dead in the basement.

As soon as Druaux's attorney heard of these events, he petitioned for a new trial. Eventually, the court consented to his demand and assigned a panel of three medical experts to review the case, including Paul Brouardel. Brouardel and his colleagues noted the presence of a lime kiln next door to the Druaux apartment and the fact that under certain weather conditions, the fumes from the stack inundated the residence. On reviewing the autopsy report, Brouardel found that most of the observations were consistent with exposure to carbon monoxide—a relatively frequent occurrence at the time, given the era's improper ventilation. The colorless, odorless gas, emitted by combustion, binds with the hemoglobin in the blood more readily than oxygen. The victim suffocates because the carbon monoxide displaces the oxygen. Hemoglobin that combines with carbon monoxide instead of oxygen turns an especially bright red—hence the ruby color of the patients' blood and the red splotches on the skin. Internal organs become congested and bloody. The gas deprives the brain of oxygen, which makes the victim feel woozy and light-headed, as if drunk.

What amazed Brouardel was that even though doctors clearly described the signs of carbon monoxide poisoning, "not for a minute" did they imagine the cause. "The thing that is most extraordinary is that [Madame Druaux] was condemned to a life sentence of hard labor even though the experts could not say what poison she used." Based on the new forensic analysis, Druaux was released after serving nine years in prison and received an indemnity of forty thousand francs. There was a flurry of articles after her release, some of which recommended medical review panels, but the furor faded and nothing was done.

In another case, a woman named Adèle Bernard was imprisoned for having an abortion. After three months in jail, she gave birth to a child. The court released her.

Lacassagne routinely saw that kind of incompetence in the course of his own consultations. The reason, he felt, was not that the state of science was primitive—as he showed in the Gouffé case, it could be strikingly sophisticated—but that the awareness of that science was not widespread. Outside the great centers of learning, medical jurisprudence was a rough practice, carried out hastily by inept practitioners. The problem was not limited to France: Forensic science in England was years behind that on the Continent, in part because England's coroners, originally designated to protect the financial interests of the Crown, had only rudimentary medical training. The United States had no licensing laws or training at all for its coroners, who often were awarded their positions by the local political machine. In return, a coroner would produce findings that

agreed with those of the police, refer next of kin to well-connected under-
takers, and turn a blind eye to crimes committed by the privileged.*

Lacassagne was appalled by the typically "scandalously insufficient"
autopsy report—a few scribbled lines recorded hours or even days after
the dissection. Despite the requirement to perform an autopsy when a
body was found in their district, many doctors avoided responding. The
work paid poorly and was objectionable and potentially dangerous—
a doctor who pricked his bare finger risked coming down with fatal sep-
ticemia. Those who agreed to perform autopsies tended to be novices or
rural physicians with limited experience in criminal matters. "These are
doctors who during their studies have never seen a hanged person, a strangled person, [or a] little victim of child molestation," wrote Lacassagne.
"In some of these cases, the medical expert is nothing more than the
apprentice or a beginner." He was so disenchanted with rural practitioners that he suggested the justice system bypass them entirely and equip a
fleet of horse-drawn carriages with newly invented refrigeration units to
convey bodies directly to major hospitals and universities.

It was easy to criticize the country doctor, especially if one had not
walked in his shoes. Dr. Paul Hervé, a rural practitioner, wrote a passionate defense of himself and his colleagues, explaining that in a given
week he might have to deliver a baby, patch up a foot that had been punc-
tured with a pitchfork, or even treat a farmer's animals for infections. And
then a knock on the door would come in the middle of the night—a *garde-
champêtre,* or rural constable, summoning him to do an autopsy on a mangled body. (In this regard, Hervé echoed Dr. Coutagne's complaints about
the rigors of rural autopsy.) With no refrigeration to delay putrefaction,
he would have to respond immediately to the call. He remembered one
case on a dark, rainy late-December day, only a few hours before nightfall. Forced by circumstances, he and the officer fashioned a table from a
door and two sawhorses and set it up in the brightest place they could
find—in the middle of a field. The policeman lit lanterns in the darkening

---

*In New York, an idealistic corporate lawyer named Clark Bell tried to clean up the image and
practice of American legal medicine by heading a professional group called the New York
Medico-Legal Society. He founded a scientific periodical, the *Medico-Legal Journal,* in which
he published studies and wrote editorials urging the professionalization of the field. He urged
Harvard, Yale, and a new university, Cornell, to offer degrees in forensic science, but none
took up the challenge. (Clark Bell, "Forensic Medicine and Its Progress," *Medico-Legal Journal* [1889]: 373–374.)

gloom, but their glow changed the look of things, distorting appearances and colors. Hervé raced through the dissection, careful to avoid wounding himself. "The more that I hurried, the more my hands and forearms became soaked with blood and unnamable liquids," he wrote. From time to time, he would rinse his hands in a bucket, scribble his observations on a page, and then pick up his scalpel again. "I could barely see [when] I made my last cut."

Fearing his haste might have caused a misjudgment, he wrapped several of the organs in gauze, stuffed them in his briefcase, and took the "macabre package" back home; he would examine it the next day in his office. He felt he had every right to complain:

> Oh you knowledgeable masters who operate in the great cities . . . you ignore these problems!
>
> You have at your disposition perfectly equipped laboratories; you have morgues of the latest models—maybe even refrigerators to conserve pathological samples that you can study and review. But we, the poor disinherited, you ask us to act quickly to see a body once and come to our conclusions. What responsibility!
>
> A doctor is not God, he is a man who is fallible. And as it happens in science, despite his attention and goodwill, he can make mistakes.

When Lacassagne assumed his position in 1881, forensic education was theoretical and lecture-based—not a good fit for Lacassagne's warm, interactive personality. He felt that what students really needed was practical experience. So in addition to the conventional lectures on anatomy, law, and the physiology of wounds, he added a significant practical component, exposing his students to all sides of the criminal equation, from visiting convicts in Saint-Paul prison across town to assisting medical experts in preparing their court testimony.

The highlight of the students' training involved assisting in the eighty or more criminal autopsies Lacassagne and his staff conducted every year. Each session followed a rigid protocol. Lacassagne or his lab chief would start by describing the known facts of the case—where and when the body had been found, whether authorities suspected foul play, and what they assumed to be the cause of death. Then he would distribute "observation pages" (*feuilles d'observation*)—charts that laid out the procedures they planned to employ. Designed as a kind of flowchart, these pages would prescribe the steps that Lacassagne, his lab chief, and students would follow in investigating each possible cause of death, with a series of observations to check off along the way. Each series of observations would lead them to the next logical series, and so on, until they arrived at a conclusion. "There is nothing more indispensable, more useful to the students, than getting habituated to medical-legal protocols," Lacassagne would say.

To do such exacting work required a well-equipped facility, and Lacassagne created one of the world's most advanced criminal laboratories at his Institute of Legal Medicine. The ground floor housed a modern amphitheater for dissections, with a rotating table in the center and semicircular galleries that could hold up to one hundred observers. An elevator brought corpses up from the basement and lowered the remains after the dissections. Adjacent to the operating theater was a laboratory containing microscopes and spectroscopic equipment.

Upstairs from the laboratory was a large criminal museum that served as a reference base. There, students, colleagues, and magistrates could wander among the exhibit cases and study the variety of natural, accidental, and purposeful deaths in order to inform their own investigations. One display case, for example, held everything related to fetuses and newborns—embryonic skeletons, bones with fractures typical of infanticide, instruments used for illegal abortions, and the heads of infants at several stages of development. Enormous glass cylinders held the bodies of stillborn infants, suspended in clear liquid as though in an eternal womb. Two glass cases were devoted to skulls and their fractures—broken from accidental deaths, suicides, and crimes, including falls from high places, hammer blows, and bullets. One cabinet contained projectiles and cartridges of every known firearm. One cabinet was stocked with vials of poisons, drawers filled with microscopic preparations of human and animal hair, and fabrics stained with blood, sperm, and pus. There was a collection of various ropes and chords used in hangings, as well as Lacassagne's collection of thousands of tattoos.

Several tall cases made of wood and glass displayed skeletons of criminals who had been guillotined, the bones wired together in a standing position. Another case contained twenty-four plaster casts of the criminals' brains and reconstructed models of their heads. There were hundreds of photographs of criminals' faces, grouped according to the crimes they had committed.

The largest and most important collection exhibited body parts collected from crime scenes—some conserved in alcohol or dried, others rendered in plaster reproductions, photographs, or anatomical sketches. "One finds there wounds created by instruments sharp and blunt, wounds of all sorts: of the skin, heart, lungs, head, liver, kidneys," according to an article in the *Archives of Criminal Anthropology*. The most useful part of this exhibit was one in which various weapons were placed alongside organs with the wounds they had created. "Weapons" was quite a broad category, including revolvers, pistols, pocketknives, swords, hammers, shovels, hatchets, and other improvised implements of destruction. With cause and effect visually reunited, medical examiners could work backward from a cadaver to the weapon that might have caused the damage.*

Adjoining the museum was a library full of books, journals, and the hundreds of theses Lacassagne's students had written. The halls were festooned with more than three hundred maps representing a criminal geography of France, and charts showing trends in crime dating back to the 1820s. Those charts highlighted another of Lacassagne's life missions— not only to develop methods to solve crimes but to uncover the patterns and causes of the phenomenon. He became famous for his opposition to Cesare Lombroso, the great Italian criminologist, who held that some people were biologically "born criminals." As Lacassagne's charts and other studies showed, he sensed larger forces at work behind criminality, such as poverty, family life, times of the year, and economic cycles. The debate between Lacassagne's "Lyon School" of criminology and Lombroso's "Italian School" would become an ongoing theme in their lives and their field.

Lacassagne and his students did not confine themselves to the workrooms of the institute, but drew on the vast intellectual and material resources offered by the medical faculty and the Hôtel Dieu Hospital. As

*Envied throughout Europe, the museum became a forerunner for others in the capitals of criminal science. At the University of Turin, in Italy, Cesare Lombroso created a museum devoted to "scientific policing." Rivaling Lacassagne's in size, it was less dedicated to practical forensics than to demonstrating Lombroso's theories about the hereditary nature of crime, with numerous examples of the "criminal type." At the University of Graz, in Austria, about one hundred miles south of Vienna, the jurist Hans Gross created the Kriminalmuseum as an instructional tool for his students and for magistrates; others were built in Berlin, Würzburg, and Prague. All presented vivid displays of the seemingly endless variety of crime and science's determination to attack it.

seen in the Gouffé case, Lacassagne believed strongly in collaboration, and he readily called in experts from the faculties of surgery, anatomy, toxicology, entomology, and other disciplines. The hospital often contributed bodies. Limited data were available on the etiology of wounds, especially those caused by modern revolvers, rifles, bombs, and bayonets. Sometimes, when a mysterious wound was presented, Lacassagne and his colleagues would try to reproduce it on fresh cadavers from the hospital and work backward to the weapon and circumstance that had caused it.

All these resources gave Lacassagne the opportunity to expand the study of forensic medicine beyond the realm of ordinary investigations. He helped create a field known as "medical archaeology," in which he used the tools of modern forensics to explore the lives and deaths of historic characters. In one study, he and a colleague re-created the 1793 assassination of the French revolutionary Jean-Paul Marat, who was stabbed by Charlotte Corday as he soaked in his bathtub. There had always been questions about the nature of the fatal wound. In order to reconstruct those final moments, Lacassagne and a colleague obtained a cadaver of the same size and build as Marat, positioned it as Marat had been in his tub, and stabbed it several times with a table knife at the same angle as recorded by the original physician. When they autopsied the cadaver, they found that Corday, who had been educated in a convent and had no history of violence, had struck an exceedingly precise and lucky blow. (Indeed, it took Lacassagne and his colleagues several strikes to duplicate it.) The blade of her knife had slipped between Marat's first and second ribs, a space no wider than a twentieth of an inch, clipped the aorta, passed under the pulmonary artery, and entered the left atrium of the heart. If she had held the knife at any other angle or rotation, the ribs or the sternum would have deflected it.

A sense of excitement pervaded the institute—not the ghoulish frisson of working with body parts, but a feeling of doing creative and important research. "The medico-legal school of Lyon is indeed an active, hardworking group, full of confidence and order," infused with "the will and spirit of the master," wrote a visiting scientist from Brussels. That spirit of inquiry extended to matters beyond crime and death. One day in 1892, when Lacassagne heard that the celebrated math genius Jacques Inaudi was coming to town, he invited him to the institute, where the prodigy submitted "with much good grace" to several hours of cognitive testing.

Much to their surprise, Lacassagne and his students found that Inaudi did not process equations visually, as they had expected, but by repeating the problems over and over in an "internal dialogue." Another time, the bishop of the Basilica of Saint-Denis asked Lacassagne to investigate a shroud given to his church by Charlemagne and believed to have been worn by Jesus on the cross. Lacassagne and a colleague confirmed the age of the garment and a dye that might have come from the Sea of Galilee, but they could not be more specific about its provenance. While not ruling out the chance of authenticity, Lacassagne reminded the bishop that many such shrouds were in circulation and that from time immemorial Middle Eastern merchants had profited and taken delight from duping foreign adventurers.

The third part of Lacassagne's mission, after teaching and research, involved developing reliable and standard methodologies that ordinary doctors could use. Whenever possible, he would take evidence from a crime scene back to the lab, engage his students in investigating the larger issue that the case represented, and tabulate the results in a way that would add to the arsenal of medical expertise. Any issue that needed exploring—chemical changes in the liver at the time of death or physical signs of child molestation, for instance—could become the subject of a research thesis. (He directed 225 student theses in all.) It was for that reason that he assigned Étienne Rollet to research the relationship of long bones to body height, for although the idea had previously been written about, it had never been examined rigorously enough to use as a reliable forensic tool.

Lacassagne published his students' research in a collection called *Works of the Laboratory of Legal Medicine, Lyon*. If a thesis held promise as an investigative tool, he and his colleagues would reconfigure it as a flow-chart, or "observation table," similar to those used in class, and publish it in the *Archives of Criminal Anthropology*. In 1892, he assembled those charts and observations in his book *Vade-mecum du médecin-expert* (Handbook for the Medical Expert). Small enough to fit in a back pocket (the Latin *Vade mecum* means "Go with me"), it contained more than 250 pages of flowcharts, procedures, and background of almost every crime that a medical examiner might come across. It became a best seller in the forensic world, praised for being both comprehensive and easy to follow. More important, it contributed to the standardization of practice. By carefully following the steps in the handbook, even a harried doctor in a remote hamlet could conduct an autopsy that would lead to a righteous conviction. Given the professional nature of his exam, it is likely that Dr. Brottet used Lacassagne's *feuilles d'observation* when conducting the autopsy of Eugénie Delhomme.

A typical and notable example of that process was Lacassagne's discovery that bullets were marked by grooves, known as "rifling marks," which could link a crime to a particular gun. He had been called to a crime scene in 1888 where a seventy-eight-year-old man named Claude Moiroud had been shot dead. Lacassagne conducted the autopsy on-site and found three bullets lodged in the body: One had stopped in the soft tissue of the larynx, one had lodged up against the shoulder bone, and one had passed through the abdominal cavity, drilled through a kidney, and lodged near the spine. Examining the bullets, he found something that surprised him: Even though each bullet had passed through a different part of the body, and only one had hit solid bone, all had identical markings. "It was extraordinary," he wrote. "The bullet found in the larynx, which had not collided with anything hard, was creased along its axis with the same kind of furrow as the bullet that was lodged in the shoulder. . . . It seemed to be a kind of marking or sign of identity of the revolver."

A witness had said that the girlfriend of a young man named Echallier was hiding his gun at her home. Police seized the weapon and gave it to Lacassagne. He contacted the venerable arms manufacturer Maison Verney-Carron, which sent an expert, Charles Jeandet, to the crime scene. He explained to Lacassagne that gunmakers cut helical grooves in the barrels to cause bullets to spin, increasing their accuracy. Those grooves left characteristic markings on the projectiles—something that was common knowledge in the arms industry but not among medical professionals.

Lacassagne returned to Lyon with Jeandet, the gun, and several more bullets. In his lab, he obtained the cadaver of an eighty-year-old man from the hospital, dressed it in the same kind of clothing as the victim had been wearing, and fired two shots—one into the shoulder bone and the other into the soft tissue of the abdomen. When he retrieved the bullets, he noted that each showed identical markings and that they matched the markings on the bullets he had recovered from the victim. When he examined the bullets through a magnifying glass, he saw even smaller matching grooves within grooves. "The formations are so identical that they must have come out of the same revolver," he concluded.

Echallier was convicted and sentenced to life imprisonment. Meanwhile, Lacassagne, knowing he had stumbled upon a new vein of inquiry, assigned one of his students to research the phenomenon. After months of research and testing, his student and he published an article in the *Archives of Criminal Anthropology*, along with a chart listing twenty-six common bullets from French, American, and British pistols, as well as their weight, shape, and predominant groove patterns. More comprehensive charts would follow, until identifying the markings on a bullet became standard practice in criminal science.

Amid all his successful research and institution building, Lacassagne faced one goal that eluded him—replacing the city's notorious morgue. Morgues served a critical function, not only for public hygiene but as a place where unknown bodies could be displayed for possible identification. In Lyon, the "floating morgue," as it was called, sat on a barge in the Rhône River, chained to a pier in front of the Hôtel Dieu Hospital. The facility consisted of a wooden building twenty meters square, with a large "exhibition room" where next of kin could view the cadavers, a small autopsy room, and a bedroom for the guard. Every year, scores of bodies of the anonymous and indigent would arrive for identification and autopsy.

In 1853, when the city fathers placed the morgue in the river, it had seemed a good idea. The location was close to the two biggest sources of bodies in Lyon—the main hospital and the Rhône River itself. (Nearly thirty people drowned every year in the Rhône and the Saône, the two rivers running through Lyon.) Real estate on the river cost nothing, and the breezes drifting down the Rhône would surely carry the odors away from the city. But reality proved otherwise. The facility was a damp, stinking place, breathless during the summer and so cold in winter that surgeons had trouble holding scalpels between their fingertips. The smell of the corpses permeated the woodwork. Bilge pumps fought a constant battle against flooding. Storms on the river caused the morgue to break free, smashing against the bridgeworks and spilling its cargo. Even normal turbulence caused disarray. The Rhône was one of the most heavily freighted rivers in France. When steamships churned by, their wakes would cause the barge to heave; sometimes the chains would snap and it would drift away.

Lacassagne repeatedly wrote to city hall, urging that this unhealthy facility be replaced. He once complained that while he was giving a demonstration to several dozen students, the barge settled so deeply into the river that water began seeping up through the floorboards. The city officials ignored his requests.

It was an embarrassing contrast to the Paris morgue, which Lacassagne's Paris-based colleague Brouardel liked to boast about. Constructed in front of the city's main hospital, the capital's morgue had a large exhibition space with a dozen marble tables tipped to display bodies at a convenient viewing angle. They were separated from the public by a glass wall, similar to the display windows of the new department stores. Cadavers were chilled by modern steam-powered refrigeration units. Refrigeration proved a boon to police work, as it delayed putrefaction and kept bodies recognizable for weeks. To increase the likelihood of identifying cadavers, authorities kept the morgue open to the public from dawn to dusk. People flocked in, whether or not they had missing relatives. Thousands strolled through every day to see the latest arrivals. Workmen came by on their lunch breaks, and retirees drifted in to occupy their time. The morgue became such a citywide attraction that the Thomas Cook tour company of London included it in its Paris itinerary.

That was not at all the case in Lyon, where the dankness and stench repelled all but those who needed to be there. There was no refrigeration unit to suppress odors; only a primitive pumping system dribbled water from the river over the corpses. The only thing remotely positive about the morgue was the beloved old guardian, Delègue, who managed to live there despite the smell. He seemed to have wandered out of the Old Testament, with his white beard and hair hanging down to his chest, a pipe clamped between his teeth, and his faithful little dog. When asked about any of the bodies on board, he would respond with terse efficiency about how long it had been in the river and how long it had been putrefying—all after a quick glance at the corpse. "In order to resolve those questions it was [normally] necessary to understand many variables," recalled Edmond Locard, who trained at the morgue as a student of Lacassagne, "but this old patriarch never made a mistake."

In 1910, after nearly three decades of Lacassagne's imprecations, the city finally broke ground for a new facility on dry land near the Faculty of Medicine. One January night during construction, a violent storm ripped the barge from its mooring. Caught in the grip of a furious current, the morgue smashed against the bridge supports, its pieces scattering down-river for miles. Delègue, his dog, and three corpses were thrown over-board. The next morning, Delègue was found safe on the riverbank, but his dog and the bodies had washed away. When told what had become of his dog, the crusty old patriarch wept like a child.

Five

The Vagabond

Hours after the Eugénie Delhomme killing, Joseph Vacher washed his blood-spattered clothes in a stream, formed a haystack into a shelter on a hill overlooking the crime scene, and bedded down. The next morning, the property owner noticed the construction and figured that a hobo must have spent the night there.

Vacher walked east, a little over forty miles, to Grenoble. After a few days of fruitlessly looking for employment, he headed back into the countryside, wandering from farm to farm, asking for charity, a place to sleep, or a job. His was not a reassuring presence, since he grimaced hideously whenever he talked, and the discharge from his ear gave off a nauseating smell. If people seemed suspicious or frightened, he would show them his regimental papers, which sometimes reassured them.

Vacher had acquired the accoutrements for life on the road. He wore maroon velour pants, a black felt hat, and sturdy shoes. He carried a voluminous hobo's sack, filled with cooking utensils, bits of food and clothing, a wallet with some change, a file, a pistol, and, at various times, a razor or a knife. Somewhere along the way, he acquired an accordion, which he sometimes played—badly—while seeking alms. At some point in his journeys, he started carrying two large and deadly wooden clubs.

In May or June of 1894, a landowner near Geneva, Jules Cartier, hired Vacher as part of a hay-scything crew. The new man was not at all friendly or chatty like the other migrant laborers; he kept his head down and maintained a gloomy silence as he thrashed away. One day, he lost track of what he was doing and kept slicing right into the asparagus field. He did not take well to being corrected. "Where did you get this rhinoceros?" one of the workers asked the foreman. "I'm afraid of him."

Once, Vacher took the sheets off his bed, hid them in his suitcase, and accused a coworker of stealing them. The police discovered the truth and ordered him to leave the area immediately. He set out for France.

In doing so, he joined a flood of wretched humanity that was inundating the French countryside in the century's final decades. These were the "vagabonds"—an estimated 400,000 hard-core unemployed who were looking for housing, seeking employment, begging, and committing crimes. These drifters, part of an international phenomenon, obsessively worried Europeans, who linked them to every social evil.

Beggars had always been a fixture throughout Europe, but rapid modernization had caused huge economic dislocations, making the problem immeasurably worse. The mechanization of agriculture led to worldwide price declines, which by the 1890s had accelerated into a collapse. France was hit particularly hard: In addition to the overall drop in farm prices, the vineyards had become infested with phylloxera—a sap-sucking insect related to the aphid—which provoked a "bubonic plague" in the wine industry. Whole villages emptied. Thousands of families lost their livelihoods and land, flooding Paris, Lyon, Grenoble, and other cities in search of a new beginning. Many fell back on public assistance. Rather than increase charity to meet the need, many city fathers tightened the residency requirements so as not to attract more indigents to their towns. Many argued to eliminate aid altogether, because, they said, it only encouraged laziness.

By the mid-1890s, 1 percent of the French population was wandering the countryside, rootless and penniless. Their numbers included the mentally ill overflowing from asylums, the abandoned elderly, and anyone else who was uncared for.

In 1899, investigating magistrate Émile Fourquet (*Foorkay*) published a monograph about vagabonds, based on interviews with dozens who had been in his custody. More humanistic than some of his colleagues, he compared them not to a contagion but to migratory birds that followed the weather and the crop cycles for shelter and food. Fourquet was able to discern at least two major migratory groups, whose ragged routes intersected and overlapped. One group would spend the winter in the south of France and migrate up the Rhône Valley as various fruits and vegetables ripened for harvest. The other group would spend winters in Brittany, where the coastal winter was made mild by the Gulf Stream, and then walk to the area north of Lyon to harvest cereals, vegetables, and wheat. Later in the summer, that group would head north into Normandy and Belgium, taking jobs in small factories and harvesting sugar beets.

In August, both groups tended to converge south of Paris for the cereal harvest, then wander down to the vineyards of the Rhône Valley and the south. In October, they would drift farther south to Provence to pick chestnuts and then olives. As the fall progressed, many would traverse the country, walking back up to Brittany, while others would trudge farther south to Lourdes, near the Spanish border. Those who were too weak to walk south for the winter would get themselves arrested so they could spend the mandatory three- to six-month sentence in one of the country's special beggars' prisons, where at least they would not starve or freeze to death.

Fourquet's description was not neat or comprehensive—after all, he was generalizing about hundreds of thousands of indigents, some with families, some elderly, some young, and many of whom were mentally ill. He also noted that drifters were drawn to certain areas not by the climate, but by the reputation of the inhabitants. The citizens of some areas, such as Dauphiné and Savoie, the mountainous regions near the Swiss border, were known for hospitality, while others, such as the residents of Touraine, which encompasses the city of Tours, were not.

Vacher himself wrote about those differences in a letter to Louise:

Two years ago, with a pair of boots I bought for 40 sous, I was in Brittany, where I saw everything . . . and in Normandy, big towns and rich prairies, and cider that was every bit as good as in Brittany. I was also in Marne [a region east of Paris] where the people really are religious and humane . . . and above all the Savoie, where the people are particularly humble and loyal. This year I also saw Touraine, which they call the garden of France, but *not of humanity*. . . . I am not the only traveler who makes that observation.

In earlier days, villagers had welcomed vagabonds to their towns. Those who were craftsmen were needed for their skills while others were required for farm labor. But industrialization had reduced the need for their manual labor, and the economic depression hit farmers very hard. Those farmers who could afford to hire migrant laborers got rid of them the moment the harvest was done, lest they be saddled with beggars to care for.

"People used to be nice to us and reassure us in the past, but now we receive a glacial welcome," a man arrested for vagrancy told Fourquet.

> But how much confidence can you have in someone who looks so poor and roughly traveled . . . covered by dirt and rain, who doesn't eat a lot and is not so attractive or in a good mood? In the old days the farmers themselves had to work like this; they remembered that and welcomed us as one of them. Now the farmers who hire us themselves are unhappy. The convents used to comfort us, but not anymore. Everywhere there is suspicion and no more charity.

The vagabonds could not even rely on one another for companionship. They knew how people reacted when a score of unemployed descended on a village: They'd more likely get a job if alone. They walked through life as solitary drifters—hungry, desperate, suspicious of one another, and a worry to the settled people they encountered.

Vacher found work on a farm near Grenoble, then drifted toward the Rhône Valley for the grape harvest. For a while he identified himself as Carpentier, a vagabond whom he had befriended and whose papers he had stolen. (Investigators suspected that Vacher might have killed the man.) He made his way south along the Rhône River, where he briefly worked in a tile factory. He never stayed anywhere for long. A prodigious walker, he would cover more than twenty miles in a day, sleeping in fields or in the rustic stone shepherds' huts.

By the fall of 1894, he entered the district of Var, two days' walk from what later would become known as the French Riviera. It was a mysterious country of dry, craggy peaks surrounded by dense pine forests and precipitous chasms. A man could disappear in those gloomy valleys. Sometimes he would emerge to stop at a rural church long enough to light candles, then disappear again.

On November 20, 1894, Louise Marcel was returning from a neighboring village, where she had gone to ask if anyone had seen her lost puppy. Although only thirteen, she was known to be exceptionally lovely and physically mature beyond her years. When she did not return home by lunchtime, her parents went to look for her. When they could not find her, they organized a search party.

Two days later, searchers found the girl's body in an old sheep barn.

An autopsy revealed the likelihood of postmortem anal rape. There were blood smears on a nearby outcropping of rock where the killer must have wiped his hands.

Ever since he was a young man, Joseph Vacher had felt the pull of two warring tendencies: to lead a life of walking with God, and to satisfy a need for violent sexual gratification. The fifteenth of sixteen children (the father had married twice), he grew up in a single-room house with a red-tiled roof and massive stone walls. He seemed a bright enough child, and his parents made sure he attended school.

He might have had a typical childhood for his time and place, except for certain strange formative experiences. As a baby, he had a twin sister, Eugénie. One day, before going outside to do chores, his mother put Joseph and Eugénie on a bed and covered them with a light fabric to keep the bugs off. She was baking bread in the family's outdoor oven— enormous, heavy loaves that she sold to neighbors to supplement the family's income. When the bread was cooked, she called one of the older children to put the loaf in the house, cautioning him not to put it on the floor. The child, seeing the expanse of fabric on the bed, put the bread down to cool without noticing the infants. When his mother came in, Eugénie was dead.

Joseph would always see God's hand in his deliverance, and from an early age, he showed priestly tendencies. When he was ten years old, his class went on an outing to a church in a neighboring village. The teacher left for a moment to say hello to some friends. When he returned, Joseph had taken the class into the church, had seated them in pews, and was delivering a sermon.

The following year, Joseph was licked by what the family thought was a rabid dog. His mother panicked, sent for a folk remedy, and made the boy drink it. What was in the potion is unclear, and perhaps it did Joseph no harm, but in the months after the incident, he changed. Classmates recalled that he became sneaky and ill-tempered. Once, when he was fourteen, he was pulling a wheelbarrow with one of his brothers, who he felt was not working hard enough. Without warning, Joseph started choking him and probably would have killed him if a neighbor had not intervened. Another time, some classmates rigged up a trip wire and Joseph fell over it. Rather than laughing it off as a prank, he ran to get a gun and started shooting.

At the age of fifteen, he left his village to join the Marist monks in Saint-Genis-Laval. He loved the austere monastery environment, reveling in how his spiritual brothers praised his beautiful handwriting. On a couple of occasions, they sent him to affiliated parishes to teach. Two years later, however, they asked him to leave. Much later, when a newspaper reporter asked why, they would refer only to his inability to "resist certain temptations of the flesh." He had been caught masturbating his comrades.

Vacher, now eighteen, returned to his native town of Beaufort and started taking farm jobs. In June 1888, he tried to rape a twelve-year-old boy, but a neighbor stopped him. He fled to Grenoble, where he stayed with a sister and worked in a restaurant. The job lasted only a month before he was hospitalized for venereal disease. "We called him the Jesuit," a fellow patient later recalled, referring to Vacher's clerical pretensions. "He was sneaky and kept trying to touch the nuns." After his two months of treatment, he went to live with another sister in a village about thirty miles away, but her husband threw him out after six months.

Joseph's illness flared up again, and he checked himself in to Antiquaille Hospital in Lyon. As part of his therapy, which lasted for two months, doctors removed part of his left testicle. He then traveled to Geneva, where he stayed with another brother for several weeks, before he, too, asked him to leave. "I don't know what's wrong with me," Joseph told his brother. "I feel as though I am possessed by something evil. I'm afraid if I met someone I might do them harm."

For the next couple of years, he drifted from town to town, seeking agricultural jobs. In 1889, he visited the Universal Exposition in Paris, where, with tens of millions of people from all over the world, he must have marveled at the newly built Eiffel Tower, the world's tallest structure, and the Gallery of Machines, the world's largest enclosed space, whose steel and glass structure seemed to float over the massive steam engines and electrical dynamos. He may have walked through the popular Cairo exhibit—a reconstructed street from the Egyptian city—and the exhibits celebrating the new science of anthropology, where "primitive" people had been shipped in from the colonies to inhabit re-created villages. He may even have caught a glimpse of the criminal anthropology exhibit, where Alexandre Lacassagne, Cesare Lombroso, and others in the field displayed skulls, tattoos, and annotated maps, with which they tried to make sense of the rising crime rates.

Such pleasures were short-lived. Generally he faced a hardscrabble existence—wandering to a farm, getting a job doing manual labor, and then doing something aggressive or crazy enough to be sent away. At one of his last full-time jobs, at a farm in the Rhône Valley, he started ranting at the dinner table about anarchism and the need to cut rich people's throats. "One day my name will make history!" Joseph shouted as the farmer paid him and showed him the door.

With no likely suspects in the Louise Marcel killing, the police arrested Charles Roux, a neighbor who had discovered the body. They reasoned that he must have known the corpse's location in order to have found it in such a hidden place. The police found footprints nearby made by wooden-soled shoes—the same kind of shoes worn by Roux. They neglected to consider that probably half the townspeople wore wooden-soled shoes, the region's traditional footwear. The police eventually released Roux, but the girl's parents and neighbors never stopped blaming him.

Two weeks later, an elderly couple was slaughtered in their home about half a dozen miles away. As police reconstructed the crime, the woman must have opened the door, where she was felled by no fewer than nine stab wounds. Her husband, who was just getting into bed, had one shoe untied when the attacker burst in. He tried to shelter himself between the bed and the wall and raised his right arm to protect himself, as revealed by defensive wounds. He was killed and mutilated with fifteen savage blows. The killer or killers stole six hundred francs and made off with a sack of wheat. Witnesses reported seeing a man who matched Vacher's description in the area, along with a big blond accomplice. (At various times during the next couple of years, witnesses would report having seen the two men together, but the blond man was never implicated or arrested.)

Having committed three murders in two weeks, Vacher knew he needed to leave the area. It was late December, and vagabonds were migrating south to avoid the cold and the snow. Vacher, however, more comfortable in his native lands of Isère and Savoie, hiked north. In late 1894, a farmer outside Grenoble hired him to watch over his cows. Halfway through the agreed-upon employment period, Vacher quit. When the farmer withheld his pay, Vacher threatened him. The farmer ran to get help. By the time he returned, the vagabond had left.

When faced with the misfortune of large numbers of their citizens, societies can take one of two general approaches. They can extend a helping hand to the sufferers, or they can characterize these people as the "other," somehow deserving of their affliction. Like other countries at the time, France decided that the vagabonds were the "other"—different from settled folk and a threat to orderly bourgeois society. (America's "army of tramps" of the Gilded Age fared no better. A Chicago newspaper advocated poisoning some of them in order to discourage others; the dean of Yale Law School called them "incorrigible, cowardly, utterly depraved savage[s].") Throughout Europe, studying and analyzing the vagabonds became an obsession, as one would study an agricultural blight or a contagious disease. There were international conferences about the problem, and scholars wrote dozens of theses. In language that we now recognize as eugenic, studies referred to vagabonds not as unfortunate human beings, but as the "dangerous classes," the "inferior classes," and "social garbage."

"Vagabondage is in the blood," asserted a prominent social critic of the time, "and this axiom is no less true for children than it is for adults." Most experts felt the same way. No one denied that the phenomenon had grown with worsening economic conditions, but in the prevailing view, the economic depression had not *caused* the phenomenon, but only aggravated an inborn tendency. Like the born criminal characterized by Lombroso, there existed born vagabonds, whose numbers swelled as the economy declined. Granted, there were small numbers of "accidental" vagabonds—families who lost their small farms to debt, perhaps—but the "real" vagabonds were born with a desire to ramble and a contempt for the values of settled society. Most had some form of mental disorder, according to Drs. Armand Marie and Raymond Meunier, the reigning experts on vagabondage during the 1880s and 1890s—hysteria, epilepsy, alcoholism, mysticism, dementia, or an ingrained wanderlust.

In keeping with the "degeneracy" theory that was popular at the time, many saw vagabonds as an evolutionary accident, a throwback to a more primitive species or form of human development. Alexandre Bérard, an authority from Lyon on vagabonds, described them as "wild beasts misplaced in civilized society," victims of an ancient wandering instinct. It had been a useful instinct in its time, he asserted, one that "led primitive people across the steppes, forests, and deserts to populate the earth, create nations, found empires." But the time for that impulse had gone. With no use in a civilized and stable society, this instinct expressed itself in the root-less, maladjusted individuals who populated the byways and frightened the good folk.

Given the notion of a primitive tendency, the connection between vagabonds and crime seemed unavoidable, especially since unemployment and the sensational coverage of crime rose in tandem. Lacassagne himself, usually given to more measured assessments, described vagabonds as simple, impulsive beings who responded to two primitive stimuli: "hunger and sexual desire." That, he explained, was why theft and rape topped the list of vagabond-related crimes. Ignoring the possible complicating factors, he noted that any time a region experienced an influx of vagabonds, serious crime in that area rose, as well. So pervasive was the fear that, in 1885, France had passed a law prescribing life sentences for vagabonds and habitual criminals, many of whom went to the penal colony of Devil's Island off the coast of Guyana. Police arrested beggars by the thousands, detaining forty thousand for vagrancy in 1900 alone. Those who did not go to jail or to the colonies received one-way train tickets from cities back to the countryside.

At noontime on Easter Day, 1895, Antoinette-Augustine Marchand, a twenty-six-year-old fruit vendor and mother of four, was walking home from the farmers' market a few miles south of Lyon. She had had a profitable morning selling oranges, and her earnings made a bulge in her right pocket. As she pushed her handcart up a path near the Rhône, she noticed a vagabond dozing by the roadside. Marchand had heard rumors about a maniac on the loose, and she warily eyed the sleeping figure as she passed by. She was just about to step over some railroad tracks when she felt herself grabbed from behind. Marchand immediately threw herself up against a stone wall to protect her right pocket, but she quickly realized her assailant had another purpose.

"I felt his knee lifting my undergarment all the way up to my stomach," she said. "He had opened his trousers. He held me with his right hand around me and with his left he was touching my sexual parts. He told me to hold still."

She could smell the foul odor from Vacher's suppurating ear, see every detail of his scar and grimace. He held her so tightly that her right arm went numb. A knife blade glinted near her throat. She shrieked and thrashed wildly. She stabbed her fingernails into his eyes, which briefly loosened his grip. When he bobbled the knife, she wrenched herself away with a violent twist, dashed to the other side of the tracks, and started hurling rocks at his face. She kept him at bay until two men arrived and Vacher ran off. "I didn't stop quaking for eight hours," she said.

"I lodged a complaint [with the mayor's office]," said Marchand, "but nothing ever came of it."

Six

Identity

In all of France there could not have been two men more different than Joseph Vacher and Alexandre Lacassagne. Vacher was wild, rootless, primitive, ruled by his impulses and sexual appetite. Lacassagne personified the bourgeois qualities of order, education, and dignity; he was regular in his habits, a voluminous reader, dedicated to service, restrained, and self-deferential. They were the opposite ends of the spectrum of human nature, as exemplified by a popular book at the time, *The Strange Case of Dr. Jekyll and Mr. Hyde*.

Lacassagne was rich in family and personal relationships, but of the more than twelve thousand volumes of books and papers he left behind, almost none was of a personal nature. He defined himself by his work as a scientist and wrote about it with humility and reserve. Still, one can find hints of the man's character and life between the lines of his scientific papers, in the compassionate and heartfelt obituaries he wrote about deceased colleagues, and in the testimonials given by colleagues and former students. In 1901, to celebrate Lacassagne's induction into the Legion of Honor, more than seventy colleagues and former students gathered at the Maderni Restaurant in Lyon, where in long, formal toasts, one after another praised their "dear master" for his scientific accomplishments, his work ethic, his humility and independence, his teaching and guidance. They saw him as the father figure to an intellectual family.

Lacassagne's home life was generally a contented one, marked by hard work and the pleasures of a bourgeois intellectual existence. In 1882, two years after he moved to Lyon, he married Magdeleine Rollet, the daughter of a prominent professor of hygiene. She bore two sons and a daughter: Antoine, Jean, and Jeanne. The sons became internationally known medical researchers; Antoine, a pioneering oncologist, treated Sigmund Freud's terminal throat cancer. The Lacassagnes lived in an apartment in

Lyon and moved twice over the years into increasingly upscale neighborhoods. They spent summers in the family cottage northwest of the city, on the banks of the Loire River. Constructed of traditional plaster and stone, with a red tile roof, it stood on a knoll surrounded by ancient beech, apple, and cherry trees. Outside was a quaint little well with a decorative crank and a bell to summon their guests to dinner. The door knocker gave visitors a preview of Lacassagne's macabre sense of humor: a bronze casting of the left hand of a female criminal. It was not the only such artifact. At their apartment in Lyon, he kept a set of dinnerware on which he had reproduced criminals' tattoos. On special occasions, a guest might be just about finishing his *boeuf bourguignon*, only to find DEATH TO THE AUTHORITIES inscribed underneath.

Inside the country house, books, papers, and photographs covered the walls and every flat surface. Scientific papers competed for shelf space with poetry, philosophy, literature, and the children's drawings. There were albums stuffed with sepia-colored photos from family vacations and souvenir postcards of the Paris Exposition. In the hallway upstairs hung two formal portraits of the family dogs, Tibia and Péroné (in English, Tibia and Fibula), named for the two bones of the lower leg, perhaps because of their tendency to get underfoot. Also on the second floor was a room called the "gallery"—a long, narrow, high-ceilinged room with a wall of windows overlooking the river and three walls covered with photographs. There were numerous snapshots of Lacassagne over the years, increasingly bald-pated and portly, but always with a smile under his walrus mustache. One photo shows him and his family picnicking by the river; others show them sitting in a rowboat and standing with houseguests by the exterior rear wall. There was a photo of playful Uncle Louis, who, after visiting the Egyptian pavilion at the World Exposition, had dressed up as an Arabian sheikh smoking a water pipe. "I smoke only Nile brand" read the handwritten caption. There was a graph drawn by Dr. Lacassagne to chart Antoine's physical and intellectual progress: a line curving upward to show the child's growth from 85 centimeters to 180 centimeters, and his academic development from toddlerhood to his baccalaureate degree. There were newspaper caricatures of Lacassagne performing his famous autopsy of Gouffé. Another photo taken at a conference, with Lacassagne standing amid a cluster of bearded colleagues wearing straw hats and bowlers, features a man in the back row gaily pointing with his umbrella to a sign reading SECTION D'ANTHROPOLOGIE. The one sobering note in the collection of happy artifacts was a large black-framed photo of his wife, Magdeleine, looking thoughtful and serious in a high-buttoned black jacket. A brass plaque on the frame indicated her lifespan: 1856–1893. Her premature death was one of the few heartbreaks of Alexandre Lacassagne's life.

If identity and one's place in society was of paramount importance in the Belle Époque and Victorian eras, it was the defining issue in criminal science, as well—the keystone for the young practice of forensics and an ongoing theme at Lacassagne's institute. Its importance was obvious: Without clearly establishing the identities of the victim and the perpetrator, it was impossible to make a case for the prosecution, or to avoid wild miscarriages of justice.

Never was that principle more vividly illustrated than in the notorious Tisza-Eslar affair, solved by Lacassagne's counterpart in Vienna, Professor Eduard von Hofmann. The affair began on April 1, 1882, in the village of Tisza-Eslar in Austria-Hungary, when a fourteen-year-old housemaid named Esther Solymossy disappeared. After a month of searching yielded no results, suspicions began to focus on the village's Jewish community. Guided by rumor and prejudice, the regional magistrate decided that the town's Jews must have killed Esther, draining her blood to make unleavened bread for the Passover celebration.* He and his men produced evidence for his theory by confining and torturing several of the town's children until one of them, the feebleminded son of the rabbi's assistant, implicated his father and at least a dozen other Jewish citizens.

A month later, a body was found floating in a river, bearing Esther's clothes but no visible wounds. If this body turned out to be Esther's it would prove that she had died far from the village and would thus exonerate the Jews. Hoping that would not be the case, the magistrate brought in two local physicians to identify the body. The doctors, who had never conducted a criminal autopsy, may well have been influenced by the magistrate's opinion, for they concluded that the cadaver in the river could not possibly be that of the fourteen-year-old girl. After looking over the corpse's "general development," they concluded the growth patterns of

---

*This charge, known as the "blood libel," had been levied against Jews in Europe since the Middle Ages.

various bones, including the complete fusion of the frontal bones of the head, could belong only to an eighteen- to twenty-year-old. They also noted that the sexual organs of the corpse were so swollen that she must have had frequent sexual intercourse—highly unlikely for a fourteen-year-old child. The skin of the corpse's hands and feet, unlike that of Esther, who spent her life doing hard manual labor, was tender and white.

News of the murder caused riots in Budapest and other centers with Jewish populations. Talk of pogroms was filling the air. Meanwhile, a liberal member of Parliament asked two young forensic experts at the University of Budapest to exhume and examine the body and send their report to Professor von Hofmann. The professor had written three textbooks on legal medicine and had won international renown after the disastrous fire at the Vienna Ring Theater in 1881, when he sorted out the jumble of bones and teeth to identify the remains of more than three hundred victims.

Von Hofmann spent several weeks comparing the new report on the corpse with the original autopsy and doing his own laboratory work. He concluded that the autopsy provided by the local physicians was so rife with errors as to be useless. Among their many mistakes, von Hofmann noted, was their assertion that the fusion of skull bones did not occur until the victim's late teens. In reality, such fusion would have taken place by age two. Von Hofmann attributed the victim's vaginal swelling not to sexual activity but to prolonged submersion, which had caused the soft tissue to swell; he had seen enough drowning victims to know that. The delicate appearance of the victim's hands and feet was not due to a pampered upbringing, as the doctors had suggested, but to the sloughing off of the outer skin layers caused by extended time underwater.

Von Hofmann supplemented the reports with laboratory experiments. He obtained three cadavers from the hospital—the bodies of individuals aged fourteen, eighteen, and twenty years old—and compared their stages of development with that of the body found in the river. In every category that he could examine or measure—teeth, skeletal dimensions, individual bones—the body in the river differed markedly from those of the two young adults but correlated to that of the fourteen-year-old. The body in the river, he concluded, must have been Esther's.

When the case went to trial in 1883, von Hofmann's report shattered the prosecutor's case. The defendants were set free and a pogrom averted.

Lacassagne considered the Tisza-Eslar affair so important that he published the professor's report in the first edition of the *Archives of Criminal Anthropology,* even though the trial had taken place three years before. Von Hofmann had demonstrated a principle that Lacassagne embraced: that every physiological detail, no matter how small, was important, and that those tiny clues could add up to reveal a person's identity.

In that same first edition, he published a paper by his friend and colleague Alphonse Bertillon, who, working on another aspect of criminal identity, moved police work into the modern era. Bertillon (*Bertiyohn*) was an underachiever in a family of scientific luminaries. His father, Louis-Adolphe Bertillon, was a founding member of the Paris Anthropological Society, and his brother Jacques was a prominent doctor and medical statistician. Yet despite his scientific pedigree, Alphonse showed little promise, briefly attending medical school, drifting through several jobs in England and France, and finally getting a job at the age of twenty-six as a low-level clerk in the Paris Préfecture of Police, mainly through the influence of his father. There, in a dreary basement office where he baked in the summer and froze in the winter, he spent his days copying thousands of descriptions of known criminals onto index cards.

Then, as now, a relatively limited number of offenders committed most crimes. Under French law, first-time offenders tended to receive lenient sentences, in order to encourage their rehabilitation; repeat offenders were given long prison sentences or exiled to Devil's Island. Traditionally, the authorities had branded the people they arrested, but when they abandoned the practice as inhumane in the 1830s, recidivists would disguise their identity by changing their names, hair color, or facial hair. To fight back, police amassed huge collections of card files and photographs, sorted according to birthplace and name. Criminals, however, gave false information, rendering the entire system useless. In desperation, the police chief in Paris offered a ten-franc bonus to any officer who recognized a repeat offender.

Alone in his office with his piles of cards, Bertillon couldn't stop thinking about the information he was copying. He had grown up in a home full of calipers and gauges, of botanical specimens and scientific discussions. One of his father's mentors, the Belgian statistician Adolphe Quetelet, had told him that every human body was unique and that the chances of two adults having even one body measurement precisely in common was about one in four. Perhaps there was a way to diminish those odds, to define a person's identity more narrowly. Bertillon reasoned that if the chance of two people having one physical measurement in common, such as height, was one in four, then adding another measurement—height plus length of the skull, for example—would again reduce those odds by a fourth, making them one in sixteen. Adding a third measurement, such as the length of the left foot, would decrease them by a fourth yet again, making them one in sixty-four. Finally, he calculated that if he took eleven measurements, the odds of any two adults having all those dimensions in common would be less than one in four *million*. And so, years before the advent of fingerprinting, he devised a system that promised to become the world standard for identification.

Using Bertillonage, as the method came to be called, a trained expert would take eleven specified measurements, including the length and width of the head, height, and the length of the left foot and several other physical dimensions, and enter them all on a card, or *fiche anthropomorphique*. Police would keep this card with thousands of others, nested in overlapping categories of small, medium, and large for each head length, height, foot size, et cetera. The system was organized so logically and simply that a trained clerk could work his way through the categories and produce a positive ID in a matter of minutes. During the first year of experimental use, Bertillon identified three hundred repeat offenders. By the end of that year, the French prison system introduced the method to all the nation's penitentiaries, and in 1888 it became mandatory in all the nation's police stations. Soon police forces throughout the world adopted the system, including those in other Western European countries, India, and Russia. In 1897, it became the official technique of the FBI's forerunner, the National Bureau of Identification. Later, a method was devised to transmit Bertillon numbers as a code over telegraph. For the first time, a fleeing criminal's identity would reach police in a foreign country—even across an ocean—before he or she could arrive.

"The prisoner who passes through [Bertillon's] hands is . . . forever 'spotted,'" wrote the American journalist Ida Tarbell, who visited Bertillon in his lab.

He may efface his tattooing, compress his chest, dye his hair, extract his teeth, scar his body, dissimulate his height. It is useless. The record against him is unfailing. He cannot pass the Bertillon archives without recognition; and, if he is at large, the relentless record may be made to follow him into every corner of the globe where there is a printing press, and every man who reads may become a detective, furnished with information which will establish his identity. He is never again safe.

In time, Bertillon added photography to the practice, taking one full-on photograph of the face and one in profile. He insisted on such exactitude for the photographs that both the chair and the camera tripod were bolted to the floor. The practice became universally employed, and it was known in the United States as the mug shot. He added descriptions to the file card, such as whether the suspect had a mole or a tattoo, and called the dossier a *"portrait parlé"* ("speaking portrait").

Bertillon's most celebrated case involved the era's most notorious terrorist, a swashbuckling anarchist known as Ravachol. The anarchist movement had been growing since the 1870s—first as a political movement, then as an increasingly violent one as acts of defiance and repression escalated into bloodshed.* The terrorism was abetted by the development of dynamite, which became the first easily available weapon of mass destruction. In 1892, after clashes between anarchists and police, a bomb exploded in downtown Paris, wrecking the apartment of a judge. Then another explosion demolished the home of a prosecutor, seriously injuring several people.

After weeks of futile inquiries by police, an informant named the bomber as Ravachol, a shadowy character who presented himself as the avenger of the working class but whose true identity was unknown. Told where the suspect habitually ate lunch, police stormed the café and captured him. At the prefecture, Bertillon carefully measured the suspect, went to his files, and a few minutes later revealed that Ravachol was actually a common criminal named François-Claudius Koenigstein, a violent offender who had been arrested near Lyon three years earlier. He had been charged with several crimes, including digging up and robbing a corpse and murdering an old man and his servant with a hatchet, but released for lack of evidence.

On the eve of his bombing trial, anarchists exploded the restaurant where Ravachol was captured, in an effort to intimidate the prosecutor. It worked: The prosecutor treated Ravachol with deference and settled for

---

*The movement made its mark in the United States when an anarchist bomb killed seven policemen in Chicago in 1886 and when the anarchist Leon F. Czolgosz assassinated President McKinley in 1901.

life imprisonment rather than the mandated death penalty. But two months later, Ravachol was transferred to a provincial courthouse near Lyon, where he was tried for the crimes he had committed as Koenigstein. Unimpressed by the goings-on in Paris, the judge sent the defendant to the guillotine.

Bertillon was, along with Lacassagne, one of the founding editors of the *Archives of Criminal Anthropology.* Their one serious disagreement occurred during the notorious Dreyfus affair of the mid-1890s, when Bertillon offered his services as a handwriting expert and testified that Dreyfus had written a document giving state secrets to Germany. Lacassagne, who became a committed Dreyfusard, urged Bertillon not to get involved in graphology, an area outside his main expertise, but Bertillon blundered ahead. The resulting scandal damaged his reputation and, according to Lacassagne, destroyed his chances of winning the Nobel Prize.

While Bertillon worked to *deconstruct* a living person's identity by breaking it down into small measurable parts, Lacassagne worked in the opposite direction, *reconstructing* a corpse's identity by compiling small parts to create a whole. The most obvious way to identify a body was by appearance, which is why morgues were so important to police work. Yet relatives often found it impossible to recognize a loved one's remains. Once putrefaction took hold (which happened rather quickly in the absence of refrigeration), it was difficult even to look at the body, much less swear to an identity. Furthermore, in the cat-and-mouse game between criminals and police, dismemberment had become *"à la mode,"* wrote Lacassagne. By the late 1800s, police had learned to trace missing persons by using photography and the telegraph system. Criminals responded by decapitating or dismembering their victims, making them more difficult to identify. Oftentimes, investigators had only pieces of the body with which to reconstruct an identity.

Lacassagne and his counterparts counseled investigators to look for small, indelible clues, such as scars. The character of scars changed over time—tender, soft, and pink when fresh; harder and brownish white after a month or two; and tough, thick, white, and shiny when mature. Scars formed in childhood could disappear by adulthood. There were particular scarrings that medical examiners should know about. Flogging, common among seamen at the time, left "faint white lines extending between little circular pits made by knots," according to a forensic textbook of the period. Bloodletting, a common medical treatment, left slender white linear scars that ran along the path of a vein. Scars left by the application of leeches would shrink and become difficult to see. It would take a keen eye to spot the characteristic three-point bite marks.

Tattoos had the added advantage of revealing something about the victim's character—occupation, politics, sexual proclivities. Lacassagne referred to them as "speaking scars." (In an effort to stay ahead of the police, criminals frequently altered their own tattoos, adding to the patterns or trying to erase them.) Other skin marks gave hints as to the victim's occupation: laundrywomen and dressmakers exhibited fingertip needle punctures; violinists and other string musicians showed fingertip calluses; men who had worked in cobalt mines in the colonies had a bluish tint to their hair; copper miners would have a green tint, and aniline dye-makers' skin would bear deep brown chemical stains.

Such details offered useful clues to identity, but they lasted only as long as the skin. Thus, the durability of clues became important. As Lacassagne had showed in the Gouffé case and elsewhere, individual bones could reveal a victim's height and, to some extent, medical history. He and his colleagues also found ways to use bone fragments to estimate age.

Skeletons had long fascinated anatomists, but more for their mechanical than biological properties. Even Leonardo da Vinci, a master anatomist and anatomical illustrator, saw bones mainly as a series of levers. It was not until the nineteenth century that scientists took enough interest in bones to study their biological complexity and distinctive growth phases. They learned that certain bones solidified in the early months of life; others, which seemed to be one solid piece, such as the skull and the pelvis, actually were a combination of bones that had fused during youth. Some bones that might seem fully formed in a young adult, such as the long bones of the arms and legs, actually revealed areas of ongoing growth, called "epiphyseal plates," characterized by a groove near the ends of the bone shaft.

Lacassagne brought that knowledge to crime analysis. In his *Handbook for the Medical Expert,* he created eleven pages of charts listing the ossification rates of thirty-seven different bones of the body. He cross-referenced them with the ages when ossification typically took place—from the early years, when the main bones of the skull stitched together, to the mid-twenties, when the five vertebrae comprising the sacrum at the base of the spine fused as one. Using this information, the investigator who had collected only a fragment of a skeleton could make an educated guess about the victim's age and begin to narrow down his or her identity.

Sometimes the investigator did not even have a bone to work with. In such cases, the medical examiner would find a head, or a piece of a head, burned, thrown in a river, or (with alarming frequency) dropped into a latrine. The investigator would have to collect clues from the smallest, most durable parts of the human body. Tooth enamel, its hardest substance, consists of a mineral form of calcium that literally can last millennia. The hardness of teeth surpasses that of copper, equals that of steel, and rises almost to the level of gem-quality minerals. That durability, plus the fact that dentists kept detailed records of their patients' teeth and dental work, made them a natural tool for identification. One of the early cases of forensic dentistry occurred when Paul Revere, who worked as a dentist and as a silversmith, identified his friend Dr. John Warren, killed and buried during the Revolution, by an artificial tooth Revere had implanted.

Such primitive uses had limited applicability, since they depended on knowing the victim's identity and confirming it with his or her dentist. Many murder victims were anonymous, so, just as with bones, dental forensics would require a sophisticated understanding of teeth and how they grew. That knowledge developed in the middle of the nineteenth century when several scientists, notably Dr. Émile Magitot of Paris, studied the natural history of teeth—not as simple chewing devices, but as living human tissue with stages of growth and vulnerability to disease. Magitot was among the first to incorporate Pasteur's germ theory to explain tooth decay, explaining that cavities were not formed by a "tooth worm" or acidic foods, but by the bacterial fermentation of food bits caught between the teeth. More important, for the purposes of forensics, he traced tooth development, from the saclike dental follicles in the embryo to the "milk teeth" of childhood to the molars of youth to the wisdom teeth of adulthood and their ultimate breakdown and decay in old age.

Magitot's studies made dentistry an indispensable part of forensic analysis, and they became standard in medical texts at the time. Lacassagne directed his students to write theses on how to apply Magitot's work broadly to criminal science. He printed them as reference tables in his *Handbook*, correlating tooth development and age. Teeth gave other clues to identity, such as whether the victim smoked (tobacco stains or wear marks of a pipe stem) and the nature of his or her diet and health. Stunted teeth with thinned or pitted enamel revealed that the victim had suffered from rickets, linked to calcium deficiency. Teeth with a peglike or notched appearance indicated congenital syphilis, acquired from an infected mother while in the womb.

Magitot wrote a report in Lacassagne's journal that would become one of his most celebrated cases of odontic deduction. It involved the case of Louis XVII, son of King Louis XVI and Marie Antoinette, both of whom were executed during the French Revolution. Fearing a possible resurgence of the monarchy, the revolutionaries put the eight-year-old heir in prison, where he died two months after his tenth birthday. In 1795, he was buried in an unmarked grave near the church wall in the Sainte-Marguerite cemetery in Paris. Ever since, there had been a cultish curiosity about the location of the grave and the circumstances of the child's demise. The boy became known as the "Lost Dauphin."

In 1894, a prominent Parisian attorney got permission to excavate near the church wall, where he found a coffin marked "L . . . XVII." Could these be the remains of the child king? He assembled a forensic team, including Léonce Manouvrier, who had constructed bone-length charts similar to Rollet's, and Émile Magitot, who would evaluate the dentition.

Magitot's study was a masterpiece. He began by noting that most of the cadaver's teeth must have been present at the time of death. A few had fallen out, but because the gaps where they had been showed no sign of healing, Magitot knew they had dislodged after death. There had been twenty-seven teeth in all. Magitot then used his knowledge of the natural history of dentition to bracket the victim's age systematically. For example, the front teeth, the canine teeth, and the bicuspids all would have come into place in early childhood, which set a minimum age of five or six. There were no baby teeth—milk teeth—left in the mouth, which meant the boy must have been at least twelve years old.

Then Magitot turned his attention to the missing first molar of the lower right jaw, which left a gap between the second molar and the bicuspid. Unlike the other empty tooth sockets in the jaw, this one had healed over, indicating that the tooth had been pulled during the victim's lifetime. That set a minimum age at twelve or thirteen. After the extraction, the second molar had grown at an angle toward the gap—so much so that it completely crossed over the gap and leaned up against the bicuspid. All that would have taken several years, said Magitot, which now set the minimum age at sixteen.

Finally, he looked for the wisdom teeth, which typically would emerge in the early twenties. They hadn't appeared yet, but he did find their crowns just below what would have been the gum line. Based on those factors, he estimated the corpse's age at eighteen to twenty years old. The remains found in the coffin were certainly not those of Louis XVII.

Seven

The Oak Woods

Augustine Mortureux was the youngest of seven siblings who grew up on a farm in the village of Étaules, about six miles north of Dijon. The daughter of a woodcutter, she had inherited none of her father's or sisters' native hardiness. Even at seventeen, she was frail and often fearful. Perhaps because of that vulnerability, she was the light of her mother's eye.

Augustine woke up on Sunday, May 12, 1895, in a state of terrible anxiety. One of her sisters, who lived in a neighboring town, was ill and had asked if a family member could come visit. Neither parent could get away, so they had asked Augustine to make the trip. Even though the route followed a busy national carriageway, she had never made the walk by herself. She trembled at the thought of hiking through the Bois du Chêne, the gloomy oak woods along the way. She took her little dog, Quiqui, for protection.

She left at 9:00 a.m. The sky threatened rain, so she carried an umbrella. On the road, she passed a lumberjack named Chaignay, who promised to keep an eye on her until she was out of sight. It had been a holiday in a neighboring village and the presence of other walkers undoubtedly reassured Augustine. She passed bicyclists coming from the opposite direction, one of whom was a man named Messner, a municipal counselor from Dijon. Moments before, Messner had overtaken a vagabond, whose menacing appearance gave him a chill. Augustine kept walking. Chaignay watched her shrink into the distance. She came to a bend in the road, then disappeared from view behind a clump of trees. Chaignay turned back to his work.

A few hours later, a woman named Gaumard was walking up the carriageway with her two young daughters and her cousin, on leave from his regiment. One of the girls noticed someone lying down in the distance and mostly shielded from view by an open umbrella. "Look, Mama," she said, "it's a bicyclist taking a nap." An hour later, when they made the return trip, the children mischievously threw some pebbles to awaken the sleeper. When there was no reaction, Gaumard's cousin approached the body; then they all fled to alert the neighbors about his shocking discovery.

That afternoon, a friar named François Brûlé was strolling along the carriageway when he came upon three lively young boys who were heading to the Bois du Chêne to collect mushrooms. They all fell in together, walking and chatting. They approached a dirt road with shoulders that fell away in steep, shady embankments. One of the boys ran ahead to where a cute little dog was barking. Then he cried out.

The dog stood next to the body of a girl lying in a cavity where some boulders had been removed; she was partially hidden by an open umbrella. Her skirts had been pulled up and her blouse ripped open. Friar Brûlé straightened the clothing to restore the girl's modesty and cover her ghastly wounds. Someone, apparently, had stolen her shoes.

The friar ran to the nearest village and burst into a tavern, where Eugène Grenier, a wealthy landowner, was playing cards with some friends. On hearing the news, Grenier piled the friar and several other people into his carriage and ordered his coachman to speed them to the Bois du Chêne. As they approached the crime scene, Grenier cried out, "It's there, I see it!"

By midafternoon, a crowd began to gather. Bicyclists sped off to alert the local authorities. Within a couple of hours, nearly three hundred people were jostling for a view, including the girl's horrified parents. No one could understand how a murder could have been committed on such a busy road in the middle of the day. At one point, Madame Gaumard, who had joined the crowd, said, "We've known about this for a while," referring to the fact that they also had spotted the body.

The authorities inspected the crime scene and took the body to the city hall in Étaules, where Dr. J. Quioc, from the school of medicine in Dijon, performed the autopsy. He found that death had come quickly from a massive stab wound to the neck, though there were several other wounds and contusions. One stab wound had penetrated a lung, but this was not what had caused Augustine's death. Dr. Quioc noted that blood had pooled in the back of the lung, indicating that she had been stabbed after collapsing onto her back; blood collecting at the bottom of the lung would have indicated that the wound was incurred while she was standing. Quioc found no evidence of rape. There were pale bloody smears on her undergarments, which indicated that the killer had washed his hands and then wiped them on her clothing. The doctor finally noted that her earrings had been stolen, judging by the empty piercings in her earlobes, and removed with great dexterity, as evidenced by the absence of bruises.

Two investigators were assigned to the case—Louis-Albert Fonfrède, the local investigating magistrate, and a Dijon-based prosecutor named Tondut. They suspected the unknown vagabond whom Messner and others had seen in the area and started gathering testimony. Several people along the road that day had seen a mean-looking vagabond wearing gray pants, a tattered blue shirt, and wooden-soled shoes. Fonfrède sent out a bulletin to surrounding districts, advising people to be alert for a man who matched that description. It was carried by newspapers as far away as Paris and Lyon.

The dragnet progressed normally for the next week and a half. Police in surrounding areas captured, interrogated, and released several suspects. But a rumor began to circulate regarding Eugène Grenier. Many people in town envied him for his wealth and property and resented his youthful reputation for laziness and dissolute ways (although he was now respectably married and had children). Some began to whisper that Grenier had spotted Augustine's body so quickly because he knew precisely where to look. Gossips said Grenier must have tried to force himself on Augustine and then killed her when she refused. It did not matter that Grenier had never shown an impulse toward violence or aggression.

Fonfrède and Tondut interrogated Grenier and his wife separately and also spoke with several of their employees. Their alibis checked out, and the two were set free. But their ordeal was just beginning.

The late nineteenth century saw the sudden and wild proliferation of the penny press, the first incarnation of the modern mass media. So-called because a newspaper cost only a penny or two, this form of popular journalism was taking France by storm, just as in Britain and the United States. After decades of censorship, French journalism was invigorated by new laws prescribing broad areas of press freedom. New technologies, including the Linotype machine, which made typesetting almost as fast as typing, and the rotary printing press, made it possible to churn out huge volumes of newspapers quickly and cheaply. The telegraph enabled correspondents to wire in stories from far corners of the world and from the equally inaccessible corners of France. The skyrocketing literacy rates gave newspapers millions of new readers, and the newly developing advertising industry yielded revenue beyond what the cheap newsstand price could provide.

This confluence of social, technological, and economic factors led to the world's first media explosion. In Paris alone, there were seventy-nine daily papers at the turn of the century. *Le Petit Parisien,* the largest newspaper in the world at the time, had one and a half million readers. The "big four" newspapers in Paris* had a combined readership of more than four million. There was an explosion of 257 daily papers in the country, not counting hundreds of weeklies, biweeklies, triweeklies, leaflets, and special editions.

With millions of semi-educated readers and Darwinian competition for space on the newsstand, the newspapers ran headlines that screamed for attention, as did their American and British counterparts. A favorite subject was crime—not only because crime rates were rising, but because the stories were so melodramatic. Newspapers brayed about the "army of criminals" who were terrorizing society, be they the gangs of urban youths known as "apaches," or the uncivilized "vagabonds," who preyed upon the country folk. Crime was high drama: Nothing attracted and titillated readers more than stories of a man shot by a jealous lover or a woman ravished by a gang of thugs. *"Sang à la une!"* went the expression: the bloodiest stories should go on page one. The women victims in these dramas were always beautiful and virtuous, and fought valiantly before meeting their deaths. In the case of Augustine Mortureux, for example, even though the evidence showed that she probably died quickly, certain newspapers portrayed her as fighting courageously. Because so many cases went unsolved, the big papers would send special correspondents to the scenes of infamous crimes to see if they could crack them.

Many newspapers also published weekly literary supplements, or illustrated editions, which, using the new halftone technology, offered full-cover renditions of the biggest story of the week, along with a dramatic telling of the story. Whole families would crowd over these editions every Sunday, gasping at the latest adventure or horror tale that the artists and reporters so graphically recounted. The coverage would include ballads,

Le Petit Parisien, Le Petit Journal, Le Matin, and *Le Journal.*

called "laments," that were written to commemorate the event. One special edition of a paper was headlined TEN MURDERS FOR A PENNY and promised all the "horrible details" within.

Dijon was the battleground of a media war between two particularly feisty publications—a leftist weekly called *Le Bourguignon Salé* (The Salty Burgundian) and an archconservative daily called *Le Bien Public* (The Public Good). In an effort to gain readers, each tried to outdo the other by ramping up accusations against Grenier and fabricating stories about the incompetence of the authorities who refused to indict him. The newspapers acted as an echo chamber for every rumor from every person with a grudge against Grenier. When the police seemed reluctant to act on those rumors, the newspapers portrayed it as a sign of official corruption. "The authorities would like to pretend to believe that the assassin is some poor devil," wrote the editor of *Le Bourguignon Salé,* who believed the upper class to be the source of all evil. "But there is more vice on high than down low, and more crime as well!"

The lack of evidence against Grenier meant nothing to these columnists, who found plenty to write about by relying on innuendo. In one typical attack, the editors of *Le Bien Public* directed readers to the inevitable conclusion that Grenier *must* have committed the crime.

Who knows if he did not see the young Augustine and conceived a desire to possess her? . . .

Who knows if Augustine recognized him and, not having reason to be afraid of him, did not flee? . . .

Who knows if, facing her resistance, alarmed by her pleas and the barking of her dog, he didn't lose his head and, driven by a kind of erotic insanity, wanted to end the situation with two blows of the knife that brought immediate death?

The papers also implicated anyone known to be a friend of Grenier, such as Madame Gaumard. "Who but a woman would have taken the victim's little shoes?" argued the editors of *Le Bourguignon Salé.* "Who but a woman would detach the earrings with such delicacy?"

"Witnesses" emerged who said they could implicate Grenier in the killing. Most of them had no direct knowledge of the murder but were using the legal system to settle old grudges. Augustine's father, Émile, who quickly became convinced that Grenier was the killer, wrote anguished denunciations in the press. Grenier consulted a lawyer in Dijon about suing for slander. In his absence, authorities rifled his home and found a pair of trousers stained by a tiny drop of blood. Grenier explained that he had been standing next to his servant, who had slaughtered a rabbit for dinner one night—an alibi that his servant confirmed. At one point, when Grenier was riding on horseback, a mob surrounded him with the intention of lynching him; he managed to gallop away.

To their credit, Fonfrède and Tondut did everything in their power to quell the panic while continuing to mount a professional investigation. In the fall of 1895, however, they left on their annual vacations. Into the breach moved two inexperienced officials, who let the situation get out of hand. A simpleton named Rouard who lived in the forest now came forward to allege that he had seen Grenier crouched over Augustine's body with a knife. Much of his story did not accord with the known facts; nevertheless, it was deemed credible.

Local people had erected a crude wooden cross at the spot where Augustine had died. The cross became a magnet for pilgrims: All day long, people would place bouquets at the memorial, cross themselves, and pray for the dead girl. Many carved graffiti on the surrounding trees that said "Death to Grenier" and (loosely translated) "Grenier the scoundrel." A friend of Grenier owned the property, and he had the graffiti scratched out. The vandalism continued, however. Seeing how the graffiti tormented his friend, the property owner ordered his workers to cut down the trees in a wide perimeter around the crime scene, remove the cross, level the ground, and post NO TRESPASSING signs.

This inflamed the populace even more. Seeing a chance to latch onto public sentiment, the editors of *Le Bourguignon Salé* started a fund-raising campaign to build a permanent monument to Augustine at the crime scene. It would be a two-meter-tall obelisk of stone, surrounded on four sides by an iron railing. The memorial, wrote the editors, "will not be so easy to destroy." Erected as a "permanent protest against crime," it would be an accusatory call to a justice system that was "powerless against the rich and forceful against the poor!"

Pending the monument's construction, the newspaper declared that August 27 would be Augustine Mortureux Day, with demonstrations at the girl's grave. More than five hundred people flocked to the cemetery. All along the roadways, vendors were hawking sheet music with a lament about the atrocity; called "The Crime of the Bois du Chêne," it was set to a popular folk air. It told the story of Augustine's murder, and inserted a new character into the tale: a honeybee buzzing frantically in her ear, trying to warn her away from the oak forest: "Return, my child, with eyes so soft, to your mother. Flee far from these woods; for in the bushes waits an assassin with black intentions. Fear this hyena."

Hundreds of people sang those lines as they trudged to the cemetery. The very air vibrated with rage. Madame Ragougé, head of the local tobacco workers' union, gave a stirring eulogy, in which she promised the dead girl that her killer would not go unpunished. "Rest in peace, dear Augustine, because justice will be done." Augustine's mother, devastated at having forced her daughter to walk alone through the woods, threw herself on the grave. The father shouted, "If the judge doesn't want to cut off Grenier's head, I'll do it myself!"

"That's right!" someone yelled. "And no one would dare condemn you!"

A rumbling began somewhere in the crowd—a few harsh and scattered cries that grew into a chant and then a rhythmic roar: "Death to Grenier! Death to the assassin!" In moments, the crowd of mourners was transformed into a mob set on vengeance.

Barricaded into their house not half a mile away, Grenier and his family could hear that roar. He had called in several relatives and armed them with rifles. The police had expected trouble and had blocked the roadway with an intimidating line of armed guards.

The mob came running. Seeing the armed presence at Grenier's, they veered off to find a softer target. They found it at Madame Gaumard's unguarded home a few hundred yards away. They *knew* she had to be implicated and that Grenier must have paid her off to keep quiet. They surrounded her house and began pelting it with stones. Her husband was away at the time, and she cowered inside with her daughters. Windows began shattering. Not satisfied with mere vandalism, the mob improvised a battering ram: This was a crime that cried out for *vengeance*! Just as the heavy wooden door began cracking, a contingent of police arrived and drove the crowd away.

A couple of months after this incident, the substitute prosecutors, acting on Rouard's accusations, arrested Grenier on suspicion of murder. They put him in a cell with two petty criminals—an arsonist and a smuggler—who, in return for lighter sentences, promised to report anything he might say. The region continued to boil.

The real killer was long gone. Immediately after the murder, Vacher had fled through the oak forest. He washed in a creek, shed his bloody trousers, underneath which was a clean pair, and took a clean shirt from his bag. Breathless and hungry, he came upon a farmhouse occupied by two girls and demanded they let him in. They slammed the door in his face, locked it, and set their dog on him. Later, Vacher met a man wearing a Legion of Honor medal who was walking with two women and a child. They told him that they had heard frightening rumors of a vagabond with a terrible face who was prowling around the woods like a savage.

Vacher kept walking. He covered nearly thiry-five miles over the next day and a half, heading northeast, in the direction of Paris. On Monday afternoon, the day after the killing, he stopped at the simple home of a widow, Madame Girardot, and asked her if he could heat his lunch on her stove. He told her that he had been bitten by a dog, and she washed and bandaged the wound. She offered him bread and wine to supplement his meal. After he ate, he thanked her, blessed her, and then, feeling expansive, started making small talk. He told her about his background as a sergeant and about his wanderings through France. By the way, he asked, had she heard about the horrible crime at the Bois du Chêne, near Dijon? Someone had killed a girl by the side of the road. In fact, he himself had seen the cadaver. He knew about the crime because he'd walked by that area around ten in the morning and a crowd had already gathered.

The newspapers had not yet reported the crime, and the crowd had not gathered until late afternoon. Madame Girardot did not know that, and had no reason to doubt Vacher's story. Still, something about his tale struck her as strange, and she wanted to remember to tell her grown children next time they visited. She found a piece of paper and wrote down the date: May 13, 1895.

A week and a half later, Vacher showed up at the farm of a man named Lachereuil, about ten miles to the north. He told the farmer that he had just been in Paris; then, moments later, he corrected himself and said that he had come from Semur-en-Auxois (the location of Madame Girardot's house). The farmer noticed that Vacher was wearing shoes that were too small, with the fronts cut open to make room for his toes. Vacher told him that someone had stolen his own shoes while he was sleeping by the side of the road. The farmer gave him a pair of wooden clogs, at which point

Vacher took out his knife, cut the shoes he had been wearing into small pieces, and threw the pieces in a brook. After Vacher left, the farmer—struck by this behavior and having read about the Mortureux killing—ran to tell the mayor. The mayor sent the police after Vacher. They questioned him briefly but let him go after he showed them his regimental papers.

Life was getting too complicated in Burgundy. He started walking south.

News of the Mortureux killing and its aftermath traveled to Paris, where it made gripping tabloid copy. In September, *Le Matin* sent a star reporter to the Dijon area to investigate—Marie-François Goron, hero of the Gouffé case and many others, who recently had retired as the head of the Sûreté. *Le Matin* had hired him to cover all matters criminal. Goron interviewed everyone with any involvement in the affair, including Augustine's father, who bemoaned the lack of thorough police work. Why, he asked, hadn't the authorities confronted Grenier with Augustine's puppy, which surely would had recognized the murderer? Why had the coroner—"a man who doesn't know anything"—neglected to look closely into the murdered girl's eyes? After all, everyone knew that the eyes of the dead retained the last image they had seen.

"I tried to get him to see things with a bit more sangfroid," Goron reported, "but it was in vain."

After several days of investigation, Goron concluded that there was not one piece of evidence or reliable testimony that could connect Grenier to the crime. The local people angrily turned on Goron, accusing him of being paid off by Grenier. The local authorities had so bungled the case, and the population had become so inflamed, he wrote, that the region was condemned to "perpetual lynch law." Soon after this case, Goron retired from his brief stint as a journalist and founded one of Europe's premier detective agencies.

Some weeks later, Fonfrède and Tondut returned from their vacations. Horrified at what had taken place in their absence, they summoned Rouard to their offices for an official inquiry. Standing in front of a group of court officials, he repeated his testimony about seeing Grenier at the crime scene.

"And do you see Grenier now?" they asked him.

"Yes, there he is, right behind you."

The man behind them stood up and introduced himself as Mr. Bourdon, a substitute prosecutor.

By now, Grenier had been incarcerated for forty-five days. Questioned by officials, the two informants in his cell said there was no doubt that Grenier was the murderer—they had heard him confess in his sleep. But when police separated the informants and interviewed them, the details of their stories did not jibe. The authorities released Grenier.

Several miles away, a mob was gathering on the road that led from the courthouse to Grenier's property. In the quickening dusk, they could see the lamps of his carriage. A group of men spread out across the road. As the coachman pulled up to avoid them, several men closed in from the sides and yanked the reins from his hands. The coachman swore and reached for his pistol, but a dozen hands grabbed him. Someone cracked a baton against his head. Several men leaped onto the running boards and yanked open the doors, only to find the carriage empty. Grenier had anticipated an ambush and had escaped by train to Saint-Jean-de-Losne, where his in-laws lived, some twenty-five miles away. His wife and children joined him there, and they never returned home again.

Eight

The Body Speaks

If there was a lesson to be learned from Grenier's travail, it was that the word of a "witness," whether given in court or used to incite a mob, was not always reliable and therefore not useful in solving a crime. In recent years, legal and psychological experts were finding that even actual eye-witnesses could not fully be trusted. There were many motivations to lie—jealousy, hatred, calumny, superficiality, ignorance, fear. Magistrate Émile Fourquet, who wrote a book about false testimony, described instances in which people who knew nothing came forward, like Rouard. The man simply wanted "to play a role in a memorable affair."

Alienists were discovering that certain witnesses might lie even when they believed they were telling the truth. In an analysis of the Tisza-Eslar affair, the neurologist and hypnotism expert Dr. Hippolyte Bernheim wrote that fourteen-year-old Moritz Scharf, already a simple and sug-gestible boy, was so frightened and coerced that he fell into a kind of hyp-notic state, falsely condemning his own father for murder. Bernheim described the phenomenon as a "retroactive hallucination," in which cer-tain people, under pressure, come to believe a false version of events. (Modern psychologists use the term *false memory*.) Defense attorneys condemned the police's "preventative detention" and "pressure cooker" tactics, which forced witnesses to tell them what they wanted to hear. "What difference is there, in effect, between the [medieval] torturer . . . and the police agent who badgers the defendant without stopping to the point of exhaustion [and lack of] sleep?" wrote Maurice Lailler and Henri Vonoven in their 1897 book, *Les Erreurs judiciaires et leurs causes* (Judicial Errors and Their Causes). "Psychological torture is less brutal and more refined, but it accomplishes the same results." Others, reflecting the prej-udices of the time, asserted that certain people were unreliable to begin with. "Women lie," wrote Émile Zola, the novelist and social commentator, who normally sympathized with the powerless in society. "They lie to everyone, to judges, to their lovers, to their chambermaids, even to themselves."

People might lie, but evidence did not, and evidence was becoming the gold standard of police work. Lacassagne wrote that the time had come for "testimonial" proof to be replaced by the "silent testimony" of evidence from the crime scene. Lacassagne and his colleagues developed an intellectual process to sort it all out. They organized their inquiries as a simple series of questions: Who was the victim? When did this person die? How did he or she die? What physical traces connect the victim to the killer?

On February 18, 1896, a trunk was delivered to Lacassagne at the morgue. Inside the trunk was the body of a man named Étienne Badoil, who was lying on his right side in a fetal position. According to the only witness, his lover, Élise Piot, the man had died by a tragic mistake. The two had been having an illicit affair. They had been in her apartment the previous evening, when they heard the heavy footsteps of her common-law husband, a grocery clerk named Matillon. According to the young woman, Badoil climbed into the trunk next to the bed and wedged himself into a fetal position, and she closed and latched the lid. She and Matillon went out for a few hours, returned home, and went to sleep. It was not until the next morning, she said, that she remembered about Badoil; on opening the trunk, she found him dead of suffocation.

Lacassagne saw purple splotches on the body's back and immediately deduced that Piot was lying. When a person dies and circulation stops, gravity pulls the blood into those capillaries closest to the ground. This pooling creates purplish splotches, known as lividity, on the bottom of most skin surfaces. The stains can migrate if the body is shifted soon after death, while the blood remains liquid; but after several hours the patches become fixed, when the blood has seeped into the tissue. Badoil must have died on his back and remained in that position for eight to ten hours. After that, someone had shifted him, perhaps to fit his body more neatly into the trunk or to create a more convincing scenario.

By immediately looking for signs of lividity Lacassagne was making use of the emerging science of postmortem timing. Physicians understood that once death occurred, a biological clock began running that could be traced backward to estimate when the death had taken place. What Lacassagne and his contemporaries tried to develop was a way to narrow the postmortem time window to make it a useful crime-solving tool.

Lividity created a window of twenty-four to thirty-six hours—appearing within a half hour of death, reaching its maximum in six to twelve hours, and then gradually fading over the next day. Another window was provided by rigor mortis, the muscular stiffening that begins three to six hours after death and reaches a maximum about nine hours later. Thereafter, the muscles begin softening again, and by the second to third day, the body goes limp. Rigor mortis does not appear in all muscles at once, and scientists at the time carefully studied the phenomenon to see if they could produce a clear timetable of its progression. Many tried to develop precise timing charts based on the theory that rigor mortis began in the head and worked its way downward. Lacassagne argued that rigor mortis did not begin closest to the head, but in whichever part of the body was most elevated, and proceeded downward from there. (Both sides were wrong: The phenomenon begins at the same time in all muscles, but becomes obvious first in the small muscles, such as those of the face.)

Even within broad parameters, rigor mortis could not serve as an entirely dependable time clock. It could appear more quickly in hot weather than cold, and more rapidly in people suffering from exhaustion or disease. Nor were its characteristics completely understood.

Over the years, scientists came to see *livor mortis* (lividity), *rigor mortis*, and *algor mortis* (a dropping of body temperature) as the three main time indicators of the cessation of life. They all had limited usefulness for dating, though, because none extended beyond a couple of days. In order to date older bodies, they needed to look at other forms of life that colonized the body after death. Conceptually, this meant learning to see death not as an end, but as a pivot point when certain processes ended but others began.

The most obvious of these processes was putrefaction, the greenish color change and bloating of the body, a phenomenon that had always been surrounded by mysticism and dread. (Sir Francis Bacon described bloating as "unquiet spirits" trying to escape their worldly remains.) In the middle of the nineteenth century, Pasteur explained away the superstition by describing the fermentation of microbes. He and his successors demonstrated that in a dead body, bacteria would escape from the digestive tract, and, along with other bacteria and fungi, colonize human tissue, turning it green. Enough gas would be released to swell the skin and push blood into peripheral veins. Sometimes the blood would escape from old wounds, giving rise to the myth that a corpse would "bleed afresh" in the presence of the murderer. Very few morgues had refrigeration at the time, and doctors dreaded that first scalpel cut, when a whoosh of repellent gases would almost overcome them. Before the Paris morgue installed its refrigerators, Brouardel would make pinpricks in the cadavers and light them, allowing the combustible gases to burn off. They might burn for three or four days, producing "long bluish flames."

Scientists tried to create timetables for putrefaction by identifying the succession of bacterial species or the order in which body parts became colonized. But so many species of bacteria were involved, and the onset of putrefaction was so affected by moisture and climatic conditions, they found the task impossible. All they could say was that putrefaction generally began after rigor mortis and continued for months.

It was not until 1894 that a long-term postmortem timetable was developed by a Parisian entomologist named Jean-Pierre Mégnin. In a masterwork entitled *Fauna of the Tombs*, he described the successive waves of arthropods—insects, beetles, mites, and other creatures—that colonized corpses in orderly and highly predictable progressions. Each wave, which he referred to as a "squad," was a collection of species that thrived under certain conditions: They would eat what they could and then leave when their waste products accumulated and the body chemistry changed. That would make way for the next squad, which found the new conditions hospitable. "We have been struck by the fact that . . . the workers of death only arrive at their table successively, and always in the same order," he wrote.

Mégnin specified eight squads, or "laborers of death," whose presence could date a body within discrete time windows from one day to three years. The first squad, for example, consisted of houseflies and blowflies, which deposited their eggs at or just before the moment of death and fed on the body for about a month. Next would come several generations of brilliant metallic green bottle flies (*Lucilia*), large gray flesh flies (*Sarcophaga*), and two other species, which would dominate the cadaver from one to three months. From the third month to the sixth, a third squad would take over, comprising the larvae and adults of flesh-eating beetles. The progression would continue, one collection of species after the next, until the body was little more than a fibrous husk still being gnawed on by certain beetles and moths.

To determine how Badoil died, Lacassagne drew upon the vast amount of emerging research. Scientists worldwide were dissecting murder victims, executed criminals, cadavers from hospitals, and laboratory animals to reproduce the conditions they saw at crime scenes and learn how to interpret the results.* They did research on whether death happened quickly or slowly, and on which markings on the body revealed murder or suicide. Lacassagne was in the forefront of the endeavor. In 1888, he wrote a paper describing how the angle of a stab wound to the heart could reveal the handedness of a murderer. He wrote another paper analyzing the wound shape and lethality produced by the army's new bayonet, which was beginning to appear in civilian homicides. He wrote a series of monographs on whether chemical changes in the liver would indicate whether a victim died slowly, as in a natural death, or suddenly, as a result of murder, accident, or suicide. The liver converts glycogen, a starch, to glucose, a simple sugar, to supply the body with energy. His research showed that the absence of glycogen in the liver would indicate a slow death because the organ had continued to break it down as the body's natural processes gradually wound down. The presence of residual glycogen would show that sudden death had brought conversion to a full stop.†

Some of the most frequent cause-of-death laboratory studies involved asphyxia—the lack of oxygen that would result from hanging, strangulation, suffocation, and drowning. The mechanisms of death by asphyxia were not simple. Through laboratory experiments, von Hofmann, in Vienna, showed that hanging and strangulation not only cut off the air supply, as was commonly known; they often produced a combination of

---

*Sometimes the doctors would experiment on themselves. Dr. Graeme Hammond of New York, in order to understand a strangling victim's final sensations, had a laboratory assistant twist a towel around his throat while another marked the time. "I first noticed a sensation of warmth and tingling . . . passing quickly over my entire body," reported Hammond. "Vision partially disappeared but there was no manifestation of colored lights. My head felt as if about to burst, and there was a confused roaring in my ears. . . ." He rested a few minutes and had his assistants repeat the procedure. "Sensibility ceased in fifty-five seconds, and a stab with a knife [into my hand] sufficiently deep to draw blood caused no sensation whatever." (Frank Winthrop Draper, *A Text-Book of Legal Medicine* [Philadelphia: W. B. Saunders, 1905], p. 296.)
†Lacassagne's conclusions about glycogen have since proven invalid. Modern forensic scientists find that almost all causes of death, fast or slow, may leave residual traces of glycogen in the liver.

injuries, such as a rupturing of the carotid artery, which would stop the flow of blood to the brain, and damage to the pneumogastric nerve (now called the vagus nerve), which runs down the neck and controls many of the body's organs, including regulating the heart rate and keeping the trachea open. He and others revealed that the throat area was so important to vital functions that a sudden violent squeeze could cause a victim to drop almost immediately, which may explain why so few of Vacher's victims cried out.

Because asphyxia was so common in cases of murder and suicide, medical experts tried to characterize the various postmortem signatures of death by asphyxiation. Drowning was revealed by a frothy foam that appeared in the windpipe and bronchial tubes—the result of violent, spasmodic efforts to breathe in the water. The lungs appeared "inflated . . . spongy . . . doughy." Hanging was indicated by the oblique groove in the skin of the neck made by the rope above the thyroid cartilage and under the jawline, coupled with damage to the muscles underneath. (Von Hofmann and Parisian anatomist Auguste Tardieu did a joint study of 299 hanging victims and found that 244 exhibited this pattern.) Hanging from a drop of several feet, such as in American executions, could result in broken vertebrae, as well. Strangling by ligature differed from hanging by the angle of the groove—perpendicular to the spinal cord, as opposed to at an angle. Manual strangulation was indicated by finger and fingernail marks on the sides of the neck, which also gave clues to the killer's handedness by the orientation of his fingers and thumb. In most cases of hanging and strangulation, doctors would also find "emphysemas" in the lungs—thin, light patches caused by the rupture of air cells. Suffocation proved an especially subtle cause of asphyxia, since there usually were no external signs of damage. Auguste Tardieu found a certain pattern of bruising on the lungs that he felt could serve as a signature for suffocation. The bruises, which became known as "Tardieu spots," ranged in size from that of a pinhead to that of a pea and could be so numerous that they gave the lungs a granitelike appearance. They resulted from the rupturing of capillaries.*

Carefully examining the surface of Badoil's body, Lacassagne saw

---

*Tardieu spots were a source of controversy for years. Some experts claimed to see the spots not only in suffocation but in all forms of asphyxiation. It is now known that Tardieu spots occur in almost all cases of death and are not the result of suffocation, but of all internal forms of lividity.

numerous hints of a rapid and violent death. The eyes were bloodshot and the inner surfaces of the lids were covered with tiny red dots, or petechial hemorrhages, which occur when pressure in the blood vessels causes small amounts of blood to leak from capillaries. Both forms of damage were known to result from death from a blocked airway, as in strangling or hanging—but not from gradual suffocation. He found extensive bruising around the neck and chest. He noticed a small rip in the skin of the neck, as though it had been snagged by a fingernail. He found symmetrical abrasions on the right and left shoulders, right and left hips, and right and left sides, as though the man had been forced into the trunk while still alive.

Lacassagne proceeded with the dissection. Opening the throat, he saw that the tissues and muscle were infiltrated with blood, and he found a tear in the lining of the left carotid artery. Both were signs of manual strangulation. The lungs showed no trace of Tardieu spots, which, to his way of thinking, would have signaled gradual suffocation if present. He noted little "emphysemas" caused by a violent struggle to breathe.

Next, he moved to the chemical analysis. Tests of the liver showed the presence of glycogen as well as glucose, meaning that Badoil had died suddenly and that the conversion of sugars had come to a quick halt. As a second test for sudden death, Lacassagne asked a colleague to run a spectrographic analysis of the blood to check for oxygen. The procedure—which involved diluting a small quantity of blood and then shining a bright light into the liquid and through a series of prisms and lenses mounted on a microscope—would create a colorful spectrum that varied according to the liquid's oxygen content. In this case, the spectrum revealed two distinct black bands separated by a strip of greenish yellow light—a clear indication that the victim's blood carried the normal complement of oxygen at the time of death. In other words, the victim died suddenly, for the blood would have lost much of its oxygen if he had gradually suffocated in an enclosed space.

Lacassagne confirmed his results by reproducing the crime-scene conditions on dogs, as often was the practice at well-equipped laboratories. Gruesomely, he had three dogs strangled and then placed in a trunk (their combined weight totaled Badoil's) and had three other healthy dogs placed in a trunk, where they were allowed to suffocate over the course of several hours. One test after another confirmed his impression that Badoil had been strangled. The dogs that died from slow suffocation showed the presence of Tardieu spots in their lungs, the absence of glycogen in their liver, and low oxygen levels in their blood. In short, the suffocated dogs showed all the physiological signs that Badoil had *not*.

The body told all. Contrary to the witness's version of events, Étienne Badoil had not climbed into the footlocker and accidentally suffocated; he had been forced into the trunk and, while in that confined space, battered and strangled. The case went to trial the following November. The members of the jury had no trouble concluding that Badoil had been murdered, but they did not find enough evidence to connect Piot and Matillon directly to the killing. (The only evidence that linked them to the crime was suspicious bruising on their arms.) Matillon was set free, and Piot was sentenced to one year in prison for negligent homicide. The result must have been disappointing for Lacassagne, although, characteristically, he did not include his reaction in the report. We can assume he derived a certain satisfaction from the fact that in the case of this murder, evidence trumped the witness's lies.

Nine

The Crime in Bénonces

Vacher was a creature of the high country. Having been born in a small village in the highlands, he was drawn to the world of sleepy hillside villages and rushing mountain streams. Here he could prowl in the high meadows and forestland, shielded by the trees and interrupted sight lines. There were fewer victims here to satisfy his appetites, but fewer witnesses, as well. Here he could stalk the youngest and weakest, and pounce when he knew they were alone.

"Woe to those who crossed the path of this terrible vagabond," Albert Sarraut, a reporter for *La Dépêche de Toulouse*, later wrote about Vacher. "Wherever he goes, a cry of agony breaks the silence of the countryside."

In the months since the Mortureux murder, Vacher had not remained idle. From the Dijon area, he had set out toward Paris, then abruptly changed course and spent the next couple of weeks making his way south toward Lyon. He stayed well away from the highly trafficked Saône River, roaming instead through rural villages parallel to the river valley. Then he crossed the Rhône Valley and started meandering eastward into the foothills of the Alps.

An evil wind blew wherever he roamed. In late May, he attacked a domestic worker walking home after visiting her parents. She escaped by using her fingernails to bloody his eyes. A few weeks later, he grabbed another girl, who escaped. In late July, neighbors in the little mountain village of Chambuet found the body of a sixty-four-year-old woman, who had been stabbed repeatedly in the head and neck. In early August, he tried to lure two boys into the forest, but they fled when their older sister warned them away.

On the morning of Saturday, August 24, a young man in the village of Saint-Ours, just north of the spa town of Aix-les-Bains, came home from pasturing the family's only cow, to find his elderly mother dead on the kitchen floor, her throat slashed. Her dress had been pulled up to her chest.

"If there ever was a crime I regretted, it was that one," Vacher would later say. "Because the people of that region have such a loyal and hospitable nature."

The village of Bénonces sits on a tilted plateau in the foothills of the Alps, east of where the table-flat Rhône Valley collides with towering cliffs. Verticality rules here. Meadows that are broad and level in the valley become miniaturized and tipped at crazy angles, offering panoramic views of the farmland below. The stone houses are capped with steep red-tiled roofs.

Like many villagers of the high country, the 450 citizens of Bénonces lived in peaceful isolation. There was no telegraph, electricity, or newspaper in town, and the serpentine road leading to the hamlet made it a difficult destination. The residents were tough but hospitable people— although they were more inclined to bestow their hospitality on a stranger who showed a willingness to work. When Vacher drifted into the town during the last week of August 1895, the woman at the first house turned him away. "We give our stew to our workers, and there's none left for you," she told him. He came to another farm and asked a boy outside if they offered employment. "Certainly," the boy said. "You just have to ask." "But does one *have* to work?" Vacher asked him. "That's for sure," said the boy. "You don't stay here without doing something."

He came to the house of a family named Babola and asked a woman he met there for milk. She didn't have any. He groaned, cursed her, and kept walking.

"The thing that impressed me most were his hands," Madame Babola said later. "As soon as I saw them in front of me, I noticed that they were small compared with those of other peasants of his height. And his nails were so long . . . they reminded me of the claws of a bird of prey."

One woman took pity. "I'm not very rich," she said apologetically as she ladled a little soup for him.

"It's not the rich people who give the most," he replied.

He walked up a dirt path another mile or so and arrived at an even smaller hamlet, Onglas. He stopped at the farm of Pierre Guiffray and offered to pay a couple of pennies for some milk. Guiffray invited him in and then eyed him suspiciously as he dunked his bread in the milk and devoured it.

"Why aren't you working?" Guiffray asked. "You certainly seem strong enough."

Vacher told him that a malady prevented him from doing hard work, and he showed Guiffray his wrist, as though that would explain things.

"Where are you from?"

Vacher thought for a moment. "Seillons," he said, referring to another village in the area. Guiffray watched in silence.

The next day, Guiffray saw Vacher sitting against a chestnut tree along the path between Bénonces and Onglas. "You seem to be fine there resting in the shade."

"Not for long," Vacher said.

The farmers of Ain, the region that includes Bénonces and Onglas, have long raised an ancient breed of cow known as the Charolais. Off-white in color, the animal is heavily muscled, long-bodied, rugged, and fast-growing, and provides large quantities of milk. They are coarse-looking creatures, with rough fur that helps them endure the harsh climate.

The rhythms of the cows governed farm life. Each day at dawn, farm girls would milk the animals. At about 7:00 a.m., the shepherd boys would walk their little herds to the hillside pastures about a mile away, watch over them for several hours, and then guide them back to the stables at around 10:30. They would pasture the herd again for another three or four hours in the late afternoon and into the evening.

Despite this pacific tableau, a shepherd's life was not at all an easy one, nor was rural life a picturesque idyll. Most rural folk lived in near poverty, only a dry season away from indigence. Meat was a luxury, something to be eaten only a few times a year; a prosperous farmer ate it once a week. (The average Parisian ate nearly four times as much meat as the average rural dweller.) Their main foods were coarse bread or pancakes and soup—a broth or a stew into which they threw anything they had. Soups, which comprised the main meal of the day, were usually vegetarian. Corn, buckwheat, chestnuts, cabbage, turnips, or potatoes were cooked in salted water or with a little bit of lard. The locals drank milk or water; they could not afford wine.

Almost no one in the countryside had running water. Tuberculosis, typhoid, and cholera were common, and medical care in the provinces was poor. To live was to work, almost as a farm animal.

Many shepherds lived with their flocks for months at a time, isolated from other people. An observer in the Pyrenees in 1888 described a shepherd's dwelling as a stone hut one meter high. Inside were all the young man's worldly possessions: a pile of straw to sleep on, a small heap of potatoes, and a sack containing half a loaf of bread, some fat, and some salt. Those who lived with farm families had marginally better lives. They could bed down in the barn, in the kitchen, or in front of the hearth. Like their nomadic counterparts, they spent their days alone with their animals, exposed to the dangers of brigands, wolves, and rabid dogs.

"Such a sad existence is that of the shepherd!" wrote a columnist for *Le Petit Parisien*. "We may poeticize it but in reality it is one of the most punishing and least rewarding professions. . . . The shepherd . . . has to have varied knowledge, a gentle character, and a highly developed sense of duty."

Despite the hardships of a shepherd's existence, it was an improvement over the life Victor Portalier might have led. He was born in Trévoux, a riverside town just north of Lyon, to a woman who had married a much older man. Victor lost his father at the age of twelve and started drifting toward petty crime. His mother, reputedly a woman of low moral character, did not properly guide the boy, so the local priest took him to the Society for the Protection of Children in Lyon. He was assigned to the foster care of Jacques Berger, a farmer in Onglas, about forty miles away. The placement was successful. Now, at the age of fifteen, Victor had friends among the other shepherds and a reputation as an agreeable boy with a solid work ethic.

On the afternoon of August 31, 1895, he set out with his cows at 1:30 p.m., a half hour before the other boys. He liked to get an early start. He would lead his flock to the "big meadow," as they called it, on a hillside just over a mile from the farmhouse. There he would settle his cows and then sit under the big walnut tree at the meadow's edge. From this vantage point, he could gaze across the panorama of the forests and cliffs of the Luizet Valley. At the far end was a precipice and the Cascade of Luizet, a cataract more than three hundred feet high. In the summer, the boys liked to play under the waterfall, frolicking in the limpid pool below. It was an unusually hot day, and nothing stirred.

He heard a noise . . .

The other boys were coming up from the valley when one of Victor's cows began wandering back. Jean-Marie Robin, a friend, started coaxing the cow back up the hill, up to the big meadow. *How unlike Victor to lose track of one of his cows.* About seventy yards from the tree where Jean-Marie knew Victor would be waiting, he saw a puddle of blood. He followed that puddle to another . . . and came upon a blood-soaked shirt. He could not bear to see what his next steps would reveal to him, and he ran away, screaming. Several people came in response, including the *garde-champêtre*, who saw Victor's remains and then sought out the nearest authorities. The next morning, the police arrived from the town of Villebois, about five miles away, along with two doctors they had pressed into service as medical examiners. The body was too mangled to transport, so they conducted the autopsy right there in the meadow, in front of horrified villagers.

The depravity of this crime was truly unprecedented. No one in the region had seen anything like it before. By following the trail of forensic evidence across the meadow, medical examiners were able re-create the sequence of events, deriving facts about the killer and his method of attack.

"We arrived at a huge walnut tree situated in a clearing near a meadow of clover," wrote the doctors. "Two meters from this walnut we observed a large puddle of blood." Ten meters from the tree, they found a second pool of blood. Sixty meters from the tree, against some juniper bushes, rested the body of Victor Portalier. He lay on his back, with his pants pulled down to his shins.

The killer had sliced open the victim from sternum to pubis, like a hunter gutting an animal. "It is a complete evisceration," the doctors reported. They noted several other nonfatal stab wounds. The boy's sexual organs had been removed with a sharp instrument. The edges of the wound were neat and not hacked—a detail that would later become important in the course of evaluating the criminal.

Vacher would later say that of all his victims, Victor Portalier had suffered the most. Fittingly, this was the crime that would prove Vacher's undoing.

The community reacted in terror. These were villages without a police force, where the only security measures were dogs and flimsy locks. Formerly hospitable villagers now closed their doors to strangers and thought they saw assassins everywhere. The citizens of Onglas, unlike those in the larger towns where Vacher had struck, could not comfort themselves by arresting the usual suspects, for there weren't any.

"What demon pushed this monstrous murderer to tear his victims to shreds?" a Lyon newspaper reporter later asked when the extent of Vacher's crime spree was revealed. "The cadaver was mutilated so appallingly that it is impossible to believe in a single murderer: One would think the little one was killed by a bull who then turned its horns on him."

Within hours, more than 150 armed people from the surrounding towns organized themselves into a posse, scouring the forests, hills, and crevasses. They had a good sense of what the killer looked like. It had to be the vagabond who was begging for milk. Very few strangers came to Onglas, and this was one everyone remembered. Yet Vacher eluded them. Immediately after the killing, he fled down a gully and abandoned the high ground. Within a couple of days, he was seen crossing one of the railroad bridges over the Rhône.

In the wake of so ghastly a crime, the police promised immediate action. The procurer general of Lyon took a personal interest in the case, as he was an active member of the Society for the Protection of Children. He sent word to his subordinates to use every means at their disposal to solve the crime. The regional official who got the case, a substitute judge in one of the local towns, returned to the area several times over the next few days and interviewed local people about strangers they had seen. He sent out a strikingly accurate description to all the neighboring districts, towns, and hospitals:

Age: 30 to 35 years
Height: 1 meter 56 [about 5 feet, 2 inches]
Thick black eyebrows
Coloring: pale and sickly
White hands, indicating that he does not indulge in any hard work
Head covering: straw hat, said to be a panama, with the front pulled down over his eyes. Sometimes he wears a beret.
Distinguishing characteristics: scar across his right eye. Carries a small work bag and a club.

No lead went unexplored. On September 5, a telegram arrived from the police in Trévoux, the town where Victor was born, where anonymous tongues had been wagging about a suspect the authorities had not considered: Victor's mother, Marie Pinet.

Most people did not like her. Nor did they like that she had married Lazare Portalier, a dwarfish old man, and that during the marriage she had dallied with other suitors. After her husband died, she immediately took up with a bricklayer with a rough reputation. Her enemies in Trévoux told the police that Portalier, who ran a tailor's business, had left a small fortune of ten thousand francs to her son, which Marie never told the boy about. People asked darkly why she had given him so willingly to foster care and why she had never answered his letters. Now that the boy was approaching the age of majority, the theory went, Marie had had him killed by a vagabond so the money would be hers.

Police conducted interviews in Trévoux. Some of the rumors proved true: Marie *was* a loose woman. But the stories of the inheritance were greatly exaggerated. The father had left the family only a modest amount, and almost all had been consumed by an ongoing lawsuit against his brother. Marie scratched out a marginal existence washing linen for two francs a day. She never answered her son's letters because she was illiterate, although she kept them as a personal treasure. When she gave the packet of letters to the police to examine, she said, "Please give them back to me, because they're all I have left of him."

The most compelling piece of exonerating testimony came from witnesses who saw her reaction to Victor's death. Even though Marie had heard rumors of a shepherd's murder, she had no idea it might be her son. When Marie came by to ask Claudine Suchet, who sold newspapers, about finding someone to care for a sick relative, Claudine asked Marie to remind her of the name of the village where Victor was working and the name of his foster family. Suchet had read the news about the killing of a then-unidentified shepherd. "I must have subtly changed color," recalled Suchet, "[because] the poor woman began trembling and broke into uncontrollable sobs. Her attitude seemed completely grief-stricken." She still had not recovered by the time of the interrogation. Police eliminated Marie as a suspect.

Weeks passed. On September 30, the medical director of the Saint-Robert asylum wrote to the authorities that one of his inmates had escaped two days before the murder. The patient, named Jean-François Bravais, who had been treated for depression and a persecution complex, had much in common with the description in the bulletin, including a scar on his face from a self-inflicted gunshot. Police put out a dragnet, and five weeks later they apprehended Bravais as he got off a train about fifty miles south of

Bénonces. Bravais denied everything, and he had a reliable eyewitness to back him up—a policeman.

On November 22, 1895, with no new evidence and no new leads to pursue, authorities officially closed the investigation. The citizens of Bénonces, Onglas, and the surrounding towns would continue to live in fear. Meanwhile, Vacher would continue to stalk the countryside, preying on the innocent, the weak, and the young.

Louis-Albert Fonfrède, who had tried but failed to solve the Augustine Mortureux case, read about the Portalier killing. He started compiling a dossier.

Ten

Never Without a Trace

One of Lacassagne's treasured artifacts was the skeleton of a young man hanging in a display case, its head reattached after an encounter with the guillotine. On the inner surface of the right pelvis, the name Gaumet was inscribed in inch-high letters. It served as a reminder of a brutal crime and the power of science to use even the tiniest traces of evidence to solve it.

Annet Gaumet was a hardened criminal, with fourteen convictions by the age of twenty-four. On the night of December 21, 1898, he and several gang members broke into the apartment of the widow Foucherand above her bistro on rue de la Villette in Lyon. They strangled her, clubbed her to death, and stole her money. The police had been well versed in the management of crime scenes, so when Lacassagne arrived the next morning with the prosecuting attorney and the commissioner of police, he found the scene undisturbed. They found the woman on her back on the floor—legs splayed, skirts hiked, her right arm in a defensive position across her chest, her left extended outward, bruises on her throat, and a gaping wound on the right side of her head. Next to the body was a blood-covered wine bottle. Furniture had been turned over; drawers had been emptied.

The investigators proceeded carefully from room to room, carefully noting the position of the furniture, bloodstains, and artifacts. Yet this scene seemed abnormally free of telltale traces. The bloody bottle may have been used in the attack, but it turned out to be free of handprint and finger marks. No footprints marked the scene, despite the apparent chaos. There was no clothing that did not belong to the victim, and no bits of foreign hair were found. The one thing that struck Lacassagne as unusual was a lump of human fecal matter on the bed. He had no idea why it was there, or if it would prove useful in the investigation. He had it taken back to the institute, along with the body and the bottle.

By the mid-1890s, experts were becoming increasingly sophisticated about searching for hidden evidence at crime scenes and eager to bridge the gap between science and the law. In the introduction to the eighth volume of his journal, in 1893, Lacassagne urged greater collaboration "between men of law and men of science." Representing the law-enforcement point of view, Hans Gross, the renowned Austrian jurist and law professor, felt the same. In his book, *Criminal Investigation*, he devoted eighty-one pages to the wisdom of using scientific experts, including "The Microscopist," "The Chemical Analyst," "The Experts in Physics," and "Experts in Minerology, Zoology, and Botany." "Experts are the most important auxiliaries of an Investigating Officer," he wrote, "and in some way or other they nearly always are the main factor in deciding a case." In 1895, the International Union of Criminal Law, meeting in Linz, Austria, passed a resolution calling for "specially designed" courses for young jurists to deepen their knowledge of scientific procedures.

Part of what science can do best is show patterns where none seems to have existed and reveal what once had been impossible to see. The same held true for the growing science of forensics. Investigators were finding that no matter how careful the criminal, he or she inevitably left traces at the crime scene, or carried traces away. Years later, Lacassagne's disciple Edmond Locard would codify that observation as the "Locard Exchange Principle." Police and experts alike were fascinated by how small these bits of evidence could be. To track down a criminal through clues as tiny as a hair or some fibers approached wizardry (which is how such feats were often portrayed in the press). Knowing the importance of tiny clues, medical experts and investigators were learning to search nonobvious places, such as hat linings, cuffs, or under the fingernails of the victim and suspects. No item was too trivial to escape their attention, whether an article of clothing, the chewed end of a pipe stem, or torn bits of paper. And they were using technologies that could detect traces so small as to be virtually invisible.

The most valuable tool for this task was the microscope. Although invented centuries before, microscope technology made a huge leap in the nineteenth century as lens crafters used the new mathematical understanding of optics to replace trial and error in designing new lenses and employed new formulations to produce purer glass. By late in the century, manufacturers such as Carl Zeiss in Germany were building microscopes whose power remained unsurpassed until the development of the electron microscope in the 1960s. Gross recounted numerous investigations in which the participation of a microscopist revealed clues that were invisible to detectives. He described several cases of cleaned-off murder weapons that revealed tiny traces of blood when a microscopist examined the rivets of the knife handle or the junction between the ax handle and blade.

Microscopes proved especially effective in examining hair, which was ubiquitous to crime scenes, if one searched carefully enough. It appeared on clothing, shoes, weapons, and bone fragments. It frequently became entangled in the fingers of the deceased, which often gave a clue to the identity of the assailant. "This happens more frequently than one would believe; indeed, if the hands of the victims were more carefully examined it would be found even more frequently," wrote Gross. For that reason, he insisted that ordinary policemen stay away from victims' hands until authorized medical examiners arrived. Those experts could microscopically distinguish the varieties of hair: human hair as opposed to animal fur or vegetable fibers such as flax, corn silk, and cotton. They could identify hair from various parts of the body, from children and adults, and from various races. By the late 1800s, sexual-assault cases were being decided based on the microscopic identification of intermingled pubic hair.

The American legal writers Francis Wharton and Moreton Stille cited a case in Norwich, England, in which a little girl was found dead in a field, her throat cut. The mother seemed strangely calm about the killing, so police detained her for questioning. She claimed she had gotten separated from her child while looking for flowers and denied any knowledge of how the girl died. Police found a long knife in her possession with a few tiny hairs adhering to its handle. She said the hairs had come from a rabbit she had slaughtered for dinner. A microscopist identified the hairs as those from a squirrel. The child had been wearing a squirrel-fur scarf, and the fibers from the scarf matched those on the knife. Faced with the evidence, the mother confessed.

Other clues came to light by examining dust, which not even the most scrupulous of criminals could remove. Dust—collected in the lining of a pocket, the weave of a coat, the groove of a pocketknife—could reveal where the suspect had been or what he or she did for a living. Gross cited the case of a jacket abandoned at a crime scene. It contained no overt clue as to its owner's identity, but investigators put the coat in a heavy paper bag and beat it with sticks, then collected and analyzed the dust. It consisted largely of sawdust, which led to the preliminary deduction that the suspect was a carpenter or worked in a sawmill. But they also found gelatin and powdered glue, which carpenters did not widely use at the time. "The further deduction was drawn that the garment belonged to a joiner," wrote Gross, a fact that eventually was substantiated.

A combination of microscopic and chemical techniques helped investigators identify bloodstains. Dried blood could resemble many different substances, such as rust, spores, chewing tobacco, paint, or vegetable matter. In order to distinguish blood from the other substances, experts made use of chemical tests, most notably one developed by the Dutch scientist J. Izaak Van Deen. To a suspected blood sample, the examiner would add tincture of guaiac, a resin derived from the bark of a tropical tree, and then add hydrogen peroxide. If the sample was blood, the chemicals would react with the hemoglobin of red blood cells and within seconds turn sapphire blue. For a more sensitive diagnosis, they could use a spectroscope, as Lacassagne did in the Badoil case.

Frequently when police found a suspect with bloody clothing or hands, especially in the countryside, he or she would claim to have recently slaughtered an animal. So it became important to distinguish human blood from that of animals, which they did by having an expert microscopically examine the size and shape of the red cells. The cells of no two species are identical: Birds, fish, and reptiles have oblong red corpuscles, with noticeable nuclei; mammalian cells are disk-shaped, with a depression in the center and no apparent nuclei. Among mammals, blood cells vary according to size, although not in relation to the size of the creature: A mouse's red cells are larger than a lion's, while a human's are larger than those of an ox or a horse. George Gulliver, a British surgeon who spent decades examining the blood cells of some six hundred species, wrote that humans had the largest red cells, at $1/3200$ of an inch, followed closely by dogs, at $1/3395$ of an inch. The size difference seemed minuscule but was easily detected with the calibrated microscopes of the day. After the turn of the century, the German scientist Paul Uhlenhuth developed a fast, simple test for human blood based on antibody reactions, a method that is used to this day.

Experts learned to analyze blood *patterns*, as well. They learned to look for blood in unlikely places, such as the underside of tables, where it might have splashed up following an assault at floor level. Candlelight revealed blood on dark cloth more effectively than daylight. Patterns had meaning. Smear marks meant the body had been dragged, which argued against a finding of suicide. Blood droplets falling from a height of several feet made a larger splash pattern than those falling from only a few inches. Those falling straight down produced a round splatter, while those falling from a body in motion produced an oblong splash, with the narrower part of the drop indicating the direction.

Traces of sperm were also left at many crime scenes. In general, semen stains had irregular shapes and a sheen produced by the dried albumin. When soaked, they gave off a characteristic starchy smell. That provided a rough identification, but the only way to identify the residue positively was to microscopically identify individual spermatozoa, with their pear-shaped heads and long, whippy tails. Most examiners considered this process relatively simple, provided they viewed the entire sperm and not a collection of separated parts. It was too easy to mistake miscellaneous granules in the liquid for detached sperm heads or to mistake microscopic filaments for tails.

When the victim or his clothing had been washed, finding unbroken sperm could become almost impossible. "I . . . myself spent three weeks in isolating a few complete spermatozoa in a case of rape of a four-year-old child," wrote Dr. Albert Florence, a colleague of Lacassagne at the Institute of Legal Medicine. Lacassagne had similar experiences, and he challenged Florence to come up with a sperm test that was as simple, fast, and reliable as the Van Deen test for blood. Florence threw himself at the problem and presented a study that was as broad as it was deep. In a series of papers, he surveyed the history of human knowledge about sperm (it wasn't until 1824 that scientists discovered that the unity of sperm and egg creates life) and gave a thorough description of sperm—its structure, its chemistry, and the various stains that made it more visible under the microscope. Then he searched for simple chemical tests, experimenting with one reagent after another that would react exclusively to semen. Eventually, he found that if he prepared a solution of one part potassium and three parts iodine (potassium triiodide), chilled it, and added it to semen, dramatic brownish red crystals appeared.

He felt he had found the holy grail of testing for sex crimes. It was "incontestably the *procedure of choice*, to which it is necessary to have recourse in all difficult cases," he wrote. Unfortunately, a couple of years later a German scientist found that when he added the solution to other substances that contained decomposed albumin, such as rotten egg whites, the rhomboid crystals also appeared. Still, nothing produced crystals faster or in greater profusion than seminal fluid, and so Florence's solution remained a valuable preliminary test until a better one replaced it in the mid-1940s.

Footprints left important clues to a criminal's identity, especially in an era when shoes were custom-made. The nail patterns of no two shoes were identical, so researchers developed a variety of ways to capture footprints in the soil by using gels or plaster of Paris, or even in snow (salts created an ice layer around the impression, which allowed a mold to be taken). A surprising number of murderers went barefoot. The shape of the foot, the height of the arch, and irregularities in the soles produced a positive identity. "There is a physiognomy of the foot just as there is of the face," wrote Lacassagne's colleagues Coutagne and Florence. Lacassagne instructed that in addition to making molds of footprints in soil, one could duplicate them with a pantograph, an instrument consisting of a framework of parallelograms that made it possible to trace objects and documents. He also developed a process to make invisible prints of bare feet on a hard floor come into view. He would soak the suspect area in silver nitrate (the same chemical used on photographic plates) and leave it for several days in the light. During that time, the salt in sweat left behind by the foot would react with the chemical and a print would appear.

The interpretation of footprints became quite a subtle art. Investigators used it to determine the height, stature, and emotional state of people at the crime scene (for example, excited people tend to walk faster and take longer strides). Gross noted that a deeper footprint did not necessarily indicate obesity: In normal firm soil, an increase of twenty kilograms in body weight made no difference in depth. But he asserted that obese people tended to walk with their toes pointed outward. One German specialist maintained that an outward-pointed gait indicated a "man of distinction," in contrast to a man of the people, although French researchers disagreed.

Fingerprints would not become common in police work until the first decade of the twentieth century, although their characteristics were being studied in England, India, and Argentina. Bertillon started attaching fingerprints to his anthropomorphic cards, although his method of classi-fying the cards did not change. He also worked increasingly with photo-graphy. He developed a technique called "metric photography," whereby he mounted the camera on a large enough tripod to look down on the crime scene and circumscribed the area with measuring tape. Later, he developed metered frames, in which he could insert crime-scene photo-graphs. This, he felt, got beyond the common problem that "the eye sees only what is already in the mind."

In considering the variety of methods Lacassagne and his colleagues employed, it is impossible not to compare them to a fictional detective whose career ran contemporaneously to theirs. Arthur Conan Doyle wrote the first novel featuring Sherlock Holmes, *A Study in Scarlet,* in 1887 and sustained the character over a period of forty years—despite the author's attempt to kill him off at Reichenbach Falls in 1893, the same year that Hans Gross's book was published. Real-life investigators found the character fascinating. Lacassagne's disciple Edmond Locard said what in part motivated his career choice, aside from his mentor, was the Sherlock Holmes stories. Doyle's own inspiration came from Dr. Joseph Bell, his medical instructor at the University of Edinburgh, whose powers as a medical diagnostician translated into those of an amateur detective; in addition, he took note of contemporary experts. In more than one instance, Holmes speaks about the work of Alphonse Bertillon. In the short story "The Adventure of the Naval Treaty," Watson records a dis-cussion with Holmes: "His conversation, I remember, was about the Bertillon system of measurements, and he expressed his enthusiastic admi-ration of the French savant." In *The Hound of the Baskervilles,* Watson reports the following exchange between a client and Holmes:

"Recognizing, as I do, that you are the second highest expert in Europe—"

"Indeed, sir! May I inquire who has the honor of being first?" asked Holmes, with some asperity.

"To the man of precisely scientific mind the work of Monsieur Alphonse Bertillon must always appeal strongly."

"Then had you not better consult him?"

"I said, sir, to the precisely scientific mind. But as a practical man of affairs it is acknowledged that you stand alone. I trust, sir, that I have not inadvertently—"

"Just a little," said Holmes.

Lacassagne admired the work of Conan Doyle, but he, like his colleagues, had reservations about Holmes's methods and the misleading impression they gave to the public. Holmes worked with blinding speed, never expressed doubt, and presented his results with "mathematical" certainty (not unlike the *CSI* television shows of today). In contrast, Lacassagne's investigations could continue for weeks. He made a *point* of maintaining uncertainty, right up until the end of the investigation. He famously told students, "One must know how to doubt."

Still, Lacassagne, like many colleagues, remained fascinated with the character. He published two reviews of Holmes stories in his journal and supervised a thesis by one of his students, comparing Holmes's methods with those of actual forensic scientists. The student, Jean-Henri Bercher, archly referred to Holmes as "a veritable Robinson Crusoe of legal medicine" for his ability to accomplish alone what normally required a team of medical experts. He did find that Holmes and Lacassagne held certain values in common: their appreciation for careful observation and the methodical compilation of evidence; their belief that each case should be approached with a logical plan; their appreciation for how even the tiniest bits of evidence could point to a solution; and their belief in the necessity of preserving an untrammeled crime scene. In one story, Holmes excoriates an officer for allowing his men to trample through the site of a murder. "If a herd of buffalo had passed along there could not be a greater mess." Like real-life investigators, Holmes appreciated the value of footprints, and he used plaster of Paris to preserve them. "There is no branch of detective science which is so important and so much neglected as the art of tracing footsteps," said Holmes. "Happily, I have always laid great stress upon it."

Sometimes the opinions of Holmes and Lacassagne were strikingly similar.

Holmes (as quoted by Bercher): "It is a grave error to warm to a theory without having put together all the necessary materials: It could lead to false judgments."

Lacassagne: "Avoid hasty theories and hold yourself back from flights of imagination."

Yet their differences eclipsed their similarities. For example, Holmes deduced the height of a suspect by the length of his or her stride. Real medical examiners knew that the stride could vary depending on the suspect's walking speed and emotional state. Holmes would take a single object from a person—a watch, for example—and use it to build an entire life history. Real examiners would never base conclusions on so narrow a piece of evidence. They collected, analyzed, and filed every piece of material they could find, and couched their conclusions in the understated language of science. Holmes knew the ash content of every popular cigar and cigarette—a useless piece of knowledge in real life. He had a cavalier approach to medicine, an understanding of anatomy that Watson himself characterized as "accurate but unsystematic."

Bercher found it particularly galling that Holmes never conducted autopsies, the cornerstone of legal medicine. For example, in *A Study in Scarlet*, Holmes deduces poisoning—probably by strychnine—with an examination that takes no more than a few minutes. "Arriving at the scene of the crime, Sherlock Holmes proceeds with several preliminary investigations to inquire into the circumstances, the habits of the victim . . . and he looks to see if he can't find some suspect objects or traces of poison," wrote Bercher.

> Next he approaches the cadaver, and he makes a diagram of the position of the corpse, the state of his clothing, and traces of stains, marks of blows or wounds. . . . Moving the arms and legs, he investigates the state of rigor mortis, and gives an approximate time of death. We see him next approach the nostrils of the victim, and in one move discovers a characteristic odor.
>
> The curtain falls on the first act: The corpse is removed and the autopsy is unnecessary!
>
> There's no question of doing research on lividity to reveal the position at death, which is of considerable importance. What matters the degree of putrefaction? A Sherlock Holmes has no need to surround himself with all that information to arrive at a conclusion! It is equally unnecessary to tire himself by doing an autopsy, and to get his hands dirty with pathological lesions that could present themselves in the thoracic and abdominal organs. Why dream of withdrawing some blood or viscera to try to discover traces of toxic substance?

As it happened, the same year *A Study in Scarlet* was published, Lacassagne also investigated a sudden death that turned out to have been strychnine-related. A pregnant woman in the countryside near Lyon drank some medicine for bronchial congestion and suffered a rapid and agonizing death. Unlike Holmes, the professor did much more than sniff the victim's lips. Bringing in two other doctors as witnesses, he made extensive notes on the body's position, lividity stains, and state of rigor mortis. Then he conducted a detailed autopsy, noting any internal hemorrhaging, blood clots, or other signs that might indicate the cause of death. He removed the brain, stomach, liver, kidney, uterus, segments of intestine and spleen, sealed them in jars, and had them sent back to his laboratory. Several other jars were sent back to the lab, as well; they contained stomach liquid, amniotic fluid, urine, and blood. Back at the institute, with the help of a physiology professor, Lacassagne injected samples of the victim's stomach fluid into two frogs and into one medium-size laboratory dog. He injected a third frog with distilled water as a control. The frog injected with water survived, but all the other animals perished; the latter exhibited convulsions, contraction of the jaw muscles, stomach swelling, asphyxia, and then a rapid onset of rigor mortis—typical signs of strychnine poisoning. The same symptoms had appeared in the woman. He gave the liquids to a chemistry professor, who found strychnine in the stomach fluid. Altogether, five doctors participated in the inquiry, which took place over a period of more than two days. In the end, a court convicted the woman's pharmacist of negligence for accidentally contaminating her medicine.

Interspersed throughout the pages of Bercher's thesis are comments in Lacassagne's spidery handwriting, giving the impression that he, too, was debating Holmes's methods and philosophy. On a strictly academic point, he questioned whether Holmes used "deductive" reasoning (arriving at specifics by starting at a general principle) or "inductive" reasoning (working from specifics to a more general idea). More fundamentally, he wondered how forensic detection could ever be considered the exact, almost mathematical science that Conan Doyle portrays. To his mind, there was art and intuition involved. Lacassagne commented that legal medicine involved three important components: craft, knowledge of science, and art. "One can learn craft," he wrote. "By patience and work, one can become educated in science. But art springs from natural qualities, and is almost exclusively attributed to one's [natural] mind." He questioned whether the kind of cool, detached analysis employed by Holmes was always sufficient to arrive at the truth. "Isn't there also 'Inspiration,' a spontaneous element, that *'Quid Divinum'* [Divine Something] . . . between geometry and finesse?"

The inspirational quality pushed Lacassagne forward and resulted in his remarkable success rate. As he saw it, criminals were always moving into new territories of cleverness and depravity, and the modern investi-

gator needed to develop new ways to pursue them. "All the silent witnesses . . . the place, the body, the prints . . . can speak if one knows how
to properly interrogate them."

The "interrogation" of evidence would prove challenging in finding the
killer of Madame Foucherand, who had lain dead on the ground, a wine
bottle next to her. Lacassagne had noted bloodstains at a height of more
than five feet on the door frame and on a newspaper on top of the bar. The
shape and location of the splashes told Lacassagne that the body had not
been killed elsewhere and dragged, but struck by a blunt instrument with
such violence that the blood droplets had been splashed to their current
locations.

The examination of the body in his lab told him that at least two people had taken part in the murder. Lividity stains showed she had been killed
and left on her back on the ground. He found extensive bruising on her
wrists, stomach, and rib cage. Internal examinations showed that the
wounds penetrated deeply, with bleeding into the muscles and organs and
breaks in several ribs. All these signs indicated that an assailant had violently held the victim to the floor while kneeling on her rib cage. At one
point, he must have strangled her: The hyoid bone above the larynx had
been broken, the thyroid cartilage had been torn at its base and midsection,
and the ringlike cricoid cartilage had been torn, as well. To Lacassagne,
this indicated the presence of two killers—there were too many breaks to
be accomplished by the same pair of hands that had held her down. He
found no evidence of a sex crime. The right side of the head was one enormous concavity, which Lacassagne attributed to strikes from the bottle.
The left side of the head showed reciprocal fractures, indicating that the
left side of her face had been against the ground when she was struck. The
bottle, more bloody on one side than the other, probably was the murder
weapon, but it bore no handprints or finger marks.

Lacassagne still had no evidence to tie any specific person to the crime.
When he examined the fecal matter, however, he saw something thread-
like, white and about half an inch long. He dissolved the fecal mass, and
a dozen more appeared. Professor Lortet, an expert in parasitology, identified them as pinworms, a fairly common intestinal parasite.

The authorities, meanwhile, had detained six suspects, members of an
"apache" gang who operated in Madame Foucherand's neighborhood.

Lacassagne gained permission to examine their waste buckets. "These observations gave no results," he reported, because the suspects had contaminated the contents by throwing in bread and other bits of food. He went back to the prison. Using long swabs, he took samples directly from the suspects, which he mounted on slides and examined microscopically. Studying the swab from one suspect, Annet Gaumet, Lacassagne noticed microscopic translucent disks, which Lortet identified as pinworm eggs.

All six prisoners admitted to breaking into the apartment with the intention of robbing Madame Foucherand. Things got out of hand when she resisted, and they started to beat her. Gaumet and the gang's leader, Émile Nouguier, were particularly out of control: Gaumet threw her down and started strangling her, while Nouguier grabbed another part of her throat. Finally, he finished the job by clubbing her with a bottle. Nouguier and Gaumet were sent to the guillotine. The other four received life sentences.

On the morning of his execution, Gaumet conveyed a message to Lacassagne. He was so impressed with the power of science, he said, that he wished to donate his skeleton to the professor's laboratory. It has been hanging in the display case ever since.

Eleven

In Plain Sight

The village of Truinas sits in the semiarid hills east of the Rhône River, about halfway as the crow flies between Lyon and Marseille. On September 23, 1895, a merchant farmer named Théodor Vache was driving his carriage up a dirt road approaching the village when he saw a strange-looking man creep from behind an acacia tree, his face and hands covered with blood. He watched as the man scraped at the dirt to cover up patches of blood on the ground. He greeted the stranger and asked if he was sick. "He told me that he'd had an accident and that he was always getting a bloody nose," the man recalled. "All the while he kept scratching at the ground with one hand while he held his head with the other." Vache also noticed a big hobo's sack and a club sticking out of it. He watched for a minute, shrugged, and kept going.

If Vache had looked a few yards beyond the side of the road, he would have seen the still-warm body of Aline Alaise, the sixteen-year-old daughter of a local landowner. Moments before, Vacher had killed her.

Earlier that day, Aline had walked with her father to a neighboring village to sell eggs and cheese, then had started home alone to finish some chores. When Aline did not arrive by dinnertime, her parents went out to search for her. They did not find her body until the next morning. Authorities found a page torn from a schoolbook nearby, on which they could make out the letters "M-A-R-C." They then seized an itinerant carnival fighter named Auguste Marseille. Apparently, the letters in his last name were close enough to those on the notebook page to qualify as a clue. Eventually, he was released for lack of evidence.

Vacher, as usual, had quickly left the scene. He walked down to the Rhône Valley, across the river, and then westward up into the hills of the Ardèche. It is a place of harsh beauty, with bold granite outcroppings and cliffs, stunted high-altitude forests, and high, angled meadows with vertiginous views. A day's outing in this countryside would involve scrambling as much as walking. The diminutive pastures were barely large enough to sustain the sinewy local goats and sheep. It was in such a meadow, six days after the Alaise murder and forty miles away, that a fourteen-year-old shepherd named Pierre Massot-Pellet was pasturing his flock, along with his sheepdog. Pierre watched the sheep on Thursdays and Sundays; the other days of the week, he attended school.

Sometimes in mountains, when the weather is just right and the morning is quiet, the rocky surfaces act as an echo chamber, propelling noises great distances. Far down the mountainside, out of sight but not out of earshot, several other shepherds heard Pierre singing his usual lighthearted songs. Then they heard two horrifying screams echo across the valleys. Then they heard barking, and then a deep, unnerving silence. Some time later, a few of his sheep came wandering down.

When Pierre failed to return for the midday meal, his employer sent another boy out to find him. The boy found Pierre's mangled remains behind a boulder.

The local investigating magistrate, Morellet, believed the killing resembled those of Victor Portalier and Aline Alaise. But just as with the murder of Augustine Mortureux and the wrongful persecution of Eugène Grenier, public opinion alighted on a suspect who had nothing to do with the crime—Bernardin Bannier, a stolid, gruff fifty-four-year-old farmer and father of four who had been politically active in town.

Politics made enemies in those isolated little villages, and anonymous denunciations came flooding in. Bannier's chief tormentor was a man named Chevalier, a political enemy, who said that because Bannier's grazing lands abutted the crime scene, Bannier was worthy of suspicion. The accusations grew to such an extent that authorities felt obligated to detain Bannier for a few weeks. Absent any valid evidence, he was released.

That was when Bannier's troubles really began. Outraged that a "guilty" man had been allowed to go free, townspeople pursued justice the traditional way—by making the culprit's life so miserable as to drive him away. Neighbors shouted epithets whenever they saw him. People threw stones at him and his family. At the silk factory where his wife and one of his daughters worked, the other employees refused to stand next to them. Later, the workers all banded together and told the factory owner that if he did not fire the Banniers, they would all quit. (The wife and daughter found other employment.)

Most nights, a nasty crowd would assemble outside Bannier's door. One night, a drunken mob broke into his kitchen, gobbled everything in the cupboard, and started a fire on his floor. One Sunday, a group of his neighbors planted a tree outside his front door and festooned its branches with the intestines of a goat kid. They hung up a blood-soaked sheet, a knife, and a placard reading DEATH TO THE KILLER!

All this took place despite the fact that the mayor and prosecutors repeatedly exhorted the town folk that Bannier could not be the killer. They fined Chevalier for spreading false accusations, but he continued. At one point, Morellet asked Bannier if it wouldn't be easier just to move. "But, Judge," he replied, "where would you like me to go? I'm not rich: I have only two little plots of land and my flock. It would be impossible at my age to begin again."

"You could imagine such savage and barbaric demonstrations worthy of an earlier era," wrote a contemporary journalist named Laurent-Martin, "but it's incredible to see it in the middle of France in the nineteenth century!"

Yet turn-of-the-century France, or Europe, or, for that matter, the United States, was not at all uniform in its modernity. Rural life, as we have seen, seemed centuries behind life in the big cities, and the searing inequalities of the time must have made the condition of those in rural areas seem worse. In a period that became famous for science and progress, rural folk (and the urban poor, as well) faced a daily struggle to feed, clothe, and shelter themselves—a struggle made worse, ironically, by the "modernizing" forces of global trade and the industrial economy, which made certain labor and trades obsolete. They did not enjoy the fruits of the era, but faced unemployment and poverty, and the increasingly bold and numerous vagabonds who would drift into their towns. Morellet complained that a "cloud of vagabonds" invaded every autumn, causing a seasonal increase in crime. "The gendarmes are up to their teeth; they do what they can, but it isn't enough." At one point, Morellet was so helpless against the vagabonds that he sent word to Marie-François Goron, who at the time was still chief of the Paris Sûreté, requesting some agents to help with the crime wave.

There were deeper reasons for the kind of primitive thinking that Laurent-Martin decried. France at the time was still largely a nation of peasants, barely a generation away from medieval-era fears and superstition. People lived in a world populated by wraiths and spirits, in which real and imaginary fears played a role in daily life. It did not take much for a villager to believe that a spell had been cast on his cattle or field. Numerous studies at the time documented a shocking level of rural superstition. For example, in 1892 an agricultural commission noted with genuine surprise that farmers in southwestern France did not practice apiculture because they felt beehives attracted bad luck, and that they would hang fern leaves over their doors to ward off the evil eye. As part of an attempt to reduce the level of rural superstition, the government issued schoolbooks admonishing children not to adhere to all their folk beliefs: "Do not believe in witches. Do not believe in ghosts, in specters, in spirits, in phantoms. . . . Do not imagine one can avoid harm or accidents with . . . amulets, talismans, fetishes."

In such an atmosphere of fear and superstition, it did not take much to persuade villagers that one of their own had become damned, or, in a sense, had decided to damn them. It was comforting to seize on a suspect, even the wrong one. Certainly it was preferable to wondering which of the malignant, invisible forces was waiting to victimize others, as well.

Years later, when the case of Massot-Pellet had been solved, a reporter for *La Dépêche de Toulouse* went to interview Bannier. The reporter, Albert Sarraut, who later entered politics and eventually became prime minister of France, was shocked to find the town folk still tormenting the man.

> In the naïveté of his unjust martyrdom [Bannier] has been telling himself that when his innocence came to light, society would give him some kind of compensation, at least for the losses that he has sustained.
>
> Should I have told him to abandon this illusion; told him that there is a fatal law in every society of every age that the victims of error of the hatred of their fellow man . . . cannot count on society for reparations? Should I have told this man, whose heart was crushed by the most dreadful injustices, that society will content itself in saying that he should consider himself lucky to be publicly declared innocent, and that he has no right to expect anything more of us?
>
> I dared not.

Vacher laid low after killing Pierre Massot-Pellet. As cold weather approached, he wandered to the vagabonds' wintering grounds in Brittany. Along the way, he fashioned a hat of white rabbit fur, which became one of his trademarks. (The white fur, he said, symbolized purity.) He carried a club, on which he carved the initials M.J.L.B.G. (Investigators never figured out what all the letters stood for, but they assumed that L.B. stood for Louise Barant.) He reemerged in February 1896 at a farm near the city of Le Mans. Late one night, a woman heard a noise in her greenhouse. She went outside, spotted Vacher, and immediately fled back to her door. Before she could slam it, he shouldered his way in, grabbed her, and started dragging her to the woods, but her brother heard the screaming and drove him away.

A few days later, twelve-year-old Alphonsine Derouet was walking to church in a nearby village. She passed a man reading a newspaper, and he asked if it was a long way to the town center. No sooner did she begin to reply than he grabbed her by the throat and threw her to the ground. Her screams drew the attention of her employer's security guard, who came running and found Alphonsine struggling underneath a stranger, her skirts bunched up around her waist. He pulled the maniac off the little girl but lost his grip when he was kicked in the face. The attacker escaped. The guard then alerted the police, who learned that a man matching the attacker's description had spent the previous night at a farm, identifying himself as Joseph Vacher, a former novitiate and sergeant. They organized a manhunt and sent an arrest warrant with his name and description to neighboring towns.

Hours later and several miles away, a policeman on a bicycle pulled up to Vacher, who by then had recovered his composure. When the gendarme started questioning him, he handed over his military papers. The documents changed everything: Rather than seeing Vacher as a suspect, the gendarme, an ex–military man himself, saw Vacher as a comrade in arms. Vacher confided that he had seen a strange-looking vagabond earlier, and he gave directions that sent the gendarme far away.

A few days later, Vacher was begging at a farm when he got into a protracted fight with a watchman. He had a death grip on the man's throat and was holding him in a water-filled ditch when several other servants arrived, overpowered Vacher, and took him to the police. Arrested for vagrancy and aggravated assault, he was sentenced to a month in jail. It was a lenient sentence, given the antivagabond hysteria and the aggravated nature of the assault. Surprisingly, the jailers never made the connection between the man they were holding and the one who was being hunted just a few towns away. They certainly must have received the arrest warrant. While police in the neighboring district pursued a vigorous manhunt, Vacher had found the perfect place to hide—in plain sight.

Of all the luck—but it was something other than luck. Outside of the big cities, the French police were barely competent. (The same was true for the rest of Europe and for the United States.) Big cities had municipal police departments, but the countryside was only loosely patrolled by a network of wardens and federal police. The wardens, or *gardes-champêtres,* were equal parts game wardens and policemen. Appointed by small-town mayors, these rural guards had been a feature of French country life for centuries and addressed the everyday problems of rural living such as vandalism, poaching, and bar fights. Many were old, poorly paid, and corrupt—useless in the face of serious crime. For major crimes, the local guard would find a gendarme, a local officer of the national police. (In Britain and the United States, the sheriff was the enforcer of higher authority.) Gendarmes were generally competent, but their barracks were thinly spread throughout the countryside, mostly along the main routes.

Generally, whenever a serious crime was committed, the chance of successful prosecution was small. Only the three biggest French cities, Paris, Lyon, and Marseille, had full-time detective bureaus, a relatively new institution at the time. The rest of the country depended on a complicated legal structure that pivoted around a national network of investigating magistrates. University-educated and generally ambitious, these magistrates (*juges d'instruction*) served as both detective and grand jury. They could direct rural guards or gendarmes to bring in a suspect and to interview and detain him as long as necessary without charges. Usually, these suspects would be confined until they cracked or someone came forward with new evidence that either exculpated or condemned them. If the magistrate found enough evidence for a trial, he would write up a report, which he would then pass to the regional prosecutor, or procurer of the Republic (*procureur de la République*), who would take the case to court. An investigating magistrate could send out interrogatories to his colleagues in other districts, asking them to pick up a suspect and question the person on his behalf. Such investigators were generally supposed to keep in touch with other districts on criminal goings-on. But due to overwork or sometimes professional jealously, they often did not. All too often an investigator did not think beyond his particular jurisdiction.

Journalist Laurent-Martin, who eventually retraced Vacher's footsteps, wrote that he was stupefied that someone "in our time, in the middle of France" could commit so many crimes "without ever being reported from one locality to another and without falling earlier into the hands of justice." He blamed the magistrates:

> Each is isolated. There is no correspondence between the authorities. . . . So if a crime is committed in a commune [a village or town], all the murderer has to do is pass into the neighboring territory for the wardens and gendarmes not to have the slightest recourse against him. By the time they can alert the authorities in the neighboring district, he's long gone.

That certainly described Vacher's method of killing in one district and fleeing to another. Yet there were other reasons why police overlooked him while repeatedly jailing the wrong people as suspects. In addition to understaffing and jurisdictional limitations, they were hampered by their own *methods* of investigation. Despite the modern emphasis that Lacassagne and others placed on evidence, many police departments remained wedded to their old ways. Ever since Eugène-François Vidocq established the Paris Sûreté, the world's first detective bureau, in 1812, the French police had relied on coercive methods to solve cases: cultivating informers, pressuring suspects (including the use of thumb screws), placing stool pigeons in jail cells, and using undercover police as agents provocateurs. But those methods, questionable even on the mean streets of Paris, often proved useless among rural villagers.

Vidocq, the world's first celebrity detective, was worthy of a book— and indeed, Honoré de Balzac and Victor Hugo based characters on him. A thief, forger, and legendary escape artist, Vidocq began to cooperate with authorities as a jailhouse informer, thus shortening his sentences. Upon his release, he realized he could capitalize on his street knowledge and his friendships among criminals and became an *agent particulier* (special agent) for the Paris Préfecture of Police. He eventually formed his own bureau, called the Bureau de Sûreté (Security Bureau). Working in disguise, he and his squad of ex-cons would infiltrate taverns that criminals liked to frequent, gain their confidence, trick them into revealing information, and hustle them or their friends. Sometimes they would employ an *indicateur*—an ex-con who would walk ahead of the police and tip his hat when he passed a suspect he recognized. They frequently hired *mouchards* (snitches) and *moutons* (sheep), who would inform from within prisons. When Vidocq published his memoirs in 1829, he became the forerunner of all celebrity detectives.

Vidocq's methods became standard throughout the countryside, and in many other countries, as well. Alan Pinkerton, the detective who formed the first U.S. detective agency, referred to himself as the "Vidocq of the West." But as effective as Vidocq's methods seemed at the time, their inherent problems eventually became apparent. He ran up huge numbers of arrests, but many were false arrests or entrapments. Suspects who were pressured to confess sometimes told police what they wanted to hear, rather than the truth.

If those methods were questionable in Paris, they proved virtually useless among the rural French. Law enforcement was relatively new in many parts of the countryside, and its representatives were seen as outsiders. Certain ordnances, such as those against illegal harvesting or poaching, did not earn respect. Peasants had their own ways of dealing with offenders, whether by individual or collective violence, or the kind of ongoing harassment targeted against Grenier, Bannier, and others. To them, the law was something to avoid, or perhaps to manipulate as a way to settle grudges.

Vacher profited from it all. It was the rare magistrate who would detect a pattern, or could imagine that one man would commit so many crimes.

Sexual murderers, of course, were not completely unheard-of. In the decade prior to Vacher's rampage, Jack the Ripper had murdered and mangled five prostitutes in London. The crimes were horrific, but people could console themselves with the fact that the victims belonged to a disgraceful profession and all lived in a single small neighborhood. There had also been monsters in France, such as Louis Menesclou, who in 1880 lured a four-year-old girl into his apartment in Paris and then raped and strangled her. Part of his notoriety was due to the fact that the police broke in just as he was in the act of burning the little girl's body; one of her severed arms was protruding from his pocket. But that was a single incident. There was also Pierre Rivière, who in 1835, in his cottage in Normandy, took a pruning hook to his mother, sister, and brother. But nothing came close to what was now taking place. To imagine crimes on the scale of Vacher's, one had to cast back to 1440, when the nobleman Gilles de Rais, one of

Joan of Arc's brothers in arms, was hanged and excommunicated for the rape and murder of literally hundreds of children.

The very scale and nature of Vacher's crimes worked to his advantage. At the time of his arrest in Baugé, he had killed at least seven people and assaulted many more, in towns more than *six hundred miles* apart. One magistrate, Louis-Albert Fonfrède of Dijon, who started keeping a dossier on the killings, thought there might be a contagion of crime, what police would later call "copycat killings." People saw implications of Pasteur's germ theory everywhere, including the idea that criminality might be contagious. But the other magistrates would focus only on a murder in their particular jurisdictions.

Vacher saw his time in prison as yet another sign of benevolence from above. After his release on April 6, 1896, he wrote a letter to a friend, alluding to his feeling that somewhere, somehow, he was fulfilling a destiny. "My program never varies. Ever since my family cast me out I have continued to serve my unique master and let myself be blown by the winds of chance."

As he thought about his blessings, he decided to make a pilgrimage to a place where he could thank the Holy Mother for her protection along his strange and dangerous path. It would be a long journey, a walk of hundreds of miles, to the southern border of France. More people would die along the way, but Vacher knew that blessings would await him. He was going to Lourdes.

Twelve

Born Criminal

The 1889 Universal Exposition in Paris was renowned as an international showplace of modern technology, science, and culture, but it also served as a massive gathering place for the world's scholars and intellectuals. From May to November, when more than thirty million attended the exhibits, 120 scientific congresses took place, including the International Congress of Zoologists, the International Congress of Dermatology and Syphilology, and the International Congress for Experimental and Therapeutic Hypnotism, attended by Sigmund Freud.

One such meeting was the Second International Congress of Criminal Anthropology (the first had taken place in Rome in 1885). This was an organization founded to address central questions in the study of criminals: Why did most people live normal, peaceful lives, while a small number committed violence and mayhem? What was the seed of the criminal instinct? And what could authorities do to suppress it?

From August 10 to 17, delegates representing twenty-two countries gathered in the amphitheater of the Faculty of Medicine. They discussed important issues regarding the causes and prevention of crime, topics that included "Do Criminals Present Any Peculiar Anatomical Characteristics?"; "The Infancy of Criminals"; and "Causes and Remedies for the Repetition of Crime."

They took field trips to the Sainte-Anne asylum, where the chief physician, Valentin Magnan, introduced them to some of his patients, and to the Préfecture of Police, where Alphonse Bertillon demonstrated his method for identifying repeat offenders. They attended lavish parties, the grandest when Prince Roland Bonaparte, the great-nephew of Napoléon, held a reception at his hotel. Prince Roland, an enthusiastic follower of science and anthropology, went to great lengths to please his guests. He persuaded Thomas Edison, who was visiting Paris, to awe and entertain them by playing music on the phonograph, Edison's marvelous invention.

Prince Roland was a collector of cultural and scientific artifacts. One of his treasured items was the skull of Charlotte Corday, the assassin of Jean-Paul Marat. She had become something of a cult figure in the ninety-six years since her execution—smaller and more delicate in myth than in real life, more elegant of speech, braver in her final moments, and almost Christ-like in her readiness to forgive her executioners. To scientists devoted to understanding crime, it must have been fascinating to wonder what had turned such an "angel" into a killer. So they were thrilled when the prince allowed them to study the contours of this unique and historic skull.

That was when cordiality became strained. Cesare Lombroso examined the skull and said it bore all the physical hallmarks of what he called the "born criminal." For more than a dozen years, Lombroso had been promoting the idea that certain people were biologically destined to be criminals, and that he could identify them by physical traits. These signs, or "stigmata," as he called them, were only the surface indicators of a primitive brain, one that predisposed its owner to impulsive brutality. Now, beholding the skull of Corday, he quickly identified a host of such stigmata—the general asymmetry; the vaguely masculine appearance; the broad, flat skull cap; and, most important, an indentation at the back of the head that he called the "occipital fossette." This was beyond doubt the skull of someone destined to commit murder.

In sharp rebuttal, Dr. Paul Topinard, president of the French Anthropological Society, said that he found nothing unusual about the flattening of the skull cap or the depression at the back of the head. He proclaimed the skull "regular, harmonic, with all the delicacy and soft but correct curves of female skulls." As for the general asymmetry, nearly all human skulls "showed a difference or distinction on the one side or the other," he said. The Viennese anatomist Moritz Benedikt, while acknowledging that the skull might exhibit certain minor anomalies, saw nothing that would link them to any personality traits. As for the occipital fossette, it no more indicated a tendency to crime than a "predisposition to hemorrhoids."

Lombroso's theory of criminal anthropology had gained a wide following since he introduced it in 1876. An opposing school of thought had surfaced, as well, and, that summer in particular, had gained much support. Led by Lacassagne, the "French School," or "Lyon School," as it was called, maintained that crime did not arise from accidents of heredity, but from the social environment. Born in the wake of the theories of evolution and heredity, this was one of the earliest instances of the nature-nurture debate, which eventually would extend to almost all human behavior, from intelligence to gender differences. The debate would pit Lombroso and Lacassagne against each other for decades, arising continually in scientific meetings and after every high-profile crime. It would raise questions about human nature that remain open to this day.

Cesare Lombroso had much in common with Alexandre Lacassagne. He, too, was born to a middle-class family and had been a precocious medical student who wrote noteworthy theses at prestigious universities—in his case, the universities of Pavia, Padua, and Genoa. Like Lacassagne, he spent several years in the army, during which time he studied the men around him, measuring thousands of soldiers to chart the physical differences among people from the various regions in Italy. He also conducted a study of the soldiers' tattoos, which he correlated to criminal behavior. Later, while stationed in Pavia, he measured and studied patients in mental asylums; still later, while chair of Legal Medicine and Public Hygiene at the University of Turin, he studied the inmates of the local prison.

Unlike Lacassagne, who was large and expansive, Lombroso was a small, bearded man, modest and unpretentious. "He has a mild, attractive face," wrote a British colleague, Maj. Arthur Griffiths, "round, apple cheeks as chubby as a child's; still, quiet eyes behind his spectacles." But he shared with his French counterpart an intellectual self-confidence. Those eyes would "flash brilliantly as he warms in the fight for his principles."

Several new ideas influencing scientific thought helped shape Lombroso's thinking, as well. In the 1850s, Dr. Paul Broca founded the world's first anthropological society in Paris. Anthropology, a new branch of science, explained and categorized human culture by the use of extensive measurement and quantification. His work set off a mania for measurement of the human body. He also established the principle of cerebral localization—that different parts of the brain have specific functions—as a result of his autopsies of patients with aphasia.* Meanwhile, some people, including Darwin's cousin Sir Francis Galton, felt that the theory of evolution carried a dark corollary: If the human species evolved from a primitive form, then those primitive seeds lay dormant within all *Homo sapiens*, ready to sprout in susceptible individuals. Finally, Dr. Augustin Morel, the French psychiatrist who discovered dementia, proposed his theory of degeneration, which argued that sometimes weak traits, such as simplemindedness, become magnified from one generation to the next, so that in certain families, successive generations become increasingly defective.

This hodgepodge of emerging ideas, plus Lombroso's own observations, prompted him to see the criminal not as an individual who exercised free will, but as the product of biological and evolutionary forces. He was drawn to the possible links between brain structure and criminal behavior. In December 1871, while dissecting the body of the infamous robber Giuseppe Villella, he saw something that would change his thinking forever: a small hollow at the base of the skull, and under it an enlarged section of the spinal cord. Although abnormal in humans, the feature was common, he claimed, in the lower apes, rodents, birds, and in some "inferior races in Bolivia and Peru." He described that moment as the most exciting of his young career: "At the sight of that skull, I seemed to see all of a sudden, lighted up as a vast plain under a flaming sky, the problem of the nature of the criminal—an atavistic being who reproduces in his person the ferocious instincts of primitive humanity and the inferior animals."

He called the deformity the "median occipital fossa" (the word *fossa* means "groove" or "pit"), and he found it in one miscreant after another. To him, it was the "totem, the fetish of criminal anthropology," because it symbolized the inherited, biological nature of the criminal impulse. Because the feature normally appeared in primitive animals, he saw people who possessed it as evolutionary throwbacks, helpless in the grip of "atavistic" behaviors, such as poor impulse control, lack of empathy, bru-

---

* Joseph Franz Gall, who developed phrenology earlier in the century, had suggested the same general principle of localization. He divided the brain into twenty-seven "organs," each with character traits such as friendship, guile, word memory, and kindness. His insistence that the relative importance of each of those organs could be detected by corresponding lumps in the skull consigned his work to the realm of pseudoscience. Yet despite his derisive treatment by historians, his basic idea of localization holds true.

tality, and selfishness. "Theoretical ethics passes over these diseased brains as oil does over marble, without penetrating," he wrote. In time, he detected other primitive "stigmata," including a small skull, a low forehead, a large jaw and face, jug ears, long arms, and thick eyebrows that tend to meet in the center. These features revealed an evolutionary past that surfaced within certain unfortunate individuals.

In 1876, Lombroso published a book describing his research and hypothesis, *L'uomo delinquente* (Criminal Man). Over the years, the book grew from a first edition of 250 pages to a fifth edition of nearly 2,000 pages; published in three volumes, it was richly illustrated with photographs and measurement tables. Lombroso was tireless: He wrote more than thirty books and one thousand articles on the biological roots of criminality. In 1893, he published *The Female Offender,* which described the atavistic impulses that ruled women criminals and prostitutes. (In general, he saw women as a more primitive version of men, with their smaller skull capacity and "childlike" emotions.) Later, he wrote a book that described genius as a type of insanity. Meanwhile, he gathered a coterie of bright young scientists, including Enrico Ferri and Raffaele Garofalo, whose collective work became known as "the Italian School." In 1880, they launched a journal called *Archivio di psichiatria ed antropologia criminale* (Archives of Psychiatry and Criminal Anthropology).

Lombroso never stopped measuring, collecting data, and dissecting, and over the years he expanded what he saw as the causes of criminality. While he originally saw criminals as a single hereditary type, he eventually divided them into several categories. Some were less dangerous than others. One group, which he called "criminaloids," had none of the stigmata of the born criminal, but these individuals became involved in crime later in life and committed less serious crimes. Another group comprised criminals of passion: otherwise upstanding citizens who committed violence on impulse, perhaps against an unfaithful spouse, and immediately repented. Another group, "mattoids," included political criminals, such as anarchists and assassins, who were mentally unbalanced but not atavistic. In this group, he included Charles Guiteau, who assassinated President James Garfield. All in all, after subtracting all the less dangerous categories, Lombroso concluded that about 40 percent of lawbreakers were congenital criminals. He said that all epileptics were born criminals, as well.

Identifying the born criminal, he said, would help address the problem of rising criminality by focusing on the person and not just the crime. Physiognomy could become the prosecutor's tool. Lombroso frequently gave expert testimony, exposing the stigmata of the accused. In one case, a court in southern Italy called him in to help decide which of two brothers had murdered their stepmother. He designated the brothers as "M." and "F." After examining the siblings, Lombroso testified that "M. represented more clearly the criminal type, exhibiting huge jaws, swollen sinuses, extremely pronounced cheekbones, a thin upper lip, large incisors . . . and left-handedness." M. was convicted.

It was important to Lombroso that society could use his theory for prevention. He suggested reeducating children with atavistic tendencies and designing prison sentences to fit the convicted. He disagreed with the prevailing system of setting the punishment strictly according to the severity of the crime. Instead, he felt justice should focus on the *criminal*, giving judges wide latitude in dealing with the accused. Those who did not fit the category of congenital criminals could receive lighter sentences, or be rehabilitated by community service. Insane criminals should be sent to asylums, he argued. Natural-born criminals should receive longer sentences and be monitored after their release. The most hard-core among them would be executed, given life terms, or exiled.

It was understandable that Lombroso's work, playing as it did into the era's mania for measurement and fascination with the dark side of human nature, found widespread international support. Almost overnight, "criminal anthropology" became a respected field of scientific study. Not only did it present a longed-for explanation for crime but it played into a latent desire to see the criminals as "other."* "Beautiful faces, it is well-known, are rarely found among criminals," wrote Henry Havelock Ellis, the noted British physician and social reformer (and later, eugenicist) in his book *The Criminal*, which incorporated many of Lombroso's ideas. "The prejudice against the ugly and also deformed is not without sound foundation." He conceded that while a certain number of anomalies might be found in nor-

---

* Many people saw the mentally ill as "other," as well. Henry Maudsley, the British psychiatrist, referred to the criminally insane as a "distinct class of creatures doomed to evil" who were easily identified by their "scrofulous, often misshapen" heads. (Laurent Mucchielli, "Criminology, Hygienism, and Eugenics in France, 1870–1914," in *Criminals and Their Scientists: The History of Criminology in International Perspective*, ed. Peter Becker and Richard F. Wetzell [Cambridge: Cambridge University Press, 2006], p. 208).

mal persons, the degenerate displays "not the mere presence of such anomalies, but their presence in a more marked form and in greater frequency."

Francis Galton, who coined the term *eugenics* (and introduced fingerprint technology to Britain), thoroughly admired Lombroso's work and created a field guide to the criminal man. He collected photos of dozens of criminals and sorted them into categories, such as "bank sneaks" and "pickpockets," for easy identification. As a further aid to spotting criminals, he invented a machine that made composite photographs. He used the technique to combine all the photos of miscreants he had collected to create a composite portrait of the "master criminal," someone capable of committing a variety of crimes. Blurred and thick-browed, this was the face of depravity itself.

In the United States, experts worried about rising crime rates, and "revolvers" (recidivists) took Lombroso's ideas to heart. America was supposed to be a classless society—how comforting it must have been to use scientific measuring instruments to explain away the Gilded Age's inequities. Later, eugenicists took up the cause, arguing that born criminals should be prohibited from marriage or, in the words of one penologist, suffer "a gentle, painless death" by "carbonic acid gas." Arthur MacDonald, an American criminologist who dedicated his book *Criminology* to Lombroso, spent years petitioning Congress and President Theodore Roosevelt to set up a Lombroso-style laboratory to study the "criminal, pauper and defective classes." He had hoped to identify born criminals and, if necessary, preventively confine them. William T. Harris, commissioner of education, called it "a fiendish method of treating the unfortunate," and MacDonald's proposal was soundly rejected.

Alphonse Bertillon, who had taken more measurements of criminals than anyone, disagreed with Lombroso. "I do not feel convinced that it is the lack of symmetry in the visage, or the size of the orbit, or the shape of the jaw, which makes a man an evil-doer," he told journalist Ida Tarbell. "A certain characteristic may incapacitate him for fulfilling his duties, thus thrusting him down in the struggle for life, and he becomes a criminal because he is down." He explained:

> Lombroso, for example, might say that, since there is a spot on the eye of the majority of criminals, therefore the spot on the eye indicates a tendency to crime; not at all. The spot is a sign of defective vision, and the man who

does not see well is a poorer workman than he who has a strong, keen eye-sight. He falls behind in his trade, loses heart, takes to bad ways, and it turns up in the criminal ranks. It was not the spot on his eye which made him a criminal; it only prevented his having an equal chance with his comrades. The same thing is true of other so-called criminal signs. One needs to exercise great discretion in making anthropological deductions.

In fairness to Lombroso, there were progressive aspects to his philosophy. By focusing on the criminal and not just the crime, he encouraged other scientists to study the roots of criminal psychology and urged authorities to consider prison reform. Still, it is striking to see how thoroughly his ideas penetrated social thinking. When the Hungarian philosopher Max Nordau condemned modern art and culture as retrograde in his book *Degeneration,* he dedicated the work to Lombroso. Lombrosian villains populated literature. The leading characters in *The Strange Case of Dr. Jekyll and Mr. Hyde* (1886) exemplify the contrast between the civilized man and his atavistic counterpart, albeit within the same body. Zola's *La Bête humaine* (*The Human Beast*) borrows much from Lombroso's portrayal of the criminal, although Zola disagreed with the scientist's philosophy. Bram Stoker's 1897 novel, *Dracula,* leans heavily on Lombroso's descriptions. At one point Van Helsing, the fictional Dutch professor who pursues Count Dracula, asks the book's heroine, Mina Harker, to describe the villain.

"The Count is a criminal and of criminal type," she says. "Nordau and Lombroso would so classify him." In a 1975 annotated version of the novel, the scholar Leonard Wolf juxtaposed Harker's description of Dracula with Lombroso's portrait of the criminal man:

HARKER: "His face was . . . aquiline, with a high bridge of the thin nose and peculiarly arched nostrils."
LOMBROSO: "[The criminal's] nose on the contrary . . . is often aquiline like the beak of a bird of prey."
HARKER: "His eyebrows were very massive, almost meeting over the nose."
LOMBROSO: "The eyebrows are bushy and tend to meet across the nose."
HARKER: " . . . his ears were pale and at the tops extremely pointed."
LOMBROSO: " . . . with a protuberance on the upper part of the posterior margin . . . a relic of the pointed ear."

Lombroso was at the peak of his influence in 1885, when he and his adherents hosted the first International Congress of Criminal Anthropology in Rome. They proposed to convene an international forum every four years in a different European city. The first meeting, held at the Palazzo delle Belle Arti from November 17 to 23, "opened a new epoch in the history of crime," according to an observer from the Smithsonian Institution. "It was proposed to investigate crime scientifically, biologically, fundamentally; to investigate its origins, its causes." The main hall, crowded with graphic and disturbing exhibits, was closed to women and children. Hundreds of skulls were spread on display tables, along with body parts from criminals, epileptics, prostitutes, the mentally deficient, and others deemed undesirable. Researchers displayed brains conserved in alcohol, molded in plaster, and, using a new process, preserved in a gelatin to allow for fine slicing and microscopic examination. The prison doctors from Genoa displayed the body parts of the murderous brigand Giona La Gala: a bronze death mask of his face, a plaster cast of his skull, and several artifacts from his autopsy, including his brain, tattoos, and gallstones, all preserved in alcohol-filled jars.

Lombroso brought an impressive exhibit. He displayed seventy skulls of Italian criminals, thirty skulls of epileptics, and the entire skeleton of a thief, showing an undersize head attached to a large, solid body. He brought plaster molds of two criminals' heads, three hundred photos of epileptics, another three hundred photos of German criminals, twenty-four life-size drawings of criminals, and samples of criminal handwriting and those of preserved skin with tattoos. They were all designed to illustrate that the criminal was a physical *type*.

Lacassagne, in contrast, brought no skulls or skeletons. He set up a more modest display of twenty-six maps and charts. They were color-coded to show the level of crime in various parts of France; whether they were committed against persons or property; and their correlation with season, alcohol consumption, and the price of grain. They served to make his point that crime was not a biological phenomenon, but something related to the social milieu. He also brought a collection of about two thousand tattoo designs—some were on preserved skin samples, but the majority had been transferred onto fabric—not to show a biological tendency, but to illustrate the criminals' culture.

Early in his career, Lacassagne had "adopted with enthusiasm" Lombroso's point of view. He visited Lombroso in 1880, listened with fascination to his theory of atavism, and followed his advice on directions for his research. One of those projects was a survey in which he measured the arm spans of eight hundred criminals and found them to be expansive, like an ape's. "We can say from the point of view of criminal anthropology that criminals resemble primitive races in their large arm spans," he reported. "This observation is an additional contribution to the theory of our friend Lombroso."

Yet Lacassagne had always felt a degree of ambivalence about Lombroso's research, and as Lombroso became more entrenched in his beliefs, Lacassagne found himself pulling away. Lombroso's system was too rigid for him, too dismissive of free will and the possibility of self-improvement. Lacassagne saw the brain as a malleable organ, subject to growth if trained the right way. In one study, he compared hundreds of brains of doctors, people with a rudimentary education, illiterates, and prisoners, correlating their education levels to their brain size. Like many measurement-based studies at the time, the basis of the study was scientifically ludicrous and his methods were laughable—there was no demonstration of causality, for example. Moreover, within certain normal parameters, brain volume bears no relation to intelligence, as Lacassagne and his colleagues later came to realize. But the thought behind his study signaled his emerging belief that physiology does not equal fate. Over the years, after conducting countless autopsies, interviewing numerous criminals, and investigating scores of cases, Lacassagne saw the development of the criminal as a multifactored process. Someone might be temperamentally predisposed to criminality, but that tendency would flower only under certain social conditions, usually involving alcoholism or poverty, he believed. In sum, crime was not a product of biology, but of the conditions in which the criminal lived.

The differences between the two colleagues surfaced dramatically during the conference in Rome. At the time, Lombroso was an intellectual hero—so revered that no one in criminology circles would contradict him; Lacassagne had not yet become famous from his work on the Gouffé affair. Early in the conference, Lombroso gave a long talk, in which he described the state of the field. In addition to identifying a born criminal's physiognomy, he claimed to have detected special sensitivities, as well. According to his research, the born criminal possessed a diminished sense of smell, taste, and pain; an acute sense of sight, like that of an animal; and an inability to blush. He had conducted his research with exotic new instrumentation, such as the Zwaardemaker olfactometer for smell, the Sieveking esthesiometer for touch, and the Nothnagel thermesthesiometer for temperature sensitivity. He had tested pain sensitivity by using a Ruhmkorff induction coil to administer shocks to the gums, nipples, eyelids, soles, and genitals of "normal" volunteers. He found that they felt the electrical shocks more acutely than did prisoners and inmates of asylums. The insensitivity of criminals reminded him of tribal peoples, "who in their puberty rituals could be affronted with tortures that a man of the white race never could tolerate." To Lombroso, the born criminal was a savage out of time and place and on the loose in civilized Europe.

Lacassagne listened patiently as one speaker after another discussed the physical differences between criminals and honest folk. At one point, he cautioned against using the "seductive hypotheses" of natural selection to oversimplify the causes of crime. On the third day of the conference, Lacassagne could no longer restrain himself. He announced that having studied criminals for ten years, he could only conclude that Lombroso's hypothesis was "an exaggeration and a false interpretation" of evolution. "What is atavism, after all?" he asked. "An accidental bit of heredity that might be influenced by one's grandfather." The theory lacked proof and was scientifically unsupportable. Beyond that, he found Lombroso's theory fundamentally disheartening. Once a person was branded an atavist, the label, he said, "will become a kind of indelible scar, an original sin . . . against which there will be nothing to do." Furthermore, it would play into the worst instincts of lawmakers. "The savants could take measurements, record angles and indexes, but the legislators will do nothing but cross their arms or begin to construct prisons and asylums in which to gather these misshapen creatures." Using Pasteur's work as a metaphor, as Lombroso had used Darwin's, Lacassagne described the criminal tendency as a germ that would proliferate only if placed in a nourishing medium. In other words: "The social milieu is the bouillon of criminality; the [born] criminal has no importance until the day that it finds the bouillon that allows it to ferment."

The Italians were shocked, having expected only the elaborate collegiality that was the norm at scientific meetings. Lombroso's colleague Giulio Fioretti was "profoundly surprised" by Lacassagne's "severe" and "unjust" critique. "The criminal type is a definite fact, acquired by science," he said; "on this point no further discussion is admissible." Lombroso lamented the "disdain" his French colleague showed for his theories.

His disciple Garofalo argued that if the social milieu was responsible for crime, "in that case we would all become criminals."

Lacassagne said he regretted if his words were taken the wrong way— "I don't mean to have attacked a man for whom I have the greatest respect"—but it was clear to him that while certain biological factors might exist, social factors had to take "preponderance." As for whether he had insulted the Italian school of criminal anthropology, he asserted that "'schools' don't exist—there is only the truth."

If the Rome conference had set up the battle lines, the Paris meeting intensified the conflict. The scientific press characterized the proceedings as a "duel" between Lombroso and Lacassagne's colleague, Léonce Manouvrier. According to Manouvrier, Lombroso's criminal type was nothing more than a "harlequin" upon which to heap the faults of society. He attacked Lombroso's selective use of statistics and compared his work to Gall's discredited phrenology. French anthropologist Paul Topinard doubted whether the median occipital fossa, Lombroso's key to criminal identity, had any anatomical significance at all. During the field trip to the Sainte-Anne asylum, chief physician Magnan challenged Lombroso to find the signs of atavism in young delinquents. Lacassagne said that if criminals seemed to have a misshapen appearance, it was because "the evils of misery and deprivation" made them so. Lombroso and his followers defended themselves poorly, perhaps because their statistics had been selective and difficult to support. In the end, both sides agreed to form an international commission to study one hundred criminals and one hundred honest men and report their findings at the next congress.

The commission never completed the task. They found it impossible to carry out a study that correlated body measurements to criminality while ruling out variables such as ethnicity, psychological background, and nutrition. Lombroso took that failure as an affront. He and the Italian delegation boycotted the 1892 meeting in Brussels, calling it "barren of any foundations in facts." They came back strongly in 1896 in Geneva. "They say I am dead and buried," Lombroso proclaimed. "Do I look like it?" A French observer who watched the presentations of Lombroso and his disciple Enrico Ferri compared the two men to Don Quixote and Sancho Panza, tilting against the preponderance of social theory. The 1906 conference in Turin saw another strong showing for Lombroso, mainly because it marked the fiftieth anniversary of his scientific career. Yet by then, the energy had drained from the meetings. Each school had embraced its philosophy on crime, and each country a method for how it would deal with its criminals. The conferences limped along until World War I, when European intellectual life dissolved into chaos.

The conferences were not the only battleground of ideas. Anytime a major case came along, the arguments would reignite in the press. During the Gouffé affair, in December 1890, a correspondent for the newspaper *Le Gaulois* sent Lombroso a dossier, including photos and the handwriting of the accused. The case had received spectacular coverage. Gabrielle Bompard had cast herself as the victim of a melodrama, the pawn of her strong-willed companion, Michel Eyraud. During their interviews, police were astonished at her combination of sangfroid, self-pity, and inappropriately coquettish behavior. Not for one minute did they believe her claims of victimhood. Yet something about her captivated the public. When police took her by train to Lyon so she could show them where she had disposed of the body, mobs of well-wishers cheered her at the station. "Look at all the people!" she was heard to declare. "There wouldn't be this many for the queen of England!"

Lombroso examined the information he had received from *Le Gaulois* and reported that even though Michel Eyraud had committed the murder, the woman was the real born killer of the two. Eyraud had the physiognomy of a con man at worst. True, he possessed several "degenerative" characteristics—large ears, an asymmetrical face, and thick, sensuous lips (especially the lower one)—but none of these characteristics was especially exaggerated. "He lacks the ensemble of features that constitute, for me, the criminal type," wrote Lombroso. "Without Bompard, I am absolutely persuaded that Michel Eyraud would be nothing more than a simple crook." Bompard was another story entirely. Her thick, curly hair, large lower jaw, facial asymmetry, and generally "Mongolian" face shape truly marked her as a female born criminal. Her well-known sensuality and indifference to the suffering of others marked her as the type "very easily associated" with murder, wrote Lombroso. Her willingness to betray her accomplice and play the victim was a behavioral trait of the born criminal, he added, for it displayed a ratlike survival instinct. Lombroso did not recommend reversing the sentences—Eyraud's of death and Bompard's of twenty years. He simply wanted to make it clear that contrary to the public's sympathy for Bompard, she was "organically" more of a criminal than Eyraud.

Lacassagne published Lombroso's analysis without comment in the

Journal of Criminal Anthropology. Perhaps he felt no need to refute a pseudoscience already in decline.

In 1896, seven years after the brouhaha over the skull of Charlotte Corday, a Parisian doctor named Augustin Cabanès made a curious discovery. He had wondered about the provenance of the skull. How had it gotten from the graveyard of the Madeleine in Paris, where it was buried in 1793, to Prince Roland's collection nearly a century later? He followed the trail backward from the prince, who said that a friend named George Duruy had given him the skull after learning of his interest in anthropology. Duruy told Cabanès that he had received it from a relative, Madame Rousselin de Saint-Albin. She had inherited the skull from her husband, who had bought it from a curio dealer. Cabanès found the shop owner, who said he had purchased the skull from the estate of Baron Dominique Denon, the noted savant, collector, and friend of Napoléon. Cabanès obtained the catalog of Denon's estate, in which he found no mention of the skull. The catalog listed many fascinating relics, including bone fragments from El Cid, Héloïse and Abelard, and Molière; a clipping from the mustache of King Henri IV of France; a fragment from the Shroud of Turin; and half of a tooth from the mouth of Voltaire. But there was nothing recorded about Corday. Cabanès knew that during the Reign of Terror a lively commerce existed in selling the body parts of executed notables and that the family of Corday's executioner, Charles-Henri Sanson, had suddenly became wealthy. But there was no actual evidence that Sanson or anyone else had looted the body. In conclusion, wrote Cabanès, the skull that had caused such a furor at the conference had no proven connection to Corday. It could easily have been "an ordinary specimen from a collection or from an anatomical museum."

Contacted by a reporter, the prince readily conceded that he could not prove the artifact's identity. "An absolute proof cannot possibly exist, and so we must content ourselves with the tradition," he said. He recalled that in 1889 he had given the skull to five anthropologists, asking them if it was the skull of a criminal. "Three of them answered affirmatively and the other two said no: Which are we to believe?"

Thirteen

Lourdes

The Basilica of Lourdes was but twenty years old when Vacher found his way into the town in the winter of 1896, but already it was one of the busiest pilgrimage sites in all Christendom. Decades earlier, a sickly fourteen-year-old peasant girl named Bernadette Soubirous had seen visions of the Blessed Mother Mary in a grotto near the Gave River. The vision instructed her to tell the village priests to make this grotto the site of a holy chapel. One day, staggering in a holy trance, Bernadette fell to her knees in the grotto and started digging. The waters that bubbled forth became an infinite source of holiness and healing. The clergy built the church, and it became a gathering place for the tens of thousands of pilgrims who came to pray and to be healed by the waters. The migrating hordes gave rise to endless rows of hotels, shops, and eateries that catered to their more earthly requirements. By the time Vacher hiked into Lourdes, the village had become so commercial and crowded that a visitor might have had trouble perceiving the holiness.

A contemporary traveler from England, Monsignor Robert Hugh Benson, wrote that the crass commercialism of Lourdes initially disappointed him, with its "incalculable crowd and oppressive heat, dust, noise, weariness." The church above the grotto was a "disappointment" as well—a neo-Gothic monstrosity, all size and spires and little that spoke of grace or the soul. And yet Benson, like many people who had stayed in Lourdes for a few days, started feeling something in the air—"some great benign influence . . . soothing and satisfying"—that overcame his early disillusionment. "I cannot describe this further; I can only say that it never really left me during those days, I saw sites that would have saddened me elsewhere—apparent injustices, certain disappointments, dashed hopes that would almost have broken my heart; and yet that great Power was over all, to reconcile, to quiet and to reassure."

Vacher may have felt something similar. Like Benson, he made reference in a letter to a certain hypocrisy among the lavish displays of religion. Yet he also made it clear that he was thrilled to arrive at the place where the spirit of Mary dwelled—"the great doctor of our bodies as well as our souls. . . . What graces I asked her for this great occasion, for me, my poor parents, and my friends!"

He spent several days in the town. If he followed the pattern of the other pilgrims, he would have lined up to light a candle at the grotto, which was festooned with hundreds of crutches discarded by those who had been healed by the waters. He may have joined the masses in Rosary Square, "crowd against crowd like herds of bewildered sheep," as Benson had reported. Vacher may have volunteered to be one of the *brancardiers*—stretcher-bearers with shoulder straps and crosses who helped carry the maimed and crippled—or helped push one of the many wagonettes that deposited the sick within a hundred yards of the grotto. The suppliants lay there, "faces white and drawn with pain, or horribly scarred, waiting for some man to put them into the water." He may have joined one of the nightly processions with their torches held high: "a serpent of fire . . . each mouth singing praises to Mary."

Unlike other pilgrims, Vacher did not pray for healing. He did not ask Mother Mary to restore his disfigured face or to stop the throbbing from the bullet in his ear. He did not ask her to calm his burning soul. He did not pray for the young victims of his cruelty or for those who grieved for them. He did not pray for those falsely accused, whose lives were forever shattered, or for the villagers, their sense of safety and communal life destroyed. Vacher, in fact, came in gratitude and celebration. He came to give thanks for the blessings he enjoyed, for the protection that had been uniquely his.

It had been a long and circuitous pilgrimage that had brought him here, a walk of at least fourteen hundred miles that looped back and forth across France from the northwest to southeast. In September he had killed again—this time in Allier, a region northwest of Lyon. Marie Moussier, a just-married nineteen-year-old, was the victim. The medical examiner had never seen such savagery: Moussier's nose was disfigured by bite marks.

Through it all, Vacher continued to feel watched over, protected. A few weeks after the Moussier killing, he was wandering in a dense fog in the

Haute-Loire, about ninety miles south, when he came upon a thirteen-year-old shepherd boy, Alphonse Rodier. He was just about to throw himself at the boy when something alerted him to some witnesses nearby. He retreated. A couple of days later, still in a dense fog, he came upon the boy's fourteen-year-old sister, Rosine. This time, there were no witnesses.

After the killing, the fog became so dense that Vacher could not see more than a few yards. He despaired of being able to escape, but then, once again, came help from above. "All of a sudden, I found the route that I recognized, then I took a path that led to the railroad track that I was following before the crime," he recalled. In a few hours, he was out of the district. "On that day I really believe that God saved me."

Vacher never stopped obsessing about Louise Barant, and he wrote to her, vowing eternal love. Louise wanted nothing to do with him. Traumatized by his attack, she remained in her village, where everyone would know the assailant on sight. The wounds to her tongue and lips had given her a speech impediment, which caused her unending embarrassment. Her inability to work burdened her aging father and her family financially, but they stood by her. In order to protect his daughter, her father intercepted Vacher's letters and destroyed most of them. One, he preserved and later gave to investigators:

Dear Louise,

I don't know if you are still in your parents' village, and I don't have any news from your dear parents. But my old friends Mr. and Mrs. Genin sometimes hear from them, so I dare to send you a letter through their hands. . . .

As a consequence of our unfortunate drama, I still have some paralysis in my right cheek. But it's only apparent when I talk and pronounce certain syllables. Other than that there's no sign of it on my face.

In case you don't accept this [offer of] reconciliation, out of respect for all the blood that was spilled, so bravely and abundantly for you, I ask you not to say anything bad about me. If you do, it will only reflect badly on you. If we want to reexamine our past, atone, and have a new good life, it's important that nobody other than the two of us and your own parents know about [what happened]. . . .

We should realize that if God wanted to test us during our youth, it's only to our advantage, and for that we should take courage. . . .

Now permit me: Louise, O! Louise to ask you a single thing: Have I lost
you forever, for all eternity? Please answer me, even by a very short letter.
Only then will I be able to resign myself to forget you. . . .

                                                            Vacher Jh

Rising behind Lourdes, the majestic Pyrenees were mantled in snow.
Vacher had tired of the crowds and the chaos and felt the pull of the mountains once more. He decided to find his own place to worship, higher than
the steeples, holier than the grotto. He waited a few days for mild weather
to set in and then hiked to the top of one of the mountains. There, on the
peak, in a patch of fresh snow, he wrote the following prayer on behalf of
Louise: "Oh! Virgin Mary, mother in the sky, watch over her as you watch
over me. And with all your power before God, bring her back to me one
day as white as this snow." There he felt the presence of "this good mother
[who] held out her hand to me . . . even as I float[ed] on the dangerous
winds of chance."

Having made his obeisance, Vacher headed south across the mountain
range. He hoped to enter Spain, "a country of good oranges and nice people." But Spanish vagabonds who were leaving the country warned him
that every available man was being conscripted for the war in Cuba. His
French citizenship wouldn't protect him.

In the weeks following his visit to Lourdes, Vacher's behavior seemed
to change—on the surface at least. Witnesses noticed that he now carried
two clubs, the one with the initials and another with "Marie Lourdes"
carved into the wood. Observers reported occasional glimmers of humanity, an affectionate side. In February 1897, he spent about a week in a
remote cluster of villages in the south of France, where several people
remembered him benignly. Villagers reported having seen him amusing
groups of children by playing the accordion. Louise Farenc, the wife of a
farmer in the hamlet of Couloubrac, recalled that on a cold, rainy day a
man arrived at her house completely soaked and asked if he could dry off.
The couple invited him to dinner and to stay. "There was a wound on his
left cheek," she recalled. "One of his eyes was smaller than the other and
his mouth was twisted. We gave him a place in front of the fire that night,
and we invited him to eat soup with us." After dinner, he told them his
name ("'Vacher' or 'Acher,'" she recalled). He said he was twenty-seven
years old, had been a Marist monk, and then had joined a regiment. He

showed them his sergeant's chevrons, which he lovingly kept folded up in paper. He explained that his cheek wound had come from being kicked by a horse.

Over the next couple of days, he became part of the family, reading to the two children and hugging them. "He loved to caress the children and, most of all, my son Henri [fourteen], whom he frequently called to come sit by him," said Louise Farenc. "He told us he knew how to play the accordion, but he didn't have the instrument at the moment."

Her husband agreed that Vacher had been a polite and proper guest. Their older son, Élie, seventeen, confided that when he and Vacher were alone, the visitor boasted about his enormous strength. "He showed me his hands and his well-developed muscles. Then he told me, 'I'm as strong as two men and I've never found anyone who could resist me.'"

Several days later, Vacher returned to recover a blanket he'd forgotten. He'd had a beard during his first stay with the family, but by now he had shaved. "The children cried to him, 'You are so cute!'" recalled their mother. "We never saw him again."

Soon after that, Vacher knocked on the door of Monsieur and Madame Paul Valette. In return for a meal and a bed for the night, he gave their daughter a penmanship lesson. His handwriting was beautiful—large, gracefully formed letters, indicating a sensitive, artistic soul. On the crosshatched graph paper from the little girl's notebook, he wrote and rewrote one sentence: "Among travelers there are often great minds and sometimes even great friends of God." (*"Dans les voyageurs il y a souvent de grands esprits et quelquefois même de grands amis de Dieu."*) Across the top of the page he wrote four equations to illustrate the basic operations of mathematics: addition, subtraction, multiplication, and division. Each involved four or five digits at a time. Clearly, the visitor had a good education.

Yet for all the gentleness of those encounters, the predator lurked. Vacher walked to the market town of Lacaune, where he met up with a vagabond named Célestin Gautrais. The two had spent some time traveling together after Vacher's visit to Lourdes, and they went to a tavern to have a drink. Gautrais told Vacher that he had two hundred francs in a lockbox at the post office, and the two went to get it. The next morning, Gautrais was found dead, his skull bashed in with a club and his pants down around his ankles. The money was gone. As the villagers gathered to gawk at the cadaver, Vacher brazenly squeezed through the crowd—just as he had done after the killing of Augustine Mortureux—and offered to help carry the body to the mayor's office.

Authorities speculated that Vacher had taken Gautrais's money and used it to buy a ticket on a train heading in the direction of Lyon. Witnesses from the train recalled seeing a vagabond with a facial scar who gave off a terrible smell.

Part Two

Punishment

If we now ask, "How should an Investigating Officer set about his work?" we can come to but one conclusion: "His whole heart must be set upon success."

—Hans Gross, *Criminal Investigation*, 1906

Fourteen

The Investigating Magistrate

On April 17, 1897, the town of Belley in the foothills of the Alps hired a new investigating magistrate named Émile Fourquet. Belley, home to about four thousand people, was a market town and the capital of the region of Bugey, in the *département* of Ain. It was a scenic but undistinguished location, a jumping-off place for an ambitious young magistrate who was trying to launch his career. Fourquet, thirty-five, had earned a law degree and had served in several minor judicial roles. He was a tall and lean man, with a bald head, a flowing mustache, and spectacles. A cleft chin suggested a stubborn strength; his eyes, magnified by the spectacles, conveyed a mixture of youthful curiosity and professorial detachment. On receiving the appointment, he "burst with joy," he wrote in his memoir. "Examining magistrate! Manhunts! It was a dream of a lifetime; an opportunity to fulfill a burning passion."

Two months later, Fourquet was having morning coffee with some colleagues when prosecutor Jean Reverdet walked in with the day's newspaper. "Look at what an extraordinary crime was committed the day before yesterday near Lyon," he said.

In an article entitled "Murder of a Shepherd," *Le Lyon Républicain* reported that a thirteen-year-old shepherd had been "shamefully murdered, then defiled" in the hills several miles west of Lyon. Pierre Laurent had been returning to his village from the fruit market on the night of June 18 when a killer attacked him. The murder was described as one of "unimaginable cruelty."

> He first slit the boy's throat with a knife, then he threw himself upon him . . . [and] sawed open the throat. . . . The miserable cur had no fear in satisfying his bestial passion, defiling the body and then mutilating it. . . .

The little victim fell under the blows of an odious brute, who unfortunately has disappeared without leaving a trace of his passage. . . .

Fourquet and the others knew that the killing had taken place in another jurisdiction, so it would not be theirs to investigate. But the details reminded Reverdet of a similar case that had traumatized their own region about two years before—the murder of Victor Portalier. "Your predecessor never discovered the killer," he said to Fourquet. "They think it was a vagabond." He told Fourquet to ask his clerk for the dossier.

For the next several days, Fourquet buried himself in the Portalier file. He was struck by the similarities between this case and the current one. Both times, someone had stalked a shepherd boy with stealth and ruthlessness. Death was accomplished by a deep cut to the throat, followed by a hideous defilement and mutilation. Both times, neighbors had seen a menacing-looking vagabond who disappeared immediately after the killing. Fourquet noted that the authorities had failed to make the slightest headway in capturing, or even identifying, the murderer.

"Needless to say, this horrible situation has raised concern throughout the region," Le Lyon Républicain soon reported.

Every night, all seven brigades in the area make their rounds from farm to farm, interrogating the inhabitants, asking if they've seen anyone new. . . .
At this point, though, none of the research has amounted to anything: not the capture of a single vagabond. . . . In sum, despite all the activity, the inquest is not any further today than it was on the day of the crime.

Fourquet kept digging through the file on the Portalier case, carefully examining every deposition. He discovered a two-year-old letter from Louis-Albert Fonfrède, the investigating magistrate from Dijon who had tried to solve the Mortureux affair. Having noticed similarities between the killing in his area and the one of Portalier, Fonfrède had written to other magistrates in southeastern France, asking if they had seen similar cases. Fourquet knew that Fonfrède did not think that a single killer could have committed all the crimes. But Fourquet did not subscribe to the "contagion" hypothesis. The mention of common elements, however, was a "flash of light," indicating that several cases might be related. He wrote to Fonfrède, and within forty-eight hours he received a dossier with the details of seven murders in various parts of France. Adding the Bénonces case would bring the total to eight.

Alphonse Benoist, the investigating magistrate of Lyon (who had jurisdiction over the Laurent case), thought he saw common elements, as well, and he discussed them with a reporter from *Le Lyon Républicain*. On June 25, the newspaper listed several crimes involving "young shepherds, who after their death were defiled and mutilated." No one had actually witnessed the murders, but in many cases people had seen a menacing vagabond with dark hair, heavy eyebrows, and a scar on his cheek shortly before the attacks. The newspaper referred to him as "a new Jack the Ripper."

Because the Laurent killing had taken place in the jurisdiction of Lyon, Benoist could draw upon a resource that his counterparts in rural areas could not—Lacassagne's Institute of Legal Medicine. The day after the murder, Dr. Jean Boyer, a former student and now a collaborator of Lacassagne, arrived to examine the crime scene and the body. His training and precision were evident in his report. No wound or stain went unnoticed, undescribed, unmeasured, or untested. After noting the location, size, and shape of brown stains on the trousers, Boyer cut them out and subjected them to the Van Deen test. Within seconds, they turned sapphire blue, a positive indication for blood. Brownish stains on the victim's pocketknife tested negative. To determine their origins, Boyer treated them with a mixture of hydrochloric acid and ferrocyanide. The resulting blue—a different shade, produced by a different set of reactions—indicated the presence of iron: rust. He also found whitish stains on the seat of the pants, but microscopic examination did not reveal sperm.

Detail by detail, he proceeded, noting each blot on the blood-soaked clothing and each piece of flesh that had been spotted on the ground. The fact that the body's limbs were stiff with rigor mortis told him that the killing had taken place within the previous seventy-two hours. The mortal wound was a series of deep, hacking stabs to the left-center side of the throat. The angle of the wound and the presence of notches along its borders told Boyer that the assailant had stood behind the victim and thrust the knife into the throat with two or three deep, tearing stabs.

Unlike most medical examiners, Boyer adhered to his mentor's instructions to examine the anus if the crime scene suggested a sexually related attack—a disagreeable procedure that involved cleaning the tissue, examining it very closely, and then palpating it with the fingers to determine the muscle tone (this in an era before doctors wore gloves). Boyer performed the steps conscientiously and found small tears in the anal mucosa. Those tears would not have occurred after death, when the anus would have gone slack. The evidence led Boyer to reconstruct a scenario in which a single attacker crept up on the child, grabbed him around the throat, and then stabbed him, threw him or let him collapse to the ground, performed unspeakable sexual mutilations, and sodomized the dying body.

None of these details ran in the newspapers. Either the doctors did not release the information or it was felt that public taste could not abide it. No matter—even the vague set of facts that appeared in the press were more than enough to panic the citizenry. According to *Le Lyon Républicain*, the killing had "literally terrorized the countryside."

> The inhabitants do not dare to go out by themselves at night; shepherds find it difficult to lead their flocks away from habitation. A mother of a good family was so frightened that she removed her daughter from service as a domestic with a farming family in Courzieu. A butcher crossing the woods in a carriage was so frightened by seeing a stranger that he whipped his horse in a panic to flee. These little incidents show the state of mind of inhabitants of the region. They don't feel safe anymore. . . .

If traditional French police work had shortcomings, it also had strengths, especially in terms of amassing information. The best practitioners were connoisseurs of paperwork. Vidocq became famous for his swashbuckling exploits, but he was also a great collector of files. The floors at his headquarters in the dreary Sûreté in Paris groaned under the weight of more than three million papers pertaining to tens of thousands of criminals. Bertillon, who developed the anthropomorphic technique and quantified each criminal as a unique set of measurements, collected tens of thousands of file cards. Once arrested, a criminal's "anthropomorphic card" would follow him permanently. The central impulse of late-nineteenth-century "scientific policing" was to characterize the criminal as a series of measurements and traits and to identify his crimes by what Lacassagne referred to as a "manual of operation." For that, one needed records.

Fourquet started generating paperwork. Working alone "in the silence and solitude of the night," he created two charts for entering information. One chart was devoted to the method of the crime, and Fourquet used it to sort all the data he could find from the autopsies and police reports. He listed the eight crimes down the left side of the page. Across the top he created categories, such as the position in which the body was found, the probable murder weapon, the status of the head, neck, chest, and abdomen, and whether the victim showed signs of rape or other significant "mutilations." Within those categories he filled in the specifics of each crime.

He devoted the other chart, also a grid, to the identity of the criminal. He listed the crimes down the left side of the page and the physical characteristics of the criminal across the top, such as age, height, hair color, and scars or any other "particular signs."

Having filled both tables with rows and columns of information, Fourquet underlined in blue all the common elements. Under this spiderweb of blue lines, certain patterns emerged. For example, almost all the bodies showed huge gashes across the throat: "The placement of the wounds was essentially the same." Several bodies showed a "vast wound" from the sternum to the pubis and an "evisceration" of the abdomen.

It became clear to Fourquet that this pattern of crimes represented a single methodology. The murderer would kill his victims by slashing the throat with a very sharp knife or razor. He would kill victims in one place and drag them to another, often behind a hedge. Then he would mutilate the corpses.

There was a similar confluence of facts about the suspect. Witnesses described a vagabond of about thirty years old with black hair and eyebrows, a black beard, and dark eyes. Several described a grimacing mouth, a big sack on his shoulder, and a menacing air.

Fourquet next moved to create a more precise profile. From the dossier about the Portalier case, he chose a dozen witnesses who had given fairly clear descriptions, summoned them to his office, and led them back through their testimony. He grilled them about particulars: age, height, physical description. He asked in what manner the suspect had presented himself, how they would describe his language and attitude, and if there were any particularities about his face, such as wounds.

The work was painstaking and took weeks. Finally, on July 10, he sent out a warrant called a "rogatory letter" to 250 magistrates throughout

France. Under the heading VERY IMPORTANT he put his colleagues on alert for a vagabond about thirty years old, of medium height, with black hair and beard, black eyes, and a bony face. They should be aware of "particular signs," including "a twisted upper lip that contorts into a grimace whenever he speaks. . . . He expresses himself with some difficulty because of the deformity of his mouth. . . . His right eye is bloodshot and the lower lid of that eye is slightly scarred. . . . He carries a big hobo's sack and a large club. . . .

"This may be the man the newspapers are calling 'Jack the Ripper of the Southeast,'" Fourquet concluded. "Telegraph me in case he is discovered."

By the time Fourquet had sent out the arrest warrant, Vacher had made his way to the Ardèche, a rugged area about eighty miles south of where he had killed the Laurent boy. In July, a cobbler sold a small black-and-white dog to Vacher for four francs. Vacher named her Loulette. He also acquired a tamed magpie, which he kept tethered on a string. The next day, several people saw him begging in front of a tavern, with his animals and an accordion.

"It occurred to me to test if he really could play," a teacher named Vital Vallonre recalled. "I said, 'Play "the Marseillaise," ' but he didn't really know how."

A few days later, Vacher slept in the attic of a farming couple and their four daughters. He repaid their kindness by playing the accordion and making funny faces for the girls and other neighborhood children.

An elderly widow whom he met shortly thereafter, Madame Ranc, asked what he did for a living. "I'm looking for a position as a shepherd," he said. "You're out of luck, monsieur," she replied, "because there are no flocks around here."

She recalled: "He lowered his head and gave me a slightly vicious look and then took up his accordion and again began to play. 'Where do you come from?' I asked. 'From a mental asylum,' he replied. He seemed menacing."

On August 2, Vacher approached the farm of a man named Régis Bac and begged for some stew. He ate some and offered the rest to his dog. When the dog turned away, he said, "If you don't want to eat it, I'll kill you," and smashed in her head with his club. Then he did the same to the magpie. Bac said he was "horrified" by this brutality, and he gave Vacher a shovel so he could bury his animals. Vacher did so and left. His blood-lust was rising.

Fourquet had so little confidence that other magistrates would pay attention to his bulletin that he was pleasantly surprised when he began to get responses, even fruitless ones. Over the next several weeks, three suspects who had been arrested for vagabondage were brought to his office. The first two bore some of the physical features identified in the arrest warrant, but the key witnesses from Bénonces could not identify them. The third, whom police delivered to Fourquet's office in August, initially fit the profile so completely that Fourquet experienced "an instant of false joy." The man was the right height and had the right coloring. He had the menacing air and the hobo's sack. When police opened the sack, they found two exquisitely sharpened straight razors and a huge knife with rust-colored stains. But when Fourquet examined the knife closely, he saw that it had been made in Spain. That, plus the syle of the suspect's beret, prompted Fourquet to ask the man if he came from Basque country. The suspect confirmed that. He had come to France a few months ago, but had been living in Spain at the time of the Portalier murder.

"Is that where you got that knife?" asked Fourquet.

"Precisely."

"Are those traces of blood on the blade?"

"Yes. In fact, it's human blood."

"So, have you killed someone?"

"Yes, but it doesn't concern you. It was someone I had a quarrel with on the other side of the Pyrenees. He threw his knife at me. . . . I avoided it, picked it up, and used it to kill him, and then I saved it as a souvenir."

Fourquet let him go.

In late August, Fourquet received a letter from the magistrate in Tournon, a town on the Rhône River, about fifty miles south of Lyon. A man was being held in the local jail on a charge of "outrage to public decency"—attempted rape. He seemed to fit the profile Fourquet had circulated. Fourquet asked his colleague to send a photo. The colleague replied that the town's only photographer found the prisoner so menacing that he could not bring himself to aim a camera at his face.

The village of Champis, deep in the Ardèche, was not easy to reach. Starting from Tournon, one would have to walk or ride a horse several hours westward into desolate countryside. One would climb ridge after ridge, past looming granite cliffs and leprous old castles. Eventually, one would enter a "wild and tragic" area, oppressive in its "silence and abandonment."

"I swear that I don't know any passage that is more discouraging or punishing," wrote journalist Albert Sarraut of *La Dépêche de Toulouse* when he visited the region in the fall of 1897. Unnerved by the trek, Sarraut described the region as a "chaotic mass of hilltops and mournful peaks with somber and black ravines, enormous masses of granite." The woodlands were dense enough to form "a veritable thicket." So tangled and dark were the forests and undergrowth that Nature herself must have conspired to create a place where malefactors could dwell, "absolutely certain of impunity."

The village itself was a cluster of primitive dwellings that looked as though they had tumbled down a ravine and settled near the bottom. A short distance away, in a little stone house, lived Séraphin Plantier, his wife, Marie-Eugénie Héraud, and their three young children. It was the simplest of homes, with a kitchen, a common room, and a single bedroom.

On the morning of August 4, the family walked into the forest to collect pinecones for fuel. Séraphin and his seven-year-old son Fernand took one path; Marie and the two younger children, six and three, took another. They were separated by about fifty yards. She had put the two children down to play and was stooped over, absorbed in her work.

Suddenly, she heard a crackling of leaves and felt something heavy land on her back. "At first I thought it was an animal," she said, "but when I turned my head, I could see it was a man dressed in velour." An iron hand grabbed the nape of her neck; another locked around her throat with such force that it immediately cut off her breath. She felt herself violently thrown onto her back. She tried to defend herself, kicking, gouging, and yanking her attacker's mustache. "I could *not* let him do what he wanted with me," she said later. Unable to subdue her quickly, the attacker let go for a moment and reached for something in his bag. In that split second, she took a quick breath and started shrieking. One of her children started screaming, as well.

In a moment, her husband arrived. He was not a big man—even by the standards of the day, he was scrawny—but he fought like a lion. He started hurling rocks at Vacher and then launched himself bodily onto him. Vacher smashed Plantier in the eye with a cane and stabbed him in the knee with scissors, but Plantier kept coming. Chaos reigned, with Plantier hammering with his fists, Marie screaming and beating the stranger with a stick, and little Fernand throwing rocks, most of which were bouncing off his father. Several times Vacher nearly broke free, but each time Plantier tackled and pummeled him. During the battle, Vacher yelled that it was not he who had attacked Marie, but a comrade who had taken flight.

In a few minutes, several neighbors arrived, subdued the attacker, and dragged him to a nearby roadhouse. Plantier set off across the rugged countryside for the nearest gendarmerie, about six miles away.

The owner of the roadhouse threw Vacher into the massive stone stable that adjoined the café. In an effort to unnerve his captor and the customers, Vacher continued to utter the most vile references about Marie, and he insisted on his right to sexual gratification, adding, "although I would have preferred a thirteen-year-old girl." Sometimes he pleaded for sympathy: "I'm a poor, miserable, handicapped man. I love women, but they find me repulsive, so I attack those I can. Even in a whorehouse the women won't have anything to do with me. I'm so pitiful." Then anger: "That bitch! If she hadn't screamed so much, it all would be over and I would be in another *département* by now."

None of that endeared him to the five men who were guarding him. Twice he tried to escape; each time, the owner, Dupré Charlon, "tapped" him hard enough to thwart the attempt. Later, when Vacher asked for water, Charlon filled his glass from a bucket.

"Pig! You're giving me water from a bucket that your goats drink from."

"If it's good enough for a goat, it's good enough for you," said Charlon.

The next time he refilled Vacher's glass, he let some water slop onto Vacher's foot. Vacher threw the glass at Charlon's face, but he dodged it and hurled the bucket at Vacher's head. Vacher kicked at Charlon's stomach. Charlon parried and gave him a "tap" that sent him sprawling.

After six hours, Plantier returned with two policemen. Vacher eyed them and said with an air of self-satisfaction, "It's not you I respect, but your weapons." When he saw that the gendarmes meant business, he jokingly commanded, "Okay, let's *march*!" As they led him away, he called out in a military cadence, "One-two, one-two!"

They took him to Tournon, where a court sentenced him to three months and one day for "outrage to public decency." They would have charged him with a more serious crime if the rape had been successful, but the attempted assault qualified only as a misdemeanor.

Vacher expected an uneventful confinement. No one had ever connected his crimes before; he knew the incompetence of the rural police. He fully expected that after three months he would be free again and that he would leave the region and again give thanks to Mother Mary for watching over him. The magistrate in this town, however, read his paperwork. He remembered Fourquet's bulletin and sent back a reply with a description of his prisoner. In the course of further correspondence, he explained that Vacher still had a few months remaining in his prison term. He asked Fourquet whether he wished to wait until the sentence ran out or if he wanted to interview the suspect now. Fourquet wrote back: Transport the prisoner to Belley at once.

Fifteen

The Interview

It was a wild train ride from Tournon to Belley via Lyon. Two guards hustled Vacher into a second-class car that had been cleared of all passengers, locked the doors, and handcuffed him. During the two-hour journey from Tournon to Lyon, he jabbered about how he admired the police and how his sentence in Tournon had been overly harsh. Then, just as the train was passing over a bridge, Vacher bolted for an open window. He had almost cleared it when one of the guards latched onto his shins. For seconds, Vacher dangled over the void, the guard inside acting as a counterweight, until some passengers in a neighboring car came to help. Later, while waiting in the station in Lyon for the connecting train to Belley, he screamed anarchist slogans and cursed the vileness of the French bourgeoisie.

Now in Belley, he faced his inquisitor. For a long while, Fourquet peered at the suspect, comparing the features he saw with those on Vacher's Bertillon card. Affecting a tone of friendly interest, he looked through Vacher's bag and asked where he had acquired each of his possessions.

Hans Gross, the great Viennese criminologist, had written about the art of interrogation in *Criminal Investigation*. Gross dismissed the conventional practice of using pressure, or even torture, to force confessions. Instead, he favored employing the newly developing science of psychology—understanding and exploiting the suspect's temperament and *luring* him into revealing information. To do that required a new kind of interrogator—not the shrieking intimidator, but one who displayed a certain "absence of passion," wrote Gross. "The officer who becomes excited or loses his temper delivers himself into the hands of the accused."

In relating the characteristics of a skilled interviewer, Gross could well have been describing Fourquet. The ideal person would be one "who knows men, who is gifted with a good memory and presence of mind, who takes pleasure in his work and zealously abandons himself to it." Such a man "will not allow himself to be carried away" by anger. No matter how monstrous the crime, he must maintain his sangfroid; if necessary by "constantly repeating to himself these words, 'It is my duty.'"

Gross saw the interview as a complex discussion, or series of discussions, with a beginning, a middle, and an end. Before the session, he said, the interviewer should prepare by researching the suspect and the crimes in order to have the information readily at hand. The investigator should begin the discussion not with the crime, but with events early in the suspect's chronology. Gradually, he should lead the suspect to the crime, "in the hope that he will begin to speak about it himself." During the discussions, the interviewer should not seem threatening, but maintain a neutral, almost beneficial stance. The suspect should not get the impression of being forced to confess, but given the opportunity to *unburden* himself. The interviews should be long and repetitive. That way, the magistrate could use multiple versions of the same events to tease out the truth. "We take notes and establish certain periods," wrote Gross, "then we make him go over the story again a little later, and then note the impossibilities, the contradictions, the gaps." Thus, he concluded, one arrives at the truth— not with brutality, but with preparation, intelligence, and patience.

It is not clear whether Fourquet had read Gross's work, but he seemed to have closely followed his procedures. With a calm, easygoing manner, Fourquet began his line of questioning at a point in time well in advance of the murders. He asked Vacher how he'd spent his time since leaving the regiment.

Vacher spoke freely. He told Fourquet about his days in the army and about the "great heartbreak of love" that had caused him to shoot his fiancée and himself. He talked about the asylums at Dole and Saint-Robert and about the years he'd spent as a vagabond. He spoke about how difficult it was to get hired because "people ridiculed the deformity of my mouth . . . and because of the bad odor that came from the pus from my ear." He talked about his travels to the hinterlands of France.

"You also traversed the departments of Rhône, Loire, l'Ain, and Savoie," Fourquet interjected.

Oh, yes, replied Vacher.

And then the investigator made a mistake. Jumping ahead too quickly in the chronology, he pointedly asked Vacher about Bénonces. "You are inculpated to have been there . . . and to have killed Victor Portalier, who was living in that locality."

Vacher saw the trap and avoided it. He denied ever having traveled to Bénonces, and he dared Fourquet to produce a witness who had seen him in the area. When Fourquet brought in someone to testify the next day, the man was too shaken to be of any use.

Fourquet knew he had risked his entire case. There were no witnesses to the murders and no definitive forensic evidence. The fact that Vacher had passed through the areas where the killings had occurred would not be enough. "It was all a presumption," Fourquet admitted, "and a presumption by itself would not suffice." The only way to bring the criminal to justice was to trick him into making a valid confession. He had to get Vacher talking again.

For three weeks, they did nothing more than "squabble," as Fourquet wrote in his memoirs. Fourquet would ask questions; Vacher would evade them. Increasingly desperate, Fourquet dealt what he called his "last card": He told Vacher that he planned to release him.

"I now see that you're not the man I am looking for," he said. "They made a mistake at Tournon. You're the fourth person who's been sent to me and the fourth I will have to let go." He told Vacher he would release him in a few days, after some final interviews.

In the meantime, he asked Vacher for some assistance. For the past several months, Fourquet said, he had been gathering information for a book about vagabonds, and he would interview each vagabond who came his way. Would Vacher be interested in telling his story?

Vacher replied with a cynical smile. To prove his sincerity, Fourquet showed him the stacks of information he had been gathering. He explained a theory he was developing about vagabond migration—how they would head south for the winter and then work their way north, following a succession of harvests: grapes, chestnuts, olives, and sugar beets. "In other words, you follow the same laws that guide the migratory birds. Isn't that right?"

"Yes, it's true."

"So you see, I'm not trying to trick you."

Little by little, Fourquet won Vacher's confidence. Over the next several days, he asked him to share his observations of the countryside. It was then that Vacher explained how the people in Brittany and Savoie tended to be hospitable and how the people around Tours were standoffish with strangers. Stealthily, Fourquet began to lead him in certain directions.

"You don't really have it so bad, you vagabonds," he said. "You get to

stay for free in the Riviera when we up here are freezing in the snow. A
magistrate like me doesn't get such a nice offer. You were in Nice, weren't
you?"

"Yes. I also went to Menton to see one of my sisters who lived in that
city in 1894, once in April and another time in November."

Fourquet remembered that the murder of Louise Marcel had taken place
in that area in November 1894. He asked about other cities and locations.
Vacher mentioned that among other places, he had visited Lourdes.

"Lourdes? By foot? Impossible!"

Vacher proudly responded that not only had he made his way to
Lourdes but that he had covered much of the rest of France by foot, as
well. The judge led Vacher to a map on the wall. With Vacher's guidance,
he traced his finger over several of the departments and villages that
Vacher had visited. As his finger passed over various locales, signals went
off in Fourquet's head about the murders. Casually, so as not to alarm
Vacher, he let his finger pass over an area southwest of Lyon where a murder had taken place in the month of September. Vacher had mentioned
having taken a couple of dangerous falls in that area. By way of disguising the intent of his inquiry, Fourquet said, "There must have been snow
there when you slipped over those cliffs."

No, Vacher said, there could not have been snow because he had passed
through that area in September. *Yes,* thought Fourquet. In November, the
suspect said, he had traveled to the Var and then to Varenne. *Yes again!*
Fourquet knew of crimes at those times and locations: the murder of
Louise Marcel in the Var in November 1894; that of Marie Moussier in
September 1896, and that of Rosine Rodier a few weeks later. And so they
continued their collegial discussion, Vacher holding forth on the adven-
tures of a vagabond and Fourquet making mental notes for his list. Later,
he would construct a series of maps connecting the dots of Vacher's ragged
itinerary and the murders. "Things were lining up in a very interesting
way," he noted.

On October 7, Fourquet brought in a dozen people from Bénonces and
paraded them before the suspect, one after the other. Ten of the twelve
positively identified him as a vagabond they had seen the day of Portalier's
murder. Two had been too frightened to testify, but they later insisted that
he was indeed the man. At one point, Vacher shouted at a woman in an
effort to intimidate her.

"You dare say, madame, that you saw me in your area? You are a liar. I've never set foot there—not in 1895 or at any other time, understand?"

The woman stood firm. "It is you who are the liar, monsieur. You came to my house around eight o'clock on the morning of the crime and I gave you some soup. I can tell you the very thing that stuck in my mind: When I was serving you the soup, I said, 'I'm not very rich.' And you replied, 'It's not the rich people who give the most.'"

Vacher backed off, snarling threats.

Now came time to spring the trap. Armed with the testimony and the knowledge he had gathered about Vacher's itinerary, Fourquet ordered the guards to bring the prisoner to his office. He began a speech that he hoped would break the suspect's resistance.

"When you were first transferred here, I had an instant when I thought that you would not be here for a long stay," he began. "I imagined, in effect, that the witnesses would not recognize you. But today all that has changed. You are formally recognized by everyone without a doubt . . . it is henceforth proven without any possible argument that you are the author of the murder of a young shepherd from Bénonces."

Furthermore, said Fourquet, he knew that Vacher had killed many people in several regions throughout France. "I will prove to you that I know everything you have done. . . . You were already known to the authorities. It was only a matter of apprehending you. "

Then, in a rapid-fire delivery, Fourquet disgorged everything he knew, or thought he knew, about Vacher's bloody wanderings. In a portentous voice free of all doubt, Fourquet told how, on November 20, 1894, Vacher had killed thirteen-year-old Louise Marcel and mutilated her corpse in an isolated barn; how, on May 12, 1895, he had killed seventeen-year-old Augustine Mortureux on the side of the main road from Dijon to Paris; how, on August 24, 1895, he had killed an old woman, the widow Morand, in her house in the Savoie; and how, eight days later in Bénonces, he had killed sixteen-year-old Victor Portalier as the shepherd was guarding his cows in a meadow. He recounted to Vacher how he had gone to the Ardèche, where, on September 29, 1895, he had killed a fourteen-year-old shepherd named Pierre Massot-Pellet; how the following year he had killed nineteen-year-old Marie Moussier while she was guarding her flock; how he had killed a fourteen-year-old shepherdess named Rosine Rodier; and, most recently, how, on a road near Lyon between 11:00 p.m. and midnight on June 18, 1897, he had killed a thirteen-year-old boy named Pierre Laurent, who was walking home with two cows.

All this was said almost as a single sentence—a torrent of accusations and crimes that Vacher never imagined anyone had connected.

"I should add that you raped or defiled all these victims," said Fourquet. "Numerous witnesses have seen you and recognized you, and I will bring them here to identify you in person.

"Guards, take him back to his cell."

The effect of this recitation was "so rude, so unexpected, so disconcerting," recalled Fourquet, that the suspect did not have the strength to object. "He left our office pale and staggering like a drunk."

Around seven that evening, Fourquet was sitting down to dinner when one of the guards knocked at his door. He had a letter from Vacher—a signed confession. Barely coherent, it began with a slogan, written in block letters, that Vacher would make a trademark of his writings:

GOD—RIGHTS—OBLIGATIONS
[DIEU—DROITS—DEVOIRS]

Belley, 7 October 1897

TO FRANCE

So much the worse for you if you think I am responsible. Your way of acting by itself makes me pity you. If I kept the secret of my misfortune it's because I believed it to be in the general interest, but since apparently I am mistaken I have come to tell you the whole truth. Yes, it was I who committed all the crimes you blame me for . . . and all of this in a moment of rage. As I said to the doctor from the prison medical service, I was bitten by a rabid dog around the age of seven or eight, but I'm not so sure, although I remember taking a remedy. Only my parents can assure you of the bitings. As for myself I always believed . . . that it was the medicine that corrupted my blood.

In his rambling letter, Vacher recalled how he had told his brother in Geneva that he frequently experienced urges to kill. Even before that, as a fourteen-year-old working in the fields, he sometimes felt the need to commit murder. He would suppress the impulse by hiking to the point of exhaustion. It was lucky, he said, that he never encountered anyone during those fevered walks. At some point in his life, the compulsion became too strong to resist.

He had now decided to confess, he explained, because "I feared that the <u>malicious world</u> would lay the blame on my poor parents who have had to suffer so much . . . since I have been roaming around France like a rabid [animal] guiding myself only by the sun."

And finally, a benediction:

Let those who think they are crying over me cry over themselves.
    It would be better for them to be in my place.
    Help yourself, and God, who makes everything possible and whose reasons no human can understand, will help you.

Signed, Vacher J.

Fourquet knew the confession was only a beginning. The document was a collection of unfocused, self-justifying statements that lacked crucial details; indeed, for legal purposes, it contained only a single worthwhile sentence: "Yes, it was I who committed all the crimes you blame me for." Fourquet knew that in order to refer this case to the prosecutor, he had to build the confession into something more specific and coherent.

The next day, he tried to reason with Vacher. The confession had been very helpful, he said, but now it was time to address some specifics. He asked Vacher to walk him through the murders, one at a time, this time with all the relevant details.

"It is useless for me to give you any more explanations about the crimes, because you know as much as I do," said Vacher, who now seemed broken and disheartened.

Fourquet explained that he knew the basics but that now he really needed the details. "It's a rule of our profession," he said, trying to sound collegial. "Investigating magistrates are obligated to have the accused tell all the details of the crimes they confess to."

"It's useless, I tell you," said Vacher. "And it's too ugly. Don't ask me to return to those ugly times. I'm not saying anything more."

Once again, the situation was becoming delicate. Fourquet worried that when the story of Vacher's confession became public, the killer would see its impact and recant his statement. Conversely, Vacher might stick to the confession, which, under public scrutiny, would seem nothing more than the ravings of a madman. Fourquet's colleague, the procurer general, whose job it would be to prosecute the case, warned him to proceed carefully, as the whole case could easily collapse. Or, he wondered, were they in the hands of a faker?

Vacher, meanwhile, wrote to his family, expressing confidence that soon he would be back at Saint-Robert, that "humane and loyal asylum."

For several days, the two men were locked in a stalemate. And then, surprisingly, Vacher offered an opening. He was an avid newspaper reader—while a patient at the Saint-Robert asylum, he had read several each day. Now that word about his case was beginning to leak, he decided that he wanted to influence the coverage. If the public could see his side of the story, he felt, they would understand he was not a monster, but a damaged—even sympathetic—human being. Vacher offered to discuss the killings in detail if Fourquet could guarantee that the newspapers would publish his confession.

Fourquet could glimpse the criminal's reasoning. If convicted of a single homicide, Vacher would undoubtedly face the guillotine. But if he confessed to multiple crimes, people would say that a madman must have done it. "There's not one person in a thousand who would contend that a man who committed eight murders—of which seven were children, and horribly mutilated their bodies—was not ten times insane," he told Vacher. "And so [your] conclusion is simple: Since insane people are not responsible for their acts and the law does not punish them, they cannot condemn me. Admit that I figured out your reasoning, haven't I?"

Vacher agreed.

But there was a problem, said Fourquet, speaking now almost as a coconspirator. Although the evidence in the Portalier case was overwhelming, that regarding the other murders was weak. Vacher would have to supply many more details if he hoped to attempt an insanity defense.

On October 16, *Le Petit Journal*, with its huge circulation, published Vacher's confession in its entirety. Immediately after that, Vacher began talking—now giving all the details. He did not merely admit to the killings; he *insisted* on the veracity of his confessions, as if daring Fourquet to try to disprove them.

He began with a murder near Dijon, "a girl of fifteen or sixteen years more or less. Didn't she have a dog?" he said to the investigator. "And didn't a lot of people pass along the route that morning? And didn't I take her shoes and her earrings? . . . What does that tell you?"

Fourquet recognized the murder as that of Augustine Mortureux. "For that crime, I can say that everything you told me is exact. And for the others?"

"The old woman in Saint-Ours was eating soup when I killed her."

"That's true; pass to another one."

"In the Var, she was the prettiest victim of all, what a shame! I took the girl on the path, and I killed her in a little barn a few meters away. Just after that I met a man who was picking olives and I spoke to him, he can tell you."

Fourquet recognized the case of Louise Marcel. "That's exact. And in Allier and Haute-Loire?"

"In Allier, near Vichy, it was a young woman, about twenty years old; she was guarding her sheep in a field. I took her wedding ring, but I threw it away so as not to be taken for a thief. Regarding the affair in Haute-Loire, it was a girl, about fifteen years old or so. I cut her throat with a knife and then mutilated her. She also was guarding a flock in a field. That morning there was such a thick fog, I thought I would get lost in the woods if God had not been protecting me."

Two more cases had fallen into place: that of Marie Moussier, who had been wed shortly before her murder, and that of Rosine Rodier, whose brother Vacher had terrified during an encounter.

"And in Saint-Étienne-de-Boulogne, in the Ardèche?" asked Fourquet, referring to the murder of Pierre Massot-Pellet.

"If I'm not mistaken it was also a little shepherd; he could have been twelve or fourteen years old, guarding his flock like the others; it was in the mountains; I killed him next to a hut and I mutilated him."

"And now we arrive at the last one, near Lyon, in Courzieu," said Fourquet. He was referring to Pierre Laurent, whose murder had first drawn Fourquet to the case.

"That one . . . he was passing up the road with a pair of cows; it could not have been any later than midnight and I took him on the other side of the hedge. So . . . do you think I've been lying?"

"No, Vacher, this time, I believe you."

Later, Fourquet tried to implicate Vacher in a crime that had taken place in 1890. Vacher denied it. The first time he ever killed, he insisted, was in May 1894, a month after his release from Saint-Robert. Vacher recalled that he was walking near the village of Beaurepaire when he came upon a girl of about nineteen or twenty years old. Overtaken by a sudden rage, he beat her in the head, strangled and stomped her, and then took a razor to her throat and chest.

Fourquet had never heard of this murder. He sent a telegram to the authorities in Vienne, the administrative capital of the region that included Beaurepaire, asking if they had anything on file. Within hours, he received a telegram confirming that Eugénie Delhomme, a young woman who had worked in the silk mill, had been murdered in exactly the manner Vacher had described. A few days later, they went through the same process in uncovering the murder of Aline Alaise.

The case exploded in the national press. Under headlines such as THE SHEPHERD KILLER, VACHER THE RIPPER, and THE RIPPER OF THE SOUTHEAST, the story of the worst serial killer in centuries became a sensation, temporarily eclipsing the Dreyfus affair. Reporters flooded the small town of Belley, overwhelming the local telegraph office. People thronged around the courthouse, jostling to get a peek at the suspect and shouting abuse whenever they caught a glimpse of him. He would yell back, "Long live anarchy!" and "I am innocent before God!" The situation became so volatile that Fourquet had a secret underground passage reopened so guards could bring Vacher to his office without setting off riots. Later, Fourquet took to interviewing Vacher in his cell, unarmed and unguarded in order to maintain the prisoner's confidence.

Reporters had a field day describing the protagonists, digging deep into their supply of sensational adjectives. "He is as repugnant physically as he is morally, this being whose face convulsively contorts and grimaces, this cripple whose defects repulse even the ugliest prostitutes," wrote a reporter for *La Dépêche de Toulouse*. "His eyes shine with a savage flame," wrote a reporter for *Le Petit Parisien*. Other correspondents described him as the "bloody wanderer," "the ripper," or simply "the monster." The illustrated weeklies ran full-page lithographs portraying Vacher in the act of slaying young women, their eyes wide in terror, their mouths in mid-scream. In one paper, multiple panels showed Vacher committing a progression of murders, under the headline THE CRIMES OF A MONOMANIAC. Fourquet, in contrast, was the "man of the hour," a coolheaded, sharp-witted hero, a magistrate with a common touch who could psychologically disarm even the slyest of criminals.

Both men tried to manipulate the coverage. Fourquet granted interviews, leaked the results of some interrogations, and occasionally let reporters sit in on others. Vacher, when Fourquet allowed him to talk to reporters, tried to make his case for insanity, telling the story of the rabid dog and explaining how he was an "anarchist of God."

"My victims never really suffered," said Vacher, trying to minimize the cruelty of his acts. "With one hand I would seize their throats and with the other I would kill them [with a razor]." He claimed that the collective agony of all his victims could not have exceeded a total of ten minutes.

At one point, Vacher posed for a sketch artist from the Lyon newspaper *Le Progrès*. "Not bad," he said, looking at the picture. "But don't make the eyebrows so close together. It makes me look menacing."

Another time, Fourquet allowed photographers access to Vacher. The prisoner refused to cooperate unless they agreed to certain conditions: He had to be photographed wearing his white rabbit-fur hat—a symbol of purity—and holding a ring full of keys, which he said symbolized the keys to heaven. He had borrowed them from a prison guard.

Newspapers sent reporters into the hinterland to trace Vacher's wanderings. Some of the most vivid reporting was done by Albert Sarraut in *La Dépêche de Toulouse*. The reporter followed Vacher's "bloody odyssey," trekking to villages, interviewing family members of the victims, and portraying the widening circles of grief and chaos. Sarraut told stories of the falsely accused, such as Bannier and Grenier, the agony of their families, and the wooden-headed refusal of victims' relatives to accept the true version of events. He told of numerous small encounters with Vacher—the accordion playing, the handwriting lesson. He looked for early signs of Vacher's proclivities, interviewing Dr. Dufour of the Saint-Robert asylum, former members of Vacher's regiment, and Abbot Chevrolat, who was responsible for the Marist monastery. The abbot, not wanting to discuss any details, blandly explained that Vacher had been dismissed from the monastery because he was not "suitable" for the vocation. Overall, he added, young Vacher's conduct had been good: He was calm, and always accomplished his tasks.

"And now what do you think of him?" Sarraut asked. The abbot gave a dismissive wave of his hand.

"It doesn't much matter if he is found to be a degenerate or not. It is necessary to rid society of whatever threatens it. There is no choice but to cut off his head."

In the midst of this coverage, Sarraut received a poignant letter from two members of Vacher's family. They thanked him for not branding the entire family with Joseph's crimes as many others had done.

"You are the only one who really understands our misfortune and misery," wrote Marius and Léonie Vacher. "Whenever I see the news vendors on the way to school tears begin to well up in my eyes and I have to turn around and take another path. We are innocent of all that, but we have already begun to pay. Our lives will be sad for a very long time."

The investigation was unprecedented in the history of police work. Never had so many people over such a broad area given testimony about so many related crimes. It was propelled not only by the number of murders and the geographic area over which they had taken place but also by two modernizing developments—the telegraph system and the mass-market newspapers. The breaking news stories of Sarraut and other reporters (made possible by the telegraph network) reached millions of readers. Many readers would see a photo of the suspect, remember something, and then come forward with recollections; these, in turn, would spark others. At the same time, Fourquet sent out dozens of telegrams and interrogatories to regions where Vacher had been sighted. Huge numbers of those with information emerged who might never have heard of the case in earlier days, when rumor and word of mouth spread the news.

Normally, under French law, Vacher would have traveled for questioning to each of those departments where he was suspected of a crime. But the number of cases made that logistically impossible, so the dossiers piled up on Fourquet's desk. He spent weeks sorting through the information, working daily from 7:00 a.m until midnight, separating "true" from "maybe true" and "false" while filling in blanks of the suspect's history and crime spree. In July, when he had sent out his letter to 250 magistrates, only seven had bothered to respond. Now, in the fall of 1897, he received eighty-eight dossiers of unsolved murders from across the country that authorities thought bore the signature of Vacher.

Amid the growing public furor, Fourquet continued interviewing Vacher in his cell. Vacher recited his crimes with a brutal simplicity, as though killing someone was no more traumatic than picking fruit:

One night along the road I met a young girl of about eighteen to twenty. I attacked her like I did with all the other victims and cut her throat. . . . Several days after that I killed a young shepherd in the same manner. . . . I soiled [raped] this victim after the murder.

He described the killing of Victor Portalier with a similar eerie detachment, adding the gruesome detail, "after I killed him I . . . bit off his testicles."

That last detail, which Vacher insisted on again and again, could not have been true. Dr. Ravier Gaston, who performed the autopsy, testified to Fourquet that the wound at the site of the removal was "very neat." It bore the sign of a sharp cutting instrument, wielded with skill. Fourquet felt that the suspect had invented that detail to bolster the argument that he was insane. "It's the sickness that wants it," Vacher had told him when explaining the sudden urges. "Maybe children exert a sort of attraction for me."

Indeed, ever since his initial confession, Vacher had embarked on a campaign to prove that he was not legally responsible. In his interviews with Fourquet and the press, he asserted that a kind of "rage" sometimes came over him that he found himself powerless to resist. He elaborated on the claim when a reporter for *Le Lyon Républicain* interviewed him about his motivations:

Why did I kill? I don't know; it just came over me. I had fits; I don't know why. It's the poison that wanted to get out.

And the mutilations—how do you explain them?

I don't know what happened after the murders. But when I left, I was relieved; I felt better. Moreover, if God did not command me to kill, it wouldn't have happened.

Do you have any remorse for your victims?

No, because God wanted it.

Your fits are less frequent now that you're here. You haven't tried to kill anyone.

Yes, but look—the last person that I took I let go without harming her. It could be that the sickness has passed over me.

By late October, Vacher had confessed to ten murders. Fourquet felt he was still holding something back. When a newspaper in Lyon expressed skepticism about Vacher's confessions and accused Fourquet of being gullible, the investigator decided to use it to his advantage.

"I'm furious with these journalists," he said as he showed the article to Vacher. "What an accursed race. They always have to dirty someone."

Vacher read the article. "Those bastards," he muttered. "Listen—I've got a surprise for them. We'll see who's the liar." And he told Fourquet about a murder he had committed that no one could possibly know about.

The previous May, he had been staying in an abandoned house in a suburb just west of Lyon, and a boy dressed like a vagabond had come by. He killed the boy and threw his body down an unused well. The well was enclosed in an abandoned courtyard, said Vacher. No one would ever come upon the victim. He gave vague directions to the scene.

News of the latest confession galvanized people in greater Lyon. Police and amateur searchers alike fanned out across the countryside, peering into every abandoned well they could think of. Several newspapers sent out search teams, hoping for the scoop of the year.

People searched fruitlessly for two days. And then, on Sunday morning, October 24, the brigadier of the gendarme unit in Tassin-la-Demi-Lune, a nondescript village five miles west of Lyon, sent an officer to a location he vaguely remembered, one that bore a resemblance to the place Vacher had described. As the officer approached, he could see details click into place: a derelict house across from an old factory, set at an angle to the road; a courtyard; a well by a cherry tree and an elderberry hedge. He peered into the well and was almost knocked flat by the stench. He and a few other men borrowed a grappling hook from a neighbor and dropped it down. When they hauled it up, it was weighted with human remains.

"When will this horrible nightmare end?" wrote Albert Sarraut.

The next day, Alphonse Benoist, the investigating magistrate of Lyon, arrived at the well, along with Dr. Boyer, of the Institute of Legal Medicine, and several firemen and police. With a crowd of spectators jostling for a view, a couple of firemen pumped out the water and poured phenol down the well in order to disinfect it. They lowered a candle and determined if there was enough oxygen. A fireman climbed down a knotted rope to the bottom, then started collecting remains and putting them in a wooden box that had been lowered down next to him. When the odor became too much to bear, the first man came up and a second went down. They worked until nightfall and again the next day. A tibia came up, then a hip bone, then some vertebrae. Again and again, the empty box descended and returned with its cargo. A pile of bloody clothing was found in the house.

LEFT: Joseph Vacher's childhood home in Beaufort, a little hill town southeast of Lyon. Neighbors reported that even as a boy he showed violent tendencies.

Le Journal illustré

TRENTE-QUATRIÈME ANNÉE — N° 4-5

DIMANCHE 31 OCTOBRE 1897

PRIX DU NUMÉRO : 15 CENTIMES

Assassinat de Louise Marcel (13 ans).

VACHER, LE TUEUR DE BERGERS

RIGHT: A tabloid portrayal of the murder of thirteen-year-old Louise Marcel, Vacher's second confirmed victim. The dramatic illustration of crime was a favorite topic in the "penny press."

BELOW: Vacher and Louise Barant, whom he became obsessed with and tried to murder. Although the photo seems to depict Louise with dark hair, articles and court testimony describe it as blond.

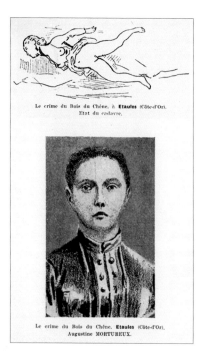

Le crime du Bois du Chêne, à **Etaules** (Côte-d'Or).
État du cadavre.

Le crime du Bois du Chêne, **Etaules** (Côte-d'Or).
Augustine MORTUREUX.

'ABOVE: Dr. Alexandre Lacassagne, circa 1901, on the occasion of his induction into the Legion of Honor

LEFT: Augustine Mortureux, Vacher's third documented murder victim, and the crime-scene diagram. Vacher confessed to eleven killings, but was thought to have committed more than twenty-five.

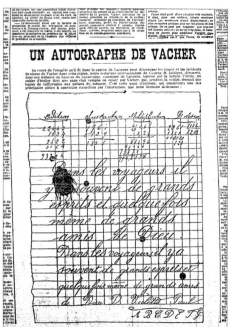

UN AUTOGRAPHE DE VACHER

Au cours de l'enquête qu'il fit dans le canton de Lacaune pour déterminer les étapes et les incidents du séjour de Vacher dans cette région, notre rédacteur-correspondant de Castres, M. Jalabert, découvrit, dans une métairie du hameau de Lacarrignac, commune de Lacaune, habitée par la famille Vitcelle, un cahier d'écolier dont une page (fait remplie en entier par Vacher, qui, pendant la veillée, donnait des leçons de calligraphie aux enfants du métayer. C'est cette page d'écriture, qui constituera une des principales pièces à conviction recueillies par l'instruction, que nous donnons ci-dessous :

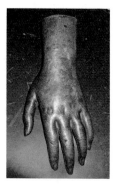

ABOVE: Lacassagne, an ardent book and art collector, also collected artifacts from crime scenes. This paperweight is a bronze casting of a female criminal's hand. A duplicate served as a door knocker at his summer home.

LEFT: Vacher sometimes took shelter with unsuspecting families. This page depicts a lesson he gave a little girl, showing his fine penmanship and mathematical skills.

A rural policeman at the Portalier crime scene, August 1895.
More than fifty meters separate the initial attack (#3)
and the final stabbing (#1).

A tabloid depiction of the Gouffé affair,
the murder investigation that made Lacassagne
internationally famous

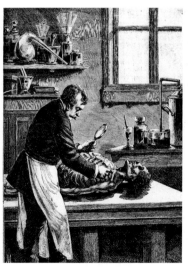

Lacassagne's autopsy of Gouffé,
who was murdered in Paris and whose
body was dumped south of Lyon.
Lacassagne's identification of the
decomposed body helped solve the case.

Lacassagne's criminal museum for the study of crime-scene and wound-pattern evidence, one of several such museums in the criminological capitals of Europe

The floating morgue of Lyon, a dank, leaky, unsanitary facility, where Lacassagne worked for nearly thirty years. Storms would sometimes wash bodies overboard.

Alphonse Bertillon developed a system of identification based on the measurements of certain body parts. It predated fingerprinting and presaged the modern use of biometrics.

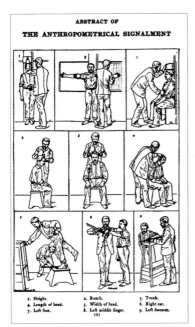

Bertillon's system, translated in an American police text. The combination of eleven critical measurements narrowed the odds of a misidentification to less than one in four million.

An ear-identification chart produced by Bertillon. He felt that ear shapes were as individual as fingerprints would later turn out to be.

ABOVE: Cesare Lombroso developed the "born criminal" theory, which stated that the tendency to commit crimes is genetic and is revealed in certain telltale body traits.

RIGHT: A diagram from a book of Lombroso's showing criminal features, which he referred to as "stigmata"

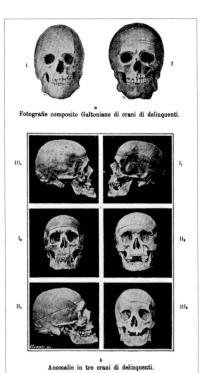

Fotografie composite Galtoniane di crani di delinquenti.

a

Anomalie in tre crani di delinquenti.

b

ABOVE: Austrian criminologist Hans Gross introduced and advocated many modern techniques, including interviews based on persuasion rather than torture.

LEFT: The skulls of "born criminals," which portray their allegedly primitive characteristics

Investigative magistrate Émile Fourquet first saw a pattern in Vacher's killing spree and played a key role in bringing him to justice.

LE « CHEMINEAU » JOSEPH VACHER

Tabloid coverage of Vacher's killing spree:
CRIMES OF A MONOMANIAC

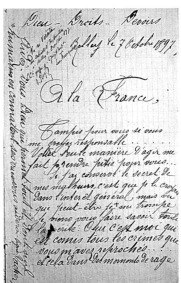

Vacher's confession: "To France: So much the worse for you if you think I am responsible," meaning responsible for his actions. The confession begins with his trademark epigram: *DIEU—DROITS—DEVOIRS* ("GOD—RIGHTS—OBLIGATIONS").

Vacher's portrait at Belley prison. He insisted on posing with a white rabbit-fur hat (a symbol of purity) and keys (to unlock the gates of heaven). He borrowed the keys from a prison guard.

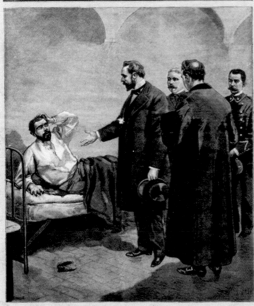

Le Petit Journal

Le Petit Journal
Le Supplément Illustré

SUPPLÉMENT ILLUSTRÉ
Huit pages : CINQ centimes

ABONNEMENTS

DIMANCHE 15 JANVIER 1899

Numéro 426

LE RÉVEIL DE VACHER

THE WAKING OF VACHER
Tabloid depiction of
officials preparing Vacher
for the guillotine

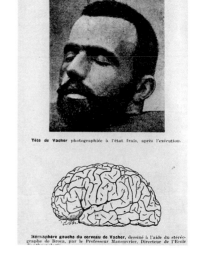

Tête de Vacher photographiée à l'état frais, après l'exécution.

Hémisphère gauche du cerveau de Vacher, dessiné à l'aide du stéréographe de Broca, par le Professeur Manouvrier, Directeur de l'École

Vacher's severed head and the postmortem diagram of his brain. After his execution, Vacher's brain, divided up and dissected by several anatomists, became the focus of a heated debate over whether it showed signs of insanity.

As people pushed for a view of the crime scene, a Madame Larraboire came forward to say she thought the clothing belonged to François Bully, who had once done some gardening for her. Bully, a seventeen-year-old, had left home to become a vagabond because his relationship with his parents was so tempestuous. He had been wandering for about a year, but he had disappeared sometime in late May.

At the institute, Dr. Boyer was separating, sorting, and identifying the body parts to determine when the murder had taken place and the victim's identity. Based on the state of decomposition, he estimated the crime had occurred a minimum of four months before the body was found.

Identifying the victim would be a more complicated task, given the fragmentary nature of the remains. Following the procedures in Lacassagne's *Handbook*, Boyer examined the growth plates a few inches from the ends of the long bones. They had not fully ossified, nor had the pieces of the hip bone, which would have tended to solidify at about age seventeen. He further noted that the two branches of the jawbone came together at an angle typical of a young adolescent. All this indicated, according to Boyer, that the victim was no older than fourteen. Dental evidence indicated that the victim was at least twelve.

To calculate the victim's height, Boyer compared key bones with the tables compiled by Rollet. He concluded that the victim had been between 1.38 and 1.42 meters tall—between four feet five and four feet seven.

In short, the victim had been killed at least four months ago, just as Vacher had confessed. He was between twelve and fourteen years old, and no taller than four feet seven. According to Boyer's anthropometrics, the victim could not have been François Bully, who was seventeen years old and at least five six.

Meanwhile, magistrate Benoist had received a letter from Belgium that, in an unexpected way, confirmed Boyer's findings:

Very surprised to hear of my murder by Wacher [*sic*]. I am eager to let you know, however, that I am quite well, but without a penny.

François Bully

Several days passed, and still no one had any idea who the victim might be. And then, at the end of October, a woman came forward to say that her fourteen-year-old son, who had been working on a farm near Tassin-la-Demi-Lune, had been missing since May. She went to the magistrate's office in Lyon, where she recognized the clothing as her son's—specifically a rip in the collar that the boy's grandmother had patched. Later, at the institute, Boyer showed her the jawbone and asked her if she recognized any dental patterns. Sobbing, she made the identification: Certain teeth were missing, and two were crossed in a particular way. Vacher's eleventh victim was a fourteen-year-old boy named Claudius Beaupied.

Newspapers now reported that Vacher displayed a new attitude. Formerly talkative and engaging, he had become taciturn and contemptuous. He ceased responding to Fourquet, declaring that he would say nothing more unless the newspapers published a new batch of his letters, which would make his case for insanity. Fourquet would not allow it. In at least fifteen more interviews over the next several weeks, he tried unsuccessfully to shake Vacher's resolve.

He knew that his part in the case was now over. It was time for the legal investigation to become a medical and psychological one. He contacted Dr. Alexandre Lacassagne.

Sixteen

Professor Lacassagne

By the time Fourquet contacted Lacassagne, the professor had reached a plateau of fame and credibility that he would occupy for the next thirty years. His books had become forensic classics; his journal was considered the authoritative source on all things related to criminal science, and his students had fanned out over Europe.

Lacassagne constantly searched for a deeper understanding of how the individual criminal developed. In the late 1890s, he embarked on a several-year experiment in which he asked notorious prisoners to write autobiographies. He provided them with notebooks and pens, gave them advice on developing their ideas, and visited every week to check on their progress. In exchange, he would give them tobacco and sweets and lend a sympathetic ear. For many of the prisoners, Lacassagne was the only person who had shown the slightest curiosity about them or their lives, and they came to see him as a friend and confessor. "Oh, dear benefactor, how much meaning you are giving to my life!" wrote one murderer.

The prisoners' musings revealed much. An anarchist named Émile Gautier, an intellectual with a law degree who spent three years in jail, wrote a forty-two-page memoir, which appeared in the *Archives of Criminal Anthropology*. He described prison as a "hothouse for poisonous plants," where anyone who was not a lifetime offender learned to become one. Gautier was well acquainted with Lombroso's hypothesis. Based on what he saw in fellow prisoners, he offered his own dissenting view of "born criminals" and their traits:

> Their cringing and timid ways, the cunning of their looks, something feline about them, something cowardly, humble, suppliant, and crushed, makes them a class apart. One would say, dogs who had been whipped; hardly, here and there, a few energetic and brutal heads of the rebels.

THE KILLER OF LITTLE SHEPHERDS

Is this a congenital type, the indication of a race, a sign of inner degeneration? Isn't this really an *acquired* characteristic?

Isn't it true that by frequent repetition the traits that are mimicked become *persistent*, even *physiological*?

Over the years, Lacassagne collected sixty-two autobiographical notebooks from more than fifty inmates of the Saint-Paul prison. The narratives showed him, one case at a time, how criminality developed. They revealed dark stories of domestic violence, disease, sporadic education, and the death of loved ones. Some of the most voluminous and revealing writing came from the hand of Émile Nouguier, the gang leader who, with Annet Gaumet, had murdered Madame Foucherand, the café owner on the rue de la Villette. During the year he spent in prison awaiting trial and execution, Nouguier filled six notebooks, which he titled "Memoirs of a Sparrow, or the Confessions of a Prisoner." The writings described a life that seemed destined to end with murder and the guillotine. Raised by an abusive criminal of a father, Émile ran away from home as a child, only to find upon his return that his father was committing incest with the boy's sister. He left home permanently at the age of twelve, working variously as a farmhand, circus worker, pimp, and thief. He flirted with anarchism, spent at least two terms in prison, reconciled briefly with his father on his release, and then became the leader of a gang in Lyon. It was at that point that he and his gang broke into Foucherand's apartment and killed her. The only tender episode in the entire life story seemed to have been the moment of his birth, which he likened to the hatching of a sparrow. Gratified by Lacassagne's attention, he tried to aid him in his research, and compiled a dictionary of criminal slang.

Henri Vidal, who stabbed four women to death on the French Riviera, wrote a 227-page manuscript for Lacassagne, striking in its self-analysis and reflection. "The thing that astonishes me most in my situation," he began, disarmingly, "is that . . . I have always had a repugnance for blood." The chapters reflected his stages of emotional development: "The Origins of the Hatred of Women," "My Regrets," "Falling Off the Bicycle," and "My Mother's Temperament." Vidal used his memoir to dispute the experts' findings that he was legally responsible and fit to stand trial. "Listening to your discourse, I simply realize that you, gentlemen, haven't understood my case as it really is: no, you do not understand because you read me too quickly," he wrote. "You do not pay attention to many details you think are important but which are precisely the ones that make my case very different from those you have come across so far."

Charles Double, a homosexual who led a notoriously dissolute life, killed his widowed mother in an argument over money and showed no remorse or reaction to the sentencing. The public reviled him for his stone-hearted demeanor. It was only in his memoir that he dropped his cool façade, revealing the depths of his tortured soul, the pain and self-loathing that a homosexual suffered at the turn of the century:

> To me, the word[s] *female-monster* seems to approach the truth. A homo-sexual is a kind of monstrosity, a castoff, a partial being, something out of step with the rest of the world, a subject of study and wonderment for science. Society does not admit these beings. It rejects and condemns them without stopping to examine them.
>
> I entered this life with a soul full of terror. . . . I have always had this secret premonition that my existence will be crossed by a great catastrophe . . . that my proud and sensual soul needed to be shattered and humiliated. Beings like me don't know middle roads or half measures. Stuck between the angel and the demon, we crawl in the fetid ruts of shameful and criminal joys. . . . Such is the destiny of poor, sick creatures like myself.

On the eve of his entry into the Vacher murder case, Lacassagne felt pulled by competing obligations. As one of the world's foremost interpreters of forensic evidence and examiner of the criminal mind, he saw lawbreakers not as biological "others" but as complex human beings influenced by their environment. He did not despise them. He believed in the rehabilitation of ex-prisoners: "to support them, direct them, counsel them, and even help them erase the memory of their punishment." Yet as a protector of the social order, he was implacable about the need to punish offenders, especially those who, in full possession of their faculties, had committed murder. "Society has the right to defend itself," he wrote. "We are far from the time when the guillotine can be relegated to the warehouse of ancient artifacts." He felt strongly that a society lacking the will for self-protection would find itself ravaged by crime, just as a person who neglected to attend to his hygiene would find himself ravaged by disease. Compassion, even pity, should not trump the values of order, self-discipline, and social responsibility. And so in this context, too, he once again employed his famous aphorism: "Societies have the criminals they deserve."

Seventeen

"A Crime Without Motive?"

The Saint-Paul prison stood near the southern edge of Lyon, steps from one of the city's two train stations and only a few blocks from its most fashionable shopping district. It was not quite twenty-five years old when Vacher arrived, but it already had taken on a look of antiquity. The high walls and towers, built of heavy brown blocks, created an oppressive Gothic appearance. The entrance, a pair of massive wooden doors set in a turret, gave the impression of a castle in a folk tale, one that did not just admit visitors but swallowed them.

As dreary and dour as the structure may have seemed, it was modern for its day. The building employed a radial architecture that was much in vogue in prison construction. Six wings of three-story cell blocks radiated out from a central structure, like the arms of a starfish. That way, guards positioned in the center could monitor activity in all the wings. Between the wings were wedge-shaped exercise yards, commonly called *camemberts* for their resemblance to cheese wedges. The most unusual feature of the prison was the chapel, fitted with special pews, boxlike partitions closed on three sides and with a shoulder-height opening at the front. The structure restricted each man's line of sight, so he could look only forward at the priest or upward to God.

Vacher was transferred there at the end of December 1897 and placed in the maximum-security wing. Lacassagne had previously visited Vacher in Belley, along with two medical collaborators—an asylum director, Dr. Fleury Rebatel, and Dr. Auguste Pierret, clinical professor of mental illness at the University of Lyon and chief medical officer of the asylum in Bron. Vacher had greeted them like saviors—at last he would be talking with people who could *understand* him.

During their visit, Vacher, over many hours, disgorged his life story, and his argument that he was not legally responsible. When the doctors returned after a lunch break, he had decorated himself and his cell, as if to present a visual montage of insanity. He had fastened a commemorative medallion of Lourdes to his shirt, and with a piece of chalk, he'd drawn a cross on one shoe and a heart on the other. He had festooned the walls of his cell with newspaper illustrations of himself. Under one he had pasted a cutout of a grandfather clock with a handwritten caption: "It is time."

The doctors felt they needed to observe Vacher over a period of weeks, or even months, and requested that he be sent to the prison in Lyon. Two weeks later, the guards woke him at five in the morning and told him to get ready. He showed no surprise, signed a release without protest, and then abruptly threw himself to the floor. Two guards bound him and carried him to a horse-drawn carriage, then bundled him onto the train. It was chaos at the station, with Vacher yelling, "The government wants my head, and they'll have it!" At the transfer station on the way to Lyon, he thrashed about and shrieked, "Make way for Vacher the Ripper! They want my head!"

The question of Vacher's legal responsibility was a key aspect in the case, and it touched on one of the most troubling issues in legal medicine. As the young sciences of neurology and psychology advanced, scientists were finding an increasing number of criminals who belonged in an asylum rather than in a penitentiary. But in the lax and insecure French asylum system, a ruling of not guilty by reason of insanity often was tantamount to early release. That raised the stakes regarding Vacher. This would be the first case involving a serial killer who claimed that, by reason of insanity, he bore no legal responsibility for his crimes.

For centuries, crime and punishment had fit a simple equation: Crime was a sin, and those who committed sins should be punished. Those who seemed to act by compulsion—against their own free will or better judgment, so to speak—were thought to be sorcerers or possessed by the devil. It was their fault if they were too weak to resist.

With the birth of the science of psychology in the nineteenth century, that point of view began to change. According to the new medical theories, it was no longer Satan who created the compulsion to do evil, but diseases of the mind. British courts acknowledged that idea in a landmark case in 1824, in which a man named Arnold shot and wounded a Lord Onslow. Arnold was clearly a raving lunatic—so much so that Onslow himself pled for the judge not to impose the death sentence. The court sentenced Arnold to life imprisonment, ruling that he was so "deprived of his understanding and memory" that he no more understood his actions than "an infant, a brute or wild beast."

The "wild beast" ruling became the standard in many countries. In most cases, it was easy to apply because judges and juries could readily see that certain defendants were insane. But sometimes a defendant's condition was less obvious.

In 1843, a Scottish woodcutter, Daniel McNaghten, shot and killed Edward Drummond, secretary to Sir Robert Peel, the former British prime minister. McNaghten, obsessed with the notion that Peel had been plotting against him, shot Drummond in a case of mistaken identity. To all appearances, McNaghten seemed a normal man. Alienists, however, testified that he was delusional. The jury acquitted him, and he was sent to Bethlem Asylum.* The queen and prime minister objected, and the case went to a highly publicized appeal. Out of that controversy emerged the "right from wrong" formulation: that a defendant could be acquitted if he was "laboring under such a defect of reason" that he did not know that what he was doing was wrong.

French law took a parallel course. Criminal insanity was not legally recognized before the French Revolution—criminals were punished regardless of their mental state—but in 1810, the post-revolutionary government passed a new legal code that spelled out citizens' rights and obligations. Article 64 of that code said an act would not be considered a crime if the accused "was in a demented state" while committing it. Like the "wild beast" standard, this rule was not difficult to apply in cases of obvious insanity; often, it was enough for neighbors and family to bear witness. But as the definition of insanity evolved from "total madness" to the less obvious "loss of reason," the article's vagueness became problematic. The issue was magnified by the fact that, unlike in England, there were no special asylums for the criminally insane in France. A man found not guilty by reason of "diminished responsibility" would be sent to an ordinary asylum (albeit to a high-security wing), where his release would depend on the judgment of the director. A murderer could be released in as little

---

* Bethlem, which received its first patients in 1403, became notorious for brutal, filthy conditions. The hospital left the English language its nickname, "Bedlam," to connote any hopelessly chaotic situation.

as a few months if the director asserted he had been cured. (Vacher's confinement after he shot Louise amounted to less than a year.) Unfortunately, as the science of psychology became more nuanced over the decades, the legal regulations did not.

This widening gap between medical science and legal codes led to wildly inconsistent verdicts. In 1885, for example, an Italian immigrant laborer went on a drunken rampage through Paris, killing one man and injuring several others. When medical experts looked into the case, they learned that he had spent weeks in a compressed-air chamber underground while laying pylons for the Pont d'Austerlitz. They concluded that changes in air pressure had made his brain so sensitive that he could not be held responsible for his behavior while drunk. The court sentenced him to five years' forced labor.

The experts' judgment was less charitable in highly publicized or notorious cases. As mentioned earlier, all France was horrified by the case of Louis Menesclou, who raped, killed, and dismembered a four-year-old child. The man was clearly deranged, but he was declared legally responsible and was guillotined. Afterward, when experts autopsied his brain and found numerous lesions, they decided, to their regret, that he probably had been insane.

A similar concession to public outrage occurred in the United States after the assassination of President James A. Garfield. The assassin, Charles J. Guiteau, shot the president, he said, on instructions from God. Guiteau, who had a history of erratic behavior, ranted during his trial, sometimes literally foaming at the mouth. Yet the prosecution's medical expert, Dr. John Gray, superintendent of the state asylum in Utica, New York, testified that Guiteau had acted entirely from wounded vanity and disappointment from not having been named ambassador to France—a position the accused somehow felt he deserved. Guiteau was found responsible, pronounced guilty, and hanged. Just as with Menesclou, the doctors who autopsied Guiteau found traces of brain damage—in this case, possibly indicating syphilis-induced insanity.*

---

* In a tragic coincidence, shortly after the trial, Dr. Gray himself was shot by an insane man. The perpetrator of this crime, Henry Reimshaw, having been released after eighteen months in an asylum, claimed to have been sent on a mission from heaven.

Clearly there was a need to align medical and judicial doctrine about criminal insanity and legal responsibility. Yet scholars could not decide how. In 1890, writing in the journal *Annales médico-psychologiques,* jurist Louis Proal summed up the dilemma.

> Public security is compromised if we wrongly consider a suspect as sick who was [legally] responsible and deserves to be punished. But can we imagine a more terrible mistake [in condemning] a sick person who deserves our pity? In which proofs can [we] be certain to condemn only the guilty ones and absolve only the sick people?

Which proofs indeed? Could the mere fact of committing a senseless murder—as opposed to a murder with motive, such as adultery, robbery, or an argument over honor or money—constitute prima facie evidence for insanity? One lawyer made that argument during a trial in the early years of the century. The man on trial had murdered two children whom he had just happened to walk past in a park. "A crime without motive? Are you not, Messieurs members of the jury, struck by all that these words mean; a crime without motive! And what a crime! The murder of two children! But who is he who does not immediately respond: This man is mad."

That may have been a compelling philosophical argument, but it never held weight with judges or juries. The legal system required a more specific approach, one in which trained experts could evaluate individual cases. Over time, high-profile murder cases in France featured panels of medical experts who would examine the defendant and give an opinion—although judges and juries were not obligated to follow them. Yet even within that well-established structure, many thought that the criminal's mental condition should not affect the verdict—that a crime was a crime, regardless of who had committed it.

"If I am bitten by a viper or a rabid dog, I do not care to know whether the animal is responsible for its misdeed or not," argued Dr. Gustave Le Bron. "I try to protect myself by preventing it from doing any further harm or harming others: This is my only concern."

Even larger questions loomed about protecting society, ones that involved citizens not yet born. This was the era of Darwin and Pasteur, and the conceptual mixing of evolution and contagion gave rise to harsh judgments about those whose existence would harm the greater good. In 1898, at the same time that Lacassagne and his colleagues were evaluating

Vacher, the alienist and writer Maurice de Fleury argued in his book *The Criminal Mind* that for the good of the human species, insane criminals should be removed from the breeding pool:

> [W]e care for them; we raise them in cages, we preserve them from death. For what purpose, God Almighty!
>
> Is it really human to allow these monsters, these creatures of darkness, these nightmarish larvae to breathe? Do you not think, to the contrary, that it would be more pious to kill them, to do away with that ugliness and unconsciousness that cannot be made noble, even by suffering? I glimpse the possibility of the legal, authorized elimination of all these incurable beings. Death without suffering, almost a consolation, a release: a gentle death, hardly sad, and annihilating useless ugliness and narrowing the intolerable field of feigned horror, of evil for no reason.

These arguments weighed heavily on Lacassagne and his colleagues as they examined Vacher. The issue was further complicated because the two alienists who had spent the most time with Vacher, the directors of the Dole and Saint-Robert asylums, had come to contradictory conclusions— the first that he was insane and the second that he was cured. And so as the media announced Vacher's arrival in Lyon, it was with full awareness of the case's implications. A columnist for *Le Petit Parisien* warned about the danger to society if Lacassagne and his colleagues decided that Vacher was not legally responsible: "Is he insane? That's the question of the day for the scientific alienist. . . . And if it should be answered by 'yes' as everyone assumes, what should one do with him? Submit him again to a healing regime so that once he is restored he will recover the right to return to his exploits?"

Albert Sarraut voiced an equal but opposite anxiety. What would it say about modern society if this "wild animal with a human face" were found to be as sane as any other citizen? "Vacher is a monster, yes; the most odious and dreadful of monsters. But is he conscious of what he does, is he in possession of his reason? For the honor of the humanity that he at least physically resembles, we must hope for the contrary."

A couple of days after his arrival in Lyon, Lacassagne and the two other experts, Rebatel and Pierret, visited Vacher. They had agreed to divide the case into three areas of investigation: Lacassagne, the lead investigator, would examine the years of Vacher's crime spree; Pierret would scrutinize Vacher's heredity and family history; and Rebatel would evaluate his behavior in prison. Vacher had calmed down considerably after the train ride, and when the three men arrived, he said he was happy to see them and generally felt well. They all chatted genially for an hour. His only complaint was that other prisoners kept asking him questions during his walks in the courtyard.

The first question the experts needed answered was whether the bullets Vacher shot into his own head had lodged in an area that could affect his behavior. Lacassagne arranged for a well-known radiographer, a Dr. Destot, to x-ray Vacher to locate the projectile. This was one of the first times in history that the new technology was used in legal medicine. An earlier case took place in 1896 during a civil suit in Nottingham, England. A dancer had fallen on some steps in the local theater and broken an ankle. The theater owners claimed she exaggerated the injury, but their argument fell apart when an X-ray showed the bone had been broken.

Vacher submitted to the forty-five-minute procedure, joking with the attendant about his days in the regiment. Vacher asked him if he had been reading the papers and seeing what people were saying about him. Then his mood suddenly darkened. "They're idiots," he snapped. "They're trying to put 200 murders on my back. I've had enough of it." And then he became cordial again.

The guards and other prisoners were discovering how volatile the new inmate could be. He might be gay and expansive and spend the day singing, then suddenly turn ugly and brutal. He treated his guards like servants, and the other prisoners like inferiors. "You don't have the right to keep me within these walls . . . and with criminals!" he wrote to the chief prosecutor of Lyon. "I think you are capable of letting an innocent man die." He demanded to be moved to a private cell.

Vacher was indeed moved to his own cell, where he spent most of his day humming contentedly. But his newfound tranquillity did not last. "Suddenly, without any apparent reason, he would become morose, sneaky, and brutal," wrote a prison official.

His outbursts were volcanic. One Sunday in March, as he was preparing to attend mass, he pushed his guards aside, kicked through the heavy wooden door to his cell, and scrambled into the hall. He was sprinting full-bore toward the chapel when one of the guards tackled him. He was returned to his cell and bound in a straitjacket. During the night, he ripped it apart. The next day, guards moved him to a special isolation cell, with a pallet instead of a bed, and shackled his hands and feet. He declared he would commit suicide and started banging his head against the wall. The jailers noticed that he was careful to let his left shoulder strike first so as not to cause himself any real harm.

He went on a hunger strike, proclaiming that he would not eat again until the authorities recognized his innocence. "For [six days] he has energetically refused all nourishment," the prison director wrote to Lacassagne. "Before I choose to force him to eat I think I should inform you of the situation to discharge my responsibilities." Lacassagne went to see the prisoner. Vacher greeted him warmly, reached out for a handshake, and then squeezed the professor's hand until it hurt. He wanted to show that despite his state of privation, God was giving him the power of a "strongman at a country fair." An alert guard later noticed a more prosaic reason for Vacher's fortitude: Other prisoners had been slipping him food. The professor was not amused.

Meanwhile, Vacher had been writing. His output was prodigious, and he made copies of most letters he wrote. He wrote to nearly everyone he had encountered in the course of his wanderings, including Louise Barant, her parents, other members of his regiment, and people in the two asylums where he had stayed, as well as to Fourquet and to himself. He wrote a two-page poem reflecting on the pleasures of roaming the countryside:

> *Oh! Lovely solitude!*
> *Element of good spirits,*
> *So many things without study*
> *You have taught me.*
>
> *My God! That my eyes are so happy*
> *To see from our mountaintops*
> *Such vast plains,*
> *Such beautiful houses! . . .*
>
> *From here I can hear thousands of noises,*
> *Hunting horns, hinds and sheep;*
> *I often find myself surprised*
> *In the midst of such reveries.*

Old ruined castles,
Old cities in decay
Against which the mutinous years
Have deployed their insolence!

He wrote to Madame Plantier, whose escape from his attack had ended the killing spree: "I am truly honored to salute you. . . . I wish that for what you did for justice God will give you back everything He owes to you for the past, present and future." But he chided her against feeling too proud. "You can congratulate yourself for my arrest, but don't forget [the role] of Divine Providence."

As part of his interest in criminals' autobiographies, Lacassagne gave Vacher a notebook. The accused filled it with scribblings over the months, eventually titling it "The Case of Joseph Vacher: His Self-Defense." Yet if Lacassagne hoped to gain any insight, expression of regret, or revelation from Vacher, he was soon disappointed. Vacher's first letter to his doctors was a tiresome recitation of previously known facts and grandiose statements. "They say that curiosity ends where concern for national safety begins," he wrote, and cataloged the misfortunes that had befallen him—all in a single run-on sentence. He said he would be willing to provide new details of his wanderings, but only if he could first release them to the press. Lacassagne, who had an abhorrence of pretrial publicity, did not agree.

Vacher wrote steadily to the doctors, with the intention of highlighting his insanity. Some letters began with the now-familiar heading of "God—Rights—Obligations" in block letters. Some bore a return address, "Lyon—Jerusalem," reflecting his religious obsession. (The town of Belley became "Bethlehem.")

"From where comes my malady?" he wrote to Drs. Lacassagne, Pierret, and Rebatel. He fell back on "the bite of a rabid dog." He enumerated certain "supplements" that had worsened his condition:

1. The bitterness of a painful operation to my sexual parts at the hospital in Lyon.
2. The bullets in my head and the infirmities that followed from the unfortunate event at Baume-les-Dames [when he shot Louise and himself].
3. Bad memories of the sad asylum at Dole.

Sometimes he would fawn over the doctors, as he had at the Saint-Robert asylum. Other times, he would remind them of their "heavy mission" in determining his sanity. Sometimes he would make quasi-religious statements about his purity: "One is truly strong when one feels innocent and has faith." Sometimes he would try to unnerve his inquisitors, as when he wrote Dr. Pierret's name on a piece of paper and drew a knife under it—"to make sure he does not betray me."

Early in his imprisonment, Vacher argued, as he had with Fourquet, that he was overcome by uncontrollable rages—proof, he said, that he was insane. By late February, though, he was advancing a theory of *temporary* insanity. Acknowledging the "sad state I was in during my wandering," he said that he had now settled into a better state of mind.

> Understand that at the present time my infirmity is not as pronounced, that I am not so repulsive to people. . . . [T]he infection of the bullets in my head that with each step made me feel closer to death [has abated, as has] the heaviness and the boiling that I always had in my head. . . . I no longer feel compelled to sleep outdoors to avoid the laughter of malevolent people.
>
> Signed: Jh Vacher
>
> PS—If under these conditions I don't deserve to be declared irresponsible, who possibly could be?

Lacassagne was unmoved. He wrote in a memo, "The real alienated do not act that way."

Eighteen

Turning Point

How the "real alienated" behaved was a grave concern to turn-of-the-century criminologists, because many offenders were faking mental illness. As asylums proliferated and medical experts increasingly became involved in trials, word had spread in the criminal world about the possibility of being sent to an asylum and the relatively easy life one could lead there. In 1888, Dr. Paul Garnier, medical director of the Préfecture of Police in Paris, wrote that in the previous two years he had noticed that criminals were employing the ruse with "uncommon frequency." He attributed the increase to the 1885 retribution law, which sentenced repeat offenders to Devil's Island. Criminals would rather spend time in an asylum than be sent to that hellhole for life.

Garnier was not alone in recognizing the problem, nor was France the only country in which it occurred. By the early 1890s, the criminal handbooks of several nations included warnings about feigned insanity and advice on how to detect it. The 1892 edition of *A Manual of Medical Jurisprudence,* a handbook used by British and American detectives, cautioned investigators to be alert for overacting. "In real insanity, the person will *not* admit that he is insane; it is in the feigned state that all his attempts are directed to make others believe that he is mad." Investigators noted a variety of faked behaviors, including mutism, paralysis, amnesia, mania, epileptic fits, melancholy, delirium, hunger strikes, and suicide attempts. Mania seemed to be the most common affectation, because "the vulgar notion of insanity is that it is made up of violent actions and vociferous and incoherent language."

Hans Gross, the Austrian criminologist, recommended that investigators carefully review a prisoner's statements, "some of which are deliberate and cunning, while others are awkward and stupid." That contradiction in tone, he said, was a sign of dissembling. He urged inspectors to observe the suspect's eyes:

> No intelligent man has an idiot's eyes, and no idiot has intelligent eyes.
> The whole physiognomy, the deportment, the gestures, may deceive, the
> eyes never; and whoever is accustomed to watch the eyes will never be taken
> in. . . . Remember also that the shammer, when he thinks no one is looking,
> casts a swift and scrutinizing glance on the Investigating Officer to see
> whether or not he believes him.

Journals were rife with cautionary reports. Richard von Krafft-Ebing, the Viennese alienist, wrote about a prisoner who killed a former mistress with a pocketknife and then simulated insanity by refusing to speak or eat and bashing his head against the wall. Later found to be eating in secret, sleeping soundly, and faking his self-battery, he was convicted and executed.

Garnier wrote a lengthy article about feigned insanity cases and how he uncovered them. One felon, a twenty-five-year-old habitual thief named Troyé, affected insanity when he learned he would be deported to a prison colony. He fell into silence and sat for days curled up in a corner of his cell, his left hand trembling. He resisted all attempts to engage him. One day, Garnier remarked to the prisoner that his right hand was now trembling instead. Having failed to keep his symptoms consistent, Troyé confessed to the sham. Another prisoner feigned hallucinations, went silent, and stopped eating. After a few visits, Garnier said to a colleague in a loud voice that he recognized this particular syndrome and that he would soon expect to see a period of mania. When the prisoner adopted the new symptoms the next day, Garnier knew the insanity was feigned. Another prisoner, who had been starving himself and banging his head against the wall, simply gave up after three days. "It's understandable that I would not want to leave for the country of savages," he explained.

Garnier's most ambiguous case involved a thirty-year-old man named Paul-Joseph Cavène. Cavène had written several threatening letters to a former mistress, who had married another man. He had also assaulted the woman's husband, for which he was arrested. Alienists who administered a psychological exam noted Cavène's turbulent youth, troubled history, and delusions of grandeur: He would spout "empty and meaningless sentences, spoken with a ridiculously emphatic tone." They concluded that Cavène was psychologically diminished, but not enough to deserve legal immunity. The court sentenced him to eight days in jail.

Shortly after his release, Cavène threw acid in his former mistress's face and tried to gouge out her eyes with his fingers. After this, his second arrest, alienists found that his symptoms had worsened. He hallucinated about his victim and ranted about seeing her perfect face in his dreams. When reminded that her face was no longer perfect and that he was the one who had disfigured her, he showed utter surprise. Routine questions drew tirades and outbursts. He wrote grandiose verses in which he compared himself to Spartacus and Toussaint-Louverture, the liberator of Haiti. He looked forward to seeing his name in the press.

Yet the alienists felt the behavior was too purposeful and systematic. Granted, Cavène was bizarre and impulsive, but the exaggerated nature of his new symptoms led them to believe that he "borrows the language and demeanor of someone who is hallucinating and haunted by ideas of persecution." A former cell mate of Cavène said he had spoken of his plan to attack his ex-mistress and "escape punishment under the pretext of mental alienation."

This was a new phenomenon for the experts: a *somewhat* alienated individual who feigned *extreme* insanity in order to escape justice. "A man presenting these deviations," they wrote, "should be placed in an asylum under the strictest surveillance."

Cavène was sent to the Bicêtre asylum in Paris and was released a few months later. He renewed his threats to his ex-mistress and her husband. This time, when Cavène went after them in a public garden in Paris, the husband shot him several times with a revolver. After a stay in the hospital, Cavène was sent to the Sainte-Anne asylum in Paris, then transferred to an asylum in the countryside. He escaped and returned to Paris for vengeance—a plan that was sidetracked by the police. At the time of Garnier's most recent report, Cavène was interned in the Sainte-Anne asylum, with no indication of how long he would remain there.

If a man like Cavène could escape and hurt people, one could only imagine the havoc that Vacher could wreak. There was a striking commonality between the behaviors in the reports of simulated insanity and Vacher's—the haughty attitude, the delusions of grandeur, the love of publicity. There were the fake hunger strikes, the periods of mutism, and phony suicide attempts. Indeed, from the time they met him, Lacassagne and his colleagues suspected Vacher of simulating insanity. "The first impression one gets from looking at Vacher with his white rabbit-fur hat, white being the color of innocence, is that this man is putting it on," wrote Lacassagne. "This is the immediate impression shared to the same degree by the most naïve observers and the most suspicious specialists." Lacassagne seemed to have taken an early dislike to him. "We have rarely seen a defendant at the same time more haughty and more suspicious, more prudent with his words and at the same time such a ridiculous faker in his actions. He affected an inappropriate familiarity and an arrogant tone toward authority."

Later, when he elaborated on the signs that he saw in Vacher, Lacassagne could almost have been quoting Gross's description of the typical malingerer:

> From time to time, Vacher forgets his amateur dramatics and the role he is playing and spontaneously makes quite sensible statements and comes out with quite clever replies, or with a crafty smile parries arguments directed against him and avoids leading questions. Often, when he feels himself being drawn away from the position he has consistently determined to take, Vacher will remain cautiously silent [or] make sporadic, deliberately unreasonable remarks, behind which he takes shelter.

It troubled Lacassagne that unlike other prisoners, whose stories evolved as he got to know them, Vacher adhered to an unchanging script. He refused to answer any questions about his crimes; he would invariably refer back to his original confession letter. "He always resorts to the main theme: bitten by a mad dog, and blood-poisoned," Lacassagne reported. Vacher repeated this story in every correspondence and every conversation, and in the memoir he eventually submitted. If pressed to be more precise, he became irritable and menacing. Lacassagne also noted fundamental inconsistencies within Vacher's story. He was bitten by a mad dog and abused at the mental asylums but was operating under the guidance and protection of "Divine Providence." Vacher's narrative was at once "hypochondriac and megalomaniac." That particular combination of symptoms had never been reported by psychologists before, which made Lacassagne doubt its authenticity. It certainly was "not in agreement with his diagnosis at Dole."

What most struck Lacassagne and his colleagues, however, was the evidence that Vacher was building a case. When Vacher arrived at the jail in Belley, the prison doctor, Bozonet, conducted a quick examination and concluded that the prisoner's responsibility was "notably diminished." A few weeks later, Dr. Léon Madeuf, an opponent of capital punishment, came unannounced from Paris to interview Vacher. (Fourquet had banned him as an unauthorized visitor, but during one of Fourquet's brief absences, Madeuf, claiming to have been given Fourquet's permission, tricked Bozonet into letting him in.) Madeuf never wrote a report, but he made his sympathies clear. Sensing an ally, Vacher later wrote to Madeuf that it was "absolutely necessary" to begin using the press to publicize his situation. If Madeuf could get the Lyon newspapers to publish his letter, then "the biggest part of [our case] will be made." Now in Lyon, Vacher wrote to the authorities that Madeuf could bring some truth to the case.

Lacassagne and his colleagues had never seen anyone work so methodically to be sent to an asylum. It was "his only objective," wrote Lacassagne. "He has not forgotten how easy it was to be let out." Vacher sensed that concern, and he made a counterargument to the medical team: "Why haven't I been sent to an asylum yet? I'll tell you why: It's because you are afraid I'll escape. Escape . . . but why? Right now I am so well known that if I ever escaped, I would be captured immediately. No, no, I would not try to escape."

Unlike scores of other prisoners at Saint-Paul, Vacher never admired Lacassagne—perhaps because of the professor's skepticism. Once Vacher realized that Lacassagne was not an ally, he decided he would tell him nothing more. There would be no meeting of the minds, not even temporarily, as with the prisoner and Fourquet. The daily interviews would produce no catharsis or confession, just a repetitive hammering away between two men of unbendable wills. Vacher seemed to take pride in the challenge and saw their interaction as a game. "So you see, Monsieur le Docteur," he said one morning to Lacassagne, assuming an air of bravado, "the most difficult part of your mission will be to get to know my state of mind."

Once, Lacassagne thought he saw an opening. He was questioning Vacher about a murder for which he was suspected but had not confessed. Every time the professor had brought up the subject previously, Vacher had retreated into petulant silence. This time, however, Vacher seemed to listen, his head tilted attentively and his hands clasped behind his back. Lacassagne thought the prisoner might finally say something on the subject. Suddenly, Vacher shrugged his shoulders melodramatically, started pacing, and blurted, "You know something—I've really had enough of you. I'm only going to say what I want to and no more. I've spoken enough. Consult my interrogatories with the judge. It's over; I have nothing to add." And then he shut down again.

In an attempt to break down Vacher's defenses, Lacassagne started a conversation about the members of Vacher's old regiment. The effort brought a rebuke from the prisoner:

The lack of confidence you have in me is something that you deserve. Do you remember the day when you allowed yourself to almost offend my self-respect and patriotism, speaking of the little and big victories of my colleagues during my military service? You were right to ask my opinion but chose [the wrong tone and] moment to do it.

Lacassagne wrote with equal irritation:

Here is the theory of Vacher: I am not responsible because I was insane. It was necessary to know my mental state, during my wandering life. . . .

Vacher has always counted on the impunity that he gained during his stay in a mental asylum. The doctor declared him cured, but today he [insists] that he was still sick when they let him go.

We have seen that he knows how to organize his thoughts toward simulating a delirium, disguising or blocking his confession, and his insistence on being declared nonresponsible during his wandering life. All this is too adept to be coming from an insane person.

That is not to say that Lacassagne's visits convinced him that Vacher was legally responsible. What they showed the professor was that he could not draw conclusions from *conversations* with Vacher. The suspect would always dissimulate and would always weigh the effect of his words. No, in order to get to the bottom of this case, to determine if the accused was insane, Lacassagne would have to let the evidence speak. He now turned to analyzing the forensic evidence gathered at the crime scenes.

Not having conducted the autopsies himself, Lacassagne had no guarantee of their quality or precision. Aside from two that his colleague Jean Boyer conducted, all the procedures were carried out by doctors with varying levels of expertise and took place in rough rural settings. The body of Vacher's first victim, Eugénie Delhomme, was not examined until four days after the body was found. Rosine Rodier's body was examined in a foggy pasture in the middle of the night, the area lit poorly with lanterns.

There were so many lapses in forensic technique. In Lacassagne's *Handbook* he had stressed, for example, the importance of checking for anal rape, as pederasty was becoming more widely recognized as a crime motive. Since Vacher had a bottle of lubricating oil among his possessions, and doctors had found traces of oil on some of the bodies, it was particularly important in this case. Yet in only two instances had doctors checked for anal rape. Lacassagne showed the eleven crime-scene reports to a sketch artist, who drew the bodies in the positions they had been found. Using the drawings, autopsy reports, and Vacher's confessions, Lacassagne started to list common elements.

All the victims had been killed in isolated areas without any witnesses. All were much smaller and weaker than Vacher—thus clearly not capable of effective self-defense. Ten of the victims' bodies had massive cuts to the side of the throat, accompanied by other brutalities. (The body of the eleventh victim, recovered from the well, was nothing more than bones.) At ten of the crime scenes, investigators had found one or more huge puddles of blood, at a distance from where the body lay. The body itself was almost always hidden—either under a bush, as in the case of Vacher's first victim, Eugénie Delhomme, or in a deserted shed, as with his second victim, Louise Marcel. Only two of the victims showed defensive wounds on the inner surfaces of their fingers or palms. None of the bodies had contusions on the back or the back of the head. In cases where the crime had taken place in enclosed areas, such as in shepherds' huts, there were no traces of blood on the walls.

These forensic details gave Lacassagne enough information to recreate Vacher's method of attack. "One can see in the circumstances of the killings that the victims were assaulted and murdered in almost identical conditions," he wrote. "Vacher did not improvise: He always follows the same method."

According to Lacassagne's reconstruction, Vacher would walk for miles along commonly traveled roads but leave for his "hunt" along paths that skirted the edge of forests. There, he would prowl for solitary adolescents, whose "young flesh fascinated and appealed to him." (Lacassagne pointed out that with the exception of one victim, the sixty-eight-year-old widow Morand, all Vacher's victims had been young.) Vacher would approach a shepherd and take a quick look to make sure there was no one around. (The young shepherd Alphonse Rodier was spared an attack by the last-minute appearance of some workers in the distance.) Then he would violently seize the victim's throat. Vacher was strong and had unusually long fingernails, and his first victim displayed telltale scratches. Later, as he gained confidence and practice in stabbing, he made throat wounds so large that they obliterated the scratches. Autopsies revealing crushed larynxes nonetheless demonstrated that strangulation had taken place.

Vacher would seize his victims so quickly and powerfully that almost none had the chance to struggle or scream. Most blacked out or went limp, at which point he placed them on the ground and slit their throats. Lacassagne deduced that Vacher always proceeded in this manner because, as noted earlier, only one of the bodies displayed the kind of contusions on the back or the back of the head that a violent fall would have produced. Only one victim, the widow Morand, showed the kind of contusions that would have resulted from a fall, as Vacher seemed to have immediately stabbed her as he broke into her kitchen. Moreover, if the victims had been stabbed while in an upright position, the blood from the jugular vein would have spurted, possibly to a distance of several feet. The lack of blood spatter at any of the crime scenes ruled that out.

Vacher's "maneuver of choice," wrote Lacassagne, was so efficient that he never was wounded or scratched. In two cases—those of Louise Marcel and Pierre Laurent—strangulation was incomplete, and although the victims struggled, as indicated by defensive wounds, they were not able to resist in any serious way. In only one case, that of Madame Plantier, did the victim escape as Vacher was executing the first part of his maneuver.

"It is certain that Vacher was behind the head or on one side of the victim [when he slashed them]; otherwise, he would have been literally covered with blood," wrote Lacassagne. "The blood spread onto the earth without reaching Vacher. This would explain why there was very little blood on his clothing."

Medical examiners noted that the backs of the clothing were blood-saturated and that the organs and hearts of the victims had been completely drained. As for the puddles of blood, Lacassagne deduced that the first one revealed the initial attack, where Vacher killed the victim and let as much blood as possible drain away. He would then drag the body out of the puddle to a second spot, where, now that it was lifeless, he would proceed with mutilation or rape. Finally, he would move the body to a hiding place—behind rocks, under bushes, or in a hollow covered with branches or leaves. In some cases, he would make a hasty attempt to cover the bloody puddles with dirt.

Then he would walk for many miles, often through the night, putting enough distance between himself and the crime scene to escape the initial search parties. He always carried a change of clothing and frequently shaved and then regrew his mustache and beard.

"One has to ask," wrote Lacassagne, "if the constant repetition of this series of bloody maneuvers is the work of a cannibal—but a responsible cannibal—or, to the contrary, of an unconscious lunatic." To the professor, the entire progression of the crimes, despite their perversity, indicated the kind of planning and presence of mind that only a sane man could possess. "There is no doubt he chose the hour, the victim, the place." From the moment Vacher began stalking each victim, "he obeyed a preconceived plan that followed a deliberate and logical process according to systematic ideas. . . . He encountered numerous travelers along the main routes, but his rage never overtook him. It only happened far from habitation."

His killing technique was fast and efficient, executed with a "precision and practice" that demonstrated a "calm, imperturbable intent." The killer's actions "would take audacity, sangfroid, a total self-possession."

Lacassagne pointed out that during the course of Vacher's peregrinations, there were particular episodes when he demonstrated the kind of lucidity one did not associate with a madman. After he killed the widow Morand, he locked her door and threw away the key, prolonging the gap between crime and discovery. Minutes after he killed Aline Alaise, when a farmer in a horse-drawn carriage came upon him, Vacher had the presence of mind to make up a story about having an accident that gave him a bloody nose. When a policeman caught up with him after he attacked twelve-year-old Alphonsine Derouet, he was clever enough to win the officer's confidence and send him off on a chase for the "real" suspect.

Once Vacher killed his victim, he would sometimes slip into an erotic frenzy. Yet, even those actions, in Lacassagne's view, would not exempt Vacher from legal responsibility, for they took place after his carefully planned executions. At that point, "the complete possession of the cadaver exalts him; then, and only then, can he freely deliver the blows [that excite him], localized at the genital organs." According to Lacassagne, those actions portrayed sadism, a recently coined term to describe people who took pleasure inflicting pain. The term "does not in any way imply insanity," wrote Lacassagne, and those who engaged in such practices did not deserve society's protection. If their predilections took them into the realm of criminal behavior, then as criminals they should be judged.

Lacassagne, like Fourquet, felt that Vacher had committed many more crimes than he had confessed to. The dossiers that came in from around the country indicated to him that Vacher had probably committed twenty-five to twenty-seven murders, rapes, and other violent felonies. Yet Vacher had confessed to only eleven, all of which occurred after his attempted shooting of Louise. Lacassagne suspected that Vacher was compiling a selective confession—a menu of crimes specifically chosen to portray an uncontrollable lunatic. Interestingly, although some of his alleged crimes involved theft—Augustine Mortureux's earrings and shoes, Marie Moussier's wedding band, and the vagabond Gautrais's two hundred francs—Vacher adamantly denied having stolen. Fourquet had seen this denial as stemming from a perverse sense of honor, but Lacassagne disagreed. He saw it as a way for Vacher to deny ever having had a logical motive.

"Finally," wrote Lacassagne, "and this is an important point—he always had enough money to not be arrested as a vagabond." That, along with his military papers, helped him evade arrest for three years.

After four months of studying Vacher—visiting his family, evaluating his heredity, observing his behavior, analyzing crime scenes, and poring over volumes of testimony, confessions, and medical reports—the experts were ready to submit their analysis. Using the terminology of the day, they concluded that he was "not an epileptic, not an impulsive." He was an immoral and violent person. He occasionally suffered temporary attacks of "melancholic delirium with ideas of persecution and suicide." Yet, if at any point in his life he was alienated, he was "cured and was in a responsible state by the time he had left the Saint-Robert asylum. If he acted insane during his incarceration, it was [only] because he simulated insanity." Vacher was, to put it simply, a criminal. "[He] should be considered as responsible, and this responsibility is in no way attenuated by any preceding psychological troubles." In the eyes of the experts, the killer of little shepherds was legally accountable, and ready to stand trial.

Nineteen

The Trial

On Wednesday, October 26, 1898, dawn brought an overcast sky in Bourg-en-Bresse, a market town about sixty miles northeast of Lyon and capital of the department of Ain. Nevertheless, a sense of festivity filled the air. Wednesday was market day, when people from all over the district thronged the streets. But there was another reason for the carnival atmosphere: On this particular Wednesday, the trial of the most fearsome murderer of the century would begin.

Portraits of Vacher were displayed in the stores; street vendors hawked special newspaper editions and pamphlets heralding "The Crimes of Vacher, the Jack the Ripper of the Southeast." Their verses titillated the public with a flavor of the upcoming testimony.

> *He begins the series*
> *Of crimes so perverse*
> *And strikes with such fury,*
> *Such fury, such fury . . .*

Another:

> *Little shepherds full of sorrow*
> *At night, take care of yourselves.*
> *There are human beasts*
> *Inhumane, inhumane,*
> *Cowardly or insane assassins*
> *More terrible than wolves.*

So many journalists had arrived that not a room in the entire town remained free. Authorities added equipment to the local telegraph office so the correspondents' dispatches would not overwhelm it. Reporters arrived from all the major French newspapers and most of the regional ones, from Italian and Swiss papers, and from the *New York Herald* and the *New York Times.* The *Times* man explained to his readers why he had traveled all the way to a provincial French town to see the trial of a man no American had heard of. Vacher, he proclaimed, would rank among "the most extraordinary criminals that has ever lived, who throws the exploits of a Jack the Ripper and almost of a Nero into the shade, and whose name will certainly be identified, like that of Bluebeard, with the legendary idea of a monster for succeeding generations."

It was a busy time for news in the French press. A few weeks earlier, a dispute between France and Britain over a colonial outpost in eastern Africa had brought the two countries to the brink of war. In Paris, several ministries were in a state of crisis in the aftermath of a failed attempt to build a canal across Panama, and the Dreyfus Affair continued to divide and scandalize the nation. In fact, the Supreme Court of Appeal in Paris was scheduled to review the Dreyfus case the day after Vacher's trial began, which made for some busy travel for the press corps. Albert Bataille, the correspondent for *Le Figaro,* advised his readers that he would attend the first day of the Vacher trial and then catch the night train to Paris for the Dreyfus appeal. He compared it to two plays opening on the same night: "The directors should have been in touch with each other!"

For Vacher, the lead-up to the trial had been less exciting. After spending four months in Lyon, he had been sent back to the little prison in Belley, where he waited another four dreary months for a trial date. Fourquet continued visiting him, in an ongoing attempt to elicit more information. But confronting a magistrate in a backwater prison was nothing like sparring with the world's greatest criminologists, and Vacher languished under confinement.

One day, Fourquet was in Vacher's cell, idly chatting, when the inmate asked, "Are you not afraid to be in here with me?"

"Should I be?" Fourquet replied.

"Do you have a revolver?"

"No," said Fourquet. Like Hans Gross, he felt a detective should never carry weapons while interviewing a suspect. He inverted his pockets and jangled his keys. "These are my only weapons," he said, joking.

Vacher reached under his mattress and pulled out a knife. Fourquet was "suffocated" by surprise; he knew that if he showed any fear, he would die. Instantly, he made up a story. "Listen, Vacher—I have just received the report from the experts. They have declared you insane, and by consequence legally nonresponsible. But if you try to kill me, regardless of what the report says, your head will fall. When one kills a magistrate, one is always condemned to death."

Taking advantage of Vacher's momentary indecision, Fourquet sprang forward and snatched away the weapon. Vacher confessed that he had been hiding the knife for the past six weeks, having kept it after one of his meals. The jailer should have been fired for his negligence, but the man wept so piteously for his job that Fourquet let him go with a severe reprimand.

Now, as the noise swelled in the courtroom in Bourg-en-Bresse, Vacher made ready for his entrance. The crowd was huge and boisterous, shoving, gossiping, ready for a show. Outside the building, a mob surged against the entrance, calling for the criminal's death. Soldiers of the Twenty-third Regiment, from the garrison of Bourg, a famously tough contingent, were having trouble holding the mob at bay.

At 8:40 a.m., Vacher, surrounded by guards, marched into the courtroom, dressed in velour and wearing his white rabbit-fur hat. With his head up, eyes directed halfway to heaven, he seemed to affect the posture of a saint. But his portrayal was unconvincing. His raggedy beard, which came to a point under his chin, made him appear slightly satanic. His right eye, half-closed with paralysis, exaggerated the emotions portrayed by the left, which, in its frantic wandering, gave Vacher an alternately ferocious and desperate look. With his clawlike fingernails and hyperactive limbs, he seemed less a martyred saint than a barely controlled animal. He brandished a rolled-up sheaf of papers. "Glory to Jesus!" he proclaimed. "Long live Joan of Arc! Glory to the great martyr of our times! Glory to the great Savior!" And, incongruously, "He who only hears the bell ring only hears a sound."

The audience started laughing and making gestures to the press gallery. Vacher took his place on a raised platform surrounded by waist-high bars. At 9 a.m., the bailiff announced, "Court is in session! Hats off!"

Vacher briefly fumbled with his cap as the president of the court, Adhémar de Coston, entered, wearing the traditional red robes. He had heard the commotion, and he did not intend to tolerate indignities. He pinned Vacher with a stare. "Listen to me well," he commanded the defendant. "I will not put up with any violence in this room. On your part, all your gestures and demonstrations will be useless. You are not going to behave here as you often did in prison. I'm absolutely firm and will use, if the case warrants, all the powers of the law and restrain you by force if necessary. Remember that."

Vacher remained silent. De Coston turned his attention to the audience and warned them not to misbehave. "I notice several ladies in the room," he added. "I should warn them that during these discussions there will be some things that are a bit difficult for feminine ears. So I would encourage them to leave."

"We waited several minutes," wrote a reporter. "Nobody left, and then everyone laughed."

In the French criminal court system, the judge plays a more active role than in the Anglo-American system, acting more as inquisitor than as a referee. (The French and Continental structure is known as the "inquisitorial" system, while the Anglo-American is known as the "adversarial.") Referred to as the "president of the court," he or she questions witnesses and defendants, based on the dossiers prepared by the investigating magistrate. The prosecuting and defense attorneys say relatively little. They make opening and closing statements, add their own questions for the witnesses, and can object or offer supplementary information in the course of the trial. It's the president's job, through questions, to develop a body of facts that the attorneys can try to interpret for the nine jurors.

Typically, the defendant testifies first in the inquisitorial system (in contrast to the American system, in which the defendant likely testifies at the end of the trial, if at all). De Coston had scheduled the trial for three days, the first of which he would devote to Vacher's testimony. During the second day, he would begin questioning the forty-nine scheduled witnesses, including Vacher's childhood acquaintances, regimental comrades, and people who had encountered him as a vagabond. During the third day, the president would call medical experts to testify about the defendant's mental state.

The bailiff now read the charges against Vacher. It was a long, discursive document, recounting the murder of Portalier, the discovery of his body, the sightings of Vacher in the area, the details of his crime spree, and the experts' conclusions about his sanity. The president explained that even though the defendant was alleged to have committed many crimes, for the purposes of this trial he was being charged with only the killing at Bénonces, which fell within this court's jurisdiction. Reading the charges took a half hour. Vacher had remained silent under the reproachful eye of the president, but he pantomimed his objections by smacking his lips, making throat-slitting gestures, and biting his thumb—all to the "general hilarity" of reporters.

At that point, Vacher's defense attorney, Charbonnier (his first name was never recorded, either in the press or in official documents), rose to his feet. He was an aging legal lion known for his gravitas, eloquence, and opposition to capital punishment. Some said he resembled an elderly Victor Hugo, with his thick white beard, piercing eyes, and craggy face. Charbonnier told the court that the treatment Vacher had received in Saint-Paul prison had been so deplorable as to invalidate the results of the medical exams. Charbonnier asked the president to appoint a new team of alienists to examine his client in a medical setting—preferably in Paris, where, he believed, Vacher would be treated more fairly. The prosecuting attorney, Louis Ducher, whom newspapers described as an "incontestable authority with a real talent for words," asserted that justice already had been too long delayed. De Coston denied Charbonnier's motion.

Vacher interjected that he had something to say. With the court's permission, he began to read from a prepared statement. In a voice sometimes mumbling and sometimes uncomfortably loud, he retold the now-familiar story of his life and the circumstances that led to his insanity. After several minutes, the president interrupted.

"Is this going to take much longer?" he asked.

"Please, Monsieur le Président, I have only three pages to read. My case is serious—I need to be understood."

"Do it quickly, then."

Vacher kept reading, his strange intonation drawing snickers from members of the audience, who quieted when the president shot them menacing glances. Vacher lashed out against those who had wronged him, including Louise Barant and Dr. Dufour, who had pronounced him cured at the Saint-Robert asylum. He saved most of his venom for Lacassagne, who, after four months of observation, had never showed any "confidence" in him. He continued for half an hour, then suddenly stopped.

Then de Coston commenced the formal questioning. Beginning with the standard questions of identity (name, birthplace, age, occupation), he led the suspect step-by-step through his personal background, up to the crime at Bénonces. Despite the simple, factual nature of the questions, Vacher kept returning to the issue of his insanity, saying it had all begun with the incident with the dog. But now he added a new element to the story:

> Ever since then, at certain times, and especially when I'm exposed to the sun in the countryside, I would feel this rage and an immediate violent insanity. I fought it! Oh! Yes, I fought it! Terrible battles raged within me. . . . The sickness would take me all of a sudden at the moment when I least expected it. And then without even being conscious of it, I threw myself on my first victim. I stabbed, I killed the innocents!

In other words, it was not just the dog bite, the medicine, the bullet in his head, and his mistreatment at the asylum that triggered his "rages," but exposure to bright sun, as well. This reverse vampirism was all the more striking because Bram Stoker's popular novel about a monster who became active in the *absence* of sunlight had been published just the year before.

At noon, the court recessed.

Court was scheduled to reconvene at 1:00 p.m., but the mob clamored so loudly at the courthouse entrance that things had to be delayed for an hour. The morning market had closed by now, and the crowds who had been there now flooded to the courthouse. De Coston sat impatiently for a few minutes, then strode to the front door and angrily confronted the hundreds of people. He berated them for wasting their day by trying to force their way into an overcrowded courtroom. They should go to work and provide for their families! He ordered the soldiers to push the crowd away, slammed the front doors, and marched back inside.

Now de Coston focused his questions on the crime at Bénonces. The bailiff had given the jury maps of the town, with each important site marked by a red *X*. By way of setting the context, the president told the jury about Victor Portalier, how the boy who came from questionable family circumstances had turned himself around to become an exemplary young man. He described the murder and explained how the boy's friend came upon the horrific crime scene. Turning to Vacher, he asked, "And the author of this abominable crime—was it you? Were you the one who chose the victim?"

Vacher shook his head: "*Chose*, you say?"

"How would you like me to put it?" asked de Coston.

"As you know, it was my sickness that chose my victims. . . . "

"In any case, witnesses saw you wandering around the area of the murder."

"I don't know how to respond to that," said Vacher. "I crossed the paths of many people."

"And so you do not deny having passed by Bénonces?"

"Without doubt, because I confessed to it."

The president asked him to describe in his own words what happened when he crossed Portalier's path.

"I don't know exactly what I did, but I do know that I gave him a terrible death. It was the fit that came over me . . . what do you want? When one is afflicted like I am, one suffers terribly."

Several audience members began snickering.

"This demonstration is disgraceful!" snapped de Coston. "Anyone capable of laughing at such a moment perhaps ought to be seated with the accused."

The audience muttered in protest and then quieted down. The president turned back to Vacher. He asked him how, if he was in the grip of insanity, he could have had the presence of mind to drag the body under a hedge and then exercise such skill in making an escape. Vacher replied that after the murder he experienced a brief moment of clarity. De Coston suggested that the real reason Vacher acted so effectively was that he understood full well the crime he had committed and dreaded the punishment.

"Punishment! I don't give a damn about punishment," Vacher said. "I am justified in the eyes of God. I acted in a rage. That is my misfortune. I was agitated, and trembling."

"If you are not afraid of punishment," asked the president, "why did you not confess during your first interview to the assassination of Victor Portalier? At first, you denied it."

"I confessed when I realized that I was not responsible, that I was no more guilty than those who let me out of the asylum of Saint-Robert."

"And after your confession, in order to cast doubt on your sanity, you [suddenly admitted to] a quantity of other crimes."

"I never use the word *quantity*," Vacher said. The audience started muttering.

De Coston was incredulous. "You wandered to nineteen departments, killing and eviscerating. During that time, did you not know you were committing these crimes?"

"Yes, but if I'd wanted to, I could have committed many more, because I had one hundred chances to kill. But I killed only when my sickness came over me."

There was grumbling from the audience, curses and shouts. Vacher turned to the spectators and yelled, "I will defend my innocence as I want to!"

Now the president broadened the line of questioning, eliciting testimony about Vacher's three-year killing spree. The bailiff distributed maps to the jury, with a red cross marking each place where a body had been discovered. De Coston asked Vacher how many murders he had committed. Vacher counted on his fingers: eleven.

De Coston: "Including Portalier?"

Vacher: "Including Portalier."

"Now I'm going to see how good your memory is," said de Coston. "The count is this: six girls, four boys, one old woman."

"Yes, it is I who did that," said Vacher. With each new recitation of the murders, he became increasingly vexed: How could the president fail to understand his state of mind during the killing spree? He was insane: legally irresponsible. "Yes, I killed, and then I soiled and mutilated the cadavers. But the guilty ones, the only guilty ones, are the doctors from the Saint-Robert asylum, who, instead of keeping me locked up, let me go running into the countryside!"

His complaint was now blossoming into a tirade. He insisted that he was an instrument of God, because the horror of his crimes would awaken society to the horrible conditions in the lunatic asylums. He served as a living example of the asylums' neglect. "I'm not a rogue! Yes, I fell upon these people and gave them a terrible death, the details of which I don't even remember. I did this, I did that. What do you want, when a fit comes over you, when you have a rage like mine! Do I know what got hold of me? I was like a beast!"

"A ferocious beast," added de Coston.

"Yes, because I was *bitten* by a ferocious beast."

Charbonnier stood up to remind the jury that Vacher was charged with a single crime—the murder at Bénonces. The president had no business bringing in all the others, he asserted. "You are putting questions to my client that are aside from the fact," he told de Coston.

"He's right!" said Vacher. "All that is none of your business."

De Coston snapped that it was up to him to determine which questions were relevant. More to the point, Vacher based his insanity defense on having committed multiple crimes, which made those murders the business of the court.

The president was growing edgy. Rather than being allowed to run a smoothly professional and dispassionate trial, he was being dragged into exactly the kind of circus he had been determined to avoid. His nerves were rubbed raw by Vacher's intransigence and the audience's disrespectful behavior, and he found himself drawn into unnecessary and nonsensical exchanges. Late in the day, Vacher seemed to have trouble understanding a question. "Can you repeat that?" he said. "I am so tired."

"So am I," said de Coston, "tired and disgusted at having been bathed in blood from the beginning of this day."

Vacher: "And whose fault is that?" It was the president, after all, who had directed this line of questioning.

Enough. Court was adjourned at 6:15 p.m. The spectators filed out and the correspondents rushed off to file their stories. The reporter from *Le Lyon Républicain,* openly siding with the prosecution, thought Vacher seemed "intimidated" by the court and by "this man in the red robe who spoke to him in a severe tone. He seemed a bit disoriented." Albert Bataille of *Le Figaro* skewered Vacher's outrageous behavior. Even those doctors "who are inclined to see the alienated everywhere were not duped by this monster," he wrote. "I wasn't either. I could see it in a single audience—and after all the nitpicking in the jousting with the president, my judgment is fixed." Bataille, like so many others who watched the performance, already had decided that Vacher was faking.

The second day began more calmly than the first. Vacher, still dressed in velour and his trademark white hat, entered without making any proclamations. He joked with the officers and offered autographs to soldiers and correspondents. Sidling up to Charbonnier, he examined his attorney's ermine robe, felt the fur, and assured him it was of very good quality but that he preferred rabbit fur. An even bigger crowd packed the courtroom, attracted by the gossip and news reports, with more women in attendance. When the proceedings began, Vacher offered to read another statement, but the president cut him off. He hoped to move briskly to the witnesses.

But first he needed to question the defendant about his professed insanity. He reviewed Vacher's dog-bite story and the other factors that Vacher said caused his mental alienation. Then he asked him about his contention that the sheer magnitude of his killing spree demonstrated insanity.

"You invoke the number of your crimes as proof of your irresponsibility," said de Coston.

"Of course," said Vacher. "I invoke their number and their atrocity. A person in a normal state would not be able to do that."

Then de Coston asked Vacher about his obsession with Joan of Arc. Vacher explained that one of his cell mates in Belley had loaned him a biography, "and I was struck by the resemblance of the missions between that young woman and me." The spectators began muttering. "Yes," Vacher insisted over the noise, "she was a great martyr like me, who came in another form and another time.... I love her like I love Christ, who was another great savior in his day."

De Coston continued: "According to medical experts, you are a simulator. Your two systems of defense are based, one, on the professed dog bite and, the other, on the professed providential mission. And yet, they don't go together."

"That's easy for you to say," replied Vacher, becoming agitated. "You don't know what I think or what I thought. But if you had seen me out there as a wild beast, when the sun was striking my poor head half to death, you would not say that I had my sanity, you monster." He shouted, "Yes . . . *monster!*"

The audience members started yelling their objections.

"The insults from a wretch like you cannot be allowed to enter this courtroom," said de Coston over the rising storm.

"Don't say that I'm a wretch! But if I am, it's your fault—yes, *you* as the representative of society!"

"We can't let you go on like that! We can't let you continue disturbing this courtroom!"

"Do what you want, you *misérable*! As for me, I am right before God, and I don't give a damn about what people think!"

De Coston threatened to have the defendant removed and to continue the trial without him. Charbonnier begged the court to be patient with his client. The man was agitated and needed some rest. He spoke quietly to Vacher and managed to calm him. It was ten in the morning.

The president spent the rest of the morning interviewing witnesses from Bénonces. Portalier's boss, Jacques Berger, told how Victor was a timid and gentle young man. Victor's young friend Jean-Marie Robin described how he had gone looking for Victor when his cows wandered down from the meadow, and then found his friend's eviscerated body. The country guardian, Joseph Marcel, testified about arriving at the meadow and summoning the gendarmes. Others placed Vacher in the area during the hours just before the killing. One woman described how Vacher came begging for milk on the day of the killing and became furious when she told him she did not have any. Vacher tried to turn her words against her. If only she had given him milk, he said, the crime might never have been committed. He explained that when the sun made him crazy, milk would sometimes calm him. The woman's lack of generosity made her equally as complicit in the murder as he was. Then a young shepherd named Alexandre Léger nervously testified about how Vacher had tried to lure him into the woods.

"Don't be afraid, my little one," said the president, motioning to Vacher. "He is well guarded."

Vacher rolled his eye grotesquely at the witness and yelled, "Look at me!"

"Do *not* try to intimidate this child," said the president.

"I'm not," said Vacher. "You're the one who is influencing him. What he's saying is false."

After the lunch break, Vacher returned quietly to his bench. He held up a hand-lettered sign: "Joseph Vacher, the great martyr of our turn-of-the-century society and instrument of divine will." He shook it at the press section to emphasize its importance.

As the spectators filed in, they left their sense of decorum outside. Perhaps it was a reaction to the horrifying testimony and the sensational newspaper coverage, or a collective unraveling from years of pent-up terror, but whatever the reason, there was more noise on this day than on the previous one, more jostling and gossiping—so much so that it became difficult to hear witnesses. People seemed barely under control. The pushing and shoving spilled into the press section, but the reporters were too busy gossiping to notice. The president called in the regiment to eject the miscreants, but after a brief lull, the ruckus began anew. "It was absolutely scandalous," wrote the *Petit Journal* correspondent. Many of the women, laughing and chatting, had elbowed their way to the front rows. At one point, a witness named Marcellin Bourdin described how, when they were adolescents, Vacher tried to anally rape him. The telling was so vivid, so coarse in its details, that several women fled the courtroom, their kerchiefs pressed to their faces. The president was unforgiving. "I'm sorry, mesdames, but you were warned. This is no place for you."

There were light moments as well, usually when a witness poked fun at the authorities, purposely or not. At one point, Charbonnier was questioning a witness who had gone to elementary school with Vacher.

"You were in class with him. Was he intelligent? Did he win prizes?"

"In our school everybody won prizes," said the witness, triggering laughter.

A Madame Declérieux had employed young Joseph Vacher as a home helper before he joined the Marist monastery. In her deposition, she had said that she'd been afraid to leave him alone with her children, and that she'd been glad when he finally left. But on the witness stand she became confused. When the president asked her whether her statement had been true, she said, "No, monsieur," and the audience started laughing.

"Maybe you did not understand my question," de Coston said, trying to be helpful. "What I said was, Were you glad when he left?"

"No, monsieur." The audience laughed heartily. Vacher guffawed with his mouth open and slapped himself repeatedly on his forehead, as if to pantomime the woman's feeblemindedness.

The day wore on, the testimony numbing. Of course there was no doubt that Vacher was the killer, but no one had clarified the key issue before the court: whether the defendant was legally responsible. Late in the day, several members of Vacher's former regiment approached the issue when they spoke about his irrational behavior. Vacher's former captain, Joseph Greihammer, testified that although Vacher had been regular and punctual with his service, his brutality toward his underlings inspired such concern that it was necessary to report him to the company commanders. A soldier named Louis Guiermet, who had been Vacher's sergeant when he entered the regiment, described how Vacher had attacked him with a razor, roaring like a beast. "It was a terrible cry, the likes of which I have never heard and which I will never forget."

"You are mistaken," said Vacher. "I didn't want to hurt you. I was furious at not having been named corporal and wanted to kill myself."

De Coston: "You wanted to kill yourself in the person of your sergeant?" Laughter.

"I maintain that I did not want to hurt you," Vacher said to the witness. "I respected you then, and still do to this day." Then, motioning to his former captain, he added, "I can't say the same about that one." More laughter.

The final and most dramatic witness of the day was Séraphin Plantier, whose battle with Vacher had led to Vacher's arrest. He recounted the attack on his wife and his wild brawl with the defendant. At the end of his testimony, the president thanked him in the name of the court. "You have done a great favor to society," he said.

"For me, too!" Vacher exclaimed. As the audience applauded Plantier, Vacher stood up and clapped the loudest of all, yelling, "Bravo! Bravo!"

"Except," he added, "it was a little too late." And then, tapping the shoulder of one of the guards, he said, "These are the guys who should have arrested me." The audience dissolved into hilarity yet again, and on that note the day's session concluded.

Twenty

Judgment

At the beginning of the third day of the trial, Vacher entered the court-room and held up two signs he had printed in red crayon:

"To my parents, poor victims of the mistakes of the asylums."

"I did not sleep one hour last night, but here I am, ready to fight."

This was to be the day of the doctors, the witnesses who might finally shed light on the question of Vacher's sanity. The bailiff called Dr. Lacas-sagne. He entered the courtroom with the gravitas of a man of his illus-trious reputation, wearing a long, dark jacket, a white shirt, and a black tie. "The doctor's outfit should always be dignified, as for a man practicing our strict profession," he once wrote. "You would recognize it as resem-bling that of professors of the faculty."

Lacassagne had given much thought to the appearance and conduct of doctors in court. Truth be told, not everyone gave medicolegal specialists the respect they deserved. There had been several mistaken judgments over the years that had damaged the young profession's credibility. In the United States, where the adversarial legal system made it customary for each side to hire its own authority, people saw medical experts as corrupt-ible quacks.

Lacassagne felt that in order to maintain the profession's credibility, the expert should take great care in how he presented himself. Several years earlier, he had published a lengthy journal letter to his students and col-leagues on exactly how they should appear and behave. Preparation was key: The doctor should never testify offhandedly, but should rigorously prepare by reading and rereading his report before the court date. He should study it so carefully that he would be able to discuss it conversa-tionally with the jury, without committing the "grave error" of reading every word or dwelling on every detail of the analysis. Therefore, he should make a broad but logical presentation, outlining his assignment,

listing the findings, and describing the reasoning that led him to his conclusions. He should use examples and illustrations along the way.

The manner of the expert's delivery was almost as important as the substance. It would be wrong "to seem passionate, and to come across like
an auxiliary prosecutor," wrote Lacassagne. The expert should "neither
plead nor accuse." It would be "pedantic and ridiculous. . . . to give a lesson to the jury on a scientific subject and speak to them as though they
were students." The doctor should use ordinary language and avoid tech-
nical expressions and jargon. "The members of the jury are good people
who need clarification, but who may not be current with scientific terms,"
he said. "One can be clear without being pedantic."

The medical expert should demonstrate "prudence, sangfroid, and
patience," he wrote. "You should never advance facts of which you are not
absolutely sure." When cross-examined by judges or lawyers, "before
responding, take time to reflect . . . take care to repeat the question to yourself, to prove that you have really understood it. Respond to all objections
with calm." He urged his colleagues to remember that lawyers "are only
exercising their profession. Don't blame them if they pose questions to us
that are embarrassing and entangling."

Lacassagne concluded that the medical expert must remain "cool and
calm," a model of impartiality whose scientific analysis would reveal the
objective truth. After all, it was the truth that should stay in the minds of
the jury, despite "the talented oratory of the prosecutor, or the irresistible
charm of the defense attorney." Properly presented, science alone would
provide the basis for determining innocence or guilt.

Lacassagne's demeanor exemplified those instructions as he entered the
courtroom—his dress sober, his stride confident, his gaze conveying
authority and intelligence. To the judge's questions, he responded clearly
and without arrogance; to the jury, he spoke simply and with respect. He
never raised his voice or became agitated or perturbed. He felt that he represented the cool light of science, and he wanted the jury to feel that, as
well. Evidently, he succeeded. According to the correspondent for *Le Lyon
Républicain*, "his deposition was made with great precision and organization and made a vivid impression on the listeners."

The boisterous crowd had gone quiet when Lacassagne was sworn in.
The bailiff handed each juror a copy of the sketches Lacassagne had com-
missioned to illustrate the crime scenes. No one recorded the jurors' reac-

tions, but one can assume they were horrified. When they recovered their composure, his testimony began.

Lacassagne described the role of the experts in this case, as well as his own job of analyzing Vacher's behavior during the years of the killing spree. He began his narrative with Vacher's release from the Saint-Robert asylum and described how he killed his first victim, Eugénie Delhomme. He described the forensic signs that portrayed the strangling, throat slitting, and mutilation of the body. "We found this characteristic in all the crimes that followed," he said. Then he guided the jury through the horrifying sketches, taking them through the subsequent crime scenes one by one. He described in detail the murder of Louise Marcel and that of Augustine Mortureux, whose shoes and earrings were stolen, and how Vacher used an umbrella to hide Mortureux's body. He continued with the murder of the widow Morand, then that of Victor Portalier, and described how the killer had used a razor to mutilate the boy's corpse. Each time, he explained how the physical evidence at the crime scene helped him recreate the killer's methods and state of mind.

Vacher, who had been sitting quietly for a time, now started shaking his fist at the doctor and trying to interrupt him by yelling, "Hou! Hou! Hou!"

Lacassagne moved on to the other crime scenes. He directed the jury's attention to the sketch of Marie Moussier, who was found murdered in September 1896. He pointed out the half-moon of hatch marks on the left side of her nose, which indicated the wound pattern left by the killer's teeth. No other cadaver exhibited those marks. The evidence showed that contrary to Vacher's claim that he always bit his victims, she was the only victim who actually was bitten. Lacassagne noted that in the case of Victor Portalier, the mutilations were carried out with a knife or a razor, "not with the teeth, as the accused would pretend."

"Hou! Hou! Hou!" hollered Vacher. "Wait a minute! Wait a minute while I respond! Hou! Hou!"

His yelping made a strange, rhythmic counterpoint to Lacassagne's calm analysis. Lacassagne led the jury through the sketches of the remaining crime scenes. The common elements were so clear, he said, that it was impossible not to notice the "systematic nature" of the killing spree. "Vacher chose the sex and the age of his victims." Gasps of horror rose from the audience. Lacassagne continued, explaining about blood patterns and the positions of wounds.

"Oh, that's very strong!" said Vacher.

Lacassagne ignored him. "Everything was thought out by Vacher," he continued. He explained that Vacher's system was so brutally efficient that "none of the victims could move once the attack began." After the murder, Vacher would disguise himself by changing his outfit and coiffure. He would put great distances between himself and the bodies, which he took care to hide "prudently" in the woods. In short, the crimes of Vacher "were not those of an alienated man, but of a sadistic, antisocial individual. He is responsible."

"He lies!" yelled Vacher. "Come on, that's false! Oh, my aching head!" He raised his arms in supplication to the sky and then poked his right cheek repeatedly, as if to emphasize the role of the bullet.

"The jury paid no attention to him," wrote the correspondent for *Le Lyon Républicain*. "They were captivated by the powerful reasoning of Dr. Lacassagne."

De Coston asked if Vacher bore any signs of degeneracy.

"Absolutely not. He carries no sign of hereditary damage. He is responsible."

The judge asked about the dog bite and the remedy. Lacassagne responded that it would not be possible for a dog bite, even a rabid one, to produce the kind of transformation Vacher alleged. "In any case, he was not bitten, but licked." He knew of no cases in which a folk remedy produced the alleged effect.

Vacher stood up with a big piece of paper, but the judge motioned for the guards to sit him back down.

Now the judge asked Lacassagne to explain sadism, which was an entirely new concept to the court. The doctor proceeded to give testimony that was so shocking that although newspapers alluded to his remarks, not a single one chose to recount them in detail. (Lacassagne later reproduced the substance of his testimony in a book.)

In 1892, Richard von Krafft-Ebing scandalized and titillated Europe with his study of deviant sexual behavior. Entitled *Psychopathia Sexualis*, it daringly explored the era's taboos. (It quickly sold out in numerous editions and was translated into several languages.) Among the many perversities Krafft-Ebing described was sadism, which he named after the Marquis de Sade, who had practiced and written about sexual cruelty at the turn of the previous century. According to Krafft-Ebing, the two strongest impulses in human beings were anger and the sexual urge, and it was not unusual for them to be interwoven. Often these impulses overlapped in mild, healthy ways—thus the playful wrestling of lovers and young married couples, he wrote. In certain individuals the anger component became overwhelming. Those people could achieve "the state of exaltation, an intense excitation of the entire psychomotor sphere," only by pairing or replacing the sexual act with acts of extreme cruelty.

Lacassagne explained that several varieties of sadists existed. There was the "imaginary sadist," who, although perverted, confined his sadistic deeds to his mind; then there was the "active sadist," who pinched or pricked women with pins. (Sadists were overwhelmingly male.) And there were "sanguinary sadists," who committed true horrors—either torturing their victims before and during sex or killing them and sexually mutilating their bodies. These included several well-known lust murderers: Gilles de Rais, the fifteenth-century killer of children; the still-at-large Jack the Ripper of London; Vincenzo Verzeni of Italy, convicted of attacking three women and suspected of killing and mutilating three more; or young Jesse Pomeroy of Boston, fifteen years old at the time of his sentencing, who killed three children and tortured several others. All employed similar methods—murder followed by the sexual gratification achieved by mutilating the corpse. Lacassagne noted that lust murders tended to be crimes of repetition. Each attack was "accomplished in the same circumstances, executed in the same way, and showed an identical operating procedure." Clearly, Vacher's crimes fit that pattern, said Lacassagne, which put him in the category of a "sanguinary sadist." Alienists did not consider sadists insane, he said, and neither should the court.

After an hour of speaking, Lacassagne stepped down. The effect of his testimony was "terrible for the accused," according to the reporter from *La Dépêche de Toulouse*.

Next, Lacassagne's colleague Dr. Fleury Rebatel took the stand. He testified about his study of Vacher's youth and family history, which indicated that the defendant was of sound body and mind. His shooting of Louise Barant might have demonstrated temporary insanity, but his time at the Saint-Robert asylum had cured him. Dr. Auguste Pierret, the third member of the study group, spoke of Vacher's "genuine preoccupation" with proving his insanity. "He kept saying words like 'the proof that I am irresponsible is . . .' Never does a real alienated person act that way. Vacher is a simulator, perfectly conscious of the responsibility that he incurred."

The last witness of the morning was Dr. Lannois, who with the aid of an X-ray, found that the bullet lodged in Vacher's ear canal did not press on any nerves that would cause cerebral problems or insanity.

The court was adjourned for lunch. The guards were leading Vacher to a holding cell when a woman burst from the crowd and threw herself upon him, hugging and sobbing. It was his sister Olympe. "Oh, my poor brother!" she cried. "It was Dr. Dufour who, by letting you free, is the cause of this dishonor to our family!" The guards pried her off and led him away.

With the court in recess, the correspondents dashed off to file their morning dispatches. Most agreed that whatever hope Vacher might have harbored had been obliterated by the medical experts' testimony. "The audience that just ended was by far the most important of the affair," *Le Lyon Républicain* said of the morning's proceedings. "It totally destroyed a system of defense in which Vacher pretended to be irresponsible for his acts, in which he said he was sick but not criminal. After the depositions of the experts there is nothing left of the defendant's assertions."

Still, a sliver of hope remained for Vacher. Two doctors who doubted his sanity were scheduled to testify that afternoon. When the court reconvened, the bailiff called Dr. Bozonet to the stand. It was Bozonet who had examined Vacher at the prison in Belley and opened the door to Dr. Madeuf, who had come from Paris to examine the prisoner. Questioned by the judge, Bozonet testified that his observations of the defendant led him to a conclusion of "diminished responsibility."

The president offered Bozonet little of the reverence he had shown for Lacassagne. He asked Bozonet how much time he had spent with the prisoner.

"Ten minutes," responded Bozonet.

"One single visit of ten minutes sufficed?"

"Perfectly."

"Really, I admire the competence and rapidity of judgment of certain people." Laughter arose from the audience.

Charbonnier interjected that Bozonet's diagnosis, rapid though it was, matched that of the director of the Dole asylum. De Coston seemed to pay no attention, but he badgered the doctor about how Madeuf had been able to enter the jail without official permission. After some back-and-forth, Charbonnier rose to object: Did all this really matter? Given that Fourquet freely allowed reporters and photographers access to the prisoner, did it matter that a man of science had entered uninvited?

The president cut him off. "That's an administrative question. Call Dr. Madeuf," he ordered the bailiff.

After Madeuf was sworn in, de Coston grilled him about his unauthorized entry. Madeuf said that Fourquet had told him that he had no objection to his visit as long as the prison doctor approved—which was the opposite of what Dr. Bozonet had said.

"Actually, you lied to the doctor," said de Coston, "and now you are lying again." He held up a deposition signed by Fourquet; it stated that he had surprised Madeuf inside the prison and that he immediately protested the unauthorized presence. "Now, what do you have to say?"

Madeuf said that none of this mattered compared with the good that came from his visit. After all, it was he, Madeuf, who had discovered the bullet in the defendant's ear.

"That's false!" asserted the president. Vacher had been complaining about the bullet ever since his days at the Dole asylum. Doctors there had proposed to remove it, but Vacher had not consented.

Madeuf argued that regardless of any procedural infraction, researchers should have access to criminals like Vacher. Madeuf, as an ear, nose, and throat specialist, was working on a theory that certain damage to the inner ear might somehow trigger insanity. "In my opinion, if one had removed the bullet from Vacher, one might have avoided all the crimes." Did the judge want to preside over another case like Menesclou's, when it was only after the autopsy that doctors realized the killer probably was insane? Did he want that kind of injustice on his hands?

"Enough!" commanded the judge. "Just respond to my questions."

Madeuf bemoaned the backward state of criminal science, explaining that his motive in sneaking in to examine the prisoner grew from a "hope to do service to French medicine." The issue was larger than this particular defendant. Studies like his might help prevent "the hatching of future Vachers."

It was a passionate argument and, in retrospect, an enlightened one, but the judge, the jury, and spectators showed no indication of taking it seriously. The audience sat mute as Madeuf left the witness stand. Only Vacher applauded.

As the day wore on, Vacher grew tired and dispirited. He listened to the remaining few witnesses with a distracted air, without gestures or clownish miming. At four o'clock, Ducher began his closing statement for the prosecution. With a solemn air and "grand gestures that seemed the result of studied preparation," he described Vacher as "probably the great-est criminal in history." He reminded the jury of the defendant's life story, from his early days as a malicious, violent child to his troubled adoles-cence and then his violent behavior in the regiment. Ducher spoke about the shooting of Louise and how afterward Vacher simulated insanity. On hearing her name, Vacher sprang to life. He took off his hat, balled it up, and reared back to throw it at Ducher. Instantly, the guards pounced. In the melee that followed, the rabbit-fur hat was ripped to shreds. "Now look what you've done!" wailed Vacher. The judge warned Vacher that if he did not calm down, he would tell the guards to shackle him in irons. "I'd rather you did that than rip up my hat," he cried.

Ducher continued with his summation. He reminded the jury of Vacher's time in the asylums, where, regardless of whether he was insane or merely faking, he was released with a document attesting to his cure. Ducher reviewed the circumstances of the Portalier murder. Then he recounted the rest of the killing spree and the experts' evaluation of the crimes. "All have the same characteristics, the mark of the monster," he said. "Each one required a sangfroid, and remarkable presence of mind in preparation and execution."

Ducher asserted that when Vacher originally confessed to Fourquet, he had hoped that the sheer number of his crimes would make a case for insanity. "But he could feel that the system was not succeeding," said Ducher. "So he retreated into absolute silence and set himself to simulat-ing insanity, but awkwardly, and with a visible lack of conviction."

Vacher was no lunatic, Ducher concluded, but a conscious, calculating predator "who spilled so much blood, and so many tears. You are his judges; you have seen all the examples. Then be without pity, members of the jury. His victims deserve it; you have that obligation to society. Ren-der the verdict that society requires without pity!" Ducher had spoken for an hour and a half.

The audience applauded long and enthusiastically, despite the presi-dent's attempts to silence them.

Now it was Charbonnier's turn. His sonorous voice, with its great ability to communicate emotion, "impressed everyone," according to reporters. Motioning to Vacher, he intoned, "This is not a great criminal, but a poor, sick man whom I have come to defend. If for three days we have been in an atmosphere of carnage and blood, we still do not have proof of his complete responsibility."

Like Ducher before him, Charbonnier reviewed Vacher's life history for the jury, but through a radically different lens. He said that many of the stories about the defendant's childhood had been exaggerated. Speaking of Vacher's time in the regiment, he noted that the defendant had been a "good soldier" who had risen in the ranks and received an honorable discharge. "How could this man so proud of his sergeant stripes . . . find himself in the status of a vagabond living off of charity? Does that not certainly indicate some aberrations of his sanity?"

Vacher listened, occasionally sobbing.

Charbonnier spoke about Vacher's rough treatment at the asylums, and cast doubt over whether the defendant had been cured. He questioned Dr. Dufour's decision to release him: Perhaps Dufour had been so busy with other matters at the asylum that he had not given sufficient attention to Vacher. "Was he cured?" Charbonnier said of the defendant. "How much do you know about that? Where's the proof?" Or could it be that once he was out of the asylum he experienced a relapse?

The attorney took the jury through each of the murders, pointing out places where one could find fault with the experts. True, "all the crimes he committed were done in an automatic fashion," but that indicated the behavior of an insane man rather than a rational one. He cautioned the jury that experts could make mistakes, even the redoubtable Dr. Lacassagne. He described an occasion in which an anthropological society had given Lacassagne a skull to examine, which he pronounced as that of a woman, whereas the skull actually had been that of an old man.

Then Charbonnier made an interesting argument. This trial involved the fifth crime in Vacher's killing spree, which had occurred a year and five months after his release from the Saint-Robert asylum. But what if he had been tried for his first crime—the murder of Eugénie Delhomme? That crime had occurred mere weeks after his discharge. Wouldn't that murder, so soon after Vacher's release, indicate that he had never been cured, that he was still alienated when he attacked her? And if he had been insane during that first killing, wouldn't he still have been insane for all those that followed?

This was not the first time that the question of timing had come up in an insanity trial. Eight years before, an inmate named James Dougherty escaped from the Flatbush asylum in Brooklyn, New York. Several weeks later, he returned and shot the director to death. When authorities tried him in criminal court, the Medico-Legal Society of New York objected.

They said it was absurd to consider an escaped lunatic sane enough for a trial, when several weeks earlier he had been officially alienated. "Had the homicide occurred while he was an inmate it seems incredible that he would have been tried at all," said an editorial in the society's journal. (The court sentenced him to life in an asylum.)

Meanwhile, European experts increasingly worried about how and when to declare an alienated person cured. More and more crimes seemed to be committed by former patients or escapees from asylums. One journal, *Les Annales médico-psychologiques* (The Annals of Medical Psychology), featured a monthly column highlighting the predations of "insane people on the loose" (*"aliénés en liberté"*). Professional societies conducted earnest debates about how to determine when a lunatic had been cured. In Britain, the one country with a prison for the criminally insane, the inmates were given an indeterminate sentence literally at the "pleasure of the Queen," which often meant perpetual confinement. In France, the United States, and many other countries, the individual asylum directors made the assessments, which, lacking firm benchmarks, often had dangerous consequences for society. Not only was Charbonnier's argument intriguing but it touched on some of the deepest anxieties of the era's medico-legal experts.

Charbonnier spoke for three and a half hours, impressing everyone with his intelligence and humanity. He called for the jury to rise above their natural instinct for vengeance and serve justice in a higher way. "I don't come to demand justice for one person, but for the honor of his family of fourteen brothers and sisters," he said. He implored jurors not to think, "This is a wild beast, we must dispose of it," but to temper their justice with understanding. "Vacher was insane, he still might be, and you have no right to suppress that fact in the interest of society." He begged the jurors not to apply the death sentence. Acknowledging their fears of releasing a homicidal maniac to the questionable security of the state-run asylum system, he asked them to sentence his client to a lifetime of forced labor in prison. He reminded the jurors that "the court is not an abattoir, but a place where human beings are judged." It was 9:00 p.m. by the time he sat down.

In the French trial system, juries do not decide the simple question of innocence or guilt, but receive a list of questions from the judge to consider.

Often this list can be rather long; not so in the Vacher case. De Coston asked the jury two simple questions: Did Vacher kill Victor Portalier on August 31, 1895? Did he commit the crime with premeditation?

In the end, Charbonnier's eloquence and appeal to the jurors' humanity was trumped by the horror of the crimes and the authority of the experts. Surely the visual impact of the forensic sketches must have played a role, as did the overriding ethos at the time that the legal system must first and foremost protect society. It took the jury only fifteen minutes to return with their answers: yes to the killing; yes to premeditation. As Ducher had asked, the jurors delivered a verdict without pity; or rather, they had reserved their pity for the victims. The judge turned to the defendant.

"What have you to say, Vacher?"

"Are you condemning me to death?"

"One has requested the death penalty for you."

"So be it," Vacher replied calmly. "I say: curses to those who would condemn me."

On hearing the news, the mob outside began cheering wildly, chanting "Death! Death!" and surging against the cordon of soldiers. Inside, the spectators applauded raucously. As Vacher was led from the courtroom, he turned to them and shouted, "Good-bye!"

A correspondent for *Le Petit Bourguignon* followed Vacher back to his cell. He reported that the convict sat down on his bench and, a few minutes later, asked for his dinner and heartily ate it. Then he lay down and started complaining about his hat. "Those bastards really fixed things for me, my poor hat! Of all the things they've done that's the one that really gets me, because I'm a little superstitious. . . . And then, my lawyer! He's a clever one to speak of the 'great principles of the Revolution'—it's not strong! He turned them against me for sure. It would have been better to speak about Jesus Christ. . . . Anyway, I don't give a damn, because I am condemned to death just like Him!" Then he rolled over. Moments later, the reporter could hear him rhythmically snoring.

Twenty-one

A Question of Sanity

Immediately after the verdict, Charbonnier started working on an appeal. He published a forty-five-page booklet outlining the flaws in the prosecutor's case as he saw them and sent it to the Justice Ministry. He also distributed it to the press. Charbonnier argued that the very premise of the trial was a sham. How could the judge try a man for a single homicide but admit selected evidence from ten others? Conversely, how could he have let ten murders go unexamined when the pattern of those murders, if carefully probed, could have shed light on the killer's mentality?

Charbonnier argued that even within the limited scope of the trial one could find evidence for Vacher's insanity. He reprinted the testimony of former comrades in the regiment who described Vacher as "manic, deranged," and "abnormal." "We took him for a madman," one former soldier had said. Charbonnier reprinted one of Vacher's letters to his friends. "Who would dare say, after reading this letter, that Vacher was sane?" He reprinted the medical report by Dr. Guillemin at the asylum in Dole, highlighting the conclusions that Vacher suffered "attacks of mental alienation" that made him "irresponsible for his acts." He devoted a section of his booklet to Dr. Dufour's report from the Saint-Robert asylum, which certified that Vacher was cured. Charbonnier argued that the report was erroneous in its foundation. He cited an affidavit from Dr. Dufour, which said that when he admitted Vacher, he had no idea of the severity of his illness, because the patient arrived with the sketchiest of medical records. Based on those documents and discussions with Vacher, Dufour concluded that the patient suffered from a depression brought about by his broken engagement; he was certainly not someone with homicidal tendencies. With no information about Vacher's past or his violent behavior at Dole, Dufour never realized how dangerous a man he had been dealing with. So when Vacher gave the *appearance* of rationality, it was enough for Dufour to order his release.

Having made his argument for Vacher's insanity, Charbonnier turned his attention to the medical experts, who he felt had acted less like scientists and more like hired guns. Going through the reports of Lacassagne and his colleagues, he found numerous places where they used prejudicial language, such as "vampire, cannibal, antisocial" and "anarchist." He attacked the core of Lacassagne's findings—that the methodical nature of Vacher's actions ruled out the possibility of insanity. But was that assertion scientifically true? Several years earlier, in fact, Lacassagne had made the *opposite* case. In 1888, a doctor named Lamotte faced prosecution for raping three of his child patients. The doctor was clearly mentally impaired: Among other symptoms, he could not remember the names of his own children, or do simple addition and subtraction. Despite his infirmity, the prosecution argued that the doctor was rational because he made appointments in advance with his victims—which indicated planning, which, in turn, indicated premeditation. When the jury found the doctor guilty and legally responsible, Lacassagne protested, arguing that even though certain insane people retained the ability to plan and to distinguish right from wrong, they were helpless to resist certain impulses. That, he said, rendered them insane and legally irresponsible. Charbonnier argued that according to that reasoning, Lacassagne should have found Vacher legally irresponsible, as well. Why had the medical expert exhibited so much understanding for Dr. Lamotte and so little for a vagabond like Vacher? No doubt because of the severity of the crimes. "It would seem that the experts, despite the gravity of their mission, let themselves be influenced by public opinion," he wrote. It was doubly absurd for the experts to contend that "Vacher did not kill in the manner of an insane person . . . as though it were perfectly ordinary for someone to cut throats, disembowel, and mutilate . . . without motive."

Charbonnier was not alone in his objections. Dr. Édouard Toulouse, medical director of the Villejuif asylum in Paris and a prominent opponent of capital punishment, wrote a letter supporting Charbonnier, stating, "It is absolutely necessary to pardon this insane man." Other alienists weighed in for the defense, including Dr. Lombroso, who classified Vacher as an epileptic, and Dr. Bonne, the current director of the Saint-Robert asylum. In the journal *Opinion médicale,* a Dr. Fourchon launched a broadside against the proceedings and Lacassagne, and he praised Dr. Madeuf for withstanding the judge's "veritable fury" by daring to contradict the experts' report.

Lacassagne did not respond to the criticism. He saw his role as that of a medical expert who presented the science and remained above the fray. But others did not hesitate to engage. Ducher warned the Justice Ministry in Paris not to be fooled by the defense's imprecations or by Vacher's theatrics:

> I have no trouble believing that Vacher never was insane, but has been feigning insanity since 1893 [after shooting Louise Barant]. In any case, I am convinced that when he committed the crime at Bénonces he was not acting under an irresistible compulsion, but in full consciousness, taking all possible precautions, and yielding to his sexual perversion with the goal of satisfying his abominable passions. Under these conditions I feel that Vacher deserves not the slightest indulgence and . . . should be executed.

The state prosecutor general, Moras, wrote a sixty-eight-page report minutely examining the evidence and offering not a sliver of tolerance for an insanity defense. De Coston sent a long and angry report to Paris, arguing that Vacher's simulated insanity "was apparent, both to experts and inexperienced observers alike." The killer's legal responsibility was "affirmed by three eminent experts, established in the course of the trial, made clear by the discussions, and correctly proclaimed by the verdict of the jury." De Coston pointed out that the issue had repercussions far beyond the courtroom. Vacher's killing spree had spread terror throughout the countryside, and "the atrocities that surpassed all human imagination call out for the supreme expiation. Public opinion would certainly rise up in indignation if it were otherwise."

On December 2, the appeals court in Paris found no legal irregularities in the trial and upheld the conviction. The case moved to the office of Félix Faure, president of the Republic, who had the power to grant clemency. Charbonnier bombarded Faure's office with reports and letters from supporting alienists. "Vacher is insane. That is the conviction of Dr. Toulouse and most of his colleagues," he insisted in one of his missives. "That is the opinion of all men who reflect on it."

Two days later, he wrote again to Faure, worried that his client's spirits had collapsed. Vacher, "who formerly would flood my office with correspondence, has completely stopped writing to me." Vacher's last communication had been a simple, terse telegram: "I am innocent. You are free to do what you have to do." Charbonnier continued: "Isn't this attitude strange on the part of the man who ought to be motivated by the instinct for self-preservation?"

Meanwhile, Dr. Madeuf had stayed true to his commitment to use science to prove his case. He contacted Vacher's brother and sister and asked for exclusive permission to autopsy their brother's brain in the event of his execution. Eager to protect the family's honor, they agreed. Furthermore, under the agreement, the three alienists who prepared the expert report on their brother could neither touch his body nor be present at the autopsy. If Madeuf could not prove Vacher's insanity during the man's lifetime, he would not abandon the effort after his death.

In mid-December, three officials in the Justice Ministry who gave advice on presidential pardons reviewed the Vacher case. There, in the tranquil halls of Paris, hundreds of miles away from the screaming mobs and traumatized villagers, they looked dispassionately at Charbonnier's documents, and saw merit. They concluded that the multiplicity and nature of the crimes "cast doubt on whether [Vacher] was in full possession of his mental faculties." Rather than impose the death penalty, they recommended a life sentence of forced labor. This recommendation was a strange compromise. While recognizing the defendant's insanity, it did not adhere to Article 64 of the French legal code, which stipulated that if the accused was insane at the time of the incident, a crime was not considered to have been committed. The panel was attempting to work around that provision: acknowledging the defendant's insanity while somehow protecting the citizens from its consequences.

The compromise could not work. President Faure knew that Vacher might escape, and should that occur, the public would demand not only Vacher's execution but, politically, his own. And so Faure, deciding to let justice "follow its course," declined to sign the recommendation. All avenues for appeal and clemency had closed. The execution was scheduled for December 31, 1898, in Bourg-en-Bresse. It would take place in a field a few blocks from the local courthouse, where the regiment had traditionally drilled.

Louis-Antoine-Stanislas Deibler was never popular with the French public, although no one would have doubted his necessity. As the country's
executioner in chief, he rid society of some if its most dangerous elements.
In the course of a forty-five-year career, Deibler dispatched more than
150 miscreants, nearly 80 in partnership with his son, who eventually succeeded him. He decapitated murderers such as Michel Eyraud, the mas-
termind of the case of the bloody trunk, and Victor Prévost, a policeman
who killed a jeweler and his wife and was caught stuffing their body parts
down a sewer. Deibler dropped the blade on the era's most dangerous ter-
rorists, too. Yet the public never found him particularly *artistic*. He cut
a dour figure with his beard, top hat, old-fashioned overcoat, and ever-
present umbrella. Also, he was clumsy and slow. During his first appearance as chief executioner, Deibler created a maladroit impression. The
convicted man struggled violently—so much so that Deibler had no
choice but to grab him by the hair, bash his head repeatedly against the
ground, and then position the stunned prisoner in the apparatus. After
that, Deibler never could shake the image of seeming gauche.

In 1897, at the age of seventy-four, Deibler was performing a routine *guillotinage,* but on a criminal who had been positioned in such a
way that when the blade fell, the man's blood showered the executioner's
face. Deibler was never the same after that. He developed a phobia
of blood, and would wash his hands compulsively, trying to remove the
imaginary stains. He retired in December 1897. But Vacher was so important that the government called Deibler back for the last execution of his
career.

To some degree, Deibler's unpopularity reflected a growing distaste for
capital punishment, as social scientists questioned the moral effects of public executions and as the seeds of an abolitionist movement were sprout-
ing. Execution—once employed for crimes as diverse as political agitation,
theft, and derailing a train—was now rarely prescribed, and often waived
for extenuating circumstances. The number of executions declined from
more than seventy per year in the early part of the century to no more
than four or five annually by the time of Vacher's trial. However, the practice still enjoyed wide support.

Even within the pro-execution majority, though, people searched for
ways to make the punishment more humane. Certainly the guillotine was
sure and swift, but did it cause even a moment of suffering? Witnesses
had observed twitching in the faces of decapitated criminals, suggesting

that the brain retained enough neural activity to give the executed person a brief awareness of his or her fate.* Subsequent experiments with laboratory animals showed that the movements were nothing more than residual reflexes and bore no relation to consciousness or pain.

Meanwhile, a new device appeared in the United States that promised to bring capital punishment into the modern era. In 1886, after a series of botched hangings in New York, the state's governor convened a commission to choose a more compassionate form of execution. At the time, Thomas Edison and George Westinghouse were marketing competing systems to distribute electricity: Edison's used direct current (DC) and Westinghouse's used alternating current (AC). Eager to portray Westinghouse's system as dangerous, Edison embarked on a campaign of publicizing AC-related deaths. An engineer from New York learned about the demonstrations and began working out of Edison's lab to develop an efficient method for capital punishment. The result was a heavy wooden chair with electrical contacts positioned at the head and at the small of the back, designed to send more than a thousand volts of AC current through the body.

The first electrocution took place on August 6, 1890, at New York's Auburn prison, where William Kemmler was executed for murdering his mistress. It required two 1,300-volt shocks over several minutes to complete, the sight of which sickened observers. A year later, four murderers were put to death more efficiently at New York's Sing Sing prison, and electrocution soon became de rigueur in the United States.

Europeans shied away from this new American technology. Henri Coutagne, a colleague of Lacassagne, worried that the effects of the device were so undramatic—a spastic stiffening of the body—that it would not discourage potential murderers. Lombroso thought it cruel to make a prisoner wait in terror during the minutes it took to adjust and test the straps and electrodes. He proposed instead an overdose of chloroform or ether, "producing asphyxiation in the course of long and pleasant hallucinations." The chaplain of La Roquette prison in Paris thought the very idea of electrocution appalling. Where was the simple purity in walking with the condemned man to the guillotine, hearing his prayers and final con-

---

* Witnesses claimed that the severed head of Charlotte Corday blushed in indignation when the executioner's assistant held it by the hair in front of the jeering mob and smacked it. ("Revue des livres: La Mort par la décapitation," *Annales d'hygiène publique et de médecine légale* 3d ser., no. 2 [1889]: 187.)

fessions, knowing the final moment would be quick? What manner of comfort could he offer the prisoner during those long minutes of being strapped to a chair?

> Electric execution is odious, and revolts me. I would never acknowledge that one could kill individuals, even criminals, like poor animals that were placed in a bell jar to be killed with an electric spark. It is against the laws of humanity and religion. One cannot refuse a man his final moments to collect himself before death.

Lacassagne, who found the technology intriguing, wrote an analysis in which he reviewed all five of the American executions to date, along with the voltages, contact times, and postmortem studies. He noted that the first execution took not one shock, but two, and that rabbits electrocuted in the lab could sometimes be revived with artificial respiration. He concluded that although electrocution seemed a promising technology, it might not be as foolproof as the Americans would like to think. And so the guillotine remained the instrument of choice.

December 31, 1898, in Bourg-en-Bresse was not the kind of day one would want to wake up to, especially if it was one's last day on Earth: dismal and cold, with heavy gray clouds and bone-chilling sleet. But the weather did not discourage thousands from gathering at the Champs de Mars, site of the execution. Hours before dawn, Deibler and his team had begun setting up the guillotine in flickering lantern light.

Executions attracted the worst kind of crowds. For years, lawmakers had tried to get the Justice Ministry to move all executions inside the prisons, but they were overruled by those who felt that public executions set an example. Still, lawmakers managed to persuade officials to stop advertising the events and to schedule them at short notice and inconvenient times.

Nonetheless, an estimated 3,500 spectators packed the two-hundred-meter-long square. People had been waiting shoulder-to-shoulder. So many had climbed the chestnut trees to watch that reporters compared them to clusters of fruit. Ladders poked up here and there in the crowd, and public benches had been piled into pyramids. As always at such events—inexplicably—the women had forced their way to the front.

There was a usual ugliness to the crowd, a nastiness that reeked of barbarity. "The spectacle of the crowd teaming around the guillotine is sad and depressing!" wrote Alexandre Bérard, a public official in the department of Ain, who had attended executions as part of his official functions. He hated those spectators, who evoked in him and his fellow officials "feelings of disgust":

> Capital execution, the supreme act of human justice, should be surrounded by a religious respect. But for the mob it is nothing but a thrilling spectacle, an occasion to demonstrate their vile appetite for blood. Surrounding the guillotine . . . prostitutes, pimps, con artists . . . those who have no moral sense and are drawn by an unseemly curiosity. For them, this is an occasion for a monstrous Saturnalia . . . an orgy [with] the most horrible and base instincts of the raging beast.

At 6:15 a.m., Louis Ducher and three other officials entered the cell where Vacher was sleeping. Ducher touched his shoulder. "Your appeal and request for pardon have been rejected," he said. "Get up and be quick about it."

Vacher awoke. "Okay, I am ready," he said. "Do with me what you will." He got up, dressed, and went to wash up. "Why did they make me leave the asylum before my complete cure?" he complained. The prison chaplain approached him with a crucifix. "Vacher, you have always shown religious sentiments. Would you like to reconcile yourself with God and accept the succor of religion?" Vacher reflected a moment but refused. "I am innocent and have no need of Christ. Death does not scare me. Soon I will meet God, and He will say mass for me."

He declined the traditional drink of rum. Then he walked to the room where Anatole Deibler, the chief executioner's son, was waiting to ritualistically cut off his shirt collar and trim the hair on the back of his neck. "I should have gotten a haircut yesterday," Vacher joked.

As they walked him through the prison door, he proclaimed to some people waiting there, "Here comes the victim of the mistakes of the asylums!"

Deibler's son and another assistant led Vacher onto the waiting buckboard. The procession clip-clopped through the cobblestone streets—Vacher lying bound in the wagon, Deibler leading the horse, the priest walking and muttering prayers, and two dozen mounted police riding in security columns alongside. Vacher asked if he could address the crowd when they arrived at the square. Deibler, against protocol, agreed. The priest offered the crucifix to Vacher, who refused to kiss it, saying, "It's useless." When the priest again tried to exhort him with prayers, Vacher told him to be quiet so he could concentrate on preparing his remarks.

Soon the narrow byway opened onto the expanse of the square. "There he is!" someone yelled out, and the crowd roared at the sight. "Death! Death to Vacher! Death to the criminal!" As Vacher approached the guillotine, the energy suddenly drained from him. Turning to the young Deibler, he said, "You know that I absolutely refuse to walk. I will not resist, but you're going to have to carry me." In that case, said Deibler, he would not allow Vacher to address the crowd. "So be it," said the prisoner. "Too bad for society."

Those were the final words of Joseph Vacher.

A cordon of soldiers had been surrounding the guillotine, watching Deibler and his assistants. They made an opening to allow the wagon through and then turned to face the mob. Vacher, now limp, seemed to lose track of his circumstances. The priest pressed the crucifix against his lips; he did not resist, nor did he kiss it. The aides hoisted Vacher out of the wagon and carried him to the death machine. He made an ungainly parcel, with his feet in the air and his head near the ground. They placed him on the hinged bench, the *bascule*, near the base of the guillotine and tipped it down to its horizontal position. Vacher was groaning like an animal whose leg had been caught in a trap. "The coward!" roared some people in the crowd. "He does not know how to die properly!" The executioners lowered the *lunette*, the wooden bracket that holds the prisoner's head in position. At exactly 7:03, Deibler senior pulled a handle. There was a swoosh and a thunk; and the mob, which had never stopped screaming, burst forth with an even wilder, unanimous "Bravo! Bravo!" Slowly, they dispersed, excitedly chattering about Deibler's farewell performance.

Vacher's body and head were taken to the local hospital. Madeuf was in charge now. He barred the three doctors who had prepared the expert report but permitted them to send representatives. (Lacassagne sent Dr. Jean Boyer, who had performed the autopsy on Pierre Laurent and had done the study of the bones in the well.) Despite being excluded, Lacassagne was more confident than ever of his conclusions—borne out, he asserted, by Vacher's final moments. "He did not die like an insane person, with a haughtiness of the mystic or the dignity of an individual who thinks himself a martyr," wrote Lacassagne, quoting a newspaper account. Like any normal person, Vacher was overcome by terror as he approached the guillotine. His very cowardice in the end demonstrated his sanity to Lacassagne.

Over the next three and a half hours, the doctors carefully dissected the body. The heart and lungs were vigorous and strong. The stomach was empty, the digestive track clean. The reproductive organs showed evidence of venereal disease: The right testicle was almost completely atrophied and the left showed signs of an old operation. That would explain why, although Boyer had noted what appeared to be semen stains on the pants of Pierre Laurent, his microscopic exam found no spermatozoa. The killer of little shepherds must have been sterile.*

Then the doctors turned their attention to the brain. A photographer made images and a craftsman made plaster casts. The doctors announced that the brain weighed a "normal" fifteen hundred grams and, to the naked eye at least, showed no abnormal adhesions or lesions. Commenting on the findings, *Le Petit Journal* concluded that the debate about Vacher's sanity effectively had ended. "The jurors of Ain can sleep without fear [knowing that] their verdict fell on a criminal and not an insane man."

But the debate was not over. That night, Madeuf boarded the train for Paris, carrying a sealed cooking pot covered with official seals and stamps. In it was the head of Joseph Vacher.

---

* Based on the autopsy, Vacher probably had advanced syphilis and advanced gonorrhea, which would have rendered him sterile.

Part Three

Aftermath

The story of this criminal, this series of heinous crimes, will always be noted as among the most astonishing examples of human perversity.

—Dr. Alexandre Lacassagne, 1899

Twenty-two

The Mystery of a Murderer's Brain

The arrest, conviction, and execution of Vacher brought little closure. After his confessions, reporters had traveled to the villages where the killer had struck to hear people's reactions to the news. The journalists were especially keen to visit places where innocent citizens had been accused of the murders. Would their neighbors apologize?

Jules Besse visited the area in southern France where thirteen-year-old Louise Marcel had been dragged into a sheep barn and slaughtered. The man who found the body, Charles Roux, had been falsely accused and imprisoned, after which his community shunned him. The trauma had broken the health of Louise's mother. Besse reported that a neighbor tried to give her the news of the execution as she lay on her deathbed. She interrupted him, crying, "Have you come to tell me that they're going to cut off the head of this criminal Charlot [Charles Roux]?"

The neighbor tried to explain that Roux had not committed the murder; a man named Joseph Vacher had confessed.

"Who is this Vacher?"

"A drifter," he said.

The poor lady raised herself out of bed and began to laugh like a madwoman. "Ah! Ah! Vacher! A drifter! Ah! Ah! It's Charlot, Charlot, Charlot! . . . Bring me this brigand, this butcher of children!"

"But I assure you, mother Marcel, it was Vacher," the neighbor said. "He confessed; he recounted it all!"

"Charlot must have paid you to say that. . . . Shut up! . . . Get out! Charlot was the assassin; leave me in peace."

For his part, Charles Roux wrote to Fourquet that although he could "breathe more freely" since the confession, many of his neighbors still treated him warily. "I will never forget what they did to me," he wrote.

Things had improved slightly for Bernardin Bannier, the stolid, gruff farmer who had been falsely accused of murdering the shepherd Pierre Massot-Pellet in the hills of the Ardèche and whose house had been mobbed and stoned by his neighbors. Shortly after Vacher's confession, Albert Sarraut of *La Dépêche de Toulouse* visited the town. The mayor told him that things had gotten calmer since the real killer confessed, but "the hate persists nonetheless. . . . [Bannier's] enemies will not leave him alone. Even if one would have brought Vacher here to re-create the crime, they will settle for nothing less than the departure of Bannier."

Fourquet wished he could have taken Vacher to all the villages where the murders had occurred. He had to settle for exchanging letters with the falsely accused and local officials, assuring them that the real killer had been found.

Besse visited the village of Étaules, near Dijon, where Augustine Mortureux had been killed as she walked through the Bois du Chêne. The townspeople and the unscrupulous local journalists who had scapegoated Eugène Grenier had eventually forced him to move to another village. Besse found Grenier's country house abandoned and vandalized. He tracked down Augustine's mother, sisters, and father and exhausted his patience trying to convince them that Vacher was the killer. "One knows what one knows," a married sister proclaimed. The mother gave a long monologue about the horror of losing her daughter and how she'd gladly sacrifice her own head if it meant that Grenier would face the guillotine. As Besse departed, she kept shouting, "Don't try to confuse us! Vacher had nothing to do with it! It was Grenier!"

Grenier, who had moved to his wife's village about twenty-five miles away, told Besse he had obtained a small measure of retribution when the editors of *Le Bourguignon Salé* retracted their stories and profusely apologized. The competing paper, *Le Bien Public,* refused to do likewise, until Grenier went to their offices and showed them the newspapers from Lyon announcing Vacher's confessions. Only then did they publish a tiny article about Vacher, buried almost invisibly on page three. "When I tell people my story, they are so astonished they think I invented it," said Grenier. "But no! It is real! My wrinkled forehead and white hair bear witness."

On arriving in Paris, Madeuf gave the left half of Vacher's brain to Dr. Édouard Toulouse at the Villejuif asylum.* With his known opposition to capital punishment and support of Charbonnier's appeal, Toulouse decided that in the interest of objectivity he would divide the brain into several parts and distribute each to a man with a particular expertise. He gave one piece to Dr. Jean-Baptiste Vincent Laborde, head of physiology in the Faculty of Medicine in Paris. He shared his portion with Dr. Léonce Manouvrier, a professor in the school of anthropology in Paris. Toulouse also gave tissue samples to several other anatomists in Paris for them to conduct microscopic exams. He sent a photo of the brain and some tissue to Lombroso, who had been pestering him with requests. Altogether, at least half a dozen scientists possessed pieces of the brain. Each would produce a study that would be united into a definitive report.

Their research reflected a fascination with the structure and function of the human brain in the late nineteenth century. Propelled in large measure by Paul Broca's discovery of the organ's speech center and the famous case of Phineas Gage,† scientists were learning that discrete parts of the brain controlled various functions. Criminologists wondered whether some portion of the brain might promote or inhibit violent behavior. In many countries, it became a matter of course to dissect the brains of executed criminals. In the United States, for example, surgeons dissected the brains of Charles Guiteau, who assassinated President Garfield, and Leon Czolgosz, who killed President McKinley. Guiteau's brain was found to be riddled with lesions, while that of Czolgosz showed "no evidence whatever of disease or deformity." (Both men were hanged.) In Vienna, neurologist Moritz Benedikt dissected scores of brains of criminals and noncriminals in an attempt to find the anatomical seat of the conscience. Doctors in France autopsied every criminal brain they could get hold of, providing that the criminal or next of kin gave permission. Lacassagne abhorred the

---

* In 1896, Toulouse gained widespread attention when he conducted a lengthy psychological study of Émile Zola, with his cooperation. The study described the famously combative and neurotic author as a "high functioning neuropath." Like many papers at the time, it pointed out the fine line between insanity and genius and in no way diminished Zola's reputation. (Henri Mitterand, *Zola: L'Honneur, 1893–1902*, vol. 3 [Paris: Fayard, 2002], pp. 228–246.)

† In 1848, Gage, a railroad worker, survived a massive brain injury when an iron rod penetrated his skull. The rod destroyed part of the frontal lobe of his brain, after which his personality changed from dependable and respectful to unstable and surly.

legal provision. He felt that condemned murderers should have no choice in the matter—cerebral autopsies would be useful to science and would serve as a further discouragement to criminals.

The most sought-after brains were those of intellectuals, which were rare and difficult to obtain. In 1876, a colleague of Broca at the Society of Anthropology in Paris tried to ameliorate the situation by organizing a group called the Mutual Autopsy Society—a circle of colleagues who pledged to dissect one another's brains after they died.* Its members included many of the era's great intellectuals, including the anthropologist Paul Topinard, Laborde, and three members of the Bertillon family— Alphonse, his father, and his brother. Broca took part in several of the society's dissections and donated his own brain to the group when he died. One of the most prominent members was Léon Gambetta, a statesman revered for his oratorical abilities. After observing the dissection of Gambetta's brain, Laborde declared that Gambetta's speech center was "the most developed and most complete that had ever been witnessed."

It was no surprise, then, that so many interested parties wanted a piece of Vacher's brain: Its tissue might hold the secrets that would explain one of the century's most notorious killers. Madeuf and other opponents of capital punishment also had a political motive. They hoped that finding lesions or deformities would discredit Lacassagne's report and prove that, just as with Menesclou, a man with brain damage had been unjustly put to death. Yet given all the manhandling Vacher's brain had endured during the examination to date, it is hard to imagine what these scientists expected to discover. Dr. Boyer, of Lacassagne's laboratory, who had taken part in the original autopsy, said the only thing the new studies would prove would be the folly of the microscopic exams.

Boyer's reservations notwithstanding, the press eagerly anticipated the studies. On January 3, *Le Petit Journal* leaked the titillating news that Toulouse had found certain "adherences" on the brain. Several days later, the newspaper came out with a contradictory report, saying that Manouvrier had found neither lesions nor depressions and that he believed

---

* The French were not alone in their fascination with the brains of intellectuals. Later in the century, the American Anthropometric Society and the Cornell Brain Association began "securing elite brains for scientific study." By 1906, they had collected more than seventy. (Edward Anthony Spitzka, "A Study of the Brains of Six Eminent Scientists and Scholars Belonging to the American Anthropometric Society, Together with a Description of the Skull of Prof. E. D. Cope," *Transactions of the American Philosophical Society* 21, no. 4 [1907], p. 175.)

in the killer's "complete responsibility." Laborde, meanwhile, promised that his group would provide some definitive answers in the next several weeks.

In early 1899, Lacassagne published a book entitled *Vacher l'éventreur et les crimes sadiques* (Vacher the Ripper and Sadistic Crimes), which told the story of Vacher's killings and his capture and reviewed the evidence that had persuaded Lacassagne that Vacher was only faking insanity. The book included Lacassagne's pen-and-ink sketches of the crime scenes. Even those simple drawings have the power to shock, and they impress the reader with their repetitive similarity. Lacassagne included writings from other authors on vagabonds and sadism, as well as an eyewitness account of Vacher's execution.

The book received laudatory reviews in the scientific and legal communities, but some colleagues, while admiring it, also expressed doubts. "Your work on Vacher is very profound and seems—at first reading—quite prudent," wrote the jurist, sociologist, and philosopher Gabriel Tarde, a friend of Lacassagne. "But I find myself on the fence on this problem of mental alienation." Dr. Paul-Louis Ladame, a neurologist at the University of Geneva, wrote a letter to Lacassagne in which he called the study "a classic." Ladame opposed the death penalty, but he admitted that, given the evidence, "it was impossible for you to pronounce anything other than what you found." Still, he pondered the question of sanity and free will: If someone seemed genuinely programmed to kill, could he still be called legally responsible? By means of analogy, he asked, "Are tigers responsible?"

On June 15, 1899, Laborde and his collaborators published the first in their collection of reports, which found no significant abnormalities. In one study, Manouvrier noted that Vacher's brain actually was "slightly larger than average," although he ascribed no particular importance to that observation. He noted the complexity of the folds, which gave the impression of "rather elevated organization." Overall, though, his findings were "negative" for pathology.

Laborde, too, found "no alterations characteristic of disease"; on the contrary, he found that certain brain areas seemed highly developed. The speech region, or Broca's area (located under the left temple, about two inches behind the eye), actually seemed larger and more convoluted than normal. Apparently mistaking Vacher's incoherent ramblings for eloquence, he linked the murderer's speech centers to an elevated verbal capacity. Laborde also found a highly developed motor center of the brain, which he linked to Vacher's ability to walk long distances.*

Lombroso, who had been hard at work microscopically examining his tissue samples, weighed in with a study that predictably classified Vacher as a born criminal. He announced that he found an atrophy of certain layers of the frontal lobe (the most "evolved" part of the brain, behind the forehead) and an unusual proliferation of microscopic pyramidal cells, which were thought to play a role in excitation. Such findings, he asserted, were characteristic of "epileptics and born criminals." The French were dismissive. "What a phony!" wrote Manouvrier after reading Lombroso's article in *La Revue scientifique*. The commentary would have a "stupefying effect if we didn't already know the value of his affirmations." A French journalist wrote, "But everyone knows that Lombroso sees born criminals everywhere."

By late July, scientists were getting no closer to consensus. Toulouse and his team released a full version of their study, which only added to the growing confusion. Despite the "adherences" they originally reported, they now found the brain to be relatively normal, despite a couple of unexpected anomalies. One of these was a thickening of the meninges, the membranes between the brain and the skull, often seen in the brain of syphilitics. Another was the proliferation of amyloid corpuscles—tiny starchy bodies commonly found in the brains of the elderly but almost never in someone Vacher's age. The killer seemed to have the brain of an old man.† One writer quipped that perhaps it was the brain of a *dirty* old man. "But one can be a dirty old man, even in a young skin, without feeling the need to eviscerate young people by the dozen."

As the discussions moved forward, the arguments became more convoluted, the passions more heated, and the public less patient with what the scientists had to say—especially since no lesions or deformities had been found in Vacher's brain. Toulouse had voiced doubts from the beginning about finding such abnormalities. He had spent years working with

---

* Although a highly developed speech center can be correlated to eloquence, the brain's motor area deals only with fine motor control. Vacher's long-distance walks were strictly a product of cardiovascular fitness.

† Actually, he might have had the brain of a syphilitic. As a teenager, Vacher had contracted syphilis, which creates a thickening of the meninges when it reaches its advanced stage. At that stage, the disease can lead to seizures, dementia, and other signs of brain damage.

patients at the asylum, many of whom died in confinement. None of their brains had revealed any lesions or deformities: Why should Vacher's be any different?

Laborde, on the other hand, had reversed his original premise to continue to make the case against capital punishment. He asserted that the lack of any lesions did not demonstrate the *absence* of insanity; it proved only that Vacher's madness arose from *invisible, functional* causes. Brain structure did not matter anymore; it was the killer's *history* and *symptoms* that proved derangement. The fact that Vacher's crimes were premeditated and systematic "does not take away from their fundamentally delusional character," he wrote. The man was insane, and rather than being sent to the guillotine, he should have been imprisoned for life, with no possibility of release. Since no suitable facility existed in France, the government could set up a colony for people like Vacher, perhaps in "a little corner of Devil's Island." Then Laborde took a swipe at Lacassagne, asserting that the professor and his colleagues would have concluded the same had they not been so influenced by "popular opinion" and the "multiplicity and horrible nature" of the crimes.

On March 20, 1900, Laborde presented an updated version of his report to the Academy of Medicine in Paris. Once again, he cast doubt on Lacassagne's ability to remain objective in such a highly fraught case. He returned to his discussion of Vacher's advanced speech centers. And then, perhaps caught up in his own soaring rhetoric, Laborde took his arguments too far. In making his point about Vacher's speech centers, he compared them to those of Léon Gambetta, who, in addition to his other distinctions, happened to have been a boyhood friend of Lacassagne. Indeed, under different circumstances, argued Laborde, Vacher could have become a statesman or orator.

With the use of that comparison, the conference erupted. Was Laborde really suggesting that a sexually depraved murderer had something in common with a founding member of the modern French Republic? The very idea insulted the other members, and threatened the credibility of the profession. Laborde had never seen Vacher or heard his rants about being an anarchist of God; how could he make such an outrageous comparison? "His argument is weak, logorrheic, and shows that he knows absolutely nothing," declared Dr. Auguste Motet, to loud applause. Manouvrier, who had seen the brains of both Vacher and Gambetta, previously had stated that the two organs had nothing in common. "I said that one could discuss the question of mental alienation indefinitely [and not] arrive at a scientific solution," he wrote to Lacassagne. As for his own feelings about Vacher's legal responsibility: "I see no reason to pit myself against the competent opinion of the experts who were there and could examine the case with their own eyes."

People were gearing up for a battle. "I think Laborde has gotten in over his head in this affair," Dr. Paul Dubuisson wrote to Lacassagne the day after the meeting. "When are you coming to Paris to defend yourself against Laborde? Let me know soon so I can help in your fight."

Motet wrote to Lacassagne, describing his confrontation with Laborde and the applause he'd received when he defended the professor. "I energetically protested . . . that [your] expertise was conducted with all prudence, with all science, and with all the conscientiousness that you bring to every affair that you take part in. . . . My dear friend, is that enough to avenge you regarding these grotesque incidents surrounding the examination of the brain of Vacher?"

Alphonse Bertillon wrote to Lacassagne that "affairs of this type" only served to make cerebral autopsies "forever seem ridiculous" and tarnished the public image of their profession. "I think Laborde missed an excellent opportunity to shut up."

There is no record of how Lacassagne responded. Perhaps with his expert testimony and his book, he felt he had written everything he needed to say about the affair. Or maybe he sensed that the public had tired of the matter. The monster was dead, citizens were safe, and it was time to move on. The popular press lost interest, as well. Indeed, if the press of the day portrayed public sentiment, people saw this kind of endless discussion as sophistry typical of the intelligentsia. The newspaper L'Écho de Paris reflected that view with a satirical column lampooning both alienists and jurists. It was no accident that the dunce cap passed so effortlessly from one expert to the other:

MAGISTRATE: *Eh bien,* my dear sir, have you examined the brain of Vacher?
DOCTOR: I know it like the inside of my own pocket.
MAGISTRATE: What is the result of this study?
DOCTOR: I will publish it in several days.
MAGISTRATE: In the meantime, just give me the headlines.
DOCTOR: You will see it in my review. That way you will understand it better.

MAGISTRATE: Will I be upset to know who it is that we have condemned to death?

DOCTOR: . . . You condemned someone to death without really knowing?

MAGISTRATE: I just need to know whether we condemned a wretch capable of all these crimes, or a lunatic, a simple lunatic.

DOCTOR: Maybe you should have learned that first!

MAGISTRATE: First it was important to avenge society. . . . Now that society has been avenged, these little scientific discussions become more interesting. And they can help us for the next time. . . .[So], yes or no, have we guillotined an insane man?

DOCTOR (coolly): No.

MAGISTRATE: Good! Because I have to say, that was bothering me a bit.

DOCTOR (exploding): No, Monsieur Magistrate, you did not cut off the head of an insane man! . . . You cut off the head of something better than that. . . . You cut off the head of a child, a veritable baby; a creature less responsible for his acts than a two-year-old, a man incapable of even killing a fly. That's what was clearly revealed by the brain of Vacher, sir!

MAGISTRATE (stunned): Nevertheless, he was the killer of shepherds . . . that is undeniable!

DOCTOR: Yes, he might have disemboweled some shepherds . . . the examination of his brain does not say that he did not . . . but [it also] indicates as clear as day that he would not have been capable of doing any harm to a fly sitting on the head of one of those shepherds.

Paul Brouardel, by then an elder scientific statesman and the recently elected president of the French Association for the Advancement of Sciences, knew that continued argument would be damaging. He urged his colleagues to de-escalate. "Laborde's intervention is very annoying," he conceded, yet to continue any further debate "would only reflect badly on us all."

In truth, they could have argued indefinitely. The mystery of what had motivated Vacher could no more be solved by dissecting his brain than it had been by interviewing him during his lifetime. Lacassagne had spent months trying to penetrate the man's thinking. Failing to make any headway with discussion, he turned to the physical evidence from the crime scenes. There he found a pattern: a systematic ability to plan; the work of a criminal who, despite the "rage" that overtook him, was conscious of his actions and stood the test of legal responsibility. One might argue that however methodical, Vacher nonetheless acted under a compulsion; or that perhaps he was only intermittently sane, as his encounters with the country's mental health institutions would suggest. Yet given the laxity of the country's asylums, Lacassagne felt that he must not err on the side of the defendant; there simply was no secure place to imprison him. The scientist retreated; the protector stepped forward . . . and so to the guillotine. Yet even Lacassagne seemed to worry if his analysis, although legally justified, was morally correct. "We are convinced at having told the truth, the whole truth, and nothing but the truth," he wrote somewhat defensively. "After having been made aware of our efforts we hope one would come to agree that if we were mistaken, it was certainly in good faith.

"It is over," he concluded. "We put down the pen and leave this long work like a nightmare; that is to say, discouraged and exhausted."

It had been a long journey, not only for Lacassagne but for the endeavor he represented. Through the centuries, his profession had come through dark times of trial by fire and of persecution through rumor and torture to a time when scientists first began to analyze evidence—and now to this golden age of forensic discovery. Science had become part of detective work, used not only to identify the "who," "when," and "how" of a crime but also to deduce the criminal's mental state based on crime-scene analysis—something unthinkable a generation earlier. Justice had been advanced by the unification of science and law. But even the best and brightest in those fields, as Lacassagne would admit, would wrestle with doubts about the moral rectitude of their decisions.

Months after the debate had died down, Émile Gautier wrote an essay about Vacher in a volume called *The Year in Science and Industry*, in which he gave the case a philosophical perspective.

"What's clear is that the most sophisticated science is still powerless to penetrate the mysteries of the human mind, which cannot be determined mathematically or by its chemical constitution, or by its molecular state," wrote Gautier. "And maybe it's there, in the regions that are still inaccessible to our sharpest senses, our most perfect instruments, and our most subtle methods—[there] that dwell the secrets of [a murderer's] psychology."

Twenty-three

Postscript

The Vacher case quickly faded from the public mind. Unlike Jack the Ripper's abominations, Vacher's crime spree had been resolved, so it no longer had the power to tantalize the public. Besides, there were always more murders and scandals for the tabloids to cover.

Vagabondage continued to be a problem in France and much of Europe. Several legislators seized on Vacher's circumstances to inflame the public against vagabonds and pass increasingly repressive measures, such as opening more "paupers' depots" and upping the quotas for exile to Devil's Island. Nothing seemed to diminish their numbers until World War I, when millions were sacrificed as cannon fodder. After the war, people began to think differently about vagabonds and the poor. They were no longer the "other," who had been put in their position by their own moral and genetic deficiencies, but, instead, unfortunate fellow citizens. Rather than using punitive measures, countries throughout Europe initiated social welfare programs to help the unfortunate get back on their feet. By the mid-1920s, nearly forty million people were receiving unemployment insurance in Europe, greatly reducing the number of drifters. After the Great Depression, the United States initiated similar social programs.

Devil's Island, where many vagabonds and criminals had been exiled, stopped taking new prisoners in 1938, and it was shut down in 1952. The former prison colony became a tourist attraction. Years later, with the advent of the space age, the French government built a rocket-launch center on the island, a facility that it shares with the European Space Agency. The island's proximity to the equator makes it ideal for shooting satellites into geosynchronous orbit.

The guillotine, already in decline when Vacher was executed, continued to wane in popularity, except for a surge during the Nazi regime. The last public execution by French civil authorities was that of the murderer

Eugène Weidman, which took place in Paris in 1939. After that, executions were moved within prison walls. France eliminated the death penalty in 1981. The asylums of Dole and Saint-Robert operate as clean, modern, humane facilities. They are no longer formally referred to as asylums, but as "specialized hospital centers" for mental disease. The Saint-Paul prison in Lyon, where Lacassagne interrogated Vacher for months, was replaced by a new facility in 2009.

After the Vacher case, Lacassagne called for the government to set up an agency to collect data nationwide on unsolved crimes, for without Fourquet's innovative data gathering and analysis, Vacher's crime spree would have remained undetected. In 1923, police forces from twenty countries formed an organization in Vienna to share such information: the International Police Commission. It fell dormant during the Nazi years, but after the war, it was reestablished in Paris under a new name: Interpol. In 1989, the organization moved its headquarters to Lyon.

Lombroso continued his illustrious career long after the Vacher case. He maintained his theory of the born criminal, although over the years he added sociological factors that brought it closer to Lacassagne's way of thinking. He tried to extend his theories beyond criminal science, pressing into the realm of art and literature, where he saw many representations of born criminals. In 1897, he had traveled to Leo Tolstoy's village to air his theories for the literary master, who he assumed would embrace them. It did not go well. "He knitted his terrible eyebrows," wrote Lombroso, and exclaimed, "All this is nonsense!" Lombroso's theories continued to irritate Tolstoy, who in 1900 referred to them as "an absolute misery of thought, of concept and of sensibility." Zola, too, had little patience for Lombroso's theories, saying he gathered evidence "like all men with preconceived theses." Lombroso had indeed been selective with his statistics—after his death, broad, rigorous studies proved him wrong.

When Lombroso died in 1909, Lacassagne had kind words for his intellectual opponent, calling him an "agitator of ideas, and exciter of wills. . . . [His] desire to solve new questions shone down on his students." Lombroso willed his body to those students, who dissected their professor and preserved the remains in his criminal museum.

Bertillon recovered from his blunder in the Dreyfus case and carried on with his work, earning decorations in France and several other countries. He expanded his identification system to include the shape of the ear, which he said was unique to each individual, and the pattern of the iris.

In that regard, he anticipated the science of biometrics by a century. In the early years of the twentieth century, most countries replaced Bertillonage with fingerprinting, which did not require finely tuned measuring devices and highly trained technicians. Bertillon saw the value of fingerprints and added them to his cards, but he continued to vigorously defend his old method. Berlin, Vienna, Budapest, Rome, and Paris, among other big cities, attempted to use both systems in tandem. But the cost in materials and manpower was prohibitive, and fingerprinting quickly won out.

The limitations of Bertillon's system became clear close to home, when a workman at the Louvre stole the *Mona Lisa* in 1911. The thief, Vincenzo Perugia, had a criminal record with Parisian police, who had recorded his fingerprints and Bertillon measurements. Unfortunately, they classified the files only by their Bertillon numbers, so when they found fingerprints on the empty picture frame, they had no way to connect them to any of their files. The painting remained missing for another two years, until Perugia was caught trying to sell it in Florence. If his records had been classified according to fingerprints, the Paris police would have identified him within half an hour. The case pointed out a serious flaw with the old system: While Bertillon measurements could be taken only from a body, fingerprints could also be lifted from the crime scene.

Bertillon pledged his brain to the Mutual Autopsy Society. When Bertillon died at the age of fifty-one, Manouvrier dissected the brain before the body was in the ground.

Émile Fourquet never got the recognition he deserved. Newspapers lauded him, and the people who had been unjustly accused thanked him profusely. But the legal bureaucracy never promoted him—perhaps because he crossed jurisdictional boundaries, or because his imagination made that of others seem pedestrian, or because of some other slight he may have committed. Whatever the reason, he spent the next several years shuttling from one provincial assignment to the next. Discouraged by his lack of advancement, he resigned from legal work in 1913. He wrote a book about the case, in which he confessed his disappointment. "The public and press . . . clamor for the magistrate who solved the Vacher case [to receive] the Legion of Honor and the promotion of his choice," wrote Fourquet, referring to himself in the third person. "In the end he received neither." In remembrance of his accomplishments, one of the hearing rooms in the courthouse in Belley was renamed in his honor and is labeled with a brass plaque.

Lacassagne's fame grew with each passing year. He worked on many more high-profile cases, including that of Luigi Richetto, who with surgical precision decapitated elderly ladies; Henri Vidal, the notorious "Killer of Women," who left four victims in his wake; and Bladier Reidal, a Lyon man who had sadistically slaughtered an acquaintance. (Lacassagne determined Reidal was legally nonresponsible.) He continued his research into the culture of criminals and the factors that cause crime, including the observation that children of alcoholics tend to be born with psychological deformities—a phenomenon that later would become known as fetal alcohol syndrome. He was named an officer of the Legion of Honor and an associate of the Academy of Medicine, and he became president of many scientific and service organizations.

The only true misstep of his career occurred in the case of "the Ogress" Jeanne Weber, who in 1905 began suffocating the little children whom relatives and friends had left in her care. (The exact number was never determined.) Police first arrested her in 1906, after a fourth child she had been babysitting was found dead. Local physicians made a determination of death by suffocation and accused her of murder. In preparing for her trial, Henri Robert, the flamboyant attorney who had defended Bompard, insisted on a second medical opinion. The court assigned the case to Paul Brouardel and his bright young colleague Léon Thoinot. They determined that there was not enough evidence to prove murder, and the court set her free.

The following year, another of her wards was found dead. This time, Lacassagne signed on to her cause by issuing a report that asserted the facts were still not sufficient to prove murder. Soon after her release, she killed yet again. It was not until 1908, when she was caught in the act of choking yet another child to death, that the legal system finally caught up with her and sentenced her to an asylum.* "History always reminds us of our limitations whenever we are in danger of forgetting them," Lacassagne said.

Lacassagne retired in 1914, at the age of seventy, yet remained as active as many full-time physicians. During World War I, he cared for the wounded in Lyon's main hospital, while his sons served as medics at the

---

* On this case, too, Lacassagne's intellectual doppelgänger Lombroso weighed in. After looking at a newspaper photo of Weber, he declared her to be a "hysterical epileptoid"—another of his many categories of born criminal.

front. In 1921, he donated his personal library of more than twelve thousand books and documents, many of great historical value, to the Bibliothèque municipale in Lyon. His vigor and intellect unabated, at the age of seventy-four he wrote a book entitled *La Verte Vieillesse* (*A Green Old Age*), about the physiology of aging and about how to age well. "Old people," he wrote, "like all living creatures, need to be active . . . they should love life and not be afraid of death." He certainly embodied that philosophy, rising at five each morning to spend several hours studying and writing, then setting out on his daily constitutional, striding vigorously up the boulevard along the Rhône. Now and then he would stop to chat with former colleagues and friends, who were delighted to have a word with the master. "Take care not to burn yourself out," he would counsel them. "Measure your efforts. Take every chance in life to live long and productively."

On February 24, 1924, at the age of eighty, he left for his usual morning walk. He was approaching one of the bridges over the river when a car swerved around the corner and struck him. He languished for several months with a brain hemorrhage, finally succumbing on September 24. Obituaries praised his scientific accomplishments, his social contributions, his personal sagacity, and his remarkable spirit. "He lived his life like a sacred flame," wrote a columnist. In his will he forbade ceremonies or speeches at his grave site. Instead, he directed that his body should be taken to the Institute of Legal Medicine, placed on the same table where he had taught for many years, and autopsied by his former colleagues and students. In that way, he wrote, one final time, "I hope to serve as both a lesson and example."

The Violent Brain

Science and law have always had an uneasy alliance.

—National Research Council, 2009

The brain of Joseph Vacher—or at least the plaster cast of that brain—sits in a display case on the eighth floor of a building at the Faculty of Medicine in Paris. The place is a remnant of the glory days of anatomical museums, when medical students and members of the public would wander among the specimens and gaze with fascination and horror. The cast of the brain keeps company with those of about fifteen other "heroes of the guillotine," as well as those of several great intellectuals—members of the Mutual Autopsy Society, such as Paul Broca—and "Tan," the man whose inability to speak led to Broca's study of aphasia.

No one visits those specimens anymore. The museum outlived its usefulness as a teaching tool and the brains sit in storage, largely unseen. A few years ago, the medical school officially closed the museum and planned to dispose of its contents. But the curators petitioned the government that the collection represented part of the nation's historical patrimony, and the brain casts were preserved.

It is an odd thing to approach the cast of Vacher's brain, knowing what its owner was capable of doing, and the controversy that surrounded its existence. It is gray, about the size of a Civil War cannonball, and unexpectedly heavy, being made of plaster and not human tissue. The circumvolutions seem thicker than one would expect, giving rise to unscientific thoughts about the primitive nature of the person who possessed it. A deep crevice separates the left and right hemispheres. It widens into a triangle at the back, through which one can see the top of the cerebellum. On that surface the master cast maker carved *"VACHER: moulé à Lyon"* ("VACHER: molded in Lyon").

In the years since that mold was formed, forensic science has reached levels of sophistication undreamed of by Lacassagne and his contemporaries. The body surrenders clues as never before, as laboratory assays deliver precise information about blood type, electrolytes, status of the organs, traces of drugs, poisons, viruses, and bacteria. Crime scenes yield information that was completely invisible to Lacassagne and his peers, even with their measuring devices and high-powered microscopes. Examiners use ultraviolet lights to luminesce blood and semen stains even after they have been scoured with bleach, and employ tapes and gels to capture invisible fingerprints. Mountains of information are shared, as agencies in many nations have pooled their resources in computerized databases. Fingerprint matches that formerly took days to ascertain as clerks sifted through their files in distant locations now can be accomplished in minutes with a computer. DNA analysis, introduced to crime labs in the mid-1980s, can link suspects to a victim or a crime scene with better than a billion-to-one probability.

All this technology and efficiency has created a fiction about forensic laboratories—a myth of wizardry and perfection exemplified by the popular *CSI* television series. These shows, watched by tens of millions of people worldwide, feature highly trained professionals working with state-of-the-art equipment, who almost always bring their suspects to justice. The episodes often pivot around a "Bingo!" or "Gotcha!" moment when a cutting-edge or even fictional technology cracks an unsolvable case. Legal professionals speak of a *"CSI* effect," in which jurors, accustomed to seeing scientific perfection on TV, demand the same from real-world prosecutors, without which they tend to acquit. In response, both prosecutors and defense attorneys increasingly use graphic presentations to emphasize or exaggerate the certainty of their evidence.

The truth is far less accommodating than television. Just as in Lacassagne's day, the state of the art far exceeds its everyday practice. Many forensic laboratories are understaffed, overburdened, and lacking in proper equipment and training. In the United States, the average forensic laboratory has a backlog of more than four hundred cases that have been waiting more than thirty days for analysis. Recent studies have cast doubt on previously "infallible" procedures such as hair matching, bite marks, handwriting analysis, and even fingerprint matching. Indeed, more than half of the more than 230 people freed by DNA analysis in recent years were found to have been convicted by faulty science, or by poorly trained or dishonest examiners. In 2009, a committee of America's National Academy of Science found so much to question about the precision of modern forensics that it recommended a wholesale revamping of the field: setting up new institutes to research, develop, and evaluate techniques; improving university training for medical examiners, and making crime labs independent of police departments. It also urged the establishment of standard procedures for all practitioners to follow rigidly, just as Lacassagne tried to do with his *Handbook*.

As for that petrified brain of the killer in Paris—what secrets are locked in its lobes, gyri, and circumvolutions? History is littered with efforts to understand the criminal mind. During and after Vacher's time, people tried to link the criminal instinct to flaws in heredity, an evil seed passed from one generation to the next. The famous "Jukes"* study, first published in the 1870s and then in a revised edition in 1914, suggested a hereditary link in an extended family of criminals. In 1912, the famous "Kallikak" study purported to track simplemindedness through several generations of an extended family. Both studies were later exposed as invalid—the Jukes were not a single family at all, and photos in the Kallikak study had been retouched to accentuate the subjects' "idiocy"—although not before authorities used their conclusions to exclude many "undesirable" immigrants from entry at Ellis Island. Then there were the infamous "XYY" studies of the 1960s, which claimed a link between criminal behavior and an extra Y chromosome, as though maleness in itself disposed people toward violence.

Only recently has valid evidence emerged that brain physiology might play a role in violent crime, as imaging technology has made it possible to see inside the living brain. Previously, scientists had to operate in the manner of Broca, finding a patient with a cognitive deficit and then, during autopsy, searching for a corresponding irregularity. Research became more sophisticated with the use of electroencephalographs (EEGs) to detect brain waves and with the study of neurotransmitters in laboratory ani-

---

* Richard Dugdale, who conducted the original study, created the name Jukes to protect the family's identity.

mals. But the science was still largely inference-based, like the fable of the blind men using their hands to explore the contours of an elephant.

In the 1980s and 1990s, however, the new technologies of the PET (positron-emission tomography) scan and MRI (magnetic resonance imaging) made it possible to observe directly the functions of the living brain. What followed was a renaissance of neurological research, some of the newest of which has compared the brains of prisoners with those of "normal" people. Many prisoners exhibit a cluster of character traits, including lack of empathy, thrill-seeking behavior, poor impulse control, and an inability to follow society's rules, collectively known as antisocial personality disorder (ASPD). The traits are so deeply embedded that most psychologists consider ASPD not an illness, but an unchangeable part of the personality.*

Scientists who have scanned the brains of prison inmates with ASPD have found deficiencies in the brain area associated with higher thought processes and self-control. Located behind the forehead and just above the eyes, the prefrontal cortex, or PFC, seems to have a governing effect on our "lower" instincts, such as fear, selfishness, and violent impulses. (Witness the personality change of Phineas Gage from pleasant to surly when his prefrontal cortex was damaged.) Those impulses originate deep in our brain, coming from an evolutionarily primitive part called the amygdala. A growing body of research suggests that the PFC inhibits the wild impulses that emerge from the amygdala. When the PFC is damaged or deficient, or the connection between the two areas becomes disrupted, a person has difficulty with delayed gratification or impulse control. Such people lack the feelings that help others obey society's rules, such as embarrassment, empathy, shame, or guilt. Other tests show that those individuals underrespond to both everyday life and stressful situations, making them at once thrill-seeking and fearless. (Scientists observe that response by measuring the electrical conduc-

---

* There is a certain degree of overlap and fuzziness in the terms antisocial personality disorder, sociopathy, and psychopathy. Those with any of these disorders share common characteristics: a deficit of empathy and an inability to follow rules or control impulses. Psychopaths, who have a more virulent form of the disorder, seem to have no conscience at all and will do whatever it takes to get what they want, even if that involves multiple murders. Sociopaths will also do what it takes, but they will exhibit a superficial intelligence and charm. None of these disorders is considered a mental illness, either by the psychiatric profession or by the legal profession.

tivity of the skin—a fascinating parallel to Lombroso's electrical-shock experiments.)

Unlike Lombroso, no one today thinks biology equals destiny. The studies of criminals' brains have not been extensive or long-running enough to have made the transition from hypothesis to fact. Researchers also need to address the problem of the chicken and the egg—whether this brain deficiency creates the behaviors or if years of bad behavior lead to the deficiency: The brain changes from experience. Furthermore, no one denies the importance of upbringing. Someone raised in an abusive, neglectful, or impoverished environment is more likely to become a criminal than someone who is not. But now, just as in Lacassagne's time, advances in science raise difficult questions about guilt and free will. As currently defined, "legally responsible" means that while committing a crime the perpetrator consciously knows it is wrong but goes ahead anyway. What if the new science indicates that certain people, knowing the wrongfulness of a violent impulse, lack the neural circuitry to resist it? Would that change the definition of legal responsibility? It's the kind of question that fascinates neuroanatomists but terrifies those who must take responsibility for judicial decisions.

Given the advances in forensics, neurobiology, and psychiatry, how would Vacher's case play out today? Probably not much differently than it did in his time. He evaded capture for years, but so do modern serial killers; they're good at what they do. Dennis Rader, the "BTK" killer who lived near Wichita, Kansas, murdered ten people over a seventeen-year period before he was arrested in 2005, and only then after he sent police an anonymous confession. Ted Bundy killed at least thirty young women over a period of five years. Andrei Chikatilo murdered fifty-two people over a period of twelve years in the waning days of the Soviet Union. Even when confronted by police, serial killers are good at evasion, as shown by Vacher and his modern counterparts. In 1991, police in Milwaukee were called to assist a bruised and naked fourteen-year-old boy fleeing from the serial killer Jeffrey Dahmer, only to have the murderer persuade them that the boy was his nineteen-year-old lover and that the two were simply having a spat. The police released them, after which Dahmer slaughtered the young man and several others in subsequent months. In the mid-1990s, Belgian police botched numerous chances to capture Marc Dutroux, the notorious head of a pedophilia-murder ring—even to the point of doing nothing when they thought they heard children's voices in his basement. Like Vacher, Dutroux had been arrested, only to be released and then begin his killing spree.

If Vacher went to trial today, the terminology of the case would be different, although the verdict probably would not change. The man whom Lacassagne labeled a "sanguinary sadist" now would be diagnosed as a psychopath, someone with no conscience or empathy, who feels no hesitation in killing, refuses to acknowledge the pain of his victims ("My victims never really suffered," said Vacher), and even sees himself as the victim ("Here comes the victim of the mistakes of the asylums!"). Psychopaths are rare—when a therapist encounters one in a prison or an asylum, the call will go out to other staff members to come and observe. Like antisocial personality disorder, psychopathology is not considered a mental illness, but a deeply rooted part of one's character. "When you sit in the presence of a psychopath, you know it," a prominent forensic psychologist told me. "You feel you're in the presence of an empty shell."

To read the affidavits and testimony connected to Vacher's case is to follow the prototypical growth of a psychopath: torturing animals as a child, finding it impossible to hold a steady job, getting into fights, abusing alcohol, imagining a relationship with a woman and trying to kill her after she rejects him, and then embarking on a multiyear killing spree, never bothered by guilt or remorse. His actions place him squarely in the company of other psychopathic killers, all of whom have been found legally responsible. What makes his case unusual, though, is that in addition to his underlying psychopathic personality, he appears to have suffered a mental disease—a "comorbidity," as psychologists put it. The doctors at the Dole and Saint-Robert asylums both noted Vacher's delusions of persecution, auditory hallucinations, and suicidal tendencies. Those symptoms suggest schizophrenia, a mental disease that can be treated with medicine, or that sometimes waxes and wanes over time. People with schizophrenia rarely commit violent acts.

Vacher's unusual combination of disorders might explain how Dr. Dufour of the Saint-Robert asylum could release him without any premonition of the tragedy to come. It is quite likely that the symptoms that Dufour observed arose from Vacher's schizophrenia. It is also quite possible that after several months of gentle treatment at Saint-Robert, those symptoms temporarily abated, or that, given the propensity of psychopaths to manipulate, Vacher faked his cure with his mild behavior and flattering letters. In either case, if Dufour were alive today, he would be relieved to learn that he had not acted negligently, given the state of knowledge at his time. It was Vacher the psychopath who killed all those people, not Vacher the schizophrenic.

Lacassagne would be gratified as well, for despite the criticism he took from his colleagues, the arguments he made would stand up in modern courts. According to most criminal codes, a person is considered legally responsible unless a mental illness renders him unable to discern the wrongfulness and illegality of his acts. Lacassagne's analysis of the crime scenes demonstrated Vacher's awareness. He stalked his victims, killed them efficiently, cleaned himself up, and quickly fled to another jurisdiction. His claims of being overcome by a rage would not stand up to modern scrutiny; countless spouse abusers who make the same argument are found competent to stand trial. One criminal psychologist observed that even if Vacher had been overtaken by rages, he sought out situations that would provoke them, as though he intentionally brought them on.

Today, as in his own time, Vacher would be found competent to stand trial, though he would be less likely to suffer the death penalty in most countries. Yet even today, common sense stumbles over a paradox: How can someone who commits such atrocities *not* be considered insane? As a nineteenth-century attorney pleaded, "A crime without motive? . . . But who is he who does not immediately respond: This man is mad!"

More than a century after that question was asked, we still ponder whether human behavior can ever be fully knowable. The legal and psychology professions have created careful distinctions between sanity and madness, legal responsibility and nonresponsibility. They are definitions with a purpose: to diagnose, to understand, to create legal protections both for society and the mentally ill. But they are acutely circumscribed; they fail to include the moral dimension of behavior—an antiquated term in this scientific age, but a valid one in the gray areas of human nature. The professionals themselves are the first to admit this. One neurologist spent hours describing the latest advances in his field, explaining how faulty brain circuitry might predispose someone to conduct heinous crimes. It brought to mind the work of Moritz Benedikt, the nineteenth-century Viennese neurologist who dissected the brains of executed criminals in his quest to find the center for morality. Have modern brain scientists come close to that goal? Have they glimpsed the neural circuitry of evil? The neurologist replied that he and his colleagues had come far, very far, in understanding the circuitry of the brain and how disruptions in those circuits could produce disastrous effects. But as to the *origins* of that malevolent impulse—that question, he said, still belonged to the philosophers and clergy.

A criminal psychologist who has extensively interviewed serial killers confronted the same question. It was she who had spoken of meeting with psychopaths and feeling herself in the presence of "an empty shell." After several hours discussing her observations, she brought up a single case in her career when she felt her scientific training briefly abandoned her. She was interviewing a notorious serial killer when, glancing into his eyes, she was overwhelmed by the feeling of "looking into pure evil." She averred that, as a scientist, she knew she should avoid such vocabulary; she was trained to see and synthesize facts. But on that one occasion, the language of science could not encapsulate what she had seen. "I swear there was something different about this one—a feeling that I was looking into the abyss."

The pursuit of knowledge about crime has involved an epic journey through the centuries: from an earlier age, when all crime was sin, to more enlightened eras, when societies developed laws to define and control criminal behavior and scientists found ways to detect and decode it. A more nuanced, humane understanding evolved, in which circumstance and state of mind became important. Yet the deepest and most troubling questions about human nature stubbornly remain rooted in the spiritual and moral worlds. Perhaps it is part of the human condition that we cannot analyze or explain that which most frightens us. We will never understand why people like Vacher arise to bring chaos and violence into a world that we struggle to keep orderly and safe. We cannot account for the source of that impulse. We can only study it and try to keep it at bay.

Acknowledgments

I would like to thank my agent, Todd Shuster, who saw promise in a topic that I'd just about given up on and guided me through its development. Without his instincts and intelligence, this book would not exist. My editor, Jonathan Segal, shared our vision and shaped the book with his usual combination of skill and tough love. I'm delighted to be working on our second project together and look forward to more. I owe an immense debt of gratitude to Leonard Rosen—friend, writer, and kindred spirit. He helped develop this project from conception to birth over four years of working lunches, as we worked on our two books in tandem. Len saw themes and connections that eluded me, and offered indispensable encouragement and feedback. Many of the ideas in this work I credit to him.

In France, I owe much to Angélique Andretto-Métrat, who did the initial groundwork for my visits, ferreted out contacts, accompanied me on research trips, served as a liaison with local experts, and provided ongoing intellectual feedback. Rémi Cuisinier, an amateur historian who lives outside Lyon and has written several books on local history (including one on the Vacher case), became my trusted guide and friend. He took me to villages, introduced me to people, and regaled me with lore that I never would have discovered on my own. Gilbert Babolat, mayor of Bénonces, a key locale in this story, introduced and endorsed me to local farmers, who would otherwise not have met or trusted this nosy American.

Dr. Daniel Malicier, director of the Institute of Legal Medicine at the University of Lyon (the position created by Dr. Lacassagne), enthusiastically supported this project, making available the resources of his institute, allowing me to sit in on criminal autopsies, and bringing important theses and documents to my attention. Muriel Salle, a Ph.D. student at the University of Lyon, who has been working on a thesis about Dr. Lacassagne, generously shared all her research material and took me on a walking tour of Lyon to point out the key locations of his life story. Dr. Lacassagne's descendants—Judge Elisabeth Biot in Lyon and Dr. Denis Muller in Villerest—generously shared their great-grandfather's artifacts and family lore that had trickled down to them. A special thanks to Professor Marc Renneville and his colleagues, creators of a remarkable online archive about the history of criminology (www.criminocorpus.cnrs.fr), who welcomed me as a colleague and facilitated my research. Marc and his colleagues had put every edition of the *Archives of Criminal Anthropology* online, which has made Lacassagne's work available. Dr. Michel Daumal, chief of the Saint-Egrève Hospital, formerly known as the Saint-Robert asylum, opened his archives, took me to the room where Vacher probably stayed, gave me a tour of the asylum, and discussed the evolution of psychiatric treatment methods. Dr.

Pierre Lamothe, medical director of the Saint-Paul prison in Lyon, took me through the prison and discussed conditions during the late nineteenth century. His wife, psychologist Christine Lamothe, shared her Ph.D. thesis on the Vacher case and spent hours speculating on the murderer's psychology. Historian Martine Kaluszynski of the Université Pierre Mendès-France in Grenoble, an expert on Dr. Lacassagne and his colleagues, shared everything she has written on the subject, and she interrupted her social schedule to spend a Saturday afternoon discussing Dr. Lacassagne's life and times. Gérard Corneloup, resident historian at the municipal library in Lyon, who wrote his own book on the Vacher case, introduced me to the library's vast archives and its extraordinary and helpful research staff. Thanks to Sophie and Olivier Roux, whose apartment became my headquarters in Lyon, and to the Roche family of Champis, whose friendship brightened every research trip.

In the United States, several people helped interpret the vast amounts of material I had collected. I cannot sufficiently thank Eva Zadeh, who at the time of my research was a visiting graduate student from Paris. Eva spent more than a year helping me review thousands of copies of handwritten documents, most of which were barely legible and in an antiquated form of the language. She organized the material, brought her considerable computer skills to bear in creating maps and interactive references, followed up on contacts, and spent countless hours helping me to understand the historical and cultural context of the materials. When she moved back to France, she continued to help with research and photography, while pursuing her own promising career in science journalism. Thanks also to Marie Dayot for help with interpretation and translations. My former graduate student Johannes Hirn, a physicist from France and now a science journalist in Canada, spent many hours translating detailed neurological and autopsical reports.

Early in my research, I contacted Nicole Rafter of Northeastern University, a widely published scholar in the history of criminology, who greeted me warmly, tolerated my naïve questions, and shared her expertise all the way through. I owe special thanks to two medical specialists—Dr. Karoly Balogh, associate professor of pathology at Harvard Medical School, and Dr. Elizabeth Laposata, who teaches pathology and forensics at Brown and Boston universities and is former chief medical examiner for the state of Rhode Island—for providing scientific expertise, thereby helping to make nineteenth-century forensic science understandable to twenty-first-century readers. Both doctors did me the extraordinary favor of reviewing the final manuscript for scientific accuracy. At Boston University, Rhoda Bilansky of the interlibrary loan department of the Mugar Memorial Library tirelessly dug up old and arcane documents, no matter where in the world they might be. Many thanks to the staff of the Francis A. Countway Library of Medicine at Harvard Medical School. My colleague Chris Daly in the Boston University journalism department shared his authoritative manuscript on the history of journalism and his knowledge of the early days of the tabloid press. Many thanks to forensic psychologists Tali K. Walters, Ph.D., and Ilizabeth Wollheim, Ph.D., who gave important insights into the criminal mind, and neurologist Dr. Daniel Press of Beth Israel Deaconess Medical Center in Boston, who helped me understand current neurological research. Professor Christian Sidor, curator of vertebrate paleontology at the Burke Museum at the University of Washington (and my nephew, I'm proud to say), provided assistance on questions of anatomy. Thanks to John Merriman and his colleagues at Yale, who welcomed me to their scholars' table and shared insights into everyday life in Belle Époque France. Personal thanks to Ellen Ruppel Shell, Larry Kahaner, and David Danforth, who gave crucial support and feedback during this process. Thanks to Steve, Chris, and Bob of the Corey Hill Surf Club for keeping it fun, and to Mishy and Wendy for keeping it real. Thanks to Seth, who gave me a push at a critical moment.

I've dedicated this book to my parents, Ruth and Arnold Starr, for their lifelong enthusiasm for every project I've ever undertaken, book-related or otherwise. Some of my earliest memories involve their taking us to our town library and showing us the shelves of writing with admiration and wonder. At home, our sons, Gordon and Gregory, contributed to this project by listening with relish to bloodcurdling scenes that their mother found difficult to tolerate at the dinner table. My wife, Monica Sidor, despite her queasiness, offered endless support and encouragement, and heroically read and commented on the manuscript. Thank you for that, and everything else.

Notes

I. THE BEAST

3 "UGLY WEATHER, ISN'T IT?": Jules Besse, *Le Tueur de bergers* (Paris: Schwarz, 1897), p. 116. Besse recounted the actions and conversations pertaining to Vacher's relationship and attempted murder of Louise Barant in detail, based on interviews with Louise, her mother, Vacher, and eyewitnesses, pp. 116–289. See also Émile Fourquet, *Vacher: Le Plus Grand Criminel des temps modernes par son juge d'instruction* (Besançon, France: Jacques et Demontrond, 1931), pp. 76–87.

4 "IT WOULD BE BEST IF YOU STOPPED WRITING TO ME": Besse, *Le Tueur de bergers*, pp. 250–51.

4 ANY OF THE SOLDIERS: Collected testimony of Vacher's comrades in Archives départementales de l'Ain, 218–48, "Le Séjour de Vacher au régiment, 16 novembre 1890–20 mai 1893"; Alexandre Lacassagne, *Vacher l'éventreur et les crimes sadiques* (Lyon: A. Storck, 1899), pp. 129–34.

5 NEIGHBORS IN BEAUFORT REMEMBERED: Lacassagne, *Vacher l'éventreur et les crimes sadiques*, pp. 9–10; Fourquet, *Vacher*, pp. 56–58; collected testimony of family and neighbors in Archives départementales de l'Ain, 72–175, "Dépositions des frères et soeurs de Vacher"; Archives départementales de l'Ain, 176–82, "Vacher séjour à Beaufort, 1869–1884."

6 "CALM, RESPONDS MEEKLY TO QUESTIONS AND REGRETS THE ACT HE HAS COMMITTED": Dr. Bécoulet, "Certificat de 24 heures," July 8, 1893, in Charbonnier, *Documents sur l'état mental de Vacher condamné à la peine de mort par arrêt de la cour d'assises de l'Ain du 29 octobre 1898* (Grenoble: Allier, 1899).

6 "CRISIS OF AGITATION": Dr. Léon Guillemin, "Rapport médico-légal constatant l'état mental du sieur Vacher Joseph inculpé de tentative d'assassinat," in Lacassagne, *Vacher l'éventreur et les crimes sadiques*, pp. 130–33.

6 "EVERYTHING THAT IS DIRTY AND ABOMINABLE": Letters from Joseph Vacher, April 10, 1898, and July 15, 1898, in Philippe Artières, *Écrits d'un tueur de bergers* (Lyon: Éditions à Rebours, 2006), pp. 109–12, 121–44.

7 "GENTLE, TOLERABLE, HUMANE": M. Jodelet, *Historique de la fondation de l'asile de Dole* (Gray: Bouffaut Frères, 1902), pp. 7–9.

7 STILL, CONDITIONS AT DOLE WERE NOT WHAT THEY SHOULD HAVE BEEN: ibid.; Henri Monod, "Aliénés recueillis après condamnation," *Annales médico-psychologiques* (1895): 186.

7 THE POPULATION OF INSANE PEOPLE: "The Views of Two French Alienists,"

American Journal of Insanity 3 (1893): 600; Edward Shorter, *A History of Psychiatry* (New York: John Wiley & Sons, 1997), pp. 33–92; Claude Quétel, "L'Asile d'aliénés en 1900," *L'Histoire*, December 1976, pp. 25–43; Marandon de Montyel, "L'Hospitalisation de la folie," *Annales d'hygiène publique et de médecine légale*, 3d ser., no. 34 (1895): 411–34; Newth, "Valeur de l'électricité dans le traitement de l'aliénation mentale," *Annales médico-psychologiques* 7 (1882): 311–17.

7 "WE WAIT FOR THEM TO DIE": Quétel, "L'Asile d'aliénés en 1900," p. 26.

7 VACHER SNEAKED OUT OF HIS ROOM: Fourquet, *Vacher*, p. 94.

8 "YOU'LL HAVE TO WAIT": Besse, *Le Tueur de bergers*, p. 303; Pierre Bouchardon, *Vacher l'éventreur* (Paris: Albin Michel, 1939), pp. 96–106; Juge d'instruction Émile Fourquet, interview with Joseph Vacher, October 11, 1897, in Archives départementales de l'Ain, 541–685, "Pièces d'information."

8 "IN THE GRIP OF MELANCHOLIC IDEAS": Dr. Bécoulet, "Certificat de situation," October 26, 1893, in Charbonnier, *Documents sur l'état mental de Vacher condamné à la peine de mort par arrêt de la cour d'assises de l'Ain du 29 octobre 1898*, p. 19.

8 "A DELIRIANT WITH A PERSECUTION COMPLEX": Guillemin, "Rapport médico-légal constatant l'état mental du sieur Vacher Joseph inculpé de tentative d'assassinat," p. 133.

8 "ENTIRE WORLD IS IN LEAGUE AGAINST HIM": ibid.

9 "CURRENTLY REALLY QUIET": Letter from Dr. Chaussimand, Asile Public des Aliénés du Jura à Dole, to Asile Saint-Robert, December 16, 1893, from the files of the Saint-Robert asylum.

9 "TO SEE BLOOD RUNNING EVERYWHERE": Fourquet, interview with Joseph Vacher, November 4, 1897, in Archives départementales de l'Ain, 541–685, "Pièces d'information"; Fourquet, *Vacher*, p. 93.

9 HE TRIED HIS "URINATION" ESCAPE: Bouchardon, *Vacher l'éventreur*, 121–22.

9 "ONE OF THE BEST INSTITUTIONS IN FRANCE": Henry C. Burdett, *Hospitals and Asylums of the World* (London: J & A Churchill, 1891), p. 367.

10 "IN TEMPORARY AND EXCEPTIONAL CASES": Dr. Edmond Dufour, "Le Congrès de Lyon à l'asile de Grenoble. Discours de M. le Dr. Dufour," *Annales médico-psychologiques*, no. 14 (1891): 350.

10 "DEAR FRIENDS, LET US PRAISE GOD": Artières, *Écrits d'un tueur de bergers*, p. 115.

12 "WHEN I ARRIVED HERE I THOUGHT I HAD ENTERED PARADISE": Letter from Joseph Vacher to the director of the Saint-Robert asylum, January 29, 1894, in ibid., p. 34.

12 "IMAGINE MY SURPRISE": Letter from Joseph Vacher to Louise Barant, June 8, 1897, in ibid., pp. 51–59.

13 WAKE-UP CALL CAME AT 5:00 A.M.: The conditions and treatment at Saint-Robert are discussed in the following sources: Muriel Santo, "Les Aliénés au XIXe siècle: L'Asile public départemental de Saint-Robert" (Ph.D. diss., Université Pierre Mendès-France, 1995), pp. 64–135, 144–63; "XIIe Congrès des médecins neurologistes et aliénistes de France et des pays de langue française . . . visite de l'asile de Saint-Robert," *Archives de neurologie* 14, no. 79 (1902): 325–29.

13 "THE TOUCH OF A BRASS PAINTBRUSH": Santo, "Les Aliénés au XIXe siècle," p. 148.

14 "ELECTRIFY PART OF MY HEAD": Letter from Joseph Vacher to the director of

the Saint-Robert asylum, January 29, 1894, in Artières, *Écrits d'un tueur de bergers,* p. 35.

14   "DOCILE AND POLITE": Fourquet, *Vacher,* p. 94.

14   "HE SHOULD BE GOVERNING ALL OF FRANCE": Letter from Joseph Vacher to Louise Barant, June 8, 1897, in Artières, *Écrits d'un tueur de bergers,* p. 54.

14   "HE ALSO MADE IT CLEAR TO ME": "Chronique: La Bête humaine," *La Dépêche de Toulouse,* November 2, 1897.

14   PRESSURING DUFOUR TO RELEASE PATIENTS: Santo, "Les Aliénés au XIXe siècle," p. 154.

14   "OPENING THE DOOR TO THE CAGE OF A WILD BEAST": "Le Tueur de bergers," *La Dépêche de Toulouse,* October 27, 1897.

2. THE PROFESSOR

15   TOUSSAINT-AUGUSTIN GOUFFÉ: Details on the case are taken from the following sources: Alexandre Lacassagne, *L'Affaire Gouffé* (Lyon: A. Storck, 1891); Edmond Locard, *La Malle sanglante de Millery* (Paris: Gallimard, 1934); *La Presse,* November 12–19, 1889; *Le Figaro,* November 10–20, 1889.

16   DR. JEAN-ALEXANDRE-EUGÈNE LACASSAGNE: Details about Lacassagne are taken from the following sources: Philippe Artières, "Dans les petits cahiers d'un savant," *Gryphe* 2 (2001): 3–9; Marc Renneville, "Alexandre Lacassagne: Un Médecin-anthropologue face à la criminalité (1843–1924)," *Gradhiva* 17 (1995): 127–40; Léon Vervaeck, "Le Professeur Lacassagne," *Revue de droit pénal et criminologie* (1924): 915–30; Martine Kaluszynski, "La Criminologie en mouvement: Naissance et développement d'une science sociale en France à la fin du XIXe siècle" (Ph.D. diss., Université Paris, Diderot, 1988); Étienne Martin, "A. Lacassagne," *Journal de médecin de Lyon* (1924); Philippe Artières, Gérard Corneloup, and Philippe Rassaert, *Le Médecin et le criminel: Alexandre Lacassagne 1843–1924, exposition de la Bibliothèque municipale de Lyon* (Lyon: Bibliothèque municipale, 2004); Henri Souchon, "Alexandre Lacassagne et l'école de Lyon," *Revue de science criminelle et de droit pénal comparé* 1 (1974): 533–59; *Souvenir du Professeur Lacassagne à ses amis & à ses élèves* (Lyon: A. Storck, 1901).

17   "STRONG, RHYTHMIC STEP AND EVER-CHEERFUL EYE": Gérôme Coquard, "Le Prof. Lacassagne," *La Revue du siècle* 43 (1890): 725–30.

17   HE LACKED THE ABILITY TO APPRECIATE MUSIC: Locard, *La Malle sanglante de Millery,* p. 56.

18   THE INSCRIPTIONS WERE EQUALLY FASCINATING: Examples of these are in the collection of Élisabeth Biot, Lacassagne's great-granddaughter, and in that of the École nationale supérieure de Police, Saint-Cyr-au-Mont-d'Or, France.

18   "ONE OF THE MOST ENTERTAINING AND INSTRUCTIVE": *Science* 28 (1883): 836.

19   "THE THODURE AFFAIR": Alexandre Lacassagne and Dutrait, "Affaire de Thodure," *Archives d'anthropologie criminelle* (1898): 419–68.

19   "THE FATHER BÉRARD AFFAIR": Alexandre Lacassagne, "L'Affaire du Père Bérard," *Archives de l'anthropologie criminelle* (1890): 407–35.

19   "THE MONTMERLE AFFAIR": Alexandre Lacassagne, "Diagnostic différentiel du suicide et de l'assassinat (Affaire de Montmerle)," *Archives d'anthropologie criminelle* (1894): 134–65.

19 "THE STUDENTS ALL FLOCKED TO HIM": Locard, *La Malle sanglante de Millery*, p. 55.

20 IT IS A MIXTURE OF EVERY REPULSIVE ODOR: ibid., pp. 59–61. Author observations at the Institute of Legal Medicine in Lyon, June 29, 2007.

20 "A BUNGLED AUTOPSY CANNOT BE REDONE": Alexandre Lacassagne, *Vade-mecum du médecin-expert* (Lyon: A. Storck, 1892), p. ii.

21 THE STATE OF ALL THOSE AGE-RELATED CHANGES: Autopsy details are taken from Lacassagne, *L'Affaire Gouffé*, pp. 29–66.

21 ROLLET OBTAINED THE CADAVERS: Étienne Rollet, "La mensuration des os longues des membres: Étude anthropologique et médico-légale," *Archives de l'anthropologie criminelle* (1889): 137–61.

23 "GRAINY, COARSE, AND DENTED": Lacassagne, *L'Affaire Gouffé*, p. 39.

24 THE RIGHT HEEL AND ANKLEBONES WERE "SLIGHTLY STUNTED": Lacassagne, *L'Affaire Gouffé*, pp. 39–41.

25 "HIS BIG TOE STUCK UP": ibid., p. 38.

25 "NOW WE CAN CONCLUDE": ibid., pp. 64, 66.

25 25,000 PEOPLE HAD FILED PAST: Jürgen Thorwald, *The Century of the Detective* (New York: Harcourt, Brace & World, 1965), p. 132.

26 "IT WAS NO MIRACLE": Locard, *La Malle sanglante de Millery*, p. 59.

27 TOY METAL CORPSE: Thorwald, *The Century of the Detective*, p. 137.

3. FIRST KILL

28 NONETHELESS, SHE AGREED TO TAKE HIM IN: Émile Fourquet, *Vacher: Le Plus Grand Criminel des temps modernes par son juge d'instruction* (Besançon, France: Jacques et Demontrond, 1931), pp. 97–98.

29 HE REALLY IS COMPLETELY CRAZY: Jules Besse, *Le Tueur de bergers* (Paris: Schwarz, 1897), p. 26.

29 EUGÉNIE DELHOMME: Fourquet, *Vacher*, p. 99; Alexandre Lacassagne, *Vacher l'éventreur et les crimes sadiques* (Lyon: A. Storck, 1899), pp. 74–78.

30 SHE WORE A RED-AND-WHITE-STRIPED SMOCK AND MOLIÈRE SHOES: ibid., p. 75.

30 "WHERE ARE YOU GOING?": Fourquet, *Vacher*, p. 99.

30 EUGÉNIE'S BODY: ibid., pp. 99–100; "Une Jeune Fille assassinée," *Le Progrès*, May 23, 1894.

31 "I CAN RECALL ALMOST NONE OF THESE OPERATIONS": Henri Coutagne, "L'Exercice de la médecine judiciaire en France: Ses conditions actuelles et les réformes nécessaires à son fonctionnement," *Archives de l'anthropologie criminelle* (1886): 50.

31 DOCTORS WOULD RECEIVE TWENTY-FIVE FRANCS: Alexandre Lacassagne, "Les Médecins-experts devant les tribunaux et les honoraires des médecins d'après le décret du 21 novembre 1893," *Bulletin du Lyon médical* (1893): 558–65.

32 BROTTET GENERALLY FOLLOWED THE PROCEDURES: Fourquet, *Vacher*, p. 103.

33 POLICE FELL BACK ON THE INVESTIGATIVE METHODS: Details regarding the botched investigation of the Delhomme case are taken from ibid., pp. 102–7.

33 "COULD IT HAVE BEEN LACOUR?": ibid., p. 105.

33 THEY MIGHT HAVE TALKED TO VICTORINE GAY: ibid., pp. 106–7.

34 THREE THOUSAND CITIZENS SIGNED A PETITION: ibid., pp. 104–5.

34 EUGÉNIE DELHOMME'S ELDERLY FATHER: ibid., p. 105.

34 "A KIND OF FEVER CAME OVER ME": Letter from Joseph Vacher, "Sa défense par lui-même," in Philippe Artières, *Écrits d'un tueur de bergers* (Lyon: Éditions à Rebours, 2006), p. 142.

35 "THIS TERRIBLE, ERRANT": ibid., pp. 142–43.

4. THE INSTITUTE OF LEGAL MEDICINE

36 INSTITUTE OF LEGAL MEDICINE: "L'Enseignement de la médecine légale à Lyon," *Le Petit Journal*, September 7, 1891; Alexandre Lacassagne, "Rapport sur l'enseignement de la médecine légale de la Faculté de médecine de Lyon," *Archives d'anthropologie criminelle* (1900): 363–72; E. Caillemer, "Revue bibliographique," *Archives de l'anthropologie criminelle* (1887): 180–85; "Le Musée du laboratoire de médecine légale à Lyon," *Archives de l'anthropologie criminelle* (1890): 364–67.

36 THE SCIENCE OF FORENSICS: Erwin H. Ackerknecht, "Early History of Legal Medicine," in *Legacies in Law and Medicine*, ed. Chester R. Burns (New York: Science History Publications, 1977), pp. 239–71; Jaroslav Nemec, *Highlights in Medicolegal Relations* (Bethesda, Md.: National Library of Medicine, 1968); Cyril H. Wecht, "The History of Legal Medicine," *Journal of the American Academy of Psychiatry and the Law* 33, vol. 2 (2005): 245–51; Julian L. Burton, "A Bite into the History of the Autopsy," *Forensic Science, Medicine, and Pathology* 1, no. 4:277–284; "History of Forensic Medicine," *Encyclopaedia Britannica*, 11th ed., s.v. "Medical Jurisprudence."

38 THE NOTORIOUS PROSECUTION OF PAULINE DRUAUX: Paul Brouardel, "Un Cas d'empoisonnement par l'oxyde de carbone," *Annales d'hygiène publique et de médecine légale*, 3d ser., no. 31 (1894): 376–89, 459–70.

39 ADÈLE BERNARD: Maurice Lailler and Henri Vonoven, *Les Erreurs judiciaires et leurs causes* (Paris: A. Pedone, 1897), p. 114.

39 NO LICENSING LAWS: Julie Johnson, "Coroners, Corruption and the Politics of Death: Forensic Pathology in the United States," in *Legal Medicine in History*, ed. Michael Clark and Catherine Crawford (Cambridge: Cambridge University Press, 1994), pp. 269–82.

40 LACASSAGNE WAS APPALLED: Alexandre Lacassagne, *Vade-mecum du médecin-expert* (Lyon: A. Storck, 1892), pp. i–iii.

41 "THE MORE THAT I HURRIED . . .": Paul Hervé, "Médecine légale et médecins légistes," *Archives d'anthropologie criminelle* (1904): 863–90.

41 THE EIGHTY OR MORE CRIMINAL AUTOPSIES LACASSAGNE AND HIS STAFF CONDUCTED: Lacassagne, "Rapport sur l'enseignement de la médecine légale de la Faculté de médecine de Lyon," *Archives d'anthropologie criminelle* (1900), 363–72.

42 "THERE IS NOTHING MORE INDISPENSABLE": ibid., p. 365.

43 "ONE FINDS THERE WOUNDS": "Le Musée du laboratoire de médecine légale à Lyon," *Archives de l'anthropologie criminelle* (1890): 366.

44 ASSASSINATION OF THE FRENCH REVOLUTIONARY JEAN-PAUL MARAT: Alexandre Lacassagne, "L'Assassinat de Marat," *Archives de l'anthropologie criminelle* (1891): 630–45.

44 "THE MEDICO-LEGAL SCHOOL OF LYON": "L'École médico-légale de Lyon," *Bulletin du Lyon médical* 85 (1897): 64.

44 JACQUES INAUDI: Laupts, "Quelques mots sur M. Jacques Inaudi," *Archives d'anthropologie criminelle* (1893): 193–94.

45 INVESTIGATE A SHROUD: Albert Florence and Alexandre Lacassagne, "La Tunique d'Argenteuil: Étude médico-légale sur son identité," *Archives d'anthropologie criminelle* (1894): 651–83.

46 "RIFLING MARKS": Alexandre Lacassagne, "De la déformation des balles de revolver, soit dans l'arme, soit sur le squelette," *Archives de l'anthropologie criminelle,* (1889): 70–79.

47 "FLOATING MORGUE": Julien Bonnot, "Le Bateau-morgue: La Morgue de Lyon, 1850–1910" (master's thesis, Université Jean Moulin Lyon III, 2003); Edmond Locard, *La Malle sanglante de Millery* (Paris: Gallimard, 1934), pp. 57–58.

48 PARIS MORGUE: Bonnot, "Le Bateau-morgue," p. 103; "La Morgue à Paris," *La Nature* (1886): 99.

48 THOMAS COOK TOUR COMPANY: Vanessa R. Schwartz, *Spectacular Realities: Early Mass Culture in Fin-de-Siècle Paris* (Berkeley: University of California Press, 1998), p. 46.

48 "BUT THIS OLD PATRIARCH": Locard, *La Malle sanglante de Millery,* p. 57.

49 WEPT LIKE A CHILD: Bonnot, "Le Bateau-morgue," p. 109n.

5. THE VAGABOND

50 VACHER WASHED HIS BLOOD-SPATTERED CLOTHES: Émile Fourquet, *Vacher: Le Plus Grand Criminel des temps modernes par son juge d'instruction* (Besançon, France: Jacques et Demontrond, 1931), pp. 107–8.

50 ACCOUTREMENTS FOR LIFE ON THE ROAD: M. Laurent-Martin, *Le Roi des assassins: La Vie errante et mystérieuse de Vacher l'éventreur* (Paris: Librairie Universelle, 1897), p. 41.

50 A LANDOWNER NEAR GENEVA: Letter from H. Lardes to Émile Fourquet, November 10, 1897, Archives départementales de l'Ain, 258–324, "Emploi du temps de Vacher, avril 1894–août 1897."

50 "WHERE DID YOU GET THIS RHINOCEROS?": ibid.

51 BEGGARS HAD ALWAYS BEEN A FIXTURE: Timothy B. Smith, "Assistance and Repression: Rural Exodus, Vagabondage and Social Crisis in France, 1880–1914," *Journal of Social History* 32 (1999): 821–46; Gordon Wright, *Between the Guillotine and Liberty: Two Centuries of the Crime Problem in France* (Oxford: Oxford University Press, 1983), pp. 145–61; Eugen Weber, *Peasants into Frenchmen: The Modernization of Rural France, 1870–1914* (Palo Alto: Stanford University Press, 1976), pp. 62–66; Émile Fourquet, *Les Vagabonds: Les Vagabonds criminels, le problème du vagabondage* (Paris: Librairie Générale de Jurisprudence, 1908); Robert A. Nye, *Crime, Madness and Politics in Modern France: The Medical Concept of National Decline* (Princeton: Princeton University Press, 1984), pp. 54–95; Herbert A. L. Fisher, "The Protectionist Reaction in France," *Economic Journal* 6 (1896): 341–55.

52 "TWO YEARS AGO, WITH A PAIR OF BOOTS": Letter from Joseph Vacher to Louise Barant, June 8, 1897, in Philippe Artières, *Écrits d'un tueur de bergers* (Lyon : Éditions à Rebours, 2006), pp. 56–59.

53 "PEOPLE USED TO BE NICE TO US": Fourquet, *Les Vagabonds,* p. 43.

53 LOUISE MARCEL WAS RETURNING: Fourquet, *Vacher,* pp. 111–16.

54 JOSEPH VACHER: His personal history is taken from the following sources: Fourquet, *Vacher,* 56–62; Alexandre Lacassagne, *Vacher l'éventreur et les crimes sadiques*

(Lyon: A. Storck, 1899), pp. 3–5; collected testimony of family and neighbors in Archives départementales de l'Ain, 72–175, "Dépositions des frères et soeurs de Vacher," and Archives départementales de l'Ain, 176–82, "Vacher séjour à Beaufort, 1869–1884."

55 "RESIST CERTAIN TEMPTATIONS OF THE FLESH": Fourquet, *Vacher*, p. 59.

55 "WE CALLED HIM THE JESUIT": Jules Bissos, deposition to Grenoble police, November 5, 1897, in Archives départementales de l'Ain, 198–201, "À l'hôpital de Grenoble, septembre 1888–25 novembre."

55 "I DON'T KNOW WHAT'S WRONG WITH ME": Fourquet, *Vacher*, 63.

56 "ONE DAY MY NAME WILL MAKE HISTORY": ibid., p. 65.

56 POLICE ARRESTED CHARLES ROUX: ibid., pp. 114–17.

56 AN ELDERLY COUPLE WAS SLAUGHTERED: ibid., p. 119.

57 "INCORRIGIBLE, COWARDLY, UTTERLY DEPRAVED": Todd Depastino, *Citizen Hobo: How a Century of Homelessness Shaped America* (Chicago: University of Chicago Press, 2003), p. 4.

57 "DANGEROUS CLASSES," "INFERIOR CLASSES," "SOCIAL GARBAGE": Smith, "Assistance and Repression," p. 832.

57 "VAGABONDAGE IS IN THE BLOOD," ibid., p. 833.

57 "WILD BEASTS MISPLACED": Alexandre Bérard, "Le Vagabondage en France," in Lacassagne, *Vacher l'éventreur et les crimes sadiques*, p. 156.

58 "HUNGER AND SEXUAL DESIRE": Lacassagne, *Vacher l'éventreur et les crimes sadiques*, p. 304.

58 IN 1885, FRANCE HAD PASSED A LAW: Smith, "Assistance and Repression," p. 836.

58 DETAINING FORTY THOUSAND FOR VAGRANCY IN 1900 ALONE: ibid.

58 "I FELT HIS KNEE LIFTING MY UNDERGARMENT": Mme. Marchand, testimony, November 23, 1897, in Archives départementales de l'Ain, 258–324, "Emploi du temps de Vacher, avril 1894–août 1897; 1895 moi d'avril."

6. IDENTITY

61 A BRONZE CASTING: Author's visit with Élisabeth Biot, Lyon, January 11, 2007.

61 DEATH TO THE AUTHORITIES: ibid.

61 INSIDE THE COUNTRY HOUSE: Author's visit with Denis Muller, Villerest, June 30, 2007.

62 NOTORIOUS TISZA-ESLAR AFFAIR: Eduard von Hofmann, "Consultation sur l'examen d'un cadavre de jeune fille retiré de la Theiss (affaire Tisza-Ezlar)," *Archives de l'anthropologie criminelle* (1886): 537–74; Jürgen Thorwald, *The Century of the Detective* (New York: Harcourt, Brace & World, 1965), pp. 141–67.

64 ALPHONSE BERTILLON: Henry T. F. Rhodes, *Alphonse Bertillon, Father of Scientific Detection* (London: Harrap, 1956); Alexandre Lacassagne, "Alphonse Bertillon," *Archives d'anthropologie criminelle* (1914): 161–66; Alexandre Lacassagne, "Un nouveau moyen de reconnaître les criminels," *Bulletin du Lyon médical* 69 (1892): 522–24; "Proceedings of the Congress of the National Prison Association of the United States, Held in Boston, 1888," *American Journal of Psychology* (1889): 339.

64 THE POLICE CHIEF IN PARIS OFFERED A TEN-FRANC BONUS: Martine Kaluszynski, "Alphonse Bertillon et l'anthropométrie," in *Maintien de l'ordre et polices en France et en Europe au XIXe siècle,* ed. Philippe Vigier (Paris: Editions Créaphis, 1987), p. 271.

65 BERTILLONAGE: Martine Kaluszynski, "Republican Identity: Bertillonage as Government Technique," in *Documenting Individual Identity*, ed. Jane Caplan and John C. Torpey (Princeton: Princeton University Press, 2001), pp. 123–38.

65 "THE PRISONER WHO PASSES:" Ida M. Tarbell, "Identification of Criminals: The Scientific Method in Use in France," *McClure's Magazine*, March 1894, pp. 355–69.

66 RAVACHOL: Rhodes, *Alphonse Bertillon*, pp. 83–84; Raymond Hesse, *Les Criminels peints par eux-mêmes* (Paris: Grasset, 1912), pp. 220–27; Henry Brodribb Irving, *Studies of French Criminals of the Nineteenth Century* (London: William Heinemann, 1901), pp. 317–19; Ernest Alfred Vizetelly, *The Anarchists, Their Faith and Their Record* (London: John Lane, 1911), pp. 110–26.

67 BERTILLON OFFERED HIS SERVICES: Jeffrey Mehlman, *Genealogies of the Text: Literature, Psychoanalysis, and Politics in Modern France* (Cambridge: Cambridge University Press, 2001), p. 73; Edmond Locard, *L'Affaire Dreyfus et l'expertise des documents écrits* (Lyon: Desvigne, 1937); Jennifer Michael Hecht, *The End of the Soul: Scientific Modernity, Atheism, and Anthropology in France* (New York: Columbia University Press, 2003), pp. 162–64.

67 URGED BERTILLON NOT TO GET INVOLVED: Rhodes, *Alphonse Bertillon*, p. 184.

67 DISMEMBERMENT HAD BECOME *"À LA MODE"*: Alexandre Lacassagne, "Du dépeçage criminel," *Archives de l'anthropologie criminelle* (1888): 231.

67 "FAINT WHITE LINES": Frank Winthrop Draper, *A Text-Book of Legal Medicine* (Philadelphia: W. B. Saunders, 1905), p. 82; "Cicatrices de sangsues," *Archives de l'anthropologie criminelle* (1887): 384.

68 "SPEAKING SCARS:" Jane Caplan, "One of the Strangest Relics of a Former State: Tattoos and the Discourses of Criminality in Europe, 1880–1920," in *Criminals and Their Scientists: The History of Criminology in International Perspective*, ed. Peter Becker and Richard F. Wetzell (Cambridge: Cambridge University Press, 2006), p. 339.

68 HINTS AS TO THE VICTIM'S OCCUPATION: Allan McLane Hamilton and Lawrence Godkin, *A System of Legal Medicine* (New York: E. B. Treat, 1900), pp. 198–200.

68 HE CREATED ELEVEN PAGES OF CHARTS: Alexandre Lacassagne, *Vade-mecum du médecin-expert* (Lyon: A. Storck, 1892), pp. 4–15.

69 DENTAL FORENSICS: Henry C. Chapman, *A Manual of Medical Jurisprudence and Toxicology* (Philadelphia: W. B. Saunders, 1892), pp. 29–30.

69 DR. ÉMILE MAGITOT: I. D. Mandel, "Caries Through the Ages: A Worm's Eye View," *Journal of Dental Research* 62 (1983), pp. 926–29.

70 CASE OF LOUIS XVII: Émile Magitot, "Notes pour servir à l'âge probable d'un squelette exhumé le 5 juillet 1894," *Archives d'anthropologie criminelle* (1894): 597–604.

7. THE OAK WOODS

72 AUGUSTINE MORTUREUX: Details on the Mortureux case are taken from the following sources: Émile Fourquet, *Vacher: Le Plus Grand Criminel des temps modernes par son juge d'instruction* (Besançon, France: Jacques et Demontrond, 1931), pp. 124–30; "Horrible crime près de Dijon," *Le Lyon Républicain*, May 14, 1895; "Jeune fille assassinée," *Le Petit Parisien*, May 14, 1895.

72 "LOOK, MAMA," SHE SAID: Fourquet, *Vacher*, p. 131.

73 FRIAR NAMED FRANÇOIS BRÛLÉ: ibid., pp. 124–25.

73 "IT'S THERE, I SEE IT!": ibid., p. 126.

73 "WE'VE KNOWN ABOUT THIS": ibid., p. 132.

73 DR. J. QUIOC: ibid., pp. 128–30; Alexandre Lacassagne, *Vacher l'éventreur et les crimes sadiques* (Lyon: A. Storck, 1899), pp. 86–88.

74 PROLIFERATION OF THE PENNY PRESS: Dominique Kalifa, *L'Encre et le sang* (Paris: Fayard, 1995); Thomas Cragin, *Murder in Parisian Streets: Manufacturing Crime and Justice in the Popular Press, 1830–1900* (Lewisburg, Penn.: Bucknell University Press, 2006); Claude Bellanger et al., *Histoire générale de la presse française*, vol. 3. (Paris: Presses Universitaires de France, 1972); Christopher Daly, *Covering America: A Narrative History of U.S. Journalism, 1704–2004* (Boston: University of Massachusetts Press, forthcomming); Gérard Corneloup, *Joseph Vacher: Un Tueur en série de la Belle Époque* (Brignais, France: Éditions des Traboules, 2007), pp. 116–25.

75 ONE AND A HALF MILLION READERS: Robert A. Nye, *Crime, Madness and Politics in Modern France: The Medical Concept of National Decline* (Princeton: Princeton University Press, 1984), p. 207.

76 TEN MURDERS FOR A PENNY: *La Feuille*, November 7, 1897. This paper is from the collection of Rémi Cuisinier.

76 "THE AUTHORITIES WOULD LIKE TO PRETEND": Émile Fourquet, *Vacher*, p. 136.

76 "WHO KNOWS IF HE DID NOT SEE": Fourquet, *Vacher*, p. 138.

76 "WHO BUT A WOMAN": ibid., p. 137.

76 "WITNESSES" EMERGED: Fourquet, *Vacher*, pp. 126–62; "Le Crime du Bois du Chêne," *Le Progrès*, October 12, 1895; Jules Besse, *Le Tueur de bergers* (Paris: Schwarz, 1897), pp. 430–663.

77 "DEATH TO GRENIER": Fourquet, *Vacher*, p. 143; "Le Crime du Bois du Chêne."

77 "WILL NOT BE SO EASY TO DESTROY": Besse, *Le Tueur de bergers*, p. 456.

77 MORE THAN FIVE HUNDRED PEOPLE FLOCKED TO THE CEMETERY: ibid., pp. 457–72; Fourquet, *Vacher*, pp. 143–44.

79 SHE FOUND A PIECE OF PAPER: Fourquet, *Vacher*, pp. 172–75.

80 "I TRIED TO GET HIM TO SEE THINGS WITH A BIT MORE SANGFROID": Besse, *Le Tueur de bergers*, p. 550.

80 THEY SUMMONED ROUARD TO THEIR OFFICES: ibid., pp. 503–19.

81 SEVERAL MEN LEAPED ONTO THE RUNNING BOARDS: ibid., pp. 568–69.

8. THE BODY SPEAKS

82 "TO PLAY A ROLE IN A MEMORABLE AFFAIR": Émile Fourquet, *Les Faux Témoins* (Chalon-sur-Saône, France: Émile Bertrand, 1901), p. 43.

82 "RETROACTIVE HALLUCINATION:" Hippolyte Bernheim, *Suggestive Therapeutics: A Treatise on the Nature and Uses of Hypnotism* (New York: G. P. Putnam's Sons, 1889), pp. 167–69.

82 "WHAT DIFFERENCE IS THERE": Maurice Lailler and Henri Vonoven, *Les Erreurs judiciaires et leurs causes* (Paris: Librairie de la Cour d'Appel et de l'Ordre des Avocats, 1897), p. 134.

82 "WOMEN LIE," WROTE ÉMILE ZOLA: G. Ferrero, "Le Mensonge et la véracité chez la femme criminelle," *Archives d'anthropologie criminelle* (1893): 138.

83 THE TIME HAD COME FOR "TESTIMONIAL" PROOF TO BE REPLACED: Alexandre

Lacassagne, "Des transformations du droit pénal et les progrès de la médecine légale," *Archives d'anthropologie criminelle* (1913): 347.

83 ÉTIENNE BADOIL: Facts and quotes regarding this case are taken from Alexandre Lacassagne, "L'Affaire de la rue Tavernier," *Archives d'anthropologie criminelle* (1897): 36–69.

84 LIVIDITY CREATED A WINDOW: Jessica Snyder Sachs, *Corpse: Nature, Forensics, and the Struggle to Pinpoint Time of Death* (New York: Basic Books, 2001), pp. 16–20; author's interview with Dr. Karoly Balogh.

84 ANOTHER WINDOW WAS PROVIDED BY: Alexandre Lacassagne and Étienne Martin, "Sur les causes et les variations de la rigidité cadavérique," *Archives d'anthropologie criminelle* (1899): 295–96; Sachs, *Corpse*, pp. 17–19; Paul Brouardel, *Death and Sudden Death* (New York: William Wood and Company, 1892), pp. 63–74; Frank Winthrop Draper, *A Text-Book of Legal Medicine* (Philadelphia: W. B. Saunders, 1905), pp. 217–24.

84 THE MOST OBVIOUS OF THESE PROCESSES WAS PUTREFACTION: Brouardel, *Death and Sudden Death*, pp. 76–98; Draper, *A Text-Book of Legal Medicine*, pp. 224–35; Alfred Swaine Taylor, *A Manual of Medical Jurisprudence*, 12th ed. (New York: Lea Brothers, 1897), pp. 70–71.

84 "UNQUIET SPIRITS": Sachs, *Corpse*, 20.

85 "BLEED AFRESH": Stanford Emerson Chaille, "Origin and Progress of Medical Jurisprudence 1776–1876," *Journal of Criminal Law and Criminology* 40, no. 4 (1949): 341.

85 "LONG BLUISH FLAMES": Brouardel, *Death and Sudden Death*, p. 80.

85 JEAN-PIERRE MÉGNIN: Mark Benecke, "A Brief History of Forensic Entomology," *Forensic Science International* 120 (2001): 2–14; Brouardel, *Death and Sudden Death*, pp. 104–9.

85 "WE HAVE BEEN STRUCK BY THE FACT": Brouardel, *Death and Sudden Death*, pp. 105–7; Jean-Pierre Mégnin, "La Faune des cadavres," *Annales d'hygiène publique et de médecine légale*, 3d ser., no. 33 (1895): 64–68.

86 ANGLE OF A STAB WOUND: Alexandre Lacassagne, "Blessure du coeur," *Archives de l'anthropologie criminelle* (1888): 356–58.

86 ARMY'S NEW BAYONET: Alexandre Lacassagne, "Des Effets de la baïonnette de fusil Lebel," *Archives de l'anthropologie criminelle* (1889): 472–76.

86 LIVER CONVERTS GLYCOGEN: Alexandre Lacassagne and Etienne Martin, "La Fonction glycogénique du foie," *Archives d'anthropologie criminelle* (1897) 446–51; Alexandre Lacassagne and Étienne Martin, "De la docimasie hépatique," *Archives d'anthropologie criminelle* (1899): 54–69.

87 MEDICAL EXPERTS TRIED TO CHARACTERIZE: Draper, *A Text-Book of Legal Medicine*, pp. 253–324; Taylor, *A Manual of Medical Jurisprudence*, pp. 398–460.

87 VON HOFMANN AND PARISIAN ANATOMIST AUGUSTE TARDIEU: Draper, *A Text-Book of Legal Medicine*, p. 283.

87 "TARDIEU SPOTS": Taylor, *A Manual of Medical Jurisprudence*, p. 404.

87 CAREFULLY EXAMINING THE SURFACE: Alexandre Lacassagne, "L'Affaire de la rue Tavernier," pp. 36–69.

88 SPECTROGRAPHIC ANALYSIS OF THE BLOOD: Allan McLane Hamilton, *A System of Legal Medicine* (New York: E. B. Treat, 1900), pp. 142–47.

9. THE CRIME IN BÉNONCES

90 "WOE TO THOSE": "Le Tueur de bergers," *La Dépêche de Toulouse,* October 25, 1897.

90 AN EVIL WIND BLEW: Émile Fourquet, *Vacher: Le Plus Grand Criminel des temps modernes par son juge d'instruction* (Besançon, France: Jacques et Demontrond, 1931), pp. 175–81.

91 "IF THERE EVER WAS A CRIME I REGRETTED": Fourquet, interview with Joseph Vacher, October 16, 1899, Archives départementales de l'Ain, 541–685, "Pièces d'information."

91 THE VILLAGE OF BÉNONCES: *Le Progrès,* November 6, 1897; l'Abbé Léon Joly, *La Paroisse de Bénonces: Étude historique* (Bourg, France: J. Dureuil, 1904); author's observations on a visit to Bénonces, July 12, 2006.

91 "WE GIVE OUR STEW TO OUR WORKERS": "Le Tueur de bergers," *Le Progrès,* November 6, 1897.

91 "BUT DOES ONE *HAVE* TO WORK?": ibid.

91 "THE THING THAT IMPRESSED ME MOST": ibid.

91 "I'M NOT VERY RICH": ibid.

92 "WHY AREN'T YOU WORKING?": ibid.

92 THE RHYTHMS OF THE COWS GOVERNED FARM LIFE: "Renseignements liés au crime de Bénonces—rythme de pâture à Bénonces et hameau d'Onglas" (a report of gendarmes Jacques Chêne and Émile-Charles Grisey on interviews with local people about shepherds' schedules), September 17, 1895, Archives départementales de l'Ain, 150–155, "Renseignements divers"; author's interviews with Mayor Gilbert Babolat of Bénonces and local farmers, July 12, 2006.

92 THE AVERAGE PARISIAN ATE: Eugen Weber, *Peasants into Frenchmen: The Modernization of Rural France, 1870–1914* (Palo Alto: Stanford University Press, 1976), p. 142.

93 MANY SHEPHERDS LIVED WITH THEIR FLOCKS: ibid., p. 14.

93 "SUCH A SAD EXISTENCE": "Bergers & Bergères," *Le Petit Parisien,* October 14, 1897.

93 AN IMPROVEMENT OVER THE LIFE VICTOR PORTALIER: "Rapport d'enquête, Gendarmerie nationale à Trévoux" (interviews with Marie Lachal, Victor Mamian, parish priest M. Morel, Claude Sevrat, and M. Chambon), September 10, 1895, in Archives départementales de l'Ain, 146–49, "Renseignements sur la mère de Portalier."

94 VICTOR'S REMAINS: Fourquet, *Vacher,* pp. 182–87; "Un Crime horrible," *Le Progrès,* September 3, 1895.

94 "WE ARRIVED AT A HUGE WALNUT TREE": Alexandre Lacassagne, *Vacher l'éventreur et les crimes sadiques* (Lyon: A. Storck, 1899), p. 90.

95 "WHAT DEMON PUSHED THIS MONSTROUS MURDERER": "Le Tueur de bergers," *Le Progrès,* November 6, 1897.

95 MORE THAN 150 ARMED PEOPLE: Fourquet, *Vacher,* p. 187.

95 HE SENT OUT A STRIKINGLY ACCURATE DESCRIPTION: "Homicide à Bénonces commis le 31 août 1895, signalement de l'auteur présumé," Archives départementales de l'Ain, 1–145, "Pièces de forme."

95 MARIE PINET: Testimony of the widow Portalier to tribunal in Trévoux, Septem-

ber 8, 1895, Archives départementales de l'Ain, 146–49, "Renseignements sur la mère de Portalier."

96   "PLEASE GIVE THEM BACK TO ME": ibid.

96   "I MUST HAVE SUBTLY CHANGED COLOR": Testimony of Claudine Suchet, September 10, 1895, Archives départementales de l'Ain, 146–49, "Renseignements sur la mère de Portalier."

10. NEVER WITHOUT A TRACE

98   RUE DE LA VILLETTE: The details of this case are taken from Alexandre Lacassagne, "Affaire de la rue Villette," *Archives d'anthropologie criminelle* (1901): 33–42.

99   LACASSAGNE URGED GREATER COLLABORATION: Alexandre Lacassagne, "Une Nouvelle Série des archives," *Archives d'anthropologie criminelle* (1893): 5.

99   HE DEVOTED EIGHTY-ONE PAGES: Hans Gross, *Criminal Investigation: A Practical Textbook for Magistrates, Police Officers and Lawyers: Translated and Adapted to Indian and Colonial Practice from the System der Kriminalistik* (Madras: A. Krashnamachari, 1906), pp. 149–230.

99   INTERNATIONAL UNION OF CRIMINAL LAW: Jean-Henri Bercher, "Étude médico-légale de l'oeuvre de Conan Doyle et de la police scientifique au XXe siècle" (master's thesis, Faculté de Médecine et de Pharmacie de Lyon, 1907), p. 66.

99   "LOCARD EXCHANGE PRINCIPLE": W. Jerry Chisum and Brent E. Turvey, "Evidence Dynamics: Locard's Exchange Principle & Crime Reconstruction," *Journal of Behavioral Profiling* 1, no. 1 (January 2000).

99   MICROSCOPE TECHNOLOGY MADE A HUGE LEAP IN THE NINETEENTH CENTURY: "Carl Zeiss—A History of a Most Respected Name in Optics," available at http://www.company7.com/zeiss/history.html.

100   "THIS HAPPENS MORE FREQUENTLY THAN ONE WOULD BELIEVE": Gross, *Criminal Investigation*, p. 134.

100   CITED A CASE IN NORWICH, ENGLAND: Frank Winthrop Draper, *A Text-Book of Legal Medicine* (Philadelphia: W. B. Saunders, 1905), p. 187.

100   GROSS CITED THE CASE OF A JACKET: Gross, *Criminal Investigation*, p. 145.

101   J. IZAAK VAN DEEN: Alexandre Lacassagne, *Vade-mecum du médecin-expert* (Lyon: A. Storck, 1892), p. 60; Alfred Swaine Taylor, *A Manual of Medical Jurisprudence*, 12th ed. (New York: Lea Brothers, 1897), p. 281.

101   GEORGE GULLIVER: Allan McLane Hamilton, *A System of Legal Medicine* (New York: E. B. Treat, 1900), p. 172; Alexandre Lacassagne, *Précis de médecine judiciaire*, deuxième édition (Paris: G. Masson, 1886), pp. 218–25.

102   "I . . . MYSELF SPENT THREE WEEKS": Dr. Albert Florence, "Du sperme et des taches de sperme en médecine légale," *Archives d'anthropologie criminelle* (1895): 418.

102   "INCONTESTABLY THE *PROCEDURE OF CHOICE*": ibid., p. 249.

103   FOOTPRINTS LEFT IMPORTANT CLUES: Lacassagne, *Précis de médecine judiciaire*, pp. 233–36.

103   A SURPRISING NUMBER OF MURDERERS WENT BAREFOOT: Lacassagne, *Vade-mecum du médecin-expert*, p. 57; R. Forgeot, "Étude médico-légale des empreintes peu visibles ou invisibles et révélées par des procédés spéciaux," *Archives de l'anthropologie criminelle* (1891): 387–404.

103   "THERE IS A PHYSIOGNOMY OF THE FOOT": Henri Coutagne and Albert Flo-

rence, "Les Empreintes dans les expertises judiciaires," *Archives de l'anthropologie criminelle* (1889): 25.

103   "MAN OF DISTINCTION": Coutagne and Florence, "Les Empreintes dans les expertises judiciaires," p. 42.

104   "METRIC PHOTOGRAPHY": Louis Tomellini, "Photographie métrique (système Bertillon)," *Archives d'anthropologie criminelle* (1908): 149.

104   "THE EYE SEES ONLY": Bercher, "Étude médico-légale de l'oeuvre de Conan-Doyle," p. 84 (Lacassagne's handwritten comment).

104   "HIS CONVERSATION, I REMEMBER": Jennifer Michael Hecht, *The End of the Soul: Scientific Modernity, Atheism, and Anthropology in France* (New York: Columbia University Press, 2003), p. 165.

104   "RECOGNIZING, AS I DO": ibid.

105   "ONE MUST KNOW HOW TO DOUBT": Jürgen Thorwald, *The Century of the Detective* (New York: Harcourt, Brace & World, 1965), p. 128.

105   "A VERITABLE ROBINSON CRUSOE OF LEGAL MEDICINE": Bercher, "Étude médico-légale de l'oeuvre de Conan-Doyle," p. 11.

105   "IF A HERD OF BUFFALO HAD PASSED": Arthur Conan Doyle, *A Study in Scarlet*, in *The Illustrated Sherlock Holmes Treasury* (New York: Chatham River Press, 1986), p. 649.

105   "THERE IS NO BRANCH OF DETECTIVE SCIENCE": ibid.

105   SOMETIMES THE OPINIONS OF HOLMES AND LACASSAGNE WERE STRIKINGLY SIMILAR: Bercher, "Étude médico-légale de l'oeuvre de Conan Doyle," pp. 16–19.

106   "ACCURATE BUT UNSYSTEMATIC": Doyle, *A Study in Scarlet*, p. 642.

106   BERCHER FOUND IT PARTICULARLY GALLING: Bercher, "Étude médico-légale de l'oeuvre de Conan Doyle," p. 20.

106   LACASSAGNE ALSO INVESTIGATED A SUDDEN DEATH: Alexandre Lacassagne, "Empoisonnement par la strychnine—erreur pharmaceutique," *Archives de l'anthropologie criminelle* (1888): 503–19.

107   "ONE CAN LEARN CRAFT": Bercher, "Étude médico-légale de l'oeuvre de Conan-Doyle," p. 13 (Lacassagne's handwritten comment).

108   THE KILLER OF MADAME FOUCHERAND: Lacassagne, "Affaire de la rue Villette," pp. 33–42.

109   "THESE OBSERVATIONS GAVE NO RESULTS": ibid., p. 39.

109   IT HAS BEEN HANGING IN THE DISPLAY CASE: Author's notes, recorded at École nationale supérieure de Police, Saint-Cyr-au-Mont-d'Or, France, June 23, 2006.

11. IN PLAIN SIGHT

110   "HE TOLD ME THAT HE'D HAD AN ACCIDENT": Émile Fourquet, *Vacher: Le Plus Grand Criminel des temps modernes par son juge d'instruction* (Besançon, France: Jacques et Demontrond, 1931), pp. 190–93.

110   BODY OF ALINE ALAISE: Alexandre Lacassagne, *Vacher l'éventreur et les crimes sadiques* (Lyon: A. Storck, 1899), pp. 29–31, 92–95.

111   FOURTEEN-YEAR-OLD SHEPHERD NAMED PIERRE MASSOT-PELLET: Details regarding the murder are taken from the following sources: ibid, 196; "Un Berger assassiné," *Le Progrès*, October 12, 1895.

111 PIERRE WATCHED THE SHEEP: M. Laurent-Martin, *Le Roi des assassins: La Vie errante et mystérieuse de Vacher l'éventreur* (Paris: Librairie Universelle, 1897), pp. 152–53.

111 PUBLIC OPINION ALIGHTED ON A SUSPECT: Fourquet, *Vacher*, pp. 198–205; "Le Tueur de bergers," *La Dépêche de Toulouse*, October 26, 1897, November 6, 1897; "Le Tueur de bergers," *Le Petit Parisien*, October 23, 1897.

112 "BUT, JUDGE," HE REPLIED: Fourquet, *Vacher*, p. 198.

112 "YOU COULD IMAGINE SUCH SAVAGE AND BARBARIC DEMONSTRATIONS": Laurent-Martin, *Le Roi des assassins*, p. 162.

112 "CLOUD OF VAGABONDS": Jules Besse, *Le Tueur de bergers* (Paris: Schwarz, 1897), pp. 806–7.

112 MEDIEVAL-ERA FEARS AND SUPERSTITION: Robert Darnton, *The Great Cat Massacre and Other Episodes in French Cultural History* (New York: Basic Books, 1984), pp. 22–37.

113 "DO NOT BELIEVE IN WITCHES": Eugen Weber, *Peasants into Frenchmen: The Modernization of Rural France, 1870–1914* (Palo Alto: Stanford University Press, 1976), p. 21.

113 "IN THE NAÏVETÉ OF HIS UNJUST MARTYRDOM": Albert Sarraut, "Le Tueur de bergers," *La Dépêche de Toulouse*, November 6, 1897.

114 TWELVE-YEAR-OLD ALPHONSINE DEROUET: Tribunal de Belley, "Tentative de viol," in "Dossier administratif de l'affaire Vacher," Archives du Rhône; Lacassagne, *Vacher l'éventreur et les crimes sadiques*, p. 7.

114 WHEN THE GENDARME STARTED QUESTIONING: Lacassagne, *Vacher l'éventreur et les crimes sadiques*, p. 7.

115 FRENCH POLICE WERE BARELY COMPETENT: Raymond B. Fosdick, *European Police Systems* (New York: Century, 1915), pp. 73–133; P. J. Stead, *The Police of France* (New York: Macmillan, 1983), pp. 54–72; Howard G. Brown, "Tips, Traps and Tropes: Catching Thieves in Post-Revolutionary Paris" in *Police Detectives in History, 1750–1950*, ed. Clive Elmsley and Haia Shpayer-Makov (Aldershot, England: Ashgate Publishing, 2006); Clive Elmsley, "From Ex-Con to Expert: The Police Detective in Nineteenth-Century France," in *Police Detectives in History*, ed. Elmsley and Shpayer-Makov, pp. 61–77; author's interview with Clive Elmsley.

116 "IN OUR TIME, IN THE MIDDLE OF FRANCE": Laurent-Martin, *Le Roi des assassins*, p. 170.

116 EUGÈNE-FRANÇOIS VIDOCQ: The informaton on Vidocq and his methods is taken from Elmsley, "From Ex-Con to Expert," pp. 64–77.

117 "VIDOCQ OF THE WEST": Robin Walz, book review of Dominique Kalifa's *Naissance de la police privée*, in *H-France Review* 1, no. 21 (2001), www.h-france.net.

118 "MY PROGRAM NEVER VARIES": Besse, *Le Tueur de bergers*, p. 818.

12. BORN CRIMINAL

119 SECOND INTERNATIONAL CONGRESS OF CRIMINAL ANTHROPOLOGY: Otis T. Moon, "Anthropology in Paris During the Exposition of 1889," *The American Anthropologist* 3, no. 1 (1890): 27–36; Thomas Wilson, "Criminal Anthropology: A Report on the Second International Congress of Criminal Anthropology, Held at Paris, August 1889," *Annual Report of the Board of Regents of the Smithsonian Institution*, July 1890, pp. 617–86.

119 "DO CRIMINALS PRESENT ANY PECULIAR ANATOMICAL CHARACTERISTICS?":
Wilson, "Criminal Anthropology," p. 625.

119 THEY ATTENDED LAVISH PARTIES: Alexandre Lacassagne, "Deuxième congrès
international d'anthropologie criminelle," *Archives de l'anthropologie criminelle*
(1889): 517–22.

120 CORDIALITY BECAME STRAINED: Paul Topinard, "Essais de crâniométrie à pro-
pos du crâne de Charlotte Corday," *Anthropologie*, January–February 1890; Pierre
Darmon, *Médecins et assassins à la Belle Époque: La Médicalisation du crime* (Paris:
Éditions du Seuil, 1989), pp. 9–15; Albert Bournet, "Chronique italienne," *Archives
de l'anthropologie criminelle* (1890): 341–43; Moritz Benedikt, "Étude métrique du
crâne de Charlotte Corday," *Archives de l'anthropologie criminelle* (1890): 293–313.

121 CESARE LOMBROSO: Alexandre Lacassagne, "Cesare Lombroso (1835–1909),"
Archives d'anthropologie criminelle (1909): 881–94; Mary Gibson, "Cesare Lombroso
and Italian Criminology," in *Criminals and Their Scientists: The History of Criminology in International Perspective*, ed. Peter Becker and Richard F. Wetzell (Cambridge: Cambridge University Press, 2006), pp. 137–58; Nicole Hahn Rafter,
"Criminal Anthropology in the United States," in *Criminals and Their Scientists*,
ed. Becker and Wetzell, pp. 159–81; Cesare Lombroso, *Criminal Man*, trans. Mary
Gibson and Nicole Hahn Rafter (Durham: Duke University Press, 2006), pp.
1–41; Marvin E. Wolfgang, "Pioneers in Criminology: Cesare Lombroso (1835–
1909)," *The Journal of Criminal Law, Criminology, and Police Science* 52, no. 4 (1961):
361–91.

121 "HE HAS A MILD, ATTRACTIVE FACE": Arthur Griffiths, *Fifty Years of Public Service* (London: Cassell, 1904), p. 382.

122 "INFERIOR RACES IN BOLIVIA AND PERU": Gibson, "Cesare Lombroso and Italian Criminology," p. 39.

122 "AT THE SIGHT OF THAT SKULL": Robert A. Nye, *Crime, Madness and Politics in
Modern France: The Medical Concept of National Decline* (Princeton: Princeton University Press, 1984), pp. 99–100.

123 "THEORETICAL ETHICS PASSES OVER THESE DISEASED BRAINS": Stephen Jay
Gould, *The Mismeasure of Man* (New York: W. W. Norton, 1981), p. 139.

123 "MATTOIDS": Lombroso, *Criminal Man*, trans. Gibson and Rafter, pp. 284–87.

123 ABOUT 40 PERCENT OF LAWBREAKERS: Mary Gibson, "Cesare Lombroso and
Italian Criminology," p. 145n. Gibson points out that Lombroso's estimate of the
percentage of born criminals ranged from a high of just over 50 percent to a low of
33 percent, depending on the edition of his book.

124 HE DESIGNATED THE BROTHERS: Lombroso, *Criminal Man*, trans. Gibson and
Rafter, p. 351.

124 "BEAUTIFUL FACES": Havelock Ellis, *The Criminal* (London: Walter Scott, 1892),
p. 80.

125 "BANK SNEAKS" AND "PICKPOCKETS": Benjamin P. Eldridge, *Our Rival the Rascal: A Faithful Portrayal of the Conflict Between the Criminals of This Age and the
Police* (Boston: Pemberton, 1893), p. 353.

125 "A GENTLE, PAINLESS DEATH": Peter Quinn, "Race Cleansing in America," *American Heritage Magazine* 54, no. 1 (2003), www.americanheritage.com.

125 ARTHUR MACDONALD: James B. Gilbert, "Anthropometrics in the U.S. Bureau of
Education: The Case of Arthur McDonald's 'Laboratory,'" *History of Education
Quarterly* 17 (1977): 169–95.

125 "A FIENDISH METHOD": "Ousted a Criminologist: Head of National Education
Bureau Objected to Scientist's Plans," *New York Times,* February 21, 1903.

125 "I DO NOT FEEL CONVINCED": Ida M. Tarbell, "Identification of Criminals: The
Scientific Method in Use in France," *McClure's Magazine,* March 1894, pp. 355–69.

126 "THE COUNT IS A CRIMINAL": Leonard Wolf, *The Annotated Dracula* (New York:
Clarkson N. Potter, 1975), p. 300.

127 INTERNATIONAL CONGRESS OF CRIMINAL ANTHROPOLOGY: The overview of
the international conferences and the competing schools of criminology is taken
from the following sources: Martine Kaluszynski, "The International Congresses
of Criminal Anthropology: Shaping the French and International Criminological
Movement, 1886 to 1914," in *Criminals and Their Scientists,* ed. Becker and
Wetzell, pp. 301–15; Nye, *Crime, Madness and Politics in Modern France,* pp. 100–131;
Olivier Bosc, "Nous nous sommes tant aimés. Cesare Lombroso et Alexandre
Lacassagne: émulation, friction et collaboration entre Turin et Lyon," *Gryphe* 8
(2004): 24–27.

127 GRAPHIC AND DISTURBING EXHIBITS: Auguste Motet, "Rapport sur l'exposition
d'anthropologie criminelle," *Archives de l'anthropologie criminelle* (1886): 88–96;
Andreas Broeckmann, "A Visual Economy of Individuals: The Use of Portrait Pho-
tography in the Nineteenth-Century Human Sciences" (Ph.D. diss., University of
East Anglia, 1995); *Actes du premier congrès international d'anthropologie criminelle
(Rome, novembre 1885)* (Turin, Rome, Florence: Bocca, 1886–1887), pp. 501–10.

127 "ADOPTED WITH ENTHUSIASM": Alexandre Lacassagne, "Gabriel Tarde: Discours prononcé à l'inauguration de son monument à Sarlat, le 12 septembre 1909,"
Archives d'anthropologie criminelle (1909): 895.

128 ARM SPANS OF EIGHT HUNDRED CRIMINALS: Alexandre Lacassagne, "Rapport
de la taille et de la grande envergure: Étude anthropologique sur 800 hommes criminels," *Extrait du Bulletin de la Société d'Anthropologie de Lyon* (Lyon: Pitrat Âiné,
1882), pp. 1–7.

128 LACASSAGNE SAW THE DEVELOPMENT OF THE CRIMINAL: Marc Renneville,
"L'Anthropologie du criminel en France," *Criminologie* 27, no. 2 (1994): 185–209.

128 CONFERENCE IN ROME: *Actes du premier congrès international d'anthropologie
criminelle.*

128 EXOTIC NEW INSTRUMENTATION: David G. Horn, "Making Criminologists: Tools,
Techniques, and the Production of Scientific Authority," in *Criminals and Their Scientists,* ed. Becker and Wetzell, pp. 321–24.

129 THE INSENSITIVITY OF CRIMINALS: Gould, *The Mismeasure of Man,* p. 126.

129 "AN EXAGGERATION AND A FALSE INTERPRETATION": This and subsequent
quotes from the debate are taken from *Actes du premier congrès international d'anthropologie criminelle,* pp. 55–56, 113, 164–68, 174–76.

130 "BARREN OF ANY FOUNDATIONS IN FACTS": Darmon, *Médecins et assassins à la
Belle Époque,* p. 96; Nye, *Crime, Madness and Politics in Modern France,* p. 109.

130 "THEY SAY I AM DEAD AND BURIED": Arthur Griffiths, *Fifty Years of Public Service,* p. 383.

131 DURING THE GOUFFÉ AFFAIR: *Le Gaulois,* December 16, 1890, cited in "Opinion
de Lombroso sur Eyraud et Gabrielle Bompard," *Archives de l'anthropologie criminelle* (1891): 38–42.

131 "LOOK AT ALL THE PEOPLE!": Edmond Locard, *La Malle sanglante de Millery*
(Paris: Gallimard, 1934), p. 89.

132 CABANÈS MADE A CURIOUS DISCOVERY: Augustin Cabanès, *Curious Bypaths of History* (Paris: Charles Carrington, 1898), pp. 187–98.

132 "AN ABSOLUTE PROOF CANNOT POSSIBLY EXIST": ibid., p. 194.

13. LOURDES

133 "INCALCULABLE CROWD": Robert Hugh Benson, *Lourdes* (St. Louis: B. Herder, 1914), p. 8.

134 "THE GREAT DOCTOR OF OUR BODIES AS WELL AS OUR SOULS": Letter from Joseph Vacher to Louise Barant, June 8, 1897, in Philippe Artières, *Écrits d'un tueur de bergers* (Lyon: Éditions à Rebours, 2006), p. 57.

134 "FACES WHITE AND DRAWN": Benson, *Lourdes*, p. 12.

134 MARIE MOUSSIER: Émile Fourquet, *Vacher: Le Plus Grand Criminel des temps modernes par son juge d'instruction* (Besançon, France: Jacques et Demontrond, 1931), pp. 221–23.

135 HE CAME UPON THE BOY'S FOURTEEN-YEAR-OLD SISTER, ROSINE: "Horrible assassinat d'une fillette," *Le Petit Parisien*, October 4, 1896.

135 "ALL OF A SUDDEN, I FOUND THE ROUTE THAT I RECOGNIZED": Fourquet, *Vacher*, p. 231.

135 TRAUMATIZED BY HIS ATTACK: Letter from Auguste Pierson, solicitor in Baumeles-Dames, to Dr. Dufour, March 6, 1894, from the files of the Saint-Robert asylum; Jules Besse, *Le Tueur de bergers* (Paris: Schwarz, 1897), p. 291.

135 "DEAR LOUISE, I DON'T KNOW IF YOU ARE STILL IN YOUR PARENTS' VILLAGE": Letter from Joseph Vacher to Louise Barant, in Artières, *Écrits d'un tueur de bergers*, pp. 49–51.

136 "OH! VIRGIN MARY": Joseph Vacher, "Inscription tracée sur la neige," in ibid., p. 47.

136 "A COUNTRY OF GOOD ORANGES AND NICE PEOPLE": Letter from Joseph Vacher to Louise Barant, June 8, 1897, in ibid., pp. 56–57.

136 LOUISE FARENC: Farenc's recollections are taken from "Le Tueur de bergers," *La Dépêche de Toulouse*, November 8, 1897, and November 15, 1897.

137 "HE SHOWED ME HIS HANDS": Fourquet, *Vacher*, pp. 237–39.

137 PENMANSHIP LESSON: "Le Tueur de bergers," *La Dépêche de Toulouse*, November 15, 1897.

137 VAGABOND NAMED CÉLESTIN GAUTRAIS: Fourquet, *Vacher*, pp. 240–41; "Le Tueur de bergers," *La Dépêche de Toulouse*, November 8, 1897.

14. THE INVESTIGATING MAGISTRATE

141 "EXAMINING MAGISTRATE! MANHUNTS!": Émile Fourquet, *Vacher: Le Plus Grand Criminel des temps modernes par son juge d'instruction* (Besançon, France: Jacques et Demontrond, 1931), p. 2.

141 "LOOK AT WHAT AN EXTRAORDINARY CRIME WAS COMMITTED": ibid., p.1.

141 "MURDER OF A SHEPHERD": "Assassinat d'un berger," *Le Lyon Républicain*, June 21, 1897.

142 "YOUR PREDECESSOR NEVER DISCOVERED THE KILLER": Fourquet, *Vacher*, p. 1.

142 "NEEDLESS TO SAY, THIS HORRIBLE SITUATION": "Assassinat d'un berger," *Le Lyon Républicain*, June 21, 1897.

142 FOURQUET KEPT DIGGING: The initial investigation is described in Fourquet, *Vacher*, pp. 1–11.

143 THE NEWSPAPER LISTED SEVERAL CRIMES: "L'Assassinat du berger," *Le Lyon Républicain*, June 25, 1897.

143 "A NEW JACK THE RIPPER": "L'Assassinat du berger," *Le Lyon Républicain*, June 26, 1897.

143 THE DAY AFTER THE MURDER, DR. JEAN BOYER: Alexandre Lacassagne, *Vacher l'éventreur et les crimes sadiques* (Lyon: A. Storck, 1899), pp. 105–11.

144 "LITERALLY TERRORIZED THE COUNTRYSIDE": "L'Assassinat du Berger," *Le Lyon Républicain*, June 24, 1897.

144 "IN THE SILENCE AND SOLITUDE": Fourquet, *Vacher*, p. 6.

145 "ROGATORY LETTER": Fourquet, *Vacher*, pp. 11–12.

146 VACHER NAMED HER LOULETTE: Testimony of Nicolas le Facteur, November 3, 1897, Archives départementales de l'Ain, 258–324, "Emploi du temps de Vacher, avril 1894–août 1897."

146 "IT OCCURRED TO ME TO TEST": Testimony of Vital Vallon, November 4, 1897, in ibid.

146 "YOU'RE OUT OF LUCK": Letter from Nicolas le Facteur to juge d'instruction Émile Fourquet, November 3, 1897, in ibid.

146 "IF YOU DON'T WANT TO EAT IT": "Emploi du temps de Vacher, établi par les gendarmes Pujel et Lavie de la brigade de St Péray, Ardèche," interview with farmer Régis Bac, Archives départementales de l'Ain, 258–324, "Emploi du temps de Vacher, avril 1894–août 1897."

147 "AN INSTANT OF FALSE JOY": Fourquet, *Vacher*, pp. 13–14.

147 FOURQUET RECEIVED A LETTER: Pierre Bouchardon, *Vacher l'éventreur* (Paris: Albin Michel, 1939), p. 72.

148 "WILD AND TRAGIC": Albert Sarraut, "Le Tueur de bergers," *La Dépêche de Toulouse*, November 3, 1897.

148 "AT FIRST I THOUGHT IT WAS AN ANIMAL": Deposition of Marie-Eugénie Héraud (Mme. Plantier), November 19, 1897, Archives départementales de l'Ain, 258–324, "Emploi du temps de Vacher avril 1894–août 1897."

149 HE STARTED HURLING ROCKS AT VACHER: Depositions of Séraphin Plantier and Henri Nodin, November 19, 1897, in ibid.; "Le Tueur de bergers," *Le Progrès*, October 23, 1897; "Le Tueur de bergers," *La Dépêche de Toulouse*, October 25 and November 3, 1897.

149 "ALTHOUGH I WOULD HAVE PREFERRED": This and subsequent quotes regarding Vacher's detainment at the roadhouse are taken from the following sources: Depositions of Victor Merle, Dupré Charlon, and Isaac Issartel, November 19, 1897, in Archives départementales de l'Ain, 258–324, "Emploi du temps de Vacher, avril 1894–août 1897"; *Le Progrès Illustré*, November 21, 1897; "Le Tueur des bergers: La Dernière Étape de l'éventreur," *La Dépêche de Toulouse*, November 3, 1897.

15. THE INTERVIEW

151 WILD TRAIN RIDE: Émile Fourquet, *Vacher: Le Plus Grand Criminel des temps modernes par son juge d'instruction* (Besançon, France: Jacques et Demontrond, 1931), pp. 17–18.

151 "ABSENCE OF PASSION": The information on interview techniques is taken from Hans Gross, *Criminal Investigation: A Practical Textbook for Magistrates, Police Officers and Lawyers: Adapted from the System der Kriminalistik* (London: Sweet & Maxwell, 1924), pp. 75–78.

152 VACHER SPOKE FREELY: Reconstruction of Fourquet's interviews with Vacher are based on the following sources: Fourquet, *Vacher*, pp. 18–31; Fourquet's interrogations of Vacher, October 7–December 12, 1897, Archives départementales de l'Ain, 541–685, "Pièces d'information."

156 "GOD—RIGHTS—OBLIGATIONS": Fourquet, *Vacher*, pp. 30–31.

157 "IT IS USELESS": Fourquet's postconfession interviews with Vacher are from Fourquet, *Vacher*, pp. 31–45.

160 THE CASE EXPLODED IN THE NATIONAL PRESS: Fourquet, *Vacher*, pp. 33, 47–55; Jean Laponce, "In the Shadow of de Sade: French Medical Responses to a Case of Serial Sexual Homicide During the Belle Époque" (Ph.D. diss., Columbia University, 2002), pp. 90–92.

160 "LONG LIVE ANARCHY!": Jules Besse, *Le Tueur de bergers* (Paris: Schwarz, 1897), p. 938.

160 "HE IS AS REPUGNANT PHYSICALLY": *La Dépêche de Toulouse*, October 25, 1897.

160 "HIS EYES SHINE": "Le Tueur de bergers," *Le Petit Parisien*, October 17, 1897.

160 THE CRIMES OF A MONOMANIAC: *Le Petit Parisien Illustré*, October 31, 1897.

161 "MY VICTIMS NEVER REALLY SUFFERED": "Le Tueur de bergers," *La Dépêche de Toulouse*, October 14, 1897.

161 VACHER POSED FOR A SKETCH: *Le Progrès*, October 24, 1897.

161 "BLOODY ODYSSEY": "Le Tueur de bergers," *La Dépêche de Toulouse*, October 11, 1897.

161 "IT DOESN'T MUCH MATTER": "Le Tueur de bergers," *La Dépêche de Toulouse*, November 7, 1897.

162 "YOU ARE THE ONLY ONE": "Le Tueur de bergers: Une Lettre de sa famille," *La Dépêche de Toulouse*, November 16, 1897.

163 THE REMOVAL WAS "VERY NEAT": Deposition of Dr. Ravier Gaston, November 18, 1897, Archives départementales de l'Ain, 541–685, "Pièces d'information."

163 "IT'S THE SICKNESS THAT WANTS IT": Fourquet's interrogation of Vacher, November 5, 1897, in ibid.

163 "WHY DID I KILL?": *Le Lyon Républicain*, October 24, 1897; Besse, *Le Tueur de bergers*, p. 841.

164 "I'M FURIOUS": Fourquet, *Vacher*, pp. 41–42.

164 HE KILLED THE BOY AND THREW HIS BODY: Fourquet, *Vacher*, pp. 42–43; "Vacher l'assassin," *Le Petit Parisien*, October 25, 1897. The search for, discovery, and autopsy of the body received voluminous coverage from October 23 to November 8 in *Le Lyon Républicain, Le Progrès*, and *La Dépêche de Toulouse*.

164 "WHEN WILL THIS HORRIBLE NIGHTMARE": Albert Sarraut, "Le Tueur de bergers," *La Dépêche de Toulouse*, October 29, 1897.

165 IDENTIFYING THE VICTIM WOULD BE A MORE COMPLICATED TASK: *Le Lyon Républicain*, October 30 and November 6, 1897; *Le Progrès*, November 3, 1897; Alexandre Lacassagne, *Vacher l'éventreur et les crimes sadiques* (Lyon: A. Storck, 1899), p. 106.

165 "VERY SURPRISED TO HEAR": "Le Tueur de bergers," *Le Progrès*, November 3, 1897.

16. PROFESSOR LACASSAGNE

167   "OH, DEAR BENEFACTOR": Philippe Artières, *Le Livre des vies coupables: Autobiographies de criminels (1896–1909)* (Paris: Éditions Albin Michel, 2000), p. 33.

167   "THEIR CRINGING AND TIMID WAYS": Émile Gautier, "Le Monde des Prisons," *Archives de l'anthropologie criminelle* (1888): 417–37.

168   THEY REVEALED DARK STORIES: Philippe Artières, "What Criminals Think About Criminology," in *Criminals and Their Scientists: The History of Criminology in International Perspective*, ed. Peter Becker and Richard F. Wetzell (Cambridge: Cambridge University Press, 2006), pp. 363–75.

168   "MEMOIRS OF A SPARROW": Philippe Artières, "'Cher Professeur A. Lacassagne, notre généreux bienfaiteur': Le Détenu écrit au criminologue," *Genèses* 25, no. 25 (1996): 143–55.

168   "THE THING THAT ASTONISHES ME": Artières, *Le Livre des vies coupables*, p. 196.

169   "TO ME THE WORD[S]": ibid, pp. 285–86.

169   "TO SUPPORT THEM, DIRECT THEM": Alexandre Lacassagne, "Congrès du patronage des libérés, session de Lyon, juin 1894, discours de M. Lacassagne, président," *Archives d'anthropologie criminelle* (1894): 404–10.

169   "SOCIETY HAS THE RIGHT TO DEFEND ITSELF": Alexandre Lacassagne, "L'Affaire Gouffé," *Archives de l'anthropologie criminelle* (1891): 205.

169   "SOCIETIES HAVE THE CRIMINALS THEY DESERVE": ibid.

17. "A CRIME WITHOUT MOTIVE?"

171   SAINT-PAUL PRISON: Author's observations; author's interview with Dr. Pierre Lamothe, medical director, January 11, 2007.

172   "IT IS TIME": Philippe Artières, *Écrits d'un tueur de bergers* (Lyon: Éditions à Rebours, 2006), p. 89.

172   "THE GOVERNMENT WANTS MY HEAD": Émile Fourquet, *Vacher: Le Plus Grand Criminel des temps modernes par son juge d'instruction* (Besançon, France: Jacques et Demontrond, 1931), p. 292; *Le Lyon Républicain*, December 31, 1897.

172   ACCORDING TO THE NEW MEDICAL THEORIES: This discussion of the criminal insanity issue as viewed at the time of the Vacher case is based on the following sources: Laurent Mucchielli, "Criminology, Hygienism, and Eugenics in France, 1870–1914," in *Criminals and Their Scientists: The History of Criminology in International Perspective*, ed. Peter Becker and Richard F. Wetzell (Cambridge: Cambridge University Press, 2006), pp. 207–29; Ruth Harris, *Murders and Madness: Medicine, Law, and Society in the Fin de Siècle* (Oxford: Clarendon Press, 1989); Louis Proal, "La Responsabilité des aliénés," *Annales médico-psychologiques* 12 (1890): 84–107; (1891): 429–37; Alfred Swaine Taylor, *A Manual of Medical Jurisprudence* (New York: Lea Brothers, 1897), pp. 675–704; Alexandre Bérard, "La Responsabilité morale et la loi pénale," *Archives de l'anthropologie criminelle* (1892): 153–78; Marc Renneville, *Crime et folie: Deux siècles d'enquêtes médicales et judiciaires* (Paris: Fayard, 2003); Nigel Walker, "The Insanity Defense Before 1800," *Annals of the American Academy of Political and Social Science* 477 (1985): 25–30; Victor Parant, "The Irresponsibility of the Insane Under the Laws of France," in *Commitment, Detention, Care and Treatment of the Insane*, ed. J. Alder Blumer and A. B. Richardson (Baltimore: Johns Hopkins Press, 1894), pp. 34–45.

173 ITALIC IMMIGRANT LABORER WENT ON A DRUNKEN RAMPAGE: Harris, *Murders and Madness,* p. 34.

173 WHEN EXPERTS AUTOPSIED HIS BRAIN: ibid., p. 95.

173 CHARLES J. GUITEAU: "The Guiteau Trial," *American Journal of Insanity* 38 (1881): 301–47.

174 PUBLIC SECURITY IS COMPROMISED: Louis Proal, "La Responsabilité des aliénés," p. 84.

174 "A CRIME WITHOUT MOTIVE?": Laurent Mucchielli, "Criminology, Hygienism, and Eugenics in France, 1870–1914," p. 212.

174 "IF I AM BITTEN BY A VIPER": ibid.

175 "[W]E CARE FOR THEM": ibid.

175 "IS HE INSANE?": *Le Petit Parisien,* December 27, 1897.

175 "WILD ANIMAL WITH A HUMAN FACE": "Le Tueur de bergers," *La Dépêche de Toulouse,* November 10, 1897.

175 LACASSAGNE AND THE TWO OTHER EXPERTS: Fourquet, *Vacher,* pp. 290–91.

176 THIS WAS ONE OF THE FIRST: F. Bordas, "Les Rayons Roentgen et leur application en médecine légale," *Annales d'hygiène publique et médecine légale* 35 (1896): 390.

176 "THEY'RE IDIOTS": "Vacher à Saint-Paul," *Le Lyon Républicain,* January 11, 1898.

176 "YOU DON'T HAVE THE RIGHT TO KEEP ME": Letter from Joseph Vacher to Procureur de la République, January 21, 1898, in Artières, *Écrits d'un tueur de bergers,* p. 94.

176 "SUDDENLY, WITHOUT ANY APPARENT REASON": "L'Assassin Vacher," *Le Lyon Républicain,* February 27, 1898.

176 ONE SUNDAY IN MARCH: "Vacher à la Prison Saint-Paul," *Le Lyon Républicain,* March 27, 1898.

177 "FOR [SIX DAYS] HE HAS ENERGETICALLY REFUSED ALL NOURISHMENT": Letter from the director of the Saint-Paul prison to Dr. Lacassagne, January 28, 1898, Archives du Rhône, 348–49.

177 "STRONGMAN AT A COUNTRY FAIR": *Le Temps,* February 2, 1898.

177 "OH! LOVELY SOLITUDE!": Artières, *Écrits d'un tueur de bergers,* p. 95.

178 "I AM TRULY HONORED TO SALUTE YOU": Letter from Joseph Vacher to M. and Mme. Plantier, January 18, 1898, in Artières, *Écrits d'un tueur de bergers,* p. 92.

178 "THE CASE OF JOSEPH VACHER: HIS SELF-DEFENSE": Artières, *Écrits d'un tueur de bergers,* p. 121.

178 "THEY SAY THAT CURIOSITY ENDS": ibid., p. 90.

178 "FROM WHERE COMES MY MALADY?": ibid.

179 "ONE IS TRULY STRONG": ibid., p. 99.

179 "TO MAKE SURE HE DOES NOT BETRAY ME": Alexandre Lacassagne, *Vacher l'éventreur et les crimes sadiques* (Lyon: A. Storck, 1899), p. 54.

179 "UNDERSTAND THAT AT THE PRESENT TIME": Letter from Joseph Vacher to doctors, February 27, 1898, in Artières, *Écrits d'un tueur de bergers,* p. 102.

179 "THE REAL ALIENATED DO NOT ACT THAT WAY": Alexandre Lacassagne, handwritten notes, Bibliothèque municipale de Lyon, Fonds Lacassagne, file MS 5283, p. 41.

18. TURNING POINT

180   CRIMINALS WERE EMPLOYING THE RUSE: Paul Garnier, "La Simulation de la folie," *Annales d'hygiène publique et médecine légale* 3d ser., no. 19 (1888): 97–119.

180   "IN REAL INSANITY, THE PERSON WILL *NOT* ADMIT": Henry C. Chapman, *A Manual of Medical Jurisprudence and Toxicology* (Philadelphia: W. B. Saunders, 1892), p. 691.

180   "SOME OF WHICH ARE DELIBERATE AND CUNNING": Hans Gross: *Criminal Investigation: A Practical Textbook for Magistrates, Police Officers and Lawyers: Adapted from the System der Kriminalistik* (London: Sweet & Maxwell, 1924), p. 222.

181   PRISONER WHO KILLED A FORMER MISTRESS: Henri Coutagne, "Revue des journaux: Von Krafft-Ebing—Assassinat, folie simulée," *Archives de l'anthropologie criminelle* (1886): 364.

181   GARNIER WROTE A LENGTHY ARTICLE: Garnier, "La Simulation de la folie," pp. 97–119.

183   "THE FIRST IMPRESSION ONE GETS": Lacassagne, quoted in Jean-Paul Vettard, "The Vacher Case," *International Criminal Police Review* (2000), p. 482.

183   "FROM TIME TO TIME, VACHER FORGETS": Alexandre Lacassagne, *Vacher l'éventreur et les crimes sadiques* (Lyon: A. Storck, 1899), p. 53.

184   "NOTABLY DIMINISHED": Gérard Corneloup, *Joseph Vacher: Un Tueur en série de la Belle Époque* (Brignais, France: Éditions des Traboules, 2007), p. 156.

184   VACHER LATER WROTE TO MADEUF: Letter from Joseph Vacher to Dr. Madeuf, November 25, 1897, in Artières, *Écrits d'un tueur de bergers*, p. 87.

184   IT WAS "HIS ONLY OBJECTIVE": Lacassagne, *Vacher l'éventreur et les crimes sadiques*, p. 283.

184   "WHY HAVEN'T I BEEN SENT TO AN ASYLUM YET?": ibid., pp. 54–55.

184   "SO YOU SEE, MONSIEUR LE DOCTEUR": ibid., p. 283.

185   "YOU KNOW SOMETHING": ibid., p. 284.

185   "THE LACK OF CONFIDENCE": Letter from Joseph Vacher to doctor, April 20, 1898, in Artières, *Écrits d'un tueur de bergers*, p. 116–117.

185   HERE IS THE THEORY: Alexandre Lacassagne, "Notes et observations medico-légales, Vacher l'éventreur," Bibliothèque municipale de Lyon, Fonds Lacassagne, file MS 5283, p. 42.

186   "ONE CAN SEE IN THE CIRCUMSTANCES": This and subsequent Lacassagne quotes in this chapter are from Lacassagne, *Vacher l'éventreur et les crimes sadiques*, p. 44–56.

19. THE TRIAL

190   THE TRIAL OF THE MOST FEARSOME MURDERER: Rémi Cuisinier, *L'Assassin des bergers* (Saint-Just-la-Pendue, France: Charat, 2002), pp. 169–71.

190   "HE BEGINS THE SERIES": Émile Fourquet, *Vacher: Le Plus Grand Criminel des temps modernes par son juge d'instruction* (Besançon, France: Jacques et Demontrond, 1931), p. 312.

190   LITTLE SHEPHERDS FULL OF SORROW: ibid.

191   "THE MOST EXTRAORDINARY CRIMINALS": Rowland Strong, "Trial of a Criminal Whose Name Will Live as a Veritable Jack the Ripper or Bluebeard," *New York Times*, November 6, 1898.

191 "THE DIRECTORS SHOULD HAVE BEEN IN TOUCH": *Le Figaro*, October 24, 1898.

191 FOURQUET WAS IN VACHER'S CELL: Fourquet, *Vacher*, p. 297.

192 "GLORY TO JESUS!": This and other quotes from the trial are taken from the following sources: *Le Petit Journal*, October 27, 28, 29, 1898; *Le Lyon Républicain*, October 27, 28, 29, 1898; *Le Progrès*, October 27, 1898; *La Dépêche de Toulouse*, October 28, 1898; *Gazette des Tribunaux*, October 31–November 1, 1898; Fourquet, *Vacher*, pp. 312–33; Alexandre Lacassagne, *Vacher l'éventreur et les crimes sadiques* (Lyon: A. Storck, 1899), pp. 65–71; Gérard Corneloup, *Joseph Vacher: Un Tueur en série de la Belle Époque* (Brignais, France: Éditions des Traboules, 2007), pp. 263–393.

20. JUDGMENT

203 THIRD DAY OF THE TRIAL: Details regarding the trial have been reconstructed from the following sources: *Le Lyon Républicain*, October 29, 1898; *Le Progrès*, October 29, 1898; *La Dépêche de Toulouse*, October 29, 1898; *Gazette des Tribunaux*, October 31–November 1, 1898; Émile Fourquet, *Vacher: Le Plus Grand Criminel des temps modernes par son juge d'instruction* (Besançon, France: Jacques et Demontrond, 1931), pp. 312–33; Alexandre Lacassagne, *Vacher l'éventreur et les crimes sadiques* (Lyon: A. Storck, 1899), pp. 65–71; Gérard Corneloup, *Joseph Vacher: Un Tueur en série de la Belle Époque* (Brignais, France: Éditions des Traboules, 2007), pp. 263–393.

203 "THE DOCTOR'S OUTFIT": Alexandre Lacassagne, "Le Médecin devant les cours d'assises," *La Revue scientifique* 26 (1883): 809.

206 SADISM: Lacassagne, *Vacher l'éventreur et les crimes sadiques*, pp. 239–43, 245–82.

211 JAMES DOUGHERTY: "Insanity as a Defense in Criminal Cases," *Medico-Legal Journal of New York* (1890): 381.

213 "THOSE BASTARDS REALLY FIXED THINGS FOR ME": Fourquet, *Vacher*, p. 334.

21. A QUESTION OF SANITY

214 A FORTY-FIVE-PAGE BOOKLET: Charbonnier, *Documents sur l'état mental de Vacher condamné à la peine de mort par arrêt de la cour d'assises de l'Ain du 29 octobre 1898* (Grenoble: Allier, 1899).

215 "IT IS ABSOLUTELY NECESSARY": Gérard Corneloup, *Joseph Vacher: Un Tueur en série de la Belle Époque* (Brignais, France: Éditions des Traboules, 2007), p. 295.

215 DR. LOMBROSO, WHO CLASSIFIED VACHER AS AN EPILEPTIC: Alexandre Lacassagne, "Vacher l'éventreur," *Archives de l'anthropologie criminelle* (1889): 653.

215 DR. FOURCHON LAUNCHED A BROADSIDE: Corneloup, *Joseph Vacher*, p. 296.

216 "I HAVE NO TROUBLE BELIEVING": Pierre Bouchardon, *Vacher l'éventreur* (Paris: Albin Michel, 1939), pp. 226–27.

216 MORAS, WROTE A SIXTY-EIGHT-PAGE REPORT: ibid., pp. 225–26.

216 DE COSTON SENT A LONG AND ANGRY REPORT: ibid., p. 224.

216 "VACHER IS INSANE": ibid., p. 222.

216 "WHO FORMERLY WOULD FLOOD MY OFFICE": ibid., p. 223.

217 HE CONTACTED VACHER'S BROTHER AND SISTER: ibid., pp. 223–24.

217 "CAST DOUBT ON": ibid., p. 227.

217 DECIDING TO LET JUSTICE "FOLLOW ITS COURSE": ibid., p. 229.

218 LOUIS-ANTOINE-STANISLAS DEIBLER: Jean-Claude Farcy, "La peine de mort en France: Deux Siècles pour une abolition (1791–1981)," available at www

.criminocorpus.cnrs.fr/article117.html; "Louis Antoine Stanislas Deibler," available at http://site.voila.fr/guillotine/Louis.html; "La Dernière Exécution à Dijon de Louis Deibler," *Le Bien Public*, February 15, 2004; Léon Blanc, "Notes sur l'exécution de Busseuil," *Archives d'anthropologie criminelle* (1894): 375; *Le Petit Journal*, December 30, 1898.

218 THE NUMBER OF EXECUTIONS DECLINED: Jean Laponce, "In the Shadow of de Sade: French Medical Responses to a Case of Serial Sexual Homicide During the Belle Époque" (Ph.D. diss., Columbia University, 2002), pp. 131–32; Farcy, "La Peine de mort en France."

219 A BRIEF AWARENESS OF HIS OR HER FATE: Laurent Mucchielli, "Criminology, Hygienism, and Eugenics in France, 1870–1914," in *Criminals and Their Scientists: The History of Criminology in International Perspective*, ed. Peter Becker and Richard F. Wetzell (Cambridge: Cambridge University Press, 2006), p. 222.

219 A NEW DEVICE APPEARED IN THE UNITED STATES: Theodore Bernstein, "The First Electrocution," *Wisconsin Engineer* (December 1974/January 1975), pp. 14–15; Craig Brandon, *The Electric Chair: An Unnatural American History* (Jefferson, N.C.: McFarland, 1999); John Miskell, "Executions in Auburn Prison, Auburn, New York: 1890–1916," available at www.correctionhistory.org/auburn&osborne/miskell/html/auburnchair_report.html.

219 WORRIED THAT THE EFFECTS OF THE DEVICE: Arthur MacDonald, "Psychological Literature: Criminological," *American Journal of Psychology* (1891): 126.

219 LOMBROSO THOUGHT IT CRUEL: Mucchielli, "Criminology, Hygienism, and Eugenics in France, 1870–1914," pp. 207–29.

220 "ELECTRIC EXECUTION IS ODIOUS": Pierre Darmon, *Médecins et assassins à la Belle Époque: La Médicalisation du crime* (Paris: Éditions du Seuil, 1989), p. 192.

220 LACASSAGNE, WHO FOUND THE TECHNOLOGY INTRIGUING: Alexandre Lacassagne, "Les Exécutions électriques aux États-Unis," *Bulletin du Lyon médical* 70 (1892): 414–15, 446–52.

220 STOP ADVERTISING THE EVENTS: Alexandre Bérard, "La Publicité des exécutions capitales," *Archives d'anthropologie criminelle* (1894): 125.

221 "THE SPECTACLE OF THE CROWD": ibid., p. 130 .

221 AT 6:15 A.M., LOUIS DUCHER AND THREE OTHER OFFICIALS: Details concerning Vacher's execution are taken from the following sources: *Le Petit Journal*, December 30, 1898, and January 1, 1899; *Le Temps*, January 1, 1899; *Le Figaro*, January 1, 1899; *Le Lyon Républicain*, December 31, 1898; *Le Progrès*, January 1, 1899.

222 "HE DID NOT DIE LIKE AN INSANE PERSON": Alexandre Lacassagne, *Vacher l'éventreur et les crimes sadiques* (Lyon: A. Storck, 1899), p. 295.

223 THE DOCTORS CAREFULLY DISSECTED THE BODY: ibid, pp. 296–96; *Le Figaro*, January 1, 1899.

223 "THE JURORS OF AIN CAN SLEEP WITHOUT FEAR": *Le Petit Journal*, January 1, 1899.

223 A SEALED COOKING POT: *Le Figaro*, January 2, 1899.

22. THE MYSTERY OF A MURDERER'S BRAIN

227 JULES BESSE VISITED THE AREA: Émile Fourquet, *Vacher: Le Plus Grand Criminel des temps modernes par son juge d'instruction* (Besançon, France: Jacques et Demontrond, 1931), pp. 116–18.

227 "BREATHE MORE FREELY": ibid., pp. 355–56.

228 ALBERT SARRAUT OF *LA DÉPÊCHE DE TOULOUSE*: ibid., p. 206.

228 FOURQUET WISHED HE COULD HAVE TAKEN VACHER: "Le Tueur de bergers," *Le Lyon Républicain,* October 20, 1897.

228 BESSE VISITED THE VILLAGE OF ÉTAULES: Jules Besse, *Le Tueur de bergers* (Paris: Schwarz, 1897), pp. 707–66.

229 TOULOUSE DECIDED THAT IN THE INTEREST OF OBJECTIVITY: "Bulletin: L'Affaire Vacher," *Revue de médecine légale et de jurisprudence médicale* 6 (1889): 66–67.

229 CHARLES GUITEAU: "The Guiteau Trial," *American Journal of Insanity* 38 (1881): 301–47.

229 THAT OF CZOLGOSZ SHOWED "NO EVIDENCE": Carlos F. MacDonald, "The Trial, Execution, Autopsy and Mental Status of Leon F. Czolgosz, Alias Fred Nieman, the Assassin of President McKinley," *American Journal of Insanity* 58, no. 3 (1902): 369–86.

229 MORITZ BENEDIKT DISSECTED: Jan Verplaetse, "Moritz Benedikt's Localization of Morality in the Occipital Lobes: Origin and Background of the Controversial Hypothesis," *History of Psychiatry* 15, no. 3 (2004): 305–28.

229 LACASSAGNE ABHORRED THE LEGAL PROVISION: Alexandre Lacassagne, "L'Affaire Gouffé: Constatations et réflexions posthumes," *Archives de l'anthropologie criminelle* (1891): 199–200.

230 MUTUAL AUTOPSY SOCIETY: Jennifer Michael Hecht, *The End of the Soul: Scientific Modernity, Atheism, and Anthropology in France* (New York: Columbia University Press, 2003), pp. 1–40.

230 "THE MOST DEVELOPED AND MOST COMPLETE": ibid., 29.

230 DR. BOYER, OF LACASSAGNE'S LABORATORY: *Le Petit Journal,* January 12, 1899.

230 "ADHERENCES" ON THE BRAIN: *Le Petit Journal,* January 3, 1900.

231 "COMPLETE RESPONSIBILITY": *Le Petit Journal,* January 7, 1900.

231 A BOOK ENTITLED *VACHER:* Alexandre Lacassagne, *Vacher l'éventreur et les crimes sadiques* (Lyon: A. Storck, 1899).

231 "YOUR WORK ON VACHER IS VERY PROFOUND": Letter from Gabriel Tarde to Dr. Alexandre Lacassagne, April 6, 1899, Bibliothèque municipale de Lyon, Fonds Lacassagne, file MS 5283, pp. 131–32.

231 CALLED THE STUDY "A CLASSIC": Letter from Paul-Louis Ladame to Dr. Alexandre Lacassagne, March 23, 1899, in ibid., 153.

231 ON JUNE 15, 1899, LABORDE AND HIS COLLABORATORS: J. V. Laborde et al., "Étude psycho-physiologique, médico-légale et anatomique sur Vacher," *Bulletins de la Société d'anthropologie de Paris* 10, no. 10 (1899): 453–95.

231 "SLIGHTLY LARGER THAN AVERAGE": ibid., p. 476.

231 "NO ALTERATIONS CHARACTERISTIC OF DISEASE": ibid., p. 481.

232 LOMBROSO . . . PREDICTABLY CLASSIFIED VACHER AS A BORN CRIMINAL: "Societé médico-psychologique, *séance du* 31 juillet 1899," *Annales médico-psychologiques:* 457–58; Cesare Lombroso, "Le Cerveau de Vacher," *La Revue scientifique* 2 (1899): 56.

232 "WHAT A PHONY!": Letter from Léonce Manouvrier to Dr. Alexandre Lacassagne, August 22, 1899, Bibliothèque municipale de Lyon, Fonds Lacassagne, file MS 5283, p. 34.

232 "BUT EVERYONE KNOWS THAT LOMBROSO SEES BORN CRIMINALS": Émile Gautier, *L'Année scientifique et industrielle* (Paris: Librairie Hachette, 1900), p. 398.

232 TOULOUSE AND HIS TEAM RELEASED A FULL VERSION: Toulouse et al., "His-
     tologie du myélencéphale de Vacher (Société médico-psychologique, séance du
     31 juillet 1899)," *Annales médico-psychologiques* (1899): 455–59.

232 "BUT ONE CAN BE A DIRTY OLD MAN": Gautier, *L'Année scientifique et industrielle*,
     p. 398.

232 TOULOUSE HAD VOICED DOUBTS: Toulouse et al., "Histologie du myélencéphale
     de Vacher," p. 459.

233 LABORDE, ON THE OTHER HAND: J. V. Laborde et al., "Étude psycho-
     physiologique, médico-légale et anatomique sur Vacher," *Bulletins de la Société de
     l'anthropologie de Paris*, pp. 481–94.

233 ON MARCH 20, 1900, LABORDE PRESENTED AN UPDATED VERSION: J. V.
     Laborde, "Le cas de Vacher, état mental, criminalité, responsabilité, examen du
     cerveau (séance du 20 mars)," *Bulletin de l'Académie de médecine*, 3d. ser., vol. 43
     (1900): 341–348.

233 THE CONFERENCE ERUPTED: ibid., pp. 348–51; "Le Cerveau de Vacher," *Le Matin*,
     March 21, 1900; "Académie de médecine—Le cerveau de Vacher," *Le Petit Temps*,
     March 21, 1900; "Académie de médecine," *Le Soleil*, March 21, 1900.

233 "HIS ARGUMENT IS WEAK": Letter from Dr. Auguste Motet to Dr. Alexandre
     Lacassagne, March 21, 1900, Bibliothèque municipale de Lyon, Fonds Lacassagne,
     file MS 5283, p. 37.

233 "I SAID THAT ONE COULD DISCUSS": Letter from Léonce Manouvrier to Dr.
     Alexandre Lacassagne, August 22, 1899, in ibid., p. 34.

234 "I THINK LABORDE HAS GOTTEN": Letter from Paul Dubuisson to Dr. Alexandre
     Lacassagne, March 23, 1900, in ibid., p. 29.

234 "I ENERGETICALLY PROTESTED": Letter from Dr. Auguste Motet to Dr. Alexan-
     dre Lacassagne, March 21, 1900, in ibid., p. 37.

234 "AFFAIRS OF THIS TYPE": Letter from Alphonse Bertillon to Dr. Alexandre Lacas-
     sagne, undated, in ibid., p. 46.

234 "*EH BIEN*, MY DEAR SIR," *L'Écho de Paris*, January 5, 1899, cited in Pierre
     Bouchardon, *Vacher l'éventreur* (Paris: Albin Michel, 1939), p. 246.

235 "LABORDE'S INTERVENTION IS VERY ANNOYING," Letter from Paul Brouardel
     to Dr. Alexandre Lacassagne, March 29, 1900, Bibliothèque municipale de Lyon,
     Fonds Lacassagne, file MS 5283, p. 27.

236 "WE ARE CONVINCED AT HAVING TOLD THE TRUTH": Lacassagne, *Vacher l'éven-
     treur*, p. iii.

236 "WHAT'S CLEAR IS THAT THE MOST SOPHISTICATED SCIENCE": Gautier, *L'An-
     née scientifique et industrielle*, p. 399.

23. POSTSCRIPT

237 BY THE MID-1920S, NEARLY FORTY MILLION PEOPLE: *Social Security Board,
     Unemployment Compensation: What and Why?* (Washington, D.C.: Government
     Printing Office, 1937).

237 FRENCH GOVERNMENT BUILT A ROCKET-LAUNCH CENTER: "Installation of CSG
     in French Guyana," available at www.cnes-csg.fr/web/CNES-CSG-en/4681
     -installation-of-csg-in-french-guiana.php.

237 THE LAST PUBLIC EXECUTION: Jean-Claude Farcy, "La Peine de mort en France:

Deux Siècles pour une abolition (1791–1981)," available at www.criminocorpus
.cnrs.fr/article117.html.

238 SAINT-PAUL PRISON IN LYON: "Un transfert de détenus sans précédent à Lyon,"
Le Figaro, May 3, 2009.

238 INTERNATIONAL POLICE COMMISSION : Alexandre Lacassagne, *Vacher l'éventreur
et les crimes sadiques* (Lyon: A. Storck, 1899), p. 306; see also http://www.britannica
.com/EBchecked/topic/291580/Interpol?view=print.

238 HE HAD TRAVELED TO LEO TOLSTOY'S VILLAGE: Paolo Mazzarello, "Lombroso
and Tolstoy: An Anthropologist's Unwitting Gift to Literature," *Nature* 409 (2001):
983.

238 ZOLA, TOO, HAD LITTLE PATIENCE: Alison Abbott, "Hidden Treasures: Turin's
Anatomy Museum," *Nature* 455 (2008): 736.

238 "AGITATOR OF IDEAS, AND EXCITER OF WILLS": Alexandre Lacassagne, "Cesare
Lombroso (1835–1909)," *Archives d'anthropologie criminelle* (1909): 883.

239 THE LIMITATIONS OF BERTILLON'S SYSTEM: Raymond B. Fosdick,"The Passing
of the Bertillon System of Identification," *Journal of the American Institute of Law
and Criminology* 6, no. 3 (1915): 363–69.

239 BERTILLON PLEDGED HIS BRAIN: "Bertillon's Brain Weighed," *New York Times,*
February 16, 1914.

239 "THE PUBLIC AND PRESS . . . CLAMOR FOR THE MAGISTRATE": Émile Fourquet,
Vacher: Le Plus Grand Criminel des temps modernes par son juge d'instruction
(Besançon, France: Jacques et Demontrond, 1931), p. 357.

240 LUIGI RICHETTO: Philippe Artières, Gérard Corneloup, and Philippe Rassaert, *Le
Médecin et le criminel: Alexandre Lacassagne 1843–1924, exposition de la Bibliothèque
municipale de Lyon* (Lyon: Bibliothèque municipale, 2004), pp. 188–91.

240 HENRI VIDAL: Alexandre Lacassagne, Jean Boyer, and Fleury Rebatel, "Vidal le
tueur des femmes," *Archives d'anthropologie criminelle* (1902): 645–98.

240 CHILDREN OF ALCOHOLICS: Marc Renneville, "Alexandre Lacassagne: Un
Médecin-anthropologue face à la criminalité (1843–1924)," *Gradhiva* 17 (1995): 134.

240 "THE OGRESS" JEANNE WEBER: Jürgen Thorwald, *The Century of the Detective*
(New York: Harcourt, Brace & World, 1965), pp. 156–75; "Notes et observations
médico-légales: Affaire Weber," *Archives d'anthropologie criminelle* (1908): 329–99.

240 "HISTORY ALWAYS REMINDS US": Thorwald, *The Century of the Detective,* p. 156.

241 "OLD PEOPLE," HE WROTE: Artières, Corneloup, Rassaert, *Le Médecin et le Criminel,* p. 54.

241 "TAKE CARE NOT TO BURN YOURSELF OUT": *Le Progrès,* September 25, 1924.

241 "HE LIVED HIS LIFE": ibid.

241 "I HOPE TO SERVE": Louis Vervaeck, "Le Professeur Lacassagne," *La revue de
droit pénal et de criminologie* (1924): 929.

EPILOGUE. THE VIOLENT BRAIN

242 SITS IN A DISPLAY CASE: Observations and notes courtesy of Eva Zadeh, Paris.

243 *"CSI* EFFECT": Kit R. Roane, "The *CSI* Effect," *U.S. News & World Report*
(April 17, 2005); Tom R. Tyler, "Viewing *CSI* and the Threshold of Guilt: Manag-
ing Truth and Justice in Reality and Fiction," *The Yale Law Journal* 115 (2006):
1050–85.

243 THE STATE OF THE ART FAR EXCEEDS: National Research Council, *Strengthening Forensic Science in the United States: A Path Forward* (Washington, D.C.: National Academies Press, 2009), pp. S4–S24.

244 "JUKES" STUDY: Nicole Hahn Rafter, *The Criminal Brain: Understanding Biological Theories of Crime* (New York: NYU Press, 2008), pp. 106–8.

244 "KALLIKAK" STUDY: Stephen Jay Gould, *The Mismeasure of Man* (New York: W. W. Norton, 1981), pp. 168–71.

245 SCIENTISTS WHO HAVE SCANNED: Antonio R. Damasio, "A Neural Basis for Sociopathy," *Archives of General Psychiatry* 57 (2000): 128–99; Adrian Raine and Yaling Yang, "Neural Foundations to Moral Reasoning and Antisocial Behavior," *Social Cognitive and Affective Neuroscience* (2006): 203–13; Adrian Raine, "The Biological Basis for Crime," in *Crime: Public Policies for Crime Control,* ed. James Q. Wilson and Joan Petersilia (Oakland, Calif.: ICS Press, 2002), pp. 43–74; author's interview with Dr. Daniel Press, neurologist, Beth Israel Deaconess Medical Center, Boston.

246 LACK THE NEURAL CIRCUITRY TO RESIST: Robert M. Sapolski, "The Frontal Cortex and the Criminal Justice System," *Philosophical Transactions of the Royal Society of London* 359 (2004): 1787–96.

247 "WHEN YOU SIT": Author's interview with Ilizabeth Wollheim, Ph.D., clinical and forensic psychologist.

247 "COMORBIDITY": ibid.

248 ONE CRIMINAL PSYCHOLOGIST OBSERVED: Author's interview with Tali K. Walters, Ph.D., forensic psychologist.

248 "A CRIME WITHOUT MOTIVE?": Laurent Mucchielli, "Criminology, Hygienism, and Eugenics in France, 1870–1914," in *Criminals and Their Scientists: The History of Criminology in International Perspective,* ed. Peter Becker and Richard F. Wetzell, (Cambridge: Cambridge University Press, 2006), p. 212.

248 ONE NEUROLOGIST SPENT HOURS: Author's interview with Dr. Daniel Press.

249 "LOOKING INTO PURE EVIL": Author's interview with Tali K. Walters.

Bibliography

VACHER CASE: PRIMARY SOURCES

Archives départementales de l'Ain. Located in the region's capital city of Bourg-en-Bresse, these archives contain thousands of pages of court records and supporting documents related to Vacher's murder trial, including affidavits, psychiatric reports, testimony, and investigator's notes.

Artières, Philippe. *Écrits d'un tueur de bergers*. Lyon: Éditions à Rebours, 2006. A collection of Vacher's writings, including his letters and confession.

Besse, Jules. *Le Tueur de bergers* (Paris: Schwarz, 1897). A voluminous account of Vacher's life and crimes. Although parts of the book seem dramatized, Besse scrupulously documented and listed his interview sources for certain sections, such as the attempted murder of Louise Barant.

Bibliothèque municipale de Lyon, Fonds Lacassagne. Located in a special wing of the library, this archive contains more than twelve thousand documents, books, case files, and manuscripts donated by Alexandre Lacassagne in 1921.

"Dossier administratif de l'affaire Vacher." Located in the Archives départementales du Rhône in Lyon, this file contains documents relating to the Vacher investigation and trial, including Fourquet's interview notes, maps on which he traced Vacher's travels, and the psychological report of Drs. Lacassagne, Pierret, and Rebatel.

Fourquet, Émile. *Vacher: Le Plus Grand Criminel des temps modernes par son juge d'instruction*. Besançon, France: Jacques et Demontrond, 1931. A firsthand account by the magistrate who brought Vacher to justice.

Lacassagne, Alexandre. *Vacher l'éventreur et les crimes sadiques*. Lyon: A. Storck, 1899.

Laurent-Martin. *Le Roi des assassins: La Vie errante et mystérieuse de Vacher l'éventreur*. Paris: Librairie Universelle, 1897. A contemporary account of Vacher's life and crimes, written after Vacher's capture but before the trial.

Newspaper reports: Contemporary accounts of the investigation, trial, and aftermath appeared in many newspapers, including *La Dépêche de Toulouse*, *La Croix*, *Le Figaro*, *Le Temps*, *Le Matin*, *Le Petit Journal*, *Le Petit Parisien*, *Le Progrès* (Lyon), and *Le Lyon Républicain*.

VACHER CASE: SECONDARY SOURCES

Bouchardon, Pierre. *Vacher l'éventreur*. Paris: Albin Michel, 1939.

Corneloup, Gérard. *Joseph Vacher: Un Tueur en série de la Belle Époque*. Brignais, France: Éditions des Traboules, 2007.

Deloux, Jean-Pierre. *Vacher l'assassin: Un* serial killer *français au XIXe siècle*. Paris: Claire Vigne, 1995.

Laponce, Jean. "In the Shadow of de Sade: French Medical Responses to a Case of Serial Sexual Homicide During the Belle Époque." Ph.D. diss., Columbia University, 2002.

Tavernier, René, and Henri Garet. *Le Juge et l'assassin*. Paris: Presses de la Cité, 1976.

GENERAL REFERENCES

Artières, Philippe. *Le Livre des vies coupables: Autobiographies de criminels (1896–1909)*. Paris: Éditions Albin Michel, 2000.

Artières, Philippe, Gérard Corneloup, and Philippe Rassaert. *Le Médecin et le criminel: Alexandre Lacassagne, 1843–1924, exposition de la Bibliothèque municipale de Lyon*. Lyon: Bibliothèque municipale, 2004.

Becker, Peter, and Richard F. Wetzell, eds. *Criminals and Their Scientists: The History of Criminology in International Perspective*. Cambridge: Cambridge University Press, 2006.

Bellanger, Claude et al. *Histoire générale de la presse française*, vol. 3. Paris: Presses Universitaires de France, 1972.

Bergeron, Henri, et al. *Médecine légale et jurisprudence médicale*. Paris: A. Maloine, 1897.

Berlanstein, Lenard. *The Working People of Paris, 1871–1914*. Baltimore: Johns Hopkins University Press, 1998.

Bernaldo de Quirós, C. *Modern Theories of Criminality*. Translated by A. de Salvo. Boston: Little, Brown , 1912.

Bernheim, Hippolyte. *Suggestive Therapeutics: A Treatise on the Nature and Uses of Hypnotism*. New York: G. P. Putnam's Sons, 1889.

Brouardel, Paul. *Death and Sudden Death*. New York: William Wood and Company, 1892.

Burdett, Henry C. *Hospitals and Asylums of the World*. London: J & A Churchill, 1891.

Burns, Chester R., ed. *Legacies in Law and Medicine*. New York: Science History Publications, 1977.

Cabanès, Augustin. *Curious Bypaths of History*. Paris: Charles Carrington, 1898.

Chapman, Henry C. *A Manual of Medical Jurisprudence and Toxicology*. Philadelphia: W. B. Saunders, 1892.

Chauvaud, Frédéric. *Les Experts du crime: La Médecine légale en France au XIXe siècle*. Paris: Aubier, 2000.

Clark, Michael, and Catherine Crawford, eds. *Legal Medicine in History*. Cambridge: Cambridge University Press, 1994.

Cragin, Thomas. *Murder in Parisian Streets: Manufacturing Crime and Justice in the Popular Press, 1830–1900*. Lewisburg, Penn.: Bucknell University Press, 2006.

Darmon, Pierre. *Médecins et assassins à la Belle Époque: La Médicalisation du crime*. Paris: Éditions du Seuil, 1989.

Darnton, Robert. *The Great Cat Massacre and Other Episodes in French Cultural History*. New York: Basic Books, 1984.

D'Avenel, Georges. *Le Mécanisme de la vie moderne*. Paris: Armand Colin, 1896.

Depastino, Todd. *Citizen Hobo: How a Century of Homelessness Shaped America*. Chicago: University of Chicago Press, 2003.

Dowbiggin, Ian. *Inheriting Madness: Professionalization and Psychiatric Knowledge in Nineteenth-Century France*. Berkeley: University of California Press, 1991.

Doyle, Arthur Conan. *The Illustrated Sherlock Holmes Treasury.* New York: Chatham River Press, 1986.

Draper, Fran Winthrop. *A Text-Book of Legal Medicine.* Philadelphia: W. B. Saunders, 1905.

Eldridge, Benjamin P. and William B. Watts. *Our Rival, the Rascal: A Faithful Portrayal of the Conflict Between the Criminals of This Age and the Defenders of Society—the Police.* Boston: Pemberton, 1893.

Ellis, Havelock. *The Criminal.* London: Walter Scott, 1892.

Ellis, Jack D. *The Physician-Legislators of France: Medicine and Politics in the Early Third Republic, 1870–1914.* Cambridge: Cambridge University Press, 1990.

Elmsley, Clive, and Haia Shpayer-Makov, eds. *Police Detectives in History, 1750–1950.* Aldershot, England: Ashgate Publishing, 2006.

Ferri, Enrico. *Les Criminels dans l'art et la littérature.* Paris: Alcan, 1897.

———. *Criminal Sociology.* Translated by Joseph I. Kelly and John Lisle. Boston: Little, Brown, 1917.

Finkel, Norman J. *Insanity on Trial.* New York: Plenum Press, 1988.

Fosdick, Raymond B. *European Police Systems.* New York: Century, 1915.

Fourquet, Émile. *Les Faux Témoins.* Chalon-sur-Saône, France: Émile Bertrand, 1901.

———. *Les Vagabonds: Les Vagabonds criminels, le problème du vagabondage.* Paris: Librairie Générale de Jurisprudence, 1908.

Gautier, Émile. *L'Année scientifique et industrielle.* Paris: Librairie Hachette, 1900.

Gibson, Mary. *Born to Crime: Cesare Lombroso and the Origins of Biological Criminology.* Westport, Conn.: Praeger, 2002.

Goldstein, Jan. *Console and Classify: The French Psychiatric Profession in the Nineteenth Century.* Cambridge: Cambridge University Press, 1989.

Gould, Stephen Jay. *The Mismeasure of Man.* New York: W. W. Norton, 1981.

Granier, Camille. *Essai de bibliographie charitable.* Paris: Librairie Guillaumin, 1891.

Griffiths, Arthur. *Mysteries of Police and Crime.* London: Cassell, 1899.

———. *Fifty Years of Public Service.* London: Cassell, 1904.

Gross, Hans. *Criminal Investigation: A Practical Textbook for Magistrates, Police Officers and Lawyers: Translated and Adapted to Indian and Colonial Practice from the System der Kriminalistik.* Madras: A. Krashnamachari, 1906.

———. *Criminal Investigation: A Practical Textbook for Magistrates, Police Officers and Lawyers: Adapted from the System der Kriminalistik.* London: Sweet & Maxwell, 1924.

Guilherment, Georges. *Le Milieu criminel.* Paris: Ancienne Librairie Schleicher, 1923.

Hamilton, Allan McLane and Lawrence Godkin. *A System of Legal Medicine.* New York: E. B. Treat, 1900.

Harris, Ruth. *Murders and Madness: Medicine, Law, and Society in the Fin de Siècle.* Oxford: Clarendon Press, 1989.

Hecht, Jennifer Michael. *The End of the Soul: Scientific Modernity, Atheism, and Anthropology in France.* New York: Columbia University Press, 2003.

Hesse, Raymond. *Les Criminels peints par eux-mêmes.* Paris: Grasset, 1912.

Hofmann, Eduard von. *Atlas of Legal Medicine.* Philadelphia: W. B. Saunders, 1898.

Hopkins, Tighe. *Wards of the State: An Unofficial View of Prison and the Prisoner.* London: Herbert and Daniel, 1913.

Irving, Henry Brodribb. *Studies of French Criminals of the Nineteenth Century.* London: William Heinemann, 1901.

Jones, David Arthur. *History of Criminology: A Philosophical Perspective.* New York: Greenwood Press, 1986.

Kalifa, Dominique. *L'Encre et le sang: Récits de crimes et société a la Belle Époque.* Paris: Fayard, 1995.

Kaluczynski, Martine. "La Criminologie en mouvement: Naissance et développement d'une science sociale en France à la fin du XIXe siècle." Ph.D. diss., Université Paris Diderot, 1988.

Klepinger, Linda L. *Fundamentals of Forensic Anthropology.* Hoboken, N.J.: John Wiley & Sons, 2006.

Lacassagne, Alexandre. *Précis de médecine judiciaire, deuxième édition.* Paris: G. Masson, 1886.

———. *L'Affaire Gouffé.* Lyon: A. Storck, 1891.

———. *Vade-mecum du médecin-expert.* Lyon: A. Storck, 1892.

Lailler, Maurice, and Henri Vonoven. *Les Erreurs judiciaires et leurs causes.* Paris: A. Pedone, 1897.

Levin, Miriam R. *When the Eiffel Tower Was New: French Visions of Progress at the Centennial of the Revolution.* Amherst: University of Massachusetts Press, 1989.

Locard, Edmond. *La Malle sanglante de Millery.* Paris: Gallimard, 1934.

———. *Les Grands Criminels lyonnais.* Lyon: Albums du Crocodile, 1938.

Lombroso, Cesare. *L'Homme criminel atlas.* Paris: Ancienne Librairie Germer Baillière, 1887.

———. *Criminal Man.* Translated by Mary Gibson and Nicole Hahn Rafter. Durham: Duke University Press, 2006.

Mannheim, Hermann, ed. *Pioneers in Criminology.* Montclair, N.J.: Patterson Smith, 1972.

Matsuda, Matt K. *The Memory of the Modern.* New York: Oxford University Press, 1996.

Mohr, James C. *Doctors and the Law: Medical Jurisprudence in Nineteenth-Century America.* New York: Oxford University Press, 1993.

Mucchielli, Laurent. *Histoire de la criminologie française.* Paris: Éditions l'Harmattan, 1995.

National Research Council. *Strengthening Forensic Science in the United States: A Path Forward.* Washington, D.C.: National Academies Press, 2009.

Nickell, Joe, and John C. Fischer. *Crime Science: Methods of Forensic Detection.* Lexington: University Press of Kentucky, 1998.

Nye, Robert. *Crime, Madness and Politics in Modern France: The Medical Concept of National Decline.* Princeton: Princeton University Press, 1984.

Osler, William, ed. *Modern Medicine: Its Theory and Practice.* Philadelphia: Lea & Febiger, 1914.

Price, Roger. *A Social History of Nineteenth-Century France.* New York: Holmes & Meier, 1987.

Rafter, Nicole Hahn. *Creating Born Criminals.* Chicago: University of Illinois Press, 1997.

———. *The Criminal Brain: Understanding Biological Theories of Crime.* New York: NYU Press, 2008.

Ramsland, Katherine M. *Inside the Minds of Serial Killers.* Westport, Conn.: Praeger, 2006.

Renneville, Marc. *Crime et folie: Deux Siècles d'enquêtes médicales et judiciaires.* Paris: Fayard, 2003.

Rhodes, Henry T. F. *Alphonse Bertillon, Father of Scientific Detection.* London: Harrap, 1956.

Robinson, Daniel N. *Wild Beasts and Idle Humours: The Insanity Defense from Antiquity to the Present.* Cambridge: Harvard University Press, 1996.

Romein, Jan. *The Watershed of Two Eras: Europe in 1900.* Translated by Arnold J. Pomerans. Middletown, Conn.: Wesleyan University Press, 1978.

Sachs, Jessica. *Corpse: Nature, Forensics, and the Struggle to Pinpoint Time of Death.* New York: Basic Books, 2001.

Schäfer, Edward, and George Thane, eds. *Quain's Elements of Anatomy.* London: Longmans, Green and Co., 1893.

Schiller, Francis. *Paul Broca: Founder of French Anthropology, Explorer of the Brain.* Berkeley: University of California Press, 1979.

Schmitt, Aurore, et al., eds. *Forensic Anthropology and Medicine: Complementary Sciences from Recovery to Cause of Death.* Totowa, N.J.: Humana Press, 2006.

Schwartz, Vanessa R. *Spectacular Realities: Early Mass Culture in Fin-de-Siècle Paris.* Berkeley: University of California Press, 1998.

Shorter, Edward. *A History of Psychiatry: From the Era of the Asylum to the Age of Prozac.* New York: John Wiley & Sons, 1997.

Stead, P. J. *The Police of France.* New York: Macmillan, 1983.

Taylor, Alfred Swaine. *A Manual of Medical Jurisprudence,* 12th ed. New York: Lea Brothers, 1897.

Thorwald, Jürgen. *The Century of the Detective.* New York: Harcourt, Brace & World, 1965.

Tidy, Charles. *Legal Medicine.* New York: William Wood & Company, 1882.

Tilly, Charles, Louise Tilly, and Richard H. Tilly. *The Rebellious Century: 1830–1930.* Cambridge: Harvard University Press, 1975.

Vizetelly, Ernest Alfred. *The Anarchists, Their Faith and Their Record.* London: John Lane, 1911.

Weber, Eugen. *Peasants into Frenchmen: The Modernization of Rural France, 1870–1914.* Palo Alto: Stanford University Press, 1976.

White, Peter, ed. *Crime Scene to Court: The Essentials of Forensic Science.* Cambridge: Royal Society of Chemistry, 2004.

Wilkins, Philip A. *Behind The French C.I.D.: Leaves from the Memoirs of Goron, Former Detective Chief.* London: Hutchinson, 1940.

Wilson, Colin, and Damon Wilson. *Written in Blood: A History of Forensic Detection.* New York: Carroll & Graf, 2003.

Wines, Frederick H. *Punishment and Reformation: A Historical Sketch of the Rise of the Penitentiary System.* New York: Thomas Y. Crowell, 1919.

Woodward, John, and Robert Jütte. *Coping with Sickness: Medicine, Law and Human Rights—Historical Perspectives.* Sheffield, England: European Association for the History of Medicine and Health Publications, 2000.

Wright, Gordon. *Between the Guillotine and Liberty: Two Centuries of the Crime Problem in France.* Oxford: Oxford University Press, 1983.

OTHER SOURCES

Criminocorpus (www.criminocorpus.cnrs.fr/). Directed by Marc Renneville, a researcher at the Alexandre Koyré Center for the history of science and technology in Paris, this Web site comprises an enormous body of work on the history of crime and punishment in France. In addition to scholarly papers and virtual exhibits, the site hosts a scanned collection of every edition of Lacassagne's journal, *Archives de l'anthropologie criminelle* (Archives of Criminal Anthropology) from 1886 to 1914 (from 1893 onward it's *Archives d'anthropologie criminelle*). The site also has links to scanned editions of the important criminological and psychological journals of the day, including *Annales d'hygiène publique et de médecine légale* (Annals of Public Hygiene and Legal Medicine) and *Annales médico-psychologiques* (Medico-Psychological Annals).

Index

abortions, 37, 39, 42

Academy of Medicine, 233, 240

"Adventure of the Naval Treaty, The" (Doyle), 104

adversarial system, 193, 203

age: ossification rates of bones and, 68–9; teeth and, 21, 69, 70–1

agent particulier (special agent), 116–17

aging, 241

agriculture, workforce dislocations and, 51, 52

Alaise, Aline, 110, 111, 160, 188

alcoholism, 7, 37, 128, 240

alienist, use of term, 7

amygdala, 245

anal rape: testing for evidence of, 143–4, 186; Vacher case and, 32, 54, 144, 186, 201

anarchism, 11, 56, 66–7, 123

anatomical museums, 242

Annales médico-psychologiques, Les (The Annals of Medical Psychology), 174, 212

anthropology, 55, 121–2

anthropometrics, 21–2

antibody reactions, 101

Antiquaille Hospital, Lyon, 55

antisocial personality disorder (ASPD), 245–6

Archives de l'anthropologie criminelle (Archives of Criminal Anthropology), 18–19, 43, 45, 47, 64, 67, 99, 167

Archivio di psichiatria ed antropologia

criminale (Archives of Psychiatry and Criminal Anthropology), 123

arm spans, 128

Arnold (shooter), 171–2

arsenic, 37

arthritic inflammation, 25

Article 64, 172, 217

asphyxia, 86–7; capital punishment and, 219

asylums, 51; conditions at, 6–7, 10, 197; confinement of criminally insane in, 124, 171, 172–3, 180, 182; crimes committed by former patients or escapees from, 211–12; daily routine at, 13; overcrowding at, 7; physical and psychological therapies at, 13; studies of patients in, 121. *See also* Dole asylum; Saint-Robert asylum

atavism, Lombroso's born criminal theory and, 122–3, 128, 129, 130

autopsies, 17, 38, 106; age determination and, 21; Church prohibitions on, 37; *Constitutio Criminalis Carolina* and, 36–7; Delhomme killing and, 30–2, 46, 186; *feuilles d'observation* (observation pages) for, 41–2, 46; foot and leg bones and, 24–5; fresh bodies and, 23; in Gouffé case, 16, 20–5, 26, 61, 68; hair color and, 22–3; height determination and, 21–2, 45; hospital, forensic dissections vs., 19; of intellectuals' brains, 230, 238, 239; Lacassagne's expertise in, 19–20; Lacassagne's

ILLUSTRATIONS CREDITS

Murder of Louise Marcel: *Le Journal illustré,* courtesy of Rémi Cuisinier
Vacher's childhood home: author photo
Vacher and Louise Barant: from Émile Fourquet, *Vacher: Le Plus Grand Criminel des temps modernes par son juge d'instruction* (Besançon, France: Jacques et Demontrond, 1931)
Augustine Mortureux: from Émile Fourquet, *Vacher*
Crime scene in Bénonces: from Émile Fourquet, *Vacher*
Vacher's handwriting lesson: *La Dépêche,* November 15, 1897
Lacassagne: courtesy of La Bibliothèque municipale de Lyon, Fonds Lacassagne
Gouffé affair: *Le Petit Journal,* supplément illustré, courtesy of Rémi Cuisinier
Gouffé's autopsy: courtesy of La Bibliothèque municipale de Lyon, Fonds Lacassagne
Lacassagne's criminal museum: author photo
Floating morgue: courtesy of Dr. Daniel Malicier, Institut de Médecine Légale de Lyon
Cast of hand: author photo, courtesy of Élisabeth Biot
Bertillon: author photo
Bertillon's system: from Alphonse Bertillon (trans. anon.), *Signaletic Instructions* (Chicago, New York: The Werner Company, 1896)
Lombroso: courtesy of Francis S. Countway Library of Medicine, Harvard Medical School
Criminal features: from Cesare Lombroso, *L'homme criminel atlas* (Paris: Ancienne Libraire Germer Baillière, 1887)
Skulls: from Cesare Lombroso, *L'homme criminel atlas* (Paris: Ancienne Libraire Germer Baillière, 1887)
Gross: courtesy of Hans Gross Kriminalmuseum of the Karl-Franzens-Universität, Graz, Austria
Fourquet: from Émile Fourquet, *Vacher*
Vacher's confession: Archives départementales de l'Ain, Bourg-en-Bresse, France
Vacher's spree: *Le Petit Parisien,* October 31, 1897, courtesy of Rémi Cuisinier
Vacher: courtesy of La Bibliothèque municipale de Lyon, Fonds Lacassagne
Vacher's execution day: *Le Petit Journal,* January 15, 1899
Vacher's head: from Émile Fourquet, *Vacher*

A NOTE ABOUT THE AUTHOR

Douglas Starr is a professor of journalism and codirector of the graduate program in science journalism at Boston University. His book *Blood: An Epic History of Medicine and Commerce* was published in seven languages; it won the *Los Angeles Times* Book Prize (science category). In 2002, it was adapted by PBS as a four-part documentary series that aired on more than three hundred PBS stations nationwide and internationally. A former newspaper reporter and field biologist, Starr has written about medicine, public health, science, and the environment for *The New Republic, Science, Smithsonian,* PBS, NPR, *Wired,* the *Los Angeles Times,* the *Christian Science Monitor,* and the *Boston Globe Sunday Magazine.* He lives outside Boston with his wife and two sons.

A NOTE ON THE TYPE

Pierre Simon Fournier *le jeune,* who designed the type used in this book, was both an originator and a collector of types. His types are old style in character and sharply cut. In 1764 and 1766 he published his *Manuel typographique,* a treatise on the history of French types and printing, and on what many consider his most important contribution to typography—the measurement of type by the point system.

Composed by
Creative Graphics, Allentown, Pennsylvania

Designed by M. Kristen Bearse